CW0922282

Walking With Paul Through the Book of Romans

GEORGE R. KNIGHT

REVIEW AND HERALD® PUBLISHING ASSOCIATION
HAGERSTOWN, MD 21740

The author assumes full responsibility for the accuracy of all facts and quotations as cited in this book.

All Bible quotations, unless otherwise noted, are from the King James Version. One exception to that rule is that a reference to alternate translations is not supplied when quotations are repeated from the given text for the day.

This book was
Edited by Gerald Wheeler
Copyedited by Jocelyn Fay and Lori Halvorsen
Interior design by Mark O'Connor
Cover design by William Tymeson
Electronic makeup by Shirley M. Bolivar
Type: 11/13 New Times Roman

PRINTED IN U.S.A.

07 06 05 04 03   5 4 3 2 1

R&H Cataloging Service
Knight, George R.
      Walking with Paul through the book of Romans.

      1. Bible. N.T. Romans—Study and teaching.   2. Devotional
literature.   3. Devotional calendars—Seventh-day Adventist.
I. Title.

                        227.1

ISBN 0-8280-1646-1

Dedication

Dedicated to Bonnie—a wife

whom it is a joy to walk with—

God's special gift to me

A Word to
My Fellow Travelers

Welcome to the journey. This year we will spend 365 days walking with Paul in the book of Romans. During the year we will journey progressively through Romans on a verse-by-verse exploration of its meaning for our lives.

The book of Romans provides an excellent basis for a year's daily study because it covers all the essential aspects of Christian belief and living. Beyond that, it contextualizes, or places, each of its doctrinal and lifestyle teachings within the framework of the gospel.

Six years ago we took a similar trip with Jesus through the Sermon on the Mount in *Walking With Jesus on the Mount of Blessing.* I trust that you will find this walk with Paul just as profitable and edifying as you did the previous one.

I have wanted to write a book on Romans ever since I was in college. For years I have studied it with enthusiasm. My prayer for you this year is that God will bless you abundantly as you wander through and meditate upon one of the most important documents you will ever read—Paul's epistle to the Romans.

The preparation of this volume would have been impossible without the skilled help of my secretary, Bonnie Beres, and my editors at the Review and Herald Publishing Association, Gerald Wheeler, Jeannette Johnson, and Richard Coffen.

George R. Knight
Andrews University
Berrien Springs, Michigan

Other books by George R. Knight (selected)

The Fat Lady and the Kingdom (Pacific Press)
I Used to Be Perfect (Pacific Press)
Millennial Fever and the End of the World (Pacific Press)
The Pharisee's Guide to Perfect Holiness (Pacific Press)
The User-friendly Guide to the 1888 Message
Walking With Jesus on the Mount of Blessing
Walking With Paul Through Romans

Books in the Ellen White series

Ellen White's World
Meeting Ellen White
Reading Ellen White
Walking With Ellen White

Books in the Adventist Heritage series

A Brief History of Seventh-day Adventists
A Search for Identity
Organizing to Beat the Devil

To order, call 1-800-765-6955.

Visit us at www.reviewandherald.com for more information on Review and Herald® products.

AN OVERVIEW OF
The Journey

STEP 1
Meeting Paul

Romans 1:1-17

HISTORY'S MOST INFLUENTIAL BOOK

The Epistle of Paul the Apostle to the Romans. Title, KJV.

WHAT! NO SCRIPTURE reading for today?

That's right! Because I want to get your full attention as we begin a yearlong study of Christianity's most influential document. Repeatedly this little book, titled "to Romans" in the original language, has changed the course of church and world history.

Take, for example, the greatest voice of the medieval period—Augustine of Hippo. "I was twisting and turning in my chains" of lust and sin, he wrote, "when I threw myself down somehow under a certain fig tree, and let my tears flow freely." Suddenly he heard a voice "repeating over and over again 'Pick up and read, pick up and read.'"

In response Augustine took his Bible and read the first passage his eyes fell on: "Not in riots and drunken parties, not in eroticism and indecencies, not in strife and rivalry, but put on the Lord Jesus Christ and make no provision for the flesh and its lusts" (see Rom. 13:13, 14). Augustine found victory over his special problems when, in the book of Romans, he met Jesus as Savior from sin.

Martin Luther more than 1,000 years later had a similar experience. A man with a tormented conscience, Luther noted that "if ever a monk got to heaven by his monkery, it was I." But religious practice just didn't do it. He was driven to despair until he discovered Christ's righteousness in Romans. "Thereupon," he wrote, "I felt myself to be reborn and to have gone through open doors into paradise. The whole of Scripture took on a new meaning." The result was the Protestant Reformation.

Two hundred years later John Wesley, who had struggled to be righteous for years, found himself in utter despair. In that condition on May 24, 1738, he went to a chapel on Aldersgate Street in London. There he heard someone reading Luther's *Preface to . . . Romans.* "I felt," he penned, "my heart strangely warmed. I felt I did trust in Christ, Christ alone, for salvation; and an assurance was given me that he had taken away my sin, even mine, and saved me from the law of sin and death." The result was the rise of the Methodist movement.

Beware! Reading Romans changes people. My prayer this year is that our daily reading of Romans will transform each of our lives.

WHO WANTS TO BE A SLAVE?

This letter is from Paul, Jesus Christ's slave. Rom. 1:1, NLT.

WHAT A WAY to begin a letter!

Paul doesn't beat around the bush. He is not one to hide his allegiance to Jesus. To the contrary, he wears it, so to speak, on his forehead. At the very beginning of his letter he indicates that the most important thing we can know about him is that he is a Christian—that everything he is and has belongs to Jesus. Thus slavery to Jesus is the keynote of what may be Paul's most important letter.

Many modern translations seek to soften the word "slave" by rendering it as "servant." But the Greek word *doulos* primarily means "slave." Paul tells us that he is not a hired man working with Christ for wages, but a slave who totally belongs to Him.

Concepts related to slavery stand at the heart of Paul's letter to the Romans. Thus when he talks about God redeeming sinners in Romans 3:24 he uses the vocabulary of the marketplace. "Redemption" in his day meant to buy at the market, particularly to purchase a slave. Central to Paul's life and message was the fact that he had been redeemed by the blood of Jesus on Calvary's cross.

The idea of a Christian's slavery to God rises again in Romans 6, in which Paul tells his readers that every human being is a slave to either Satan or Christ, that all of us belong to someone, that no person is a totally free agent, and that every individual becomes the slave of either "sin, which leads to death, or of obedience, which leads to righteousness" (see Rom. 6:16-23, RSV).

But slavery to Christ, Paul tells us, is not bondage. To the contrary, it is how a person gains freedom. It will climax in eternal life (verse 23). Thus even Paul's slavery is good news.

How is it with us? What is it that I want people to know about me? My accomplishments? My good looks? My possessions? My Christianity?

It is not a question I should try to avoid. As with Paul, it stands at the heart of my life and its meaning. Today is a day to get real with God—and with myself.

Lord Jesus, help me to realize my helplessness, that by creation and redemption I am totally Yours, and that like Paul I need to be first and foremost Your "slave."

WHAT'S AN APOSTLE, ANYWAY?

Paul, . . . called to be an apostle. Rom. 1:1.

HAVE YOU EVER THOUGHT about the meaning of the word "apostle"? Or is it just one more word that you banter around without really knowing its significance? The dictionary defines the biblical word as one who is "sent out."

But an apostle is not merely any Christian who gets sent somewhere, nor is it the equivalent of "disciple." To the contrary, in the Bible an apostle is a disciple with great authority. According to Acts 1:15-26, an apostle was one who had personally known the Lord and had been a "witness to his resurrection" (verse 22, RSV). In addition, an apostle was a disciple who had received a call "not from men nor through man, but through Jesus Christ and God the Father" (Gal. 1:1, RSV).

Paul repeatedly asserts that God had called him to be an apostle (see, e.g., 1 Cor. 1:1; 2 Cor. 1:1).

Wow! Do you see a problem here? Perhaps even a contradiction?

After all, first Paul tells us he is a "slave." And then he declares that he is an "apostle." The first is a term of great humility that expresses Paul's sense of personal insignificance. The second is a title of great authority—so much authority that Paul could claim equality with the disciples whom Jesus chose while on earth.

In actuality, Paul's claim to be an apostle lined up in one sense with his claim to be a slave of God, since the Old Testament also identified Joshua and other prophets as "slaves" of God (Joshua 24:29; Amos 3:7). Thus Paul in describing himself as both a slave and an apostle was placing himself in the succession of the prophets. As a result, he could assert that "the gospel which was preached by me is not man's gospel. For I did not receive it from man, nor was I taught it, but it came through revelation" (Gal. 1:11, 12, RSV).

Paul had no doubt that his message was from God. Are we ready for that message? Are we prepared to let God's authoritative Word speak to our hearts and minds? In particular, are we ready for Romans, which has advice and counsel for nearly every aspect of our religious experience and daily life? Let us pray that we might be responsive to God's Word and will as we walk with Paul through the corridors of his letter to the Romans.

SET APART FOR WHAT?

Paul, . . . set apart for the gospel of God. Rom. 1:1, RSV.

PAUL IS TELLING the Romans about himself. So far he has stated that: (1) he is Jesus Christ's slave, and that (2) God has called him to be an apostle.

Now he claims that (3) he has been set apart for the gospel.

We find two ideas in this third identifying factor. First, Paul was "set apart" for the gospel. That is an interesting phrase, since set apart has the same root meaning as Pharisee (one who is separated). With that in mind, Anders Nygren writes that "even before his becoming a Christian [Paul] had been 'set apart.' As a Pharisee he had set himself apart for the law. But now God had set him apart for something entirely different. . . . Paul, who had set himself apart for the law, is [now] set apart by God for the gospel." Thus the very first verse of the Epistle raises the tension between law and gospel as ways of approaching God, a tension that runs through-out the entire letter.

The second idea contained in Paul's third description of himself is "the gospel of God." In that phrase we not only meet the first usage of the word "gospel" in the Epistle but also the understanding that the gospel comes from God.

At this point we will not say much about the word gospel (literally, "good news"), since that word and the meaning behind it lies at the heart of the book of Romans and we will discuss it at great length as we move through the Epistle. Rather, we want to note that the gospel comes from God. "God" is the most important word in the Epistle. Not only did God call Paul, but God is the author of the gospel. Paul and the other apostles did not invent the good news. Rather it was revealed to them by the God, who also called them and set them apart to preach it.

The fact that God is the author of the gospel is the first point of a six-part analysis of the gospel that Paul sets forth in Romans 1:1-6. We will examine the rest of the points in the next few days. But for the present it is vital to recognize the fact that the most important thing in Paul's life was the gospel message. It changed him from a Pharisee to a Christian. The gospel summoned him to dedicate his life to preaching the gospel. That summons is ours also. And just as it was for Paul, the gospel in our lives will shape everything we do or think. As Paul notes in Romans 1:16, there is "power" in God's gospel.

14

THE GOOD NEWS ISN'T AN AFTERTHOUGHT

Set apart for the gospel of God, which He promised beforehand through His prophets in the holy Scriptures. Rom. 1:1, 2, NASB.

THE SECOND THING PAUL wants us to know about the gospel is that it wasn't something new, something invented by the disciples. To the contrary, the entire Old Testament points to the Christ and His work. The first allusion appears in Genesis 3:15, in which God promised that the seed of the woman would eventually defeat the devil. The last is in Malachi 4:5, which promises Elijah, the forerunner of the Messiah.

To put it bluntly, "the gospel . . . He promised beforehand through His prophets" is the key to understanding the entire Old Testament. The Old Testament points toward Christ, while the New expounds and expands upon the implications of God's good news in Jesus.

It was no accident that John the Baptist, upon first seeing Jesus, cried out, "Behold the Lamb of God, which taketh away the sin of the world" (John 1:29) or that Paul referred to Jesus as our "passover" (1 Cor. 5:7). The central symbol of the Old Testament is the sacrificial system pointing to the substitutionary sacrifice of Christ who would die for the world's sins.

That Jesus died for each and every human being—that He died our death, that we might have His life—stands at the very foundation of Paul's understanding of the gospel.

The fact that the Old Testament promised the gospel provides one of the major themes of the sermons in the New Testament. We see this in Peter's Pentecostal sermon of Acts 2, Paul's preaching in Acts 13, and Philip's dialogue with the Ethiopian official concerning Isaiah 53 and the sheep led to slaughter (Acts 8:32, 33).

Jesus Himself helped His followers recognize that the Old Testament pointed to His work. Describing Jesus' conversation with the two He met on the road to Emmaus, the Bible tells us that "beginning at Moses and all the prophets, he expounded unto them in all the scriptures the things concerning himself" (Luke 24:27).

We thank You today, Father, for not only sending Jesus, but for anchoring our faith in the corridors of Old Testament history. Thank You for the knowledge that the gospel was not an afterthought, but at the heart of Your providence from the beginning.

WHO IS JESUS? PART 1

*Set apart for the gospel . . . regarding his Son, who as to
his human nature was a descendant of David." Rom. 1:1-3, NIV.*

THIS VERSE COMES IN the midst of Paul's six-point preliminary analysis of the gospel to which God had set him apart. His first point is that the gospel came from God, the second is that the Old Testament predicted it, and the third (today's passage) is that Jesus is the gospel's focal point.

But who is this Jesus? Paul answers that question in Romans 1:3-5. The first part of his answer is that Jesus is David's Son, according to the flesh or human nature.

Now, you may be thinking that that is a strange way to talk about Jesus. After all, don't we all have human nature? Yes, but not just like Jesus.

In today's verse Paul tells us two things about Jesus—one in a straightforward manner and the other in a more veiled way. The veiled allusion appears in the words "as to his human nature." Paul reminds us of the fact that Jesus was not merely a human being, the Son of David, but also the Son of God. One of the great teachings of the Gospel of Matthew is that Jesus was Mary's son but not Joseph's—that is, He was the son of Mary and the Holy Spirit (Matt. 1:18). Thus Jesus was not exactly like other human beings. He was both human and divine, or as Matthew puts it, "God with us" (verse 23). As a result, the incarnate Jesus was in a position to "save his people from their sins" (verse 21).

Praise God! Jesus is not only the Son of David, but also the Son of God. As such He becomes the agent of God's salvation. That is truly good news—truly gospel.

But the Son of David aspect of Jesus is also crucial. "Son of David" was a universally recognized messianic title going back to 2 Samuel 7:12, 13, in which God promised to establish David's throne forever.

Jeremiah refers to that accepted understanding when he prophesies:
" 'The days are coming,' declares the Lord,
    'When I will raise up to David a righteous Branch,
  A King who will reign wisely
    and do what is just and right in the land. . . .
  This is the name by which he will be called:
    The Lord Our Righteousness' " (Jer. 23:5, 6, NIV).
Paul will build the book of Romans on the fact that Jesus is indeed "our righteousness," our hope, our Savior.

WHO IS JESUS? PART 2

*Jesus Christ our Lord was shown to be the Son of God
when God powerfully raised him from the dead by
means of the Holy Spirit. Rom. 1:4, NLT.*

YES, JESUS IS THE SON of David, but even more important is the fact that he was "declared with power to be the Son of God by his resurrection from the dead" (Rom. 1:4, NIV). The good news centers not only on His incarnation but also on His resurrection.

Nothing is more useless than a dead Savior. That is not good news. If Jesus had come to earth and merely lived a good (even perfect) life and died a heroic death, He would have been merely one more good and heroic man. But dead like the rest of them.

The good news, Paul tells us, is that Jesus is not merely another good man who came to an unjust end. To the contrary, His resurrection demonstrates Him to be the powerful Son of God. The good news is that Jesus lives on to continue His work for those who have accepted Him.

Christ's resurrection was central to Paul. In 1 Corinthians 15:1-4 he specifically identifies it as an essential part of the gospel message and notes that "if Christ has not been raised, our preaching is useless and so is your faith" (verse 14, NIV).

Christianity is built upon the fact that Jesus had victory over death itself, a fact that transformed the sniveling post-Calvary disciples into the courageous crusaders that we find in the early chapters of the book of Acts. Jesus, they realized, was truly the Christ and their Lord and Savior. His resurrection from the dead demonstrated that fact.

"Fear not," Jesus tells us, "I am the first and the last, and the living one; I died, and behold I am alive for evermore, and I have the keys of Death and Hades" (Rev. 1:17, 18, RSV). The gospel of His resurrection is also good news for us. His resurrection is a guarantee of our own. He won the victory for us. Thus we have hope, even as we stand at the graves of our loved ones (1 Thess. 4:13-18). Jesus is the "firstfruits of those who have fallen asleep" in Him (1 Cor. 15:20, NIV). Those who accept Him will be resurrected when He comes again (verses 23, 52).

The resurrection of Christ is the hinge of history. "Before that," Anders Nygren points out, "He was the Son of God in weakness and lowliness. Through the resurrection He became the Son of God in power."

Thank You today, Lord, for power, for hope, for the gospel.

THE OBEDIENCE OF WHAT?

Jesus Christ our Lord, through whom we have received
grace and apostleship to bring about the obedience of faith
for the sake of his name among all the nations. Rom. 1:4, 5, RSV.

A FIFTH POINT TO NOTE in Paul's initial analysis of the gospel is that its purpose is "the obedience of faith." The phrase is an especially interesting one because it shows up both at the beginning of Romans and at its very end (Rom. 16:26). Thus "the obedience of faith" is a central idea in Romans, the phrase bracketing the entire book.

Wait a minute, you may be thinking. *I thought that the whole point of Romans was that justification is through faith alone.* Yet here Paul seems to be saying that it is not by faith alone, but by "the obedience of faith." Are we dealing with a confused apostle?

Not really. The New International Version captures Paul's idea when it translates the phrase as "the obedience that comes from faith." Paul declares that it is impossible to claim Jesus as Savior without surrendering to Him as Lord of our lives. Obedience to Jesus as Lord is the faith response of those who have been justified freely by His grace. Thus it was in the case of Abraham, who "by faith . . . obeyed" (Heb. 11:8, RSV).

Please underline the fact that we are not here dealing with legalistic obedience of law but the obedience that results from faith. Paul teaches throughout the entire book of Romans that obedience flows out of a saving faith relationship with Jesus. The apostle is adamant that genuine Christian obedience rises from faith and is never independent of a saving relationship with Jesus as Lord. Thus he writes that "whatever does not proceed from faith is sin" (Rom. 14:23, RSV). Any so-called obedience that takes place outside of a faith relationship with God is nothing but the sinful arrogance of unrenewed individuals who think that they can be good without God.

Paul's sixth and final point in his analysis of the gospel in Romans 1:1-5 is that the goal of the gospel is the glorification of Christ's name throughout the world.

Thus while our immediate purpose in preaching the gospel is to bring people to faith and then into the obedience of faith, our ultimate goal, writes John Stott, "is the greater glory of the name of Jesus Christ."

Lord, help me this day that I might not only have faith, but that that faith will direct my every action for Your glory.

WHO CALLS WHOM?

*And you also are among those who are called
to belong to Jesus Christ. Rom. 1:6, NIV.*

WITH ROMANS 1:6 the letter makes a radical shift. The first five verses dealt with Paul and his understanding of the gospel. In verse 6 he begins to focus on the recipients of his letter—the believers in Rome.

This text contains two great ideas. The first is that God had *called* the Romans. That is a powerful idea. Sometimes we get the idea that we have to do something before God loves us. I remember some time ago reading the headline in a tabloid: "Hubby Crawls 900 Miles to Beg Forgiveness."

Many people have a similar idea about God. If I crawl far enough, work hard enough, or become good enough, perhaps He will finally accept me. But that is not Paul's picture. He makes it plain that it is God who initiates our personal salvation. *God calls us.*

The Bible portrays this from beginning to end. It is God who searches out Adam and Eve in the Garden of Eden; God who seeks the lost sheep, the lost coin, and the rebellious son in Luke 15; and God who arrests Paul's attention on the road to Damascus. Jesus said it concisely in Luke 19:10 when He told Zacchaeus that "the Son of man is come to seek and to save that which was lost."

Salvation is God's initiative. "God so loved the world, that he gave his only begotten Son, that whosoever believeth in him should not perish, but have everlasting life" (John 3:16). "God shows his love for us in that while we were yet sinners Christ died for us" (Rom. 5:8, RSV). It is God who does the searching. He is the one who does the calling. Our part is to respond to His invitation.

The second central idea in Romans 1:6 is that those in Rome who had responded to God's gracious invitation "belong to Jesus Christ." The words "belong to" refer back to verse 1, in which Paul tells us he is Christ's slave. To belong to someone implies ownership. Thus each Christian in Rome, like Paul, was a slave of Christ because Jesus had purchased or redeemed them by His blood. The same can be said for each of us.

Thank You, Lord, for both Your calling and Your redemption. Help me to so live today that those around me will recognize that I truly belong to You and no one else. And beyond that, please use me today as a channel for extending Your call to others who have not heard it yet.

Saint George of Berrien Springs

*To all in Rome who are loved by God
and called to be saints. Rom. 1:7, NIV.*

JUST THINK. THE BELIEVERS in Rome were not merely called, but were summoned to be "saints."

What do you think of when you hear the word "saint"? A special person? A Mother Teresa? Individuals who have been martyred for their faith? A hero of the Christian faith, such as Saint Peter or Saint Paul?

The Bible answer is much different. The basic meaning of the word is to be "set apart." The idea is that Christians are set apart for God. The word in the Greek also implies to be holy. Thus a saint is one whom God has set apart for holiness.

"Saint" comes from the same root word as "sanctification," which also means to be set apart for holy use. Thus in the Old Testament God sanctified, dedicated, and set apart the wilderness tabernacle, Solomon's Temple, the Levites, and the priesthood for His holy use. The Lord also told Moses to "sanctify" ("consecrate," RSV) the entire people of Israel to Him (Ex. 19:10). Thus the Jewish people were God's Old Testament saints.

The New Testament regards those who believe in Jesus as Savior and Lord as the saints. Thus Paul could note that even the individuals in the rather disorderly Corinthian church were "called to be saints" (1 Cor. 1:2). So am I! That's good news. Just as with Paul in Romans 1:1, God has called us and set us apart for holy service to Him.

In one sense we as saints have been called from something (the principles and ways of "the world"). But even more important is the idea that each Christian has been called to God.

God's saints are His people. Thus the title of today's reading. I am Saint George of Berrien Springs. You may be Saint Gerald of Hagerstown or Saint Nancy of Sydney. But we all have one thing in common. We are God's servants; we have been set apart to do His will; we have been called and put on the path of God's salvation.

And what is my response?

Take me today, God, and use me for Your glory. Help me to be like You. Amen.

THREE SPECIAL WORDS

Grace to you and peace from God our Father,
and the Lord Jesus Christ. Rom. 1:7.

WITH ROMANS 1:7 PAUL ends his greetings to the Christians at Rome. But in his concluding words we find three ideas that will be central in the letter that follows.

First is the word "grace," which Paul uses more than 20 times in Romans. In its Christian sense grace is God's gift of salvation to us. Romans 6:23 makes it clear that salvation is a gift: "The wages of sin is death, but the free gift of God is eternal life in Christ Jesus our Lord" (RSV). God in His love doesn't give us what we deserve (death) but what we don't deserve (eternal life). That's grace.

Second is the word "peace." In Paul's thinking peace has a close connection with grace. Thus he writes in Romans 5:1 that "since we are justified by faith, we have peace with God through our Lord Jesus Christ" (RSV).

Peace is a beautiful New Testament word. For the pagan world of the first century peace meant the absence of war. But in the New Testament the word has a positive connotation related to the Hebrew concept of *shalom*. The Hebrews and the New Testament writers consider peace not so much the absence of strife as the presence of positive blessing.

In Paul's greetings, "peace" (when used) always follows "grace." Only God's grace can bring about genuine peace in the human heart.

The third great word in our passage for today is "Father." All the way through the New Testament the term expresses God's love and tender care for each of His children. God doesn't ignore our plight. As our Father He is actively on our side and cares for us with the strength of a true father's love. The thought of the Fatherhood of God climaxes in Romans 8, when Paul talks about Christians becoming a part of the family of God. When that happens, he asserts, nothing "will be able to separate us from the love of God in Christ Jesus" (Rom. 8:39, RSV).

Paul's use of "grace" and "peace" in his greetings was not new with him. We find it in the blessing that Aaron was to use to bless the Israelites.

"The Lord bless you and keep you;
the Lord make his face shine upon you and be gracious to you;
the Lord turn his face toward you and give you peace" (Num. 6:24-26, NIV).

A REPUTATION WORTH HAVING

First, I thank my God through Jesus Christ for you all,
that your faith is spoken of throughout the whole world. Rom. 1:8.

WITH ROMANS 1:8 WE find Paul moving from the generalities of a greeting to the business at hand. First he commends the Romans. There is a lesson in that for us. All of us see both good and bad things in people. I imagine the same held for Paul and the Romans. He probably could have found fault with something they were doing or believing. But he chose to begin with the positive rather than the negative.

I wish that everyone could learn that lesson. Unfortunately, I know some church members who always greet me with the negative. In place of a good word, it is always what's wrong with the world, the church, or other people. Sometimes these "apostles of joy" even start with what's wrong with me. Now what they have to say may be important or even true, but psychologically I find it easier to listen to them if we can start out on a positive note. The other stuff may have its place—after we have established a relationship.

Paul's letter can teach us some things about communication. Here is something you can practice in your family or work place: Discover and mention the good in other people. Start on the positive. For some of us, given our reputations, our positive attitude and words might actually send shock waves through those who have to deal with us. If so, praise God! God wants to transform His saints even in their conversation. Thanks, Paul, for the side lesson.

The main lesson of verse 8 is also important. The Romans, he claimed, had a reputation for genuine faith recognized far and wide. Their "faith" was "being reported all over the world" (NIV). That is a reputation worth having.

Paul's commendation should raise questions in each of our minds. What do people say when they speak about us? What comes to their minds when they think of our local church?

Evangelism does not begin when the great evangelist finally arrives in town. Rather, it starts with our reputation as men, women, and children of faith.

Lord, help me today not only to be more like Paul in my attitudes and communication, but help me know how I can best let my light shine to those around me, how I can develop a reputation as a person of faith.

THE MINISTRY OF PRAYER

God, whom I serve with my whole heart in preaching the
gospel of His Son, is my witness how constantly I remember
you in my prayers. Rom. 1:9, NIV.

PAUL NOT ONLY HAS a positive compliment for the Romans, as we saw yesterday, but he also wants them to know that he is praying for them. Paul was a man of intercessory prayer.

The apostle was well aware of the fact that "prayer moves the arm of Omnipotence" (*Christ's Object Lessons,* p. 172). He spent much time in prayer for other people because he knew that his ministry of prayer helped people.

The realization of the power of intercessory prayer has inspired people to pray for others across the ages. It has been especially true of parents. "The mother of Augustine," penned Ellen White, "prayed for her son's conversion. She saw no evidence that the Spirit of God was impressing his heart, but she was not discouraged. She laid her finger upon the texts, presenting before God His own words, and pleaded as only a mother can. Her deep humiliation, her earnest importunities, her unwavering faith, prevailed, and the Lord gave her the desire of her heart. Today He is just as ready to listen to the petitions of His people. His 'hand is not shortened that it cannot save; neither his ear heavy, that it cannot hear;' and if Christian parents seek Him earnestly, He will fill their mouths with arguments [to help their children], and for His name's sake will work mightily in their behalf in the conversion of their children" (*Testimonies for the Church,* vol. 5, pp. 322, 323).

Augustine truly looked like a hopeless case. Caught in the web of sensuality and drunkenness, he didn't appear a very likely candidate for church leadership. But God honored his mother's prayers. He would in his later years become, next to Jesus and Paul, perhaps the most well-known leader of the Christian church.

Intercessory prayer is important. That is why Paul constantly remembered the Romans in prayer.

How is it with me? Who is on my prayer list? Is it my children? my parents? my pastor? my neighbor? my church? my government?

Am I following Paul's example? Jesus said that we should even pray for those who persecute us (Matt. 5:44). The age of miracles isn't over yet. God is able to use our prayers to change the world. Will we let Him?

23

THE PURPOSE OF PAUL'S LETTER

I pray that now at last by God's will the way may
be opened for me to come to you. Rom. 1:10, NIV.

PAUL HAS REACHED A critical juncture in his ministry. His evangelization thus far had covered the Roman provinces of Galatia, Asia, Macedonia, and Achaia (territories that cover roughly the modern nations of Turkey, Greece, and Macedonia), and he was preparing to move the focus of his ministry to Spain.

But before going to Spain, the apostle needed to visit two other places. The first was Jerusalem, so that he could deliver the contribution for the poor among the Jewish Christians that he had collected from the Gentile churches. His second visit on the way to Spain would be Rome (Rom. 15:23-28).

Those two forthcoming visits set the stage for Paul's letter to the Christians in Rome. He had at least three goals in the letter. First, he wanted the Romans to pray for his ministry to the Jewish Christians in Jerusalem and that he might "be rescued from the unbelievers in Judea" (verses 30, 31, NIV). It was no small thing for Paul to go to Jerusalem. The non-Christians there viewed him as a troublemaker and many of the Christians regarded him as a liberalizer who had been disloyal to their Jewish heritage. To accept a gift from such a person, some evidently feared, might seem to be agreeing with Paul's theological perspective. Thus the apostle asked for the prayers of the Romans.

Beyond that, however, Paul also requested that the Roman church "assist" him in his mission to Spain (verse 24, NIV). That appeal for help provides the second reason for writing the letter. He apparently hoped that they would support his ministry to Spain with their encouragement, prayers, and finances.

In order to gain that assistance, Paul felt that he needed to establish his apostolic credentials. As a result, he wrote a letter that set forth his view of what C.E.B. Cranfield calls "the inner logic of the gospel."

As he explained the gospel, Paul hoped to accomplish a third goal by healing the evident rift between the Jewish and Gentile Christians in the Roman Church through demonstrating that the good news of salvation was for all people (see Rom. 1:16, 17; 11:32).

To the best of our knowledge, Paul never made it to Spain. But his letter to Rome has influenced the church for 2,000 years.

24

THE HEART OF PAUL'S MINISTRY

I am longing to see you so that I may share with you
some spiritual gift to strengthen you. Rom. 1:11, NRSV.

THE GOAL OF THE APOSTLE Paul's life was ministry—service to others.

When he planned his trip to Rome, it was not to go as a tourist to see the famous Appian Way, the Forum, the Colosseum, or the chariot races. No, his primary purpose was to be a blessing to the Roman Christians. As he put it, he wanted to impart to them "some spiritual gift."

Service to others was a keynote in the apostle's experience. We see his selfless giving vividly reflected in 2 Corinthians, in which he wrote: "I will gladly spend myself and all I have for your spiritual good, even though it seems that the more I love you, the less you love me" (2 Cor. 12:15, NLT).

Perhaps the tenderness of Paul's loving spirit shows up most beautifully in his first letter to the Thessalonians. "We proved to be gentle among you," he penned, "as a nursing mother tenderly cares for her own children. Having so fond an affection for you, we were well-pleased to impart to you not only the gospel of God but also our own lives, because you had become very dear to us. For you recall, brethren, our labor and hardship, how working night and day so as not to be a burden to any of you, we proclaimed to you the gospel of God" (1 Thess. 2:7-9, NASB).

That same spirit of loving service surfaces in the Epistle to the Romans, to whom Paul wants to impart "some spiritual gift." The term *spiritual gift* could imply a special charismatic gift, such as prophecy or the generosity that he later mentions in Romans 12:6-8, but the book also uses the idea of spiritual gift in other ways. In Romans 5:15, for example, Paul speaks of justification by faith as a gift. It appears that he employs the phrase in Romans 1:11 in the sense of those things that build up spiritual life.

That is the central goal in Paul's life—he wants to build up people in Christ. He not only sought to do it for the Romans, but he wants to do it for me as an individual.

He could, of course, visit with the Romans in person. But the good news is that the apostle still meets with us today—not in person, but through the pages of his letters.

Thank you, Paul, for your ministry to me. Help me to pass on the blessing.

MINISTRY IS A TWO-WAY STREET

*That we may be mutually encouraged by each other's faith,
both yours and mine. Rom. 1:12, RSV.*

HERE IS HUMILITY!

Listen to the great apostle! Listen to the man directly called by God on the road to Damascus! Listen to the man greatly used of God! Listen to one of the most influential voices in the history of civilization!

Paul never thought that he was above being spiritually edified by the people in the pews. He hoped to learn from them as well as to teach them. The Romans could bless him even as he blessed them. For Paul, ministry was a two-way street.

In reflecting on this verse, John Calvin the Reformer wrote: "See to what degree of modesty his pious heart submitted itself, so that he [refused] not to seek confirmation from unexperienced beginners: nor did he speak [falsely] for there is no one so void of gifts in the Church of Christ, who is not able to contribute something to our benefit: but we are hindered by our envy and by our pride from gathering such fruit from one another. Such is our high-mindedness, such is the [intoxication] produced by vain reputation, that despising and disregarding others, every one thinks that he possesses what is abundantly sufficient for himself."

Spiritual pride is about the worst of all illnesses. It is no accident that Jesus begins the Beatitudes with "Blessed are the poor in spirit: for their's is the kingdom of heaven" (Matt. 5:3). He knew that it is only the humble who can hear His voice.

Peter, who from time to time had a bit of a problem with the balance between greatness and humility, counseled that church leaders should not aim at "being dictators but examples of Christian living. . . . And then, when the Chief Shepherd reveals himself, you will receive that crown of glory which cannot fade" (1 Peter 5:3, 4, Phillips).

We need to see the church not in terms of greater and lesser members but as a mutual-enhancement society in which every person is a servant and teacher to each of the others.

That appears to have been Paul's ideal. He not only gave blessings, but he was open to receiving them from those he served.

Lord, help me today to have the spirit of service and humility that formed the very foundation of Paul's ministry.

PAUL THE FRUIT FARMER

Now I do not want you to be unaware, brethren, that I often planned to come to you (but was hindered until now), that I might have some fruit among you also, just as among the other Gentiles. Rom. 1:13, NKJV.

CHARLIE HAD BEEN PRAYING earnestly for a bicycle for Christmas. His family was poor and he not only wanted a bicycle, he *needed* one. Christmas arrived, but it brought no bike. A family friend who wasn't very sensitive said to Charlie, "Well, I see God didn't answer your prayer for a bicycle."

"Yes, He did," the boy replied. "He said no."

Not all of our prayers get a positive response. That must have been Paul's experience as he prayerfully planned a trip to Rome on several different occasions. He wanted to go, but God wasn't ready for him to leave yet.

But now at last the apostle received a green light to move west. It set the appetite of Paul's spirit on edge. His very first thought was that he might gather some "fruit" in Rome.

The Bible uses the word "fruit" in relation to spiritual things in at least three ways. First it serves as a metaphor for the attitudes that characterize the Spirit-filled person. Thus Galatians 5:22, 23 lists the "fruit of the Spirit": "love, joy, peace, longsuffering, gentleness, goodness, faith, meekness, [and] temperance."

A second meaning involves a Christian's actions. Paul writes to the Romans about having "fruit unto holiness" (Rom. 6:22).

A third meaning of spiritual fruit in the New Testament refers to the increase of converts to Christ. As a result, Paul can speak of Epaenetus as being the "firstfruits" or first convert for Christ in Achaia (Rom. 16:5).

It is undoubtedly the third meaning that Paul has in mind in today's text. The apostle wanted God to use him to help the Roman church add new members to its ranks. His heart was perpetually a soul-winning one. Nothing made Paul happier than leading individuals into a saving relationship with Jesus.

Having said that, however, does not exclude the first two meanings of fruit. He sought also to enable people to mature in Christ in both the fruits of the Spirit (character traits) and in their daily living (behavior).

Paul seeks the same thing today for me: to dedicate my life to Christ constantly and to become more like Him in character.

THE THREE "I AM"S

I am obligated both to Greeks and non-Greeks, both to the wise and the foolish. That is why I am so eager to preach the gospel also to you who are at Rome. Rom. 1:14, 15, NIV.

ROMANS 1:14-16 PRESENTS three forceful personal statements about Paul's concern to preach the gospel in Rome:

verse 14: "I am obligated"

verse 15: "I am . . . eager"

verse 16: "I am not ashamed"

John Stott points out that the reason these affirmations are so striking is that they are in direct opposition to the attitude of many in today's church. "People nowadays tend to regard evangelism as an optional extra and (if they engage in it) that they are conferring a favour on God."

Paul's attitude has a lesson for us today. Part of the secret of the success of his ministry was that he fully believed that he was under a moral obligation to preach the gospel message. For him, that obligation was not an option but a debt to the Christ who had given His life that he might have life everlasting.

But obligation for Paul did not mean dreary duty. Rather, he was "eager to preach the gospel" so that others might understand the truth that had so blessed his own personal life. When it came to Jesus, Paul was a difficult man to shut up. His eagerness kept him active.

With verses 14 and 15 we are beginning to touch upon the heart of his theme in Romans. First, this passage notes that Paul's message is for both the Greeks and the non-Greeks, the wise and the foolish. In short, he had a message for everyone—to Jews, Gentiles, the intelligent and the educated, and those who lacked education. As we shall soon see, Paul's theme in Romans is essentially that God's grace and mercy is for everyone. Paul will expound upon that idea in Romans 1:16.

Another idea in Romans 1:15 that he will develop in verses 16 and 17 is that of "gospel." We noted in our examination of verse 3 that "gospel" is best translated as "good news."

The reason for Paul's eagerness to preach is that he realizes that the good news is better than anyone can even imagine. Unable to sit still, he is impelled to tell others about Jesus.

THE THIRD "I AM"

I am not ashamed. Rom. 1:16.

PAUL'S THIRD "I AM" sounds a bit strange at first. Why should he, or anyone else for that matter, be ashamed of the gospel? After all, in other places he claims to glory and rejoice in the gospel message (see Gal. 6:14; Rom. 5:2, 11).

Perhaps the answer to the question of why Paul put the phrase about not being ashamed of the gospel at this point in his letter is that some in Rome despised the simplicity of the gospel message. It had certainly been the case in Corinth, where some saw the preaching of a crucified Savior to be "foolishness" (1 Cor. 1:18). In fact, he noted a few verses later, the preaching of "Christ crucified" was a "stumblingblock" to the Jews and "unto the Greeks foolishness" (verse 23). Again, in Athens "some mocked" "when they heard of the resurrection of the dead" (Acts 17:32).

To preach a God who became a man through a virgin birth, died as a criminal on a cross, rose bodily from the dead, went to live in heaven, and would return to earth some day didn't exactly make rational sense to the sophisticates of that day. And the self-appointed sophisticates of any age can make one feel a little squeamish with their better-than-thou attitudes and airs.

Another reason the people of Paul's time hesitated to preach Christ was that in addition to verbal abuse, it often brought physical persecution. William Barclay notes that "Paul had been imprisoned in Philippi, chased out of Thessalonica, smuggled out of Berea, laughed at in Athens."

Then again, the apostle may not have had an overly impressive physical presence. Early tradition in the apocryphal book of the Acts of Paul and Thecla describes him as "a man of short stature, with a bald head and crooked legs, . . . with eyebrows meeting and nose somewhat hooked" (par. 2).

To put it bluntly, Paul probably had all the same problems as you and I when it comes to testifying for our Lord. It has never been easy or painless to witness. We always put ourselves in danger of ridicule and jest.

Yet Paul was "eager" to preach his message. Beyond that, far from being ashamed of the gospel, he was *proud* of it. Why? Paul will answer that question in Romans 1:16 and 17 as he talks about the power and salvation of our God. By the time he finishes we all have a right to be proud of the gospel.

DEFINING THE GOSPEL

The gospel. Rom. 1:16.

YOU MAY BE WONDERING at the brevity of our scripture reading today.

Good! Keep wondering. I want you to think hard on the word "gospel" and nothing else.

Let the word itself sink in. *Gospel!* We have noted more than once that it translates from the Greek as "good news." But today we want to examine Paul's best definitions of the word.

The first is in Romans 1:16, 17, in which he describes the gospel as "the power of God for salvation to every one who has faith, to the Jew first and also to the Greek. For in [the gospel] the righteousness of God is revealed through faith for faith; as it is written, 'He who through faith is righteous shall live'" (RSV).

The second appears in 1 Corinthians 15:1-4: "Now I would remind you, brethren, in what terms I preached to you the gospel, which you received, in which you stand, by which you are saved, if you hold it fast. . . . For I delivered to you as of first importance what I also received, that Christ died for our sins in accordance with the scriptures, that he was buried, that he was raised on the third day" (RSV).

A third passage, while not mentioning the word "gospel," certainly highlights its content. "For by grace you have been saved through faith: and this is not your own doing, it is the gift of God—not of works lest any man should boast" (Eph. 2:8, 9, RSV).

Again, "but now the righteousness of God has been manifested apart from law . . . , the righteousness of God through faith in Jesus Christ for all who believe. . . . They are justified by his grace as a gift, through the redemption which is in Christ Jesus, whom God put forth as an expiation by his blood, to be received by faith" (Rom. 3:21-25, RSV).

Read those verses again and again. Meditate upon their meaning. Savor the great gospel words of "grace" and "faith." And note that the sacrifice, death, and resurrection of Christ form the foundation of Paul's understanding of the gospel.

It is a small word. But one that means everything to you and me. One that has literally changed the world. Praise God for His gift in Jesus. Praise God for the good news.

GOD'S POWER

The gospel . . . is the power of God for the salvation
of everyone who believes. Rom. 1:16, NIV.

THE FIRST THING I sensed was a blinding flash on a mountain some miles distant. Next I saw a huge cloud of dirt and debris. At that point the first sound waves shook my car, and I realized that I had witnessed a mighty explosion.

The explosive agent in this case was undoubtedly dynamite. That English word comes from the Greek *dunamis,* meaning "power." Paul uses the word in Romans 1:16 in relation to the work of salvation. He expresses the fact that the gospel carries with it the omnipotence of God, whose power alone is able to save individuals from sin and give them eternal life.

One reason that Paul is not ashamed of the gospel is that it is backed by God's power. And one thing the apostle will make crystal clear in the early chapters of Romans is that people are unable to save themselves from the ravages of sin. No matter how hard they try, they can't free themselves from the corruption that abides in their very nature.

That's where God's power comes in. He can do what we can't do. And it's very good news.

God's power, the apostle claims, is aimed at salvation, a word meaning to rescue, preserve, deliver, or save. The basic idea is that the power of God in salvation rescues people from the penalties of sin.

Salvation has both positive and negative implications. Negatively, it will—among other things—deliver people from wrath (Rom. 5:9), from hostility to God (verse 10), from sin (Matt. 1:21), from being lost (Luke 19:10), from futility (1 Peter 1:18), from a "yoke of slavery" (Gal. 5:1, NIV), from demon possession (Luke 8:36), and from sickness (verse 48). On the positive side, salvation brings reconciliation with God (Rom. 5:9, 10) and a multitude of blessings. Jesus, Matthew tells us, came to bring salvation to His people (Matt. 1:21).

Salvation, as the general work of God, has past, present, and future implications. In one sense it has already been accomplished and provided for by the once-for-all death of Jesus on the cross (Heb. 7:27). But it is also the present experience of those who accept God's gift and are learning to walk with Him (Rom. 6:1-10). Then again, salvation has a future aspect. It will not be completed in all its fulness until Jesus comes again in the clouds of heaven (1 Thess. 4:13-18; 1 Cor. 15:51-55).

THE WIDTH OF MERCY

To the Jew first, and also to the Greek. Rom. 1:16.

"SALVATION," PAUL SAID, IS for "everyone who believes: first for the Jew, then for the Gentile" (Rom. 1:16, NIV). In other words, it has a universal scope. After all, from the Jewish perspective the world had only two kinds of people—those who were Jews and those who weren't. As Leon Morris puts it, "the combination stands for the totality of mankind. The gospel is for all and knows no limitation by race." W. H. Griffith Thomas hit the nail on the head when he penned that "salvation is for everyone, from every sin, at every time, in every place, under every circumstance." A worldwide need led God to make a worldwide provision. It is little wonder that Paul refers to his understanding of salvation as the gospel or good news. Nothing could be better.

Yet salvation has one condition: it is for "everyone who believes." God doesn't force it on anyone. People must accept it as they see their need in relation to the power of the gospel and its potential for their lives.

But all who accept God's salvation by faith are on one level—they become brothers and sisters in Christ. The Jews don't have one gospel and the Gentiles another. The community of Christ erases all racial, economic, and social barriers. As Paul wrote to the Galatians, "there is neither Jew nor Greek, there is neither slave nor free, there is neither male nor female; for you are all one in Christ Jesus" (Gal. 3:28, RSV).

The idea of salvation or mercy for all becomes a major theme throughout Romans. In fact, that very thought climaxes his treatment of Jewish and Gentile inclusion in the gospel blessing that runs from Romans 9-11. He made it clear that God desires to have *"mercy upon all"* (Rom. 11:32).

On the other hand, Paul is quite clear that in one sense Jews do have a priority. Jesus taught the same when He claimed that salvation came through Israel (John 4:22). After all, God not only used the Jewish nation to preserve the covenant in Old Testament times, but He also sent the Savior of the world through a Jewish mother.

The theme of the "firstness" of the Jewish nation runs throughout the New Testament. Thus in Acts 1:8 we read that after the disciples received the power of the Spirit they were to be God's witnesses beginning with the Jews and extending to the ends of the earth.

We can be thankful today that the wideness in God's mercy includes even us.

LUTHER'S GREAT TEXT

*For in the gospel a righteousness from God is revealed,
a righteousness that is by faith from first to last. Rom. 1:17, NIV.*

TODAY'S TEXT HAS BEEN one of the most influential in the history of Christianity. An understanding of it ignited the Protestant Reformation during the early 1500s. Let's let Martin Luther tell us about it in his own words: "I greatly longed to understand Paul's Epistle to the Romans and nothing stood in the way but that one expression, 'the justice of God,' because I took it to mean that justice whereby God is just and deals justly in punishing the unjust. My situation was that, although an impeccable monk, I stood before God as a sinner troubled in conscience, and I had no confidence that my merit would assuage him. Therefore I did not love a just and angry God, but rather hated and murmured against him. Yet I clung to the dear Paul and had a great yearning to know what he meant.

"Night and day I pondered until I saw the connection between the justice of God and the statement that 'the just shall live by faith.' *Then I grasped that the justice of God is that righteousness by which through grace and sheer mercy God justifies us through faith. Thereupon I felt myself to be reborn and to have gone through doors into paradise. The whole of Scripture took on a new meaning,* and whereas before the 'justice of God' had filled me with hate, now it became to me inexpressibly sweet in greater love. The passage of Paul became to me a gate to heaven" (italics supplied).

Romans 1:17, we read in *The Great Controversy,* never lost its power upon Luther. "From that time he saw more clearly than ever before the fallacy of trusting to human works for salvation, and the necessity of constant faith in the merits of Christ" (p. 125).

It will be easier for us to understand what happened to Luther when we realize that Greek uses the same word for both righteousness and justice. Luther, who had been reading the word in terms of justice and judgment, had been overwhelmed, because no matter how hard he tried, he couldn't be good enough. All he could see were God's just judgments. His breakthrough came when he realized that Paul was not emphasizing judgment but a righteousness that comes through faith. That day Luther passed from being a judgment-oriented Christian to being a grace-oriented Christian, a shift in understanding that changed the world. It will transform your life also.

THE CENTRALITY OF FAITH

As it is written, The just shall live by faith. Rom. 1:17.

PAUL IS QUITE CLEAR throughout Romans that salvation is a matter of faith "from start to finish." As Luther finally saw, salvation or righteousness does not come from being good or trying to be good, but from faith in the power of the gospel to save (Rom. 1:16).

In order to support his claim, Paul cites the Jewish scripture of Habakkuk 2:4 that "the just shall live by faith." The original context of that passage is interesting. The prophet had complained that God was using the ruthless Babylonians to punish Israel for their sinful ways. How could that be? How could God use the wicked to punish the wicked? In that context God told Habakkuk that the proud Babylonians would eventually fall, but that the righteous among the Israelites would live by their faith through their humble and consistent trust in God's power and mercy.

Paul took Habakkuk's passage and applied it to salvation from sin. In short, though it was impossible to gain everlasting life through obedience, it was possible to do so by simple trust in God: "the just shall live by faith."

C. H. Dodd helps us here when he writes that "for Paul faith is that attitude in which acknowledging our complete insufficiency for any of the high ends of life, we rely utterly on the sufficiency of God. It is to cease from all assertion of the self, even by way of effort after righteousness, to make room for the divine initiative." The phrase "righteousness by faith" derives from that perspective.

There appears, however, to be another idea buried in today's text, since a second acceptable translation of the text is that "he that is just shall live by faith." The concept here is that righteous people live their lives by faith.

While the context demands the reading that implies how people become righteous, the idea that those who are already righteous will live by faith is quite in harmony with the overall teaching of Romans. After all, saved people live changed lives on a daily basis. Having begun in faith at their conversion, they continue to walk with God day by day. Thus they live "from faith to faith" (Rom. 1:17).

Lord, today I want to thank You for both Your righteousness and Your sustaining power. Help me to live by faith because I have been saved by faith.

STEP 2
The Sin Problem

Romans 1:18–3:20

TAKING A SECOND STEP WITH PAUL

For the wrath of God is revealed from heaven against all
ungodliness and wickedness of men who by their
wickedness suppress the truth. Rom. 1:18, RSV.

WOW!

What happened? In the past few verses we had been reading about grace and faith and salvation. The highlight was mercy. But Romans 1:18 opens with the thunder of God's wrath.

The key to the transition is the word "for." "For" links the gospel presentation of Romans 1:16, 17 to the next couple of chapters and their discussion of sin. The word "for" implies that we need the gospel of salvation by the power of the gospel because of the depth of human sin.

Thus in Romans 1:18 we come to the first great transition in the book of Romans. We have met Paul in verses 1-17, in which he introduced himself, his purpose for writing the book, and his gospel. Now we are ready for step 2 in our walk with Paul through Romans.

Our second step runs from Romans 1:18 through 3:20. In that long section Paul explores the depth and universality of the sin problem. He demonstrates that "all [both Jews and Gentiles] have sinned" (Rom. 3:23). Therefore all need God's salvation by grace through faith on the basis of Christ's death on the cross (verses 21-26).

Thus we should see Romans 1:18–3:20 as God's diagnosis of the sin problem. The rest of the book deals with the cure. But before the cure people need to see the depth of the problem. Sin is serious. We can't just overlook it. It led to the death of Christ, God's solution for a lost world.

The word "wrath" is central in today's passage. Here we encounter the judgmental side of God's character. While wrath in the final analysis has to do with the destruction of wickedness at the end of time, it also concerns the daily results of sin in our ordinary world.

One thing is certain: God hates *sin!* He hates all those things that injure His children and oppose His love. In His love God finds Himself forced to deal with the sin problem. The central part of His answer, Paul will show us, is the cross of Christ.

Meanwhile, it is in Romans 1:18 that Paul begins to deal with the problem of sin.

Our Father, today we want to thank You that You see our problems so clearly, and that You cared for us enough to send Jesus on a rescue mission.

36

GOD'S SECOND BOOK

For since the creation of the world God's invisible qualities—
his eternal power and divine nature—have been clearly
seen, being understood from what has been made, so
that men are without excuse. Rom. 1:20, NIV.

THIS INTERESTING PASSAGE tells us that even people who don't have the Bible have some word from God, some knowledge of who He is. In the previous verse Paul had noted that "what may be known about God is plain to them, because God has made it plain to them" (Rom. 1:19, NIV). Verse 20 specifies that God makes His eternal power and divine nature plain through His creation.

This is an important point, since Paul in this section of Romans is demonstrating that Gentiles, in their relative ignorance, are still responsible for rebelling against what they know about God and goodness through what they see in nature and conscience.

God's revelation of Himself in nature is what theologians refer to as "general revelation." Such revelation, of course, is far from perfect. Ellen White makes that point when she writes: "Nature still speaks of her Creator. Yet these revelations are partial and imperfect. And in our fallen state, with weakened powers and restricted vision, we are incapable of interpreting aright. We need the fuller revelation of Himself that God has given in His written Word" (*Education,* p. 17). Theologians describe God's fuller revelation of Himself in the Bible as "special revelation."

The Jews of Paul's day had both of God's books (general and special revelation), but the Gentiles had only the incomplete revelation through nature. But, Paul argues, even that partial revelation through nature and conscience left them with a responsibility.

Their real problem, he penned in Romans 1:18, was that they preferred "godlessness and wickedness" (NIV) to what they knew about God and goodness. As a result, they had chosen to "supress the truth by their wickedness" (NIV). Rejecting that general revelation, Paul will go on to say in the last part of verse 20, leaves them without excuse.

The point here is that God has given every person some information about Himself and true goodness. Each of us, no matter how limited our knowledge, has a responsibility to live according to the information that God has provided.

Help me today, Father, to utilize all the light that You have given me.

TWO NEGLECTED PRIVILEGES

For although they knew God, they neither glorified
him as God nor gave thanks to him. Rom. 1:21, NIV.

HERE IS A TRAGEDY. Even though the majesty of God's creation and the intricacies of its interworkings confront every person, most throughout history have failed to either glorify Him or give Him thanks for their bountiful blessings. Because of this, along with the deliberate rebellion pictured in Romans 1:19 and 20, Paul presents a dismal picture of the downward results of sin throughout the rest of Romans 1. But before looking at the negative, let's focus on the positive.

First, it is our privilege to glorify or honor the God of all creation. The Bible frequently urges believers to glorify the Lord. Thus the psalmist tells us to "give unto the Lord glory and strength. Give unto the Lord the glory due unto his name; worship the Lord in the beauty of holiness" (Ps. 29:1, 2). Paul's counsel reflects the same spirit: "Whether therefore ye eat, or drink, or whatsoever ye do, do all to the glory of God" (1 Cor. 10:31). Such glorification, or praise, even takes place in the heavenly realms. The book of Revelation pictures the 24 elders falling down and worshiping God, saying "Thou art worthy, O Lord, to receive glory and honour and power: for thou hast created all things, and for thy pleasure they are and were created" (Rev. 4:11).

In a "normal" world glorifying God in worship and our daily lives would be a natural expression of the human heart. But, and this point undergirds Paul's argument in Romans 1:18-32, we don't live in a normal world. Since Adam and Eve, men and women have been interested in glorifying themselves more than God. The human race has too often had the spirit of Nebuchadnezzar, who proclaimed: "Is not this the great Babylon I have built as the royal residence, by my mighty power and for the glory of my majesty?" (Dan. 4:30, NIV).

A second privilege that each person has is to give thanks to God for His many gifts. Even though we live in a world of sin, we can be thankful for bodies that generally function well, for the miracle of digestion, for the love put in our hearts as we deal with our children. Yet too often, once again, as Paul points out, people forget the Giver of all good things.

Lord, help us this day to follow the road that honors and glorifies You and that thanks You for not only life itself but for every gift that makes life meaningful. Amen.

THE DOWNWARD PATH: STEP 1

*Their thinking became futile and their foolish hearts
were darkened. Although they claimed to be wise,
they became fools. Rom. 1:21, 22, NIV.*

REBELLING AGAINST GOD (Rom. 1:18-20) and neglecting praise and thankfulness affects us. In Romans 1:21-32 Paul presents the results of sin in a series of downward consequences. First it darkens people's hearts and they become fools even as they proclaim their wisdom. Eugene Peterson translates verses 22, 23 insightfully: "When they didn't treat him like God, refusing to worship him, they trivialized themselves into silliness and confusion so that there was neither sense nor direction left in their lives. They pretended to know it all, but were illiterate regarding life" (Message).

One of the first results of sin, Paul says, is that people's thinking becomes futile or ineffective, and their minds become foolish and darkened. The apostle was well aware of the philosophic contortions of the ancient world as it speculated on the meaning and purpose of life.

Human philosophies really haven't improved much in the 2,000 years since Paul wrote Romans. Thus David Hume in the late eighteenth century claimed that he could demonstrate in his study that no such thing as cause and effect exists in the world around us. He also noted that when he left his study and entered the everyday world he had a difficult time living by his philosophic discoveries.

A century later Friedrich Nietzsche, sometime before his tragic suicide, concluded that life had no meaning. For him the purpose of history was to develop the ruthless superman who did "right" by crushing those weaker than himself. Adolf Hitler later used that philosophy to justify his actions.

The twentieth century had its own share of philosophic "breakthroughs," such as William James's foundational point that truth is that which works or Jean-Paul Sartre's dictum that "other people are hell." Sartre was also quite clear that "there is no human nature, since there is no God to conceive it. . . . Man is nothing else but what he makes of himself."

Having given up a belief in the only true God, the world has endured a series of philosophic speculations that have led it into the nooks and crannies of darkness and futility. Such has been the intellectual result of humanity's turning its back on God.

Christians should glorify God daily that He not only exists but has revealed Himself in a way that gives life meaning.

THE DOWNWARD PATH: STEP 2

[They exchanged] the glory of the immortal God for an image
shaped like mortal man, even for images like birds,
beasts, and reptiles. Rom. 1:23, REB.

IN PAUL'S MIND ONE of the best examples of the foolishness of those who turned their backs on God was idolatry. Nothing, he implied, was more irrational than ignoring the Creator while at the same time worshiping images of His creation.

That insight did not originate with Paul. Isaiah, speaking of a craftsman, writes that he takes part of a tree and "warms himself, he kindles a fire and bakes bread," but with the rest of the tree "he makes a god and worships it, he makes it a graven image and falls down before it. Half of it he burns in the fire; over the half he eats flesh, he roasts meat and is satisfied; also he warms himself and says, 'Aha, I am warm.' . . . And the rest of it he makes into a god, his idol; and falls down to it and worships it, he prays to it and says, 'Deliver me, for thou art my god!' " (Isa. 44:15-17, RSV).

The writer of the ancient book known as Wisdom of Solomon takes the foolishness of idol worship a bit further. He speaks of creating a wooden idol, covering its defects with red paint, and making a shrine for it. He then "fixes it on the wall" with nails. The idol worshiper "has to take precautions on its behalf to save it from falling, for he well knows that it can't help itself: it needs help, for it is only an image. *Yet he prays to it* about his possessions and his wife and children, and feels no shame in addressing this inanimate object; *for health he appeals to a thing that is weak, for life he prays to a thing that is dead, for aid he asks help from something utterly incapable, for a prosperous journey from something that cannot put one foot before the other"* (Wis. of Sol. 12:15-18, REB).

Paul and the ancient Jews considered idol worship the ultimate irony, the ultimate foolishness. Paul declares in Romans 1 that such foolishness resulted from people's turning their back on what they knew about God. It was a product of their darkened thinking.

Now as modern twenty-first-century people we see the foolishness of idolatry. Or have we? What do we put our trust in? Our things? Our beauty? Our wisdom? Have we merely created more foolish idols?

Today is an excellent day for each of us to examine our own lives. It is time for clear thinking and rededication to the God who created everything.

THE DOWNWARD PATH: STEP 3

*Therefore God gave them over in the sinful desires of
their hearts. . . . They exchanged the truth of God for
a lie, and worshiped and served created things rather
than the Creator—who is forever praised. Rom. 1:24, 25, NIV.*

THE CORE PROBLEM OF SIN is really worship, a truth evident from
Genesis to Revelation. At the end of time, for example, the issue will be
whether people will "worship him that made heaven, and earth, and the
sea, and the fountains of waters" or "worship the beast and his image"
(Rev. 14:7, 9). The same dynamic operated in Eden, where Adam and Eve
had the choice of following God or listening to the words of the devil
(Gen. 3:1-6).

In the light of the centrality of worship throughout the Bible, an un-
translated word in Romans 1:25 becomes significant. Most versions say
that those who are on the path of evil have traded *"the truth* of God for *a
lie."* But in the Greek the article is definite. Thus Paul is stating that they
traded "the truth" for *"the lie."* Idolatry and false worship is not one falsehood among many. Rather, it is *the* lie. And from the lie of false religion,
Paul claims, come a torrent of degradations that have inundated our world.

Three times in Romans 1:24, 26, 28 Paul claims that God has given
blatant sinners over to their "sinful desires," "shameful lusts," and "depraved mind" (NIV). At first sight, that seems quite unlike God. Does
God abandon us to evil?

The key to understanding the phrase seems to be in such words as
"sinful desires." William Barclay points out that Paul is using a word that
"makes men do nameless and shameless things. It is a kind of insanity
which makes a man do things he would never have done if this desire had
not taken away his sense of honor and prudence and decency."

At the bottom of the issue is the fact that God has given each person free
will. Furthermore, He has pledged Himself not to interfere with that liberty.
Thus God allows us to make wrong choices and do hurtful things. But He
doesn't rescue us from their harmful consequences. In fact, He has actively
"given us over" to the frightful effects of sin. He lets us reap its results.

Why? Because he hates sinners? No, because He loves them and
wants them to wake up to their need of salvation. Thus even when God
gives people up to their sins, He has a merciful purpose. When we see the
depth of our need, God hopes we will look to Him for mercy and grace.

THE DOWNWARD PATH: STEP 4

Since they did not think it worthwhile to retain the knowledge
of God, he gave them over to a depraved mind, to do what
ought not to be done. They have become filled with every kind of
wickedness, evil, greed, and depravity. Rom. 1:28, 29, NIV.

THIS IS NOT A PRETTY picture. In fact, it sounds more like front-page copy for a tabloid than it does for a proper text for devotional meditation.

But hold on. The passage gets worse. Paul gives a list of human depravity that is scandalous in its scope: "They are full of envy, murder, strife, deceit and malice. They are gossips, slanderers, God-haters, insolent, arrogant and boastful; they invent ways of doing evil; they disobey their parents; they are senseless, faithless, heartless, ruthless" (Rom. 1:29-31, NIV).

The apostle wants to show what happens to people when they leave God out of their lives. One of the grim facts of life is that sin gives birth to sin. Once a person or a society sets out on the path of sin it becomes easier and easier to practice evil. In fact, they soon come to view evil as normal.

Individuals begin sinning with what William Barclay calls a kind of "shuddering awareness" of what they are doing, but as time passes they end up sinning without a second thought. Sinning becomes a way of life.

The end result, as Paul points out later in Romans, is that a person under the rule of a depraved mind becomes a slave to sin.

Thus we can use God's gift of free will in such a manner that in the end it obliterates our free will and we become slaves to sin. And as Eve discovered, sin is always a lie. Though the serpent may have promised her that if she rejected God and His will, her eyes would be opened and she would be like God, the end result was not divinity but death. Sin promises a fuller life and happiness but delivers ruination. The prodigal son discovered that. He set out on the path of freedom, "to live it up," but he ended up drooling over hog food. At that point, the Bible tells us, "he came to himself" and consciously decided that he was better off in his father's house (Luke 15:17).

That's the point. Remember where Paul is going in Romans. It is not a letter about sin, but about salvation. Paul is describing what God wants to save us from if we will accept His offer. Just as rejecting Him led to the downward steps of sin, so accepting Him leads to righteousness. That's the message of Romans. That's the message that our world today so desperately needs. And that's the message that I need to grasp in my own personal life.

THE DOWNWARD PATH: STEP 5

They know God's decree that those who do
such things deserve to die. Rom. 1:32, RSV.

LIFE ON EARTH HAS one great certainty—it will end! The Grim Reaper never ceases. Just wait. Your turn will come.

Why? Paul provides the answer in stark simplicity in Romans 6:23: "The wages of sin is death," a text quite in harmony with today's passage. It is also in agreement with God's warning to Adam in Genesis 2:17. Death is the end result of sin, of separating ourselves from God, the source of all life.

Fortunately Romans 6:23 doesn't end with a death sentence. God doesn't want to give sinners what they deserve. The passage goes on to tell us that "the gift of God is eternal life through Jesus Christ our Lord."

While it is true that sin results ultimately in death, it is not what Paul wants to talk about. That's the bad news. The apostle desires to tell us the good news (gospel) that Jesus died in the place of every sinner, that He died "once for all" (Heb. 10:10) that we might have life.

Ellen White in *The Desire of Ages* puts it nicely when she writes: "Christ was treated as we deserve, that we might be treated as He deserves. He was condemned for our sins, in which He had no share, that we might be justified by His righteousness, in which we had no share. He suffered the death which was ours, that we might receive the life which was His. 'By his stripes we are healed'" (p. 25).

The good news about death is that Jesus triumphed over it. "Fear not," we read in Revelation 1:17, 18, "I am the first and the last, and the living one; I died, and behold I am alive for evermore, and I have the keys of Death and Hades" (RSV).

Christ not only obtained victory over death; He wants to pass that victory on to everyone who will accept His "gift" of eternal life. "For as by a man [Adam] came death," Paul wrote, "by a man [Christ] has come also the resurrection of the dead. For as in Adam all die, so also in Christ shall all be made alive" (1 Cor. 15:21, 22, RSV). When Christ returns "the trumpet will sound, and the dead will be raised" (verse 52, RSV).

Yes, sin does result in death. But for the Christian death is not the end. Christians, the book of Romans argues, are saved from both sin and its results (death).

No wonder Paul called his message the gospel.

THE DOWNWARD PATH: STEP 6

They not only do [evil things] but approve those who practice them.
Rom. 1:32, RSV.

HOW LOW IS LOW? Where is the bottom of sin, the final degradation?

Paul hints at it in the last part of Romans 1:32: "They not only do" such things as those listed in 1:24-31, but they *"approve* those who practice them" (RSV). The New English Bible captures the forcefulness of Paul's idea when it translates the phrase as "they actually *applaud* such practices."

Paul Achtemeier writes that "it may strike us odd that Paul" in verse 32 "seems to think approving such acts is worse than doing them, but what he is pointing to is the fact that those who do such things not only do them in their own lives but make them a matter of public encouragement for others to follow. Not content to let wrath take its course in their lives, such people, Paul says, seek to make the measure of their sinful conduct the norm for the conduct of others. It is the desire to make [their] private sin the measure of public conduct that Paul is condemning here."

This is a serious issue. We live in a society that approves and applauds a great deal of evil. One only has to look at what the public generally calls "entertainment." If it isn't filled with action-packed sex and violence, it hardly rates as popular entertainment. Modern society really hasn't moved beyond the ancient world in such matters. It is true, of course, that we no longer feed people to lions or let gladiators battle to the death. No, we are much more sophisticated in the sense that we do the same thing in terms of virtual reality.

But entertainment tells a great deal about a society. And it reveals a great deal about Christians confused on this topic.

The message of Romans 1 is that God finds sin to be sickening and death producing. He wants to help people move beyond approving evil. Not only does He long to save their souls; He wants to transform their minds (Rom. 12:2). The Lord wants Christian influence to be on the side of approving and applauding that which is lifegiving and upbuilding. And He wants His ways to become the social norm. As Christians we have a part in shaping society through those things that we approve.

WAKE UP, MR. AND MRS. "CLEAN"

Therefore you have no excuse, O man, whoever you are, when you judge
another: for in passing judgment upon him you condemn yourself,
because you, the judge, are doing the very same things. Rom. 2:1, RSV.

IT IS EASY TO feel superior. After all, *I* don't do the kinds of sins Paul
recorded in chapter 1. In fact, compared with life's riffraff I am pretty good.

That is just the attitude that Paul attacks in the first half of Romans 2.
In the second half of Romans 1 he presented those who blatantly sin. His
depiction prompts those in the "front pew" to shout "amens" as loud as
their judicious voices allow. But it is just that attitude of moral superiority that Paul now attacks in Romans 2:1-16.

The apostle inexorably moves toward the conclusion that all have
sinned (Rom. 3:23). He has dealt with what some see as the *real* sinners,
an approach that has won over the moralists. They have sided with Paul.
At the very point that he has them fully with him, however, he turns his
guns on them.

They also, he points out, are sinners. Of course, they are nice church
members. They don't let all their dirty laundry hang out. No, their sins are
vegetarian sins. Compared with the really nasty people, they appear good
in their own eyes.

But—and here is Paul's point—they don't look so good in God's
sight. Their airs of moral superiority are also sin, even if it is invisible to
them. Such people suffer from the *sin of goodness,* the most hopeless of
all sins. In *Christ's Object Lessons* we read that "there is nothing so offensive to God or so dangerous to the human soul as pride and self-sufficiency. Of all sins it is the most hopeless, the most incurable" (p. 154).
Such goodness feels no need to repent or to seek God's grace.

Thus Romans 2 creates a major shift in Paul's argument. Finished
with speaking to prostitutes, perverts, and thieves, he's now ready for
church members.

Are you ready? Paul wants to speak to you, dear church member. He
longs to wake you up also.

The apostle wants each of us to recognize the depth of our personal
sin. He urges us to see and feel the deceptiveness and depth of our problems so that we might recognize the greatness of His offer of salvation and
our need of it, no matter how "good" we might appear in our own eyes.

THE SIN OF GOODNESS

Now we know that God's judgment against those who do
such things is based on truth. So when you, a mere man,
pass judgment on them and yet do the same things,
do you think you will escape God's judgment? Rom. 2:2, 3, NIV.

"HE ALSO TOLD THIS parable to some who trusted in themselves that they were righteous and despised others: 'Two men went up into the temple to pray, one a Pharisee and the other a tax collector. The Pharisee stood and prayed thus with himself, "God, *I thank thee that I am not like other men,* extortioners, unjust, adulterous, or even like this tax collector. I fast twice a week, I give tithes of all that I get." But the tax collector, standing far off, would not even lift up his eyes to heaven, but beat upon his breast, saying, "God, be merciful to me a sinner!" I tell you, this man went down to his house justified rather than the other; for every one who exalts himself will be humbled, but he who humbles himself will be exalted'" (Luke 18:9-14, RSV).

One of the most effortless things in the world is to judge other people. In Romans 2:1-3 Paul exposes the rather twisted truth that it is easy to be critical of everybody except ourselves.

I can instantly work myself up into a state of moral indignation when my wife or children do some obnoxious thing (such as walking on a clean floor with muddy shoes) yet excuse myself. After all, I am in a hurry. John Stott suggests that "we even gain a vicarious satisfaction from condemning others in the very faults we excuse in ourselves." Philosopher Thomas Hobbes wrote of people who "are forced to keep themselves in their own favor by observing the imperfections of other men."

Well, you might be able to fool yourself, or even other people. But Paul tells us here that you can't mislead God, whose "judgment . . . is based on truth." The plain fact is, the apostle asserts, no one will escape God's judgment, no matter how often they go to church or how vegetarian their sins are. All of us are sinners. All of us will stand before God's judgment seat. Each of us can choose to either present ourselves before Him in our own goodness or in Christ's righteousness.

Our eyesight might be tilted in our favor, but God has 20/20 vision when it comes to reading not only our actions but the sentiments of our hearts and our minds.

Paul's message is that we can afford to be humble.

THE PURPOSE OF GOD'S MERCY

*Or despisest thou the riches of his goodness and
forbearance and longsuffering; not knowing that
the goodness of God leadeth thee to repentance? Rom. 2:4.*

A GOOD PSYCHOLOGIST, Paul outlined in Romans 1 the sins of the Gentiles. The Jews were quite happy with chapter 1. After all, what he said was true. The Gentiles weren't living up to the light they had. They, therefore, deserved God's wrath and judgment.

But then Paul did the unexpected: he turned his arguments on the Jews and other "good" people. He showed them that they also were liable to the same punishment.

That thought went against the Jewish way of thinking. They considered themselves to be specially privileged in their relationship to the Lord. "God," they claimed, "loves Israel alone of all the nations of the earth." "God will judge the Gentiles with one measure and the Jews with another." "All Israelites will have part in the world to come." In short, the Jews of the day believed that everyone was destined for judgment except themselves.

Paul challenged that way of thinking in Romans 2:1-3. No one, he asserted, is exempt from God's judgment—no matter what their religious or moral pedigree.

In today's text (Rom. 2:4) the apostle tells the Jews that they were in danger of despising God's goodness, His forbearance, and His patience. Paul is trying to wake them up to their real needs. Just because He was gracious did not mean they had a right to keep on sinning. Just because He was forbearing with their perverse ways did not mean that they were safe from judgment. And just because God was patient didn't mean that they were beyond punishment.

To the contrary, they needed to repent of their proud ways. They should not use God's goodness, forbearance, and longsuffering as an excuse to remain where they were spiritually, but should let God's grace inspire them to sincere repentance. As William Barclay puts it, "the mercy of God, the love of God, is not meant to make us feel that we can sin and get away with it; it is meant to break our hearts in love" and lead us to repentance.

Today is the day of our salvation. "If we confess our sins, he is faithful and just to forgive us our sins, and to cleanse us from all unrighteousness" (1 John 1:9).

SPIRITUAL ARTERIOSCLEROSIS

*But no, you won't listen. So you are storing up terrible punishment
for yourself because of your stubbornness in refusing to turn from
your sin. For there is going to come a day of judgment. Rom. 2:5, NLT.*

THE KEY WORD in today's text is "but." It contrasts the passage with
the counsel of Romans 2:4. Thus instead of God's kindness and mercy
leading to repentance, it had had the opposite effect—it had produced
hardness, impenitence, or stubbornness.

The word translated as "stubbornness" is a Greek word meaning
"hardness." From that same word we get the medical term sclerosis. Thus
arteriosclerosis refers to hardening of the arteries, a process also found in
the spiritual realm. It represents the condition of those hearts that have become unresponsive and insensitive to God. But the spiritual condition has
much more serious consequences than the physical. Physical arteriosclerosis may lead a person to the grave, but spiritual hardening may cause the
loss of eternal life.

The Bible constantly warns us about spiritual hardness. Jesus told His
hearers that it was because of the "hardness of your hearts" that Moses
permitted them to divorce their wives (Matt. 19:8). Likewise, when the
self-righteous synagogue leaders waited to see if Jesus would heal on the
Sabbath, He "looked round about on them with anger, being grieved for
the hardness of their hearts" (Mark 3:5).

Paul put his comments about hard hearts in the context of the final
judgment. Some Christians today seek to avoid any mention of the judgment. The Bible writers had no such qualms. For Paul the final judgment
was an absolute certainty that his readers were preparing for.

Each of them would be storing up one of two things: repentance or
hardness. As with them, so with us. God's will is obvious. He wants us to
let Him break up the fallow ground of our hearts—to have the new
covenant experience of a softened and repentant heart. Through Ezekiel
He promised: "A new heart I will give you, and a new spirit I will put
within you; and I will take out of your flesh the heart of stone and give
you a heart of flesh" (Eze. 36:26, RSV).

God has made the offer of salvation. But He forces no one. It is up to
us either to harden our hearts by rejecting His offer or to respond with a
yes to His gift of a new heart.

IS PAUL CONFUSED?

[On the day of judgment] God, the just judge of all the world, will judge all people according to what they have done. Rom. 2:5, 6, NLT.

IS PAUL CONFUSED? Has he taken leave of his senses? How can we relate today's text to what the apostle teaches in other places?

In the very next chapter, for example, he writes that "no human being will be justified in his sight by works of the law" (Rom. 3:20, RSV). And in Ephesians he points out that we are saved by grace through faith; "not because of works, lest any man should boast" (Eph. 2:8, 9, RSV).

How can Paul turn around and claim that people will be judged by what they have *done* or accomplished?

Before answering, we should note that Paul's words actually come from the Old Testament. He often cited Jewish scripture to nail down a point. Psalm 62:12 reads: "You will reward each person according to what he has done" (NIV). Jesus picked up that idea when He noted that "the Son of Man is going to come in his Father's glory with his angels, and then he will reward each person according to what he has done" (Matt. 16:27, NIV).

Paul is not contradicting himself. It is true that in Romans 1:16 he claimed that salvation is by faith alone. But he is not now destroying his gospel by saying that salvation results from good works after all. To the contrary, he is affirming that, as John Stott puts it, "although justification is indeed by faith, judgment will be according to works." Stott goes on to argue that it is not difficult to discover the reason. The judgment is a public occasion, and its purpose is not so much to determine God's decision as to announce it and to vindicate it.

"Such a public occasion," Stott writes, "on which a public verdict will be given and a public sentence passed, will require . . . verifiable evidence to support them. And the only public evidence available will be our works. . . . The presence or absence of saving faith in our hearts will be disclosed by the presence or absence of good works in our lives."

Thus Paul is teaching that good works are not the ground of our salvation but the fruit of a saving relationship with Jesus. Paul called it the "obedience of faith" in Romans 1:5 and 16:26 (RSV). A changed life results from giving one's heart to Jesus. Those who have died to sin will not continue to live in it. To the contrary, they will walk with Jesus "in newness of life" (Rom. 6:1-12).

MORE ON DOING

To those who by persistence in doing good seek glory,
honor and immortality, [God] will give eternal life. But for
those who are self-seeking and who reject the truth and
follow evil, there will be wrath and anger. Rom. 2:7, 8, NIV.

ROMANS 2:7-10 ELABORATES the meaning of verse 6. In other words, those verses continue expounding the principle that the basis of God's final judgment will be on what people have done. Jesus taught the same concept in the Sermon on the Mount: "Not every one who says to me, 'Lord, Lord,' shall enter the kingdom of heaven, but he who *does* the will of my Father who is in heaven. On that day many will say to me, 'Lord, Lord, did not we prophesy in your name, and cast out demons in your name, and do many mighty works in your name?' And then will I declare to them, 'I never knew you; depart from me, you evildoers.'

"Every one then who hears these words of mine and does them will be like a wise man who built his house upon the rock; and the rain fell, and the floods came, and the winds blew and beat upon that house, but it did not fall, because it had been founded on the rock. And every one who hears these words of mine and *does not do them* will be like a foolish man who built his house upon the sand; and the rain fell, and the floods came, and the winds blew and beat against that house, and it fell; and great was the fall of it" (Matt. 7:21-27, RSV).

Both Paul and Jesus were concerned that Christians do God's will. Verbal faith or even so-called Christian activity was not enough.

Some Christians seem to have the idea that it is wrong to think about rewards, but Paul in Romans 2:7 doesn't seem to have any problem with people having the goals of "glory, honor and immortality" and "eternal life." On the other hand, he would be the first to object to any idea that they can earn such rewards by their good conduct. Those things, he is clear, are God's gift (Rom. 6:23). It is impossible for humans to obtain such things through their own efforts. But the Bible is not against Christians contemplating such gifts during their daily struggles. God wants to give us all the encouragement that we need as we persevere "in doing good."

Thank You, Father, for providing us a light at the end of the tunnel of life. Help us to put that light in its proper perspective. Help us to serve You from the right motives, so that we will be found in Your will when Christ returns.

No Favored Nation Status

*There will be trouble and distress for every human being
who does evil: first for the Jew, then for the Gentile. . . .
For God does not show favoritism. Rom. 2:9-11, NIV.*

NO PARTIALITY! No favoritism!

Here is a point that must have raised eyebrows among Paul's Jewish readers. Hadn't God chosen Abraham, Isaac, and Jacob? Hadn't He selected Israel as His special covenant nation, His representative on earth?

He had, but that decision was not, so to speak, a blank check. To the contrary, God could bless Israel only if they followed His will. In Deuteronomy we read: *"If* you obey the voice of the Lord your God, being careful to do all his commandments which I command you this day, *[then]* the Lord your God will set you high above all the nations of the earth. And all these blessings shall come upon you. . . . But *if* you will not obey the voice of the Lord your God or be careful to do all his commandments and his statutes which I command you this day, *then* all these curses shall come upon you" (Deut. 28:1-15, RSV).

Unfortunately, Israel never emphasized the conditionality of God's blessings to them. Instead, they came to believe that they remained God's favored nation no matter how they lived. John the Baptist challenged that line of thought when he told the Jewish leaders that "God is able from these stones to raise up children to Abraham" (Matt. 3:9, RSV). And Jesus wept over the unresponsiveness of the Jewish leaders to His ministry (Matt. 23:37, 38). Then again, near the end of His ministry He told the parable of the wicked tenants with its frightful conclusion that "the kingdom of God will be taken away from you [Israel] and given to a nation producing the fruits of it." The Jews "perceived that He was speaking about them" (Matt. 21:43, 45, RSV), but they never really believed Him. They still assumed that their nation was beyond judgment.

It is the very idea that Paul combats in Romans 2. God, he says, has no favorites. The Lord always offers the kingdom to men and women on His conditions alone.

Here is a lesson for the church. God wants to use and bless His people. But He can do so only when they do His will. As with Israel of old, God still has no favored nation. The covenant is always expressed in "if . . . then" terms. In the end God will judge His church by its compliance with His wishes.

REWARDS FOR EVERYONE

*There will be . . . glory, honor and peace for everyone who
does good: first for the Jew, then for the Gentile. Rom. 2:9, 10, NIV.*

GOD WANTS TO BLESS His people—all of them, both Jew and Gentile. Just as we saw in Romans 2:9 that there is no favoritism in "trouble and distress" (NIV), so there is no partiality in "glory, honor and peace." All will face the judgment. All will be evaluated by what they have "done" (verse 6, NIV), whether it be evil (verse 9) or good (verse 10).

Paul leaves no rocks unturned. He has repeatedly hammered home from the beginning of Romans 2 that the Jews stand in the same position as the Gentiles regarding sin and salvation. The apostle is building an argument that will climax in the second half of chapter 3, in which he notes that everybody (both Jew and Gentile) are absolutely dependent on the salvation that comes as a gift on the basis of Christ's sacrifice.

Those found by the end-time judgment (Rom. 2:5, 6) to be doing good (living according to God's will), Paul writes, will receive "glory, honor and peace" (verse 10, NIV). Glory in this context is not a self-centered human exaltation, but rather the sharing of God's glory at the second advent of Jesus. "I consider," Paul writes in chapter 8, "that our present sufferings are not worth comparing with the glory that will be revealed in us. The creation waits in eager expectation for the sons of God to be revealed" (Rom. 8:18, 19, NIV).

"Honor," as with glory, is not a human achievement but the recognition that comes from God when He rewards His people at the Second Coming. To each, He says, "Well done, good and faithful servant; you were faithful over a few things, I will make you ruler over many things. Enter into the joy of your lord" (Matt. 25:21, NKJV).

"Peace," of course, is the ultimate reconciliation of each saved person with both God and his or her fellow beings. The basis of that peace is what Jesus described as the two great commandments—love to both God and our neighbor (Matt. 22:37-40). Those great principles of the law, interestingly enough, are also the basis of all *doing* that will stand up in the final judgment. Just as Paul talks about the "obedience of faith" (Rom. 1:5; 16:26, RSV), so he also speaks of "faith working through love" (Gal. 5:6, RSV). Christian faith is an active response to God's love. In one sense, the life of faith is a life that passes on that love to others.

JUDGMENT WITHOUT LAW

*For as many as have sinned without law shall also
perish without law: and as many as have sinned in
the law shall be judged by the law. Rom. 2:12.*

AT FIRST GLANCE today's verse may seem a bit confusing. Phillips' translation helps us see the meaning more clearly: "All who have sinned without knowledge of the Law will die without reference to the Law; and all who have sinned knowing the Law shall be judged according to the Law."

In order to understand Paul's meaning we need to remember the context. In Romans 1 Paul discussed the justifiable condemnation of the wicked Gentiles. Then in the first half of chapter 2 he brought up the rather revolutionary idea that the moralistic Jews were equally guilty and equally subject to God's judgment.

That was a revolutionary thought to the Jews. Weren't they God's special people? Although Paul does believe that they were a called-out people, at the same time he does not mean that they are exempt from sin or divine punishment. Here the Jews and Gentiles stand on the same ground, and as we read in Romans 2:11, "God does not show favoritism" (NIV).

That lack of favoritism raises an objection in the minds of Paul's Jewish readers. After all, a major difference exists between the Jews and the Gentiles. The Jews have God's law. That proves that they are His favorites and in no way can He judge them in the same manner as the Gentiles.

Wrong! claims Paul. It is true that we cannot accuse the Gentiles of breaking a law that they never formally received, yet it is also true, as Paul argued in Romans 1:19, 20 and will argue in Romans 2:15, that God has revealed to them a sense of right and wrong. The Lord will judge by that God-given sense. That is, God will evaluate them according to their response to the revelation that He has provided them.

The same is true of the Jews. But they have a wider basis for judgment. They not only have the general revelation through conscience and nature that they share with the Gentiles; they also have God's special revelation in the law.

Thus God holds all individuals responsible for the light that He has given them. On the other hand, none have to answer for what they don't know.

Our God, in spite of the complexities of the world, is indeed a just Father who has no favorites. No wonder the songs in the book of Revelation extol the justice and truthfulness of His rulings (see, e.g., Rev. 19:1, 2).

JUSTIFICATION BY LAW

For it is not the hearers of the law who are righteous before God,
but the doers of the law who will be justified. Rom. 2:13, RSV.

NOTE PAUL'S USE OF the word "hearers." Most people during his day couldn't read. Rather they heard the law read week by week in the synagogue.

But—and here we have his point—"hearing" was not enough. Having the law was not enough. It is not enough to claim Abraham as your father or Moses as your prophet or the law as your guide.

Paul is making a concerted effort to break through Jewish exclusiveness. Some Jews apparently believed that the mere possession of the law meant eternal security. But the apostle has been hammering away at them with the fact that they haven't kept it. It is not possessing the law or being a Jew that provides security, but the "doing" of the law.

At that point, the apostle sets forth an interesting idea: that "the doers of the law will be justified." What does he mean? Is he teaching that we can be justified or righteous by obeying the law?

If so, he is flatly contradicting himself in the next chapter in which he declares that "no human being will be justified in his sight by works of the law" (Rom. 3:20, RSV; cf. Gal. 2:16).

Of course, people could be justified or counted righteous by keeping the law if they obeyed it *perfectly*. But that is the very point that Paul is making. All people are sinners; none keep it perfectly. The purpose of the law is not to be a ladder to heaven but to point out our sins and lead us to salvation in Christ (Rom. 3:20-25). In actuality, trying to keep the law as a way of salvation will leave us in utter frustration and lostness, especially if we have grasped the full meaning of the law as expounded by Jesus in Matthew 5:21-48 in the Sermon on the Mount.

Well, then, if we don't get justification through lawkeeping, what does Paul mean? Remember that he is speaking in Romans 2 about the judgment in a book dedicated to teaching the gospel of righteousness by faith. In that context, it is not enough to say that we have the law or that we are Jews or Adventists or anything else. Rather, Paul is teaching that we need to live according to God's will. Just because we have Christ does not mean that we can live in flagrant disobedience. It is not "saved by grace and do as *you* please." To the contrary, if we are saved by grace, we will do as *God* pleases.

THE ROLE OF CONSCIENCE

[The Gentiles] show that what the law requires is written on their hearts, while their conscience also bears witness. Rom. 2:15, RSV.

IN ROMANS 2:14 and 15 Paul takes a little detour from his main argument concerning the Jews and their responsibility in the judgment. Briefly he turns aside to the Gentiles.

Paul has just demonstrated in verse 13 that for the Jew it is not a matter of merely hearing the law but of doing it. That raises the question about the judgment of the Gentiles who haven't even heard the law. How will God evaluate them? The apostle tackles that question in verses 14 and 15. "When Gentiles who have not the law," we read in verse 14, "do by nature what the law requires, they are a law to themselves, even though they do not have the law" (RSV).

Here Paul is telling us two things: (1) That the Gentiles do not have the written law of Moses, and (2) that they do have some knowledge of the standards of the law internally; that is, they "do by nature" some of the things that the law requires. Paul is not here making a universal claim, but stating that some Gentiles at times do some of what the law requires. Thus, for example, not all people are adulterers, thieves, or murderers. In fact, in a general sense people feel some need to honor their parents, recognize the sanctity of human life, and practice honesty, just as the last six of the commandments require. Thus, even though the Gentiles do not have the revealed law of Moses, their conduct often shows that they recognize right from wrong.

On what basis, we might ask, do they have such knowledge? Through the conscience, Paul tells us in verse 15, and the fact that God has written a sense of what the law requires in their hearts. Note that the apostle is not claiming too much for the human conscience. Rather, he is suggesting that conscience is informed to some extent by a divinely implanted (however minimal) sense of right and wrong.

In this verse we find that our conscience is a God-given blessing intended to wake us up and guide us. Fortunately, as Christians we have the privilege of enlightening our consciences through reading the Bible. A well-informed conscience—one that is not merely sensitive (1 Cor. 10:25) or not sensitive enough (1 Tim. 4:2)—is a blessing to be cherished.

Help us today, Father, to nourish the health of our conscience and then learn how to use it in conjunction with Your Word and the Holy Spirit.

THE JUDGMENT CONCLUDED

We may be sure that all this will be taken into account in the day of true judgment, when God will judge men's secret lives by Christ Jesus, as my Gospel plainly states. Rom. 2:16, Phillips.

TODAY'S TEXT BRINGS US to the end of Paul's discussion of the judgment. It started, as you will recall, in Romans 1:32, when he noted that those who were blatantly wicked sinners deserved death. The "good" people (those who had less nasty sins) and the religious people (the Jews in this case) were quite happy with such a judgment. They could fully agree on that death sentence. It was just. Outright sinners deserve to die.

But then Paul made his next move. He told the "good" people and the religious people that they also would come under judgment. The ramifications of that pronouncement have taken Paul some 15 verses to explain. In Romans 2:16 he binds off his argument: "We may be sure that all this will be taken into account in the day of true judgment, when God will judge men's secret lives by Christ Jesus."

What does the apostle mean? In the context of Romans 2:1-15, he indicates that everyone will be judged impartially (verse 11). That is, God will base every person's judgment upon what they have known. For the Jews that involves their faithfulness to God's revealed law, and for the Gentiles their faithfulness to their partially enlightened consciences.

But let's not forget verse 13, the text that tells us that it is "the doers of the law who will be justified" (RSV). For those who know the law of God, knowledge is not enough. Those who have been saved will also be found walking in God's way. That brings us back to Romans 2:6, in which we read that in the judgment "God 'will give to each person according to what he has done'" (NIV).

Thus Paul's understanding of the judgment seems clear enough. All people will face it, not merely for their actions, but for their "secret lives." And all, both Jew and Gentile according to God's reckoning, will be found guilty.

The apostle's concern with judgment, however, is not an end in itself. His real interest is the good news of full and free salvation in Christ. For Paul the importance of the judgment is that it shows up every person's weakness and guilt. He has developed the truth of universal condemnation so that every person will feel their deep need of his gospel. Paul's message always points beyond guilt and condemnation to salvation in Christ.

Be Taught Before Teaching

You [Jews] are convinced that you are a guide for the blind. . . .
You think you can instruct the ignorant. . . . Well then, if you
teach others, why don't you teach yourself? Rom. 2:19-21, NLT.

PAUL HAS FINISHED WITH the topic of judgment, but not with point-ing to the Jewish need for a greater righteousness than their law and their heritage. In fact, beginning in verse 17 he actually increases the pressure. He will do so for the rest of chapter 2 along two lines: First, the Jewish re-lationship to the law (Rom. 2:17-24), and second, the value of circumci-sion (verses 25-29).

He starts his first topic in verse 17 with the Jewish tendency to brag about their relationship to God and their reliance on the law. Then he con-tinues in verses 18-21 to chide them for their superior airs in things related to the law. If they are so full of wisdom and such great teachers, he asks them, why they are so ignorant? Or to put it in his own words, "if you teach others, why don't you teach yourself?" (verse 21).

That is an excellent question. And Paul will pick up on its implica-tions in the rest of verse 21 and on into verses 22 and 23.

But before moving on to those verses, we need to ponder a bit what he has already said. Why is it that as a religious person I think of myself as superior in my knowledge to others? Or why is it that my wife or hus-band never quite does things in the right way (the way I do it)?

Those are important questions. Jesus faced them in the Sermon on the Mount. "Why," He asked the "good" people of His day, "do you see the *speck* in your brother's eye, but do not notice the *log* that is in your own eye? . . . First take the log out of your own eye, and then you will see clearly to take the speck out of your brother's eye" (Matt. 7:3-5, RSV).

Such "good" people are still with us. Ellen White wrote about them when she noted that "it is the desire and plan of Satan to bring in among us those who will go to great extremes—people of narrow minds, who are critical and sharp, and very tenacious in holding their own conceptions of what the truth means. They will be exacting, and will seek to enforce rig-orous duties, and go to great length in matters of minor importance, while they neglect the weightier matters of the law—judgment and mercy and the love of God" (*Medical Ministry*, p. 269).

Help me today, Lord, to be taught of You in the fullest sense before I
seek to teach others. Help me to have a sense of spiritual proportion.

HYPOCRISY COMES NATURALLY

*You who preach against stealing, do you steal? You who
say that people should not commit adultery, do you
commit adultery? . . . You who brag about the law,
do you dishonor God by breaking the law? Rom. 2:21-23, NIV.*

ONE OF THE EASIEST things in the world to become is a hypocrite. In fact, it seems to come natural to us humans.

We love to preach to others. After all, I know exactly what other people should be doing, and I don't mind telling them so, sometimes with great precision and enthusiasm. We don't stand alone in this matter. The Jews of old, Paul says, had the same habit.

Their problem, he notes, was not their message but that they didn't live up to it, that they said one thing yet did another. Jesus pointed this out when He noted that "they say, and do not do" (Matt. 23:3, NKJV).

Paul highlights several examples of their problem. First, he asks: "You who preach against stealing, do you steal?" The implied answer is that they obviously do. Historically, the prophets had had to face that problem. Ezekiel rebuked those who "have made profit" from their "neighbors by extortion" (Eze. 22:12, NKJV), Amos spoke of those who made their "bushel smaller and the shekel bigger" and cheated "with dishonest scales" (Amos 8:5, NASB), and Malachi accused his fellow Jews of robbing God through the withholding of tithes and offerings (Mal. 3:8, 9).

Things hadn't changed all that much by New Testament times. Jesus censured the Temple money changers and those who sold sacrifices in the Temple for making His Father's house into a robbers' den (Matt. 21:13). On another occasion He condemned the scribes and Pharisees (the self-appointed protectors of the law) for "shamelessly cheat[ing] widows out of their property, and then, to cover up the kind of people they really are, they make long prayers in public" (Mark 12:40, NLT).

Paul's other examples were also pointed. He brought his series of questions to a conclusion by inferring that those who bragged about the law really didn't obey it. In that, he suggests, they dishonored God (Rom. 2:23). Once again, according to the argument of Romans, the Jews stood under the condemnation of God.

Today, Father, I want to rededicate my life to You. Help me not only to have high ideals, but to practice them. And when I fall short, please help me to come to You hungering and thirsting after Your righteousness.

THE BEST ARGUMENT AGAINST CHRISTIANITY

As it is written: "God's name is blasphemed
among the Gentiles because of you." Rom. 2:24, NIV.

THE ATHEISTIC PHILOSOPHER Friedrich Nietzsche once proclaimed that the best argument against Christianity is Christians. It does no injustice to extend that saying to claim that the best argument against Adventism is Adventists, or the best argument against Methodism is Methodists, or the best argument against Lutheranism is Lutherans. People who advocate a high ideal, but don't live up to it, turn others away from their way of life. Most of us have known individuals who are pious in church, but sharp dealers the rest of the week. Such persons disgust us. And the more sanctimonious they are the worse the stench they leave in our nostrils.

But the problem is deeper than what people may believe about some pious hypocrite of a church member. The ultimate difficulty is that hypocrisy reflects not only on that member but also on the God whom he or she claims to be serving. That is what Paul is talking about when he writes that "God's name is blasphemed among the Gentiles" because of Jewish hypocrisy.

The apostle has come to the end of a section in which he has been demonstrating Jewish inadequacy in relation to the law. He binds the section off with a quotation from either Isaiah 52:5 or Ezekiel 36:22. The hypocrisy problem wasn't new. It had existed earlier in Jewish history.

And if it wasn't new then, neither is it over in our day.

God desires His people to fully live for Him. There is nothing wrong with God's law. In Romans 7:12 Paul freely admits that it is "holy," "just," and "good." The problem is not in the law but in those who pride themselves in it while not living up to its precepts.

The apostle has been careful to point out in Romans that possessing the law does not make people superior. Even Christians can have "the commandments of God" (Rev. 14:12) and still be totally lost.

There is something else, something beyond the law, that we need. And that something is what Paul is driving toward step by step in Romans 2. It is found in Jesus, who provides the answer to all of our needs through His death and resurrection. And it is related to our need of His work on our behalf.

MISPLACED CONFIDENCE

Circumcision has value if you observe the law,
but if you break the law, you have become as though
you have not been circumcised. Rom. 2:25, NIV.

WITH TODAY'S VERSE PAUL has arrived at the next step in his extensive argument against Jewish exemption from God's judgment. If their possession of the law didn't protect them from the judgment of God, he argues in Romans 2:25-29, then circumcision won't either.

The Jews put a great deal of stock in circumcision. The rite in Jewish circles goes back to Abraham, the father of the nation. When God established the covenant with Abraham that made his descendants the people of God's promises, He stipulated circumcision as the outward sign of the covenant. All Jewish boys were to be circumcised on the eighth day and "any uncircumcised male who is not circumcised in the flesh . . . shall be cut off from his people; he has broken my covenant" (Gen. 17:9-14, RSV).

As a result, the Jews regarded circumcision as having the utmost importance. Leon Morris points out that "it was unthinkable that a man, duly circumcised and admitted to the covenant, should fail of his salvation." In other words, in Jewish thinking circumcision guaranteed salvation. Thus Rabbi Levi could state that "in the Hereafter Abraham will sit at the entrance to Gehenna [hell], and permit no circumcised Israelite to descend therein." And we read in the Jewish *Mishnah* that "all Israelites have a share in the world to come."

Paul in today's passage rejects such a belief. Attaching no saving value to the physical act of circumcision, he plainly states in Romans 2 and in Galatians 5:3 that circumcision had no significance unless a person obeyed the "whole law."

His position directly challenged Jewish feelings of security, because he had just demonstrated in Romans 2:17-24 that the Jews were guilty before God because they were lawbreakers. Paul then came to the frightful conclusion in verse 25 that if they broke the law they had become as if they had not been circumcised.

That was serious. If they couldn't place their trust for salvation in either the law or in circumcision, what could they do?

Paul knows the answer to that question. He can hardly keep still on the topic. But before he presents it he has to nail a few more points in place.

THE GREAT REVERSAL

If those who are not circumcised keep the law's requirements, will they not be regarded as though they were circumcised? Rom. 2:26, NIV.

WE NOTED YESTERDAY that Paul exploded the Jewish idea that equated circumcision with salvation. Today we find out that he hasn't finished shaking up the Jewish belief system. He continues to challenge their theology of circumcision and the assurance that it brought to them.

Yesterday we noted that in Romans 2:25 Paul asserted that if the Jews, who had been circumcised, broke the law, they then had become as though they had never been circumcised. Today in verse 26 he looks at the other side of that coin, indicating that Gentiles, who had not been circumcised, would be regarded as though they were circumcised if they kept the law's requirements.

What does that mean? It does not indicate that they could earn salvation by obeying the law. Paul will specifically deny that possibility in Romans 3. Rather, he is saying that the Gentiles stand on an equal footing with the Jews when it comes to God's promises. The corollary to that position is that the Jews face God's judgment just as much as the Gentiles.

What Paul said profoundly shocked his Jewish readers. Traditionally they had pictured themselves as sitting in judgment on the uncircumcised pagans. But the roles could actually be reversed. What counts with God is not the outward symbol of circumcision but an attitude of total surrender to doing His will.

This concept has a great deal of meaning for Christians in the twenty-first century. Many have thought of baptism in much the same way that the Jews did about circumcision. But baptism is not magical. It, like circumcision, is merely an outward sign of an inward dedication to God and His will.

The same applies to church membership. There is nothing salvific about belonging to a church, whether that church be Roman Catholic, Southern Baptist, or Seventh-day Adventist.

Salvation, as Paul will explain, comes from accepting God's grace through faith. A saved person will seek to do God's will. Within that context such things as baptism and church membership have genuine meaning. Outside of it they are meaningless. In all such matters all God's children—both Jew and Gentile—stand on equal footing.

INWARD IS WHERE THE ACTION IS

A man is not a Jew if he is one outwardly, nor is
circumcision merely outward and physical. Rom. 2:28, NIV.

THE GREAT REVERSAL goes on in Romans 2:27 and 28. In Romans 1
Paul made the Jews feel good by leading them to assume superiority over
the wicked Gentiles. But throughout Romans 2 he has blasted away at
Jewish self-confidence. He erased their confidence that they were beyond
God's final judgment (Rom. 2:1-16). Then he removed their confidence
based upon their possession of the law (verses 17-24). Next he undermined their confidence in the value of circumcision as guaranteeing entrance into the kingdom (verses 25, 26).

And finally in verse 27 Paul had the audacity to say that the Gentiles
who obeyed the law would sit in judgment on the Jews. That reversed everything they had been taught about the judgment. Weren't they the superior race, the "true church," the chosen ones? Weren't they supposed to sit
in judgment on the unclean, uncircumsized Gentiles? Paul had smashed
all their idols.

But wait. He isn't finished yet. In Romans 2:28 he begins to redefine
what it means to be a Jew, when he states that "you are not a true Jew just
because you were born of Jewish parents or because you have gone
through the Jewish ceremony of circumcision" (NLT).

Paul here teaches that neither birth nor formalism is the key to being
a part of God's true people. Nor do they enable anyone to pass the final
judgment. And most important, they are not the key to salvation. Religion,
Paul is telling us, is not an external matter. Rather, he will reveal in verse
29 that it is a matter of the heart.

It is all too easy to get caught up in the daily round of being religious,
of doing the right thing, of going to church, while at the same time neglecting the inner aspects of our daily experience.

Today is an excellent time to rededicate ourselves to the inward aspects of religion, to confessing to God (in light of our faults) our deep
need of Him, to putting the morning reading of His Word back where it
should be, to spending time meditating so that He can speak to us more
fully, to making prayer a priority, and to finding the real center of our existence. Just as God overturned the priorities of Jewish thought, so He
wants to do the same with ours.

A Circumsized Heart

A man is a Jew if he is one inwardly; and circumcision
is circumcision of the heart, by the Spirit. Rom. 2:29, NIV.

A CIRCUMSIZED HEART?

Sounds strange! A startling combination of words.

Today's text completes Paul's redefinition of what it means to be a Jew, what it means to be a part of God's chosen people. Yesterday we saw in Romans 2:28 that true religion was not a matter of externals. Today we find Paul emphasizing that genuine religion is a matter of the heart.

The concept of a circumsized heart was not new with Paul. The Old Testament regularly utilized it. Moses writes in Deuteronomy 30, for example, that if the Jews repented of their sin God would bless them. Furthermore, "the Lord your God will circumsize your heart and the heart of your offspring, so that you will love the Lord your God with all your heart and with all your soul, that you may live" (Deut. 30:6, RSV). In Deuteronomy 10:16 Moses appealed to the Israelites to circumsize the foreskins of their hearts, and "be no longer stubborn" (RSV). Again in Leviticus 26:41 he tells the people that God would bless them if "their uncircumsized heart is humbled and they make amends for their iniquity" (RSV).

The males that Moses was speaking to had undoubtedly been physically circumcised. They had the outward sign, but they didn't have the inward experience of religion. Using New Testament terminology, we would say that they hadn't been converted, that they needed a new heart and a new mind, and that they must be born again. That conversion experience, as Moses indicates, would be accompanied by confession and repentance and the heartfelt love for God that stands at the very foundation of the law of God.

To be a Jew, Paul notes in Romans 2:29, a person must have an experience beyond the legalisms of the "written code" of Moses. Rather, they need the converting power of the Holy Spirit in their lives. Jesus put it somewhat differently when He told Nicodemus that "except a man be born of the water and of the Spirit, he cannot enter into the kingdom of God" (John 3:5).

Religion has always been a matter of the heart. Paul is calling his Jewish readers (and us) back to that eternal truth. He wants us to experience the real thing rather than the cheap imitation that seems to satisfy so many church members.

Don't Let Sin
Follow You to Church

The real Jew . . . receives his commendation
not from men but from God. Rom. 2:29, REB.

IN ROMANS 2:28 and 29 Paul has redefined what it means to be a Jew, one of God's chosen people. He has set forth a fourfold contrast. Being a true Jew is: (1) not something outward and visible, but inward and invisible; (2) not a circumcision of the flesh, but of the heart; (3) not merely an experience with the law, but with the Spirit; (4) not focused on the approval of other people, but on an approval from God.

Unfortunately, we as humans are comfortable with the external, visible, material, and superficial. That is what God wants to change in our lives and is what Christianity is all about. Throughout the rest of Romans Paul will be helping us understand how God through His Holy Spirit seeks to transform our hearts and minds. Romans is a book about God's desire to change how we look at God, ourselves, and our fellow beings, and then how we put those new understandings into practice.

But before moving into that study, I need to take a moment to ask myself a question about today's text. Whom do I want to honor me—God or other people? Whose applause do I seek? What am I willing to do or to surrender to receive that favor or hear that applause?

Those are serious questions. Jesus faced the issue in the Sermon on the Mount. In Matthew 6 He warned His Jewish listeners not to practice their piety for the purpose of receiving commendation from other people. Thus He spoke to the same problem as Paul in Romans 2:29.

Nor is the problem restricted to the ancient Jews. We all have it. Of course, as "good" Christians we know that we should be like Jesus, who cared not a fig for human applause, but only for the approbation of the Father.

The problem is that we are not Jesus. We love to hear the words that we are "good" Christians, that we have prayed a great prayer, that we are the best of preachers. Sin follows us even into church.

That's just where the devil comes in. And it is the very reason that conversion is a daily process.

Help me today, Lord, to lay even my precious self on Your altar. Help me through Your Spirit, to truly seek only Your commendation.

OBJECTION NUMBER 1: WHY GO TO CHURCH?

What advantage, then, is there in being a Jew,
or what value is there in circumcision? Rom. 3:1, NIV.

BY THE END OF Romans 2 Paul has in fact made his point, showing that everyone needs Christ's righteousness—both Gentiles (chapter 1) and Jews (chapter 2). At this point we would expect him to summarize his conclusions. He will do that in Romans 3:9-20, but first he takes us on an eight-verse digression.

His plain speaking in Romans 2 about the Jew has raised some serious questions. The apostle places them in the mouth of a Jewish objector in Romans 3:1-8, who raises four challenges to Paul's theology. Paul had undoubtedly already met such objections in response to his preaching in various localities. In fact, James Dunn suggests that they might have been the very ones that Paul himself had had as he began to understand the gospel of God's grace. Thus, Dunn writes, we find him "expressing attitudes Paul remembered so well as having been his own." In this way Paul the Pharisee debates Paul the Christian.

The debate itself in Romans 3:1-8 goes through four cycles, with four objections being raised, and four answers being provided in turn. The objections center on Jewish superiority in relation to God's faithfulness. Paul touches upon that topic briefly in chapter 3, but he will treat it extensively in Romans 9-11. In chapter 3, however, he only has to deal with the issues to the extent that they can't be used to set aside the powerful argument he made about Jewish sin in Romans 2.

The first argument arises in Romans 3:1, in which we find the objector asking in the light of chapter 2 what advantage being a Jew or being circumcised might possibly have. Paul will answer the first part of that question in Romans 3:2 and the second part in Romans 4, in which he deals with Abraham.

Meanwhile, we find here a question for us as Christians. What advantage is there in being baptized or belonging to a church (or even in going to church) if those things don't save us? Have you ever asked such questions? You should!

My guess is that Paul would answer you in the same way that he did the Jews in Romans 3:2: "Much in every way!" (NIV). We will need to listen to Paul throughout the book of Romans to get the complete answer.

ANSWER NUMBER 1:
THE BLESSING OF THE BIBLE

Yes, being a Jew has many advantages. First of all, the Jews
were entrusted with the whole revelation of God. Rom. 3:2, NLT.

AFTER PAUL'S POWERFUL argument in Romans 2 on the inadequacy of
their possession of the law and circumcision, we would expect him to respond with a resounding no to the question of whether being a Jew had
any advantage.

Instead, we find Paul unexpectedly answering with a resounding yes,
or, more accurately, "Much in every way" (Rom. 3:2, NIV).

This point is important for both Paul's Jewish readers and for his own
theology. After all, as C. K. Barrett points out, "if the Old Testament is to
be believed God did choose the Jews out of all mankind and did bestow
special privileges upon them. To reduce them therefore to the level of
other nations is either to accuse the Old Testament of falsehood, or to accuse God of failing to carry out his plans. It is this theological objection
to his thesis that Paul" must respond to.

The apostle's answer is forceful. "First of all," he points out, "the
Jews were entrusted with the whole revelation of God." When he says
"first," we would expect a second and so on, but Paul's list of advantages
has only one item. But that single item had the potential of bringing all
other blessings in its train.

The primary advantage of being Jewish, Paul declares, is that God
gave the Bible to the world through the Jewish nation. Through it they received both the law and circumcision. But the Bible had more—it also had
God's teaching on the depth of sin and the problem of outward religion.
Beyond that, the Jewish scripture had the promises of the coming Christ
and the way of salvation.

Yes, the Jewish nation had received an inestimable blessing over
other peoples. Unfortunately, they had misused the blessing, as Paul
pointed out in chapter 2, but that did not negate their privilege. "Being a
Jew has many advantages."

As it was with the Jews of old, so it is with the Christian church,
which has not only the Jewish scripture but also the New Testament. The
church has not only the witness of the prophets but also of the apostles.

Help us today, Lord, to utilize fully the blessings of Your Word in our
lives. Help us let You make it the blessing in our lives that You want it to be.

OBJECTION NUMBER 2: REGARDING GOD'S FAITHFULNESS

What if some of them were unfaithful? Will their faithlessness cancel the faithfulness of God. Certainly not! Rom. 3:3, 4, REB.

IN ROMANS 3:1 and 2 we saw Paul address the issue of Jewish advantage by noting that they were privileged because God had given the Scriptures through the Jewish nation. That gave them a great edge over other people. As one author put it, "by their possession of the Law the Jews have an advantage over the heathen, much as the educated man has a better chance in life than one who has never been to school."

But that very privilege leads to a second objection in the minds of Paul's opponents: "What if *some* of them were unfaithful?" What if some of the Jews, not having faith, failed to properly respond to God's mercy? Will their lack of faith, or lack of a proper response, nullify God's faithfulness? Will God still be faithful to His Old Testament promises to bless those who love Him and to judge the wicked?

That question is crucial to Paul and his audience because of the fact that if God isn't faithful to His promises nothing else will make any sense. If we can't rely upon God to be true to His ways, then nothing can be trusted.

Paul responds in verse 4 with the most forceful negation at his command: "Certainly not" (REB), "God forbid" (KJV), "By no means" (RSV). Other translations have suggested "not on your life" (Message) or "not in a thousand years." "Not at all!" we read in the New International Version. "Let God be true, and every man a liar." The basic idea here is that even if every person is untrustworthy in their promises, God will be absolutely faithful in keeping His word.

Paul then goes on to quote Psalm 51:4 in Romans 3:4: " 'When you speak you will be vindicated; when you are accused, you will win the case' " (REB). In referring to Psalm 51, the apostle is alluding to the fact that even though God punished David's sin with Bathsheba, God did not withdraw His faithfulness from him. Thus God vindicated His covenant faithfulness. He had been true to His promises in spite of David's faithlessness.

Each day we can praise the Lord that we can rely on His trustworthiness. Likewise, we can rely on the promises in His Word, even if the church goes astray or many members prove unfaithful. The good news is that God can be trusted. Human faithlessness *never* cancels the faithfulness of God.

OBJECTION NUMBER 3: REGARDING GOD'S JUSTICE

If God is not just, how is he qualified
to judge the world? Rom. 3:6, NLT.

IN ROMANS 3:1-4 the apostle has successfully responded to two objections. The first (verses 1, 2) was that Paul's teaching undermined God's covenant to the Jews as a specially chosen people. The second (verses 3, 4) was that his teaching nullified God's faithfulness. We now come to a third: that his teaching thwarted God's justice (verses 5, 6).

This third objection and Paul's answer to it are not the easiest of his passages to understand in their details, but Paul's general conclusion is clear enough. The essence of the objection in Romans 3:5 is that if our wickedness brings God's justice or righteousness into focus and magnifies His glory, then it couldn't possibly be right for God to punish sinners. After all, the objection implies, if we didn't sin, God couldn't be shown to be just. And if we have thereby done God such a good favor by sinning, how can He turn around and punish us for helping Him?

Paul appears to be somewhat embarrassed for even raising such a ridiculous objection. Thus he adds the words, "I speak in a human way" (verse 5, RSV).

The apostle may have been somewhat uncomfortable about the way that he was forced to state such a foolish objection, but he was quite bold in his answer to it in verse 6. Once again he uses the "certainly not" of verse 4 (REB), indicating that he emphatically disagrees with such foolish reasoning. And then he goes on to note that "if God is not just, how is he qualified to judge the earth?" At that juncture we might have expected an affirmation of God's justice, but he and his fellow Jews were so certain about the role of God in judgment that he put his answer in a question form that implied that God was certainly just. Therefore, He was obviously qualified to judge the world.

Since no Jew doubted either the coming judgment or God's justice, the Jewish objection fell under its own weight. Paul's point in chapter 2 held. God had indeed the right to judge everybody, even Jews.

Of two things Paul is most certain: that God is just and that He will judge the world. We can be thankful we are in the hands of a merciful God. Just how merciful will be Paul's topic beginning in Romans 3:21.

OBJECTION NUMBER 4: REGARDING CHEAP GRACE

Why not say—as we are being slanderously reported as saying and as some claim we say—"Let us do evil that good may result"? Their condemnation is deserved. Rom. 3:8, NIV.

"CHEAP GRACE! HOW SWEET the sound, that saved a wretch like me! I once was lost, but now am saved by grace and can sin as much as I please."

Well, that's not exactly the way the song goes. But it does reflect the perversion represented in the fourth objection to Paul's teaching as found in today's scripture. All too often people who have followed Paul in believing that we are saved by grace alone and that human merit has no part in bringing about our salvation have also concluded that it doesn't matter if we sin or not.

It appears that some of Paul's contemporaries—at least among those who opposed him—drew exactly that conclusion. His opposition, as Paul puts it, "slanderously reported" that he was teaching that Christians should sin as much as possible so God could dispense as much grace as possible and thereby receive as much praise and honor as possible for saving such wretched sinners.

The apostle refuses to answer such a stupid and dishonest accusation. All he says is that those who pervert his teachings in such a manner will receive their deserved condemnation.

But that doesn't mean that he has no answer. In fact, he will take up that exact issue in Romans 6, in which he relates God's grace to living the Christian life. But before he gets to that explanation, he needs to expound upon his understanding of justification by faith, a task he will undertake between Romans 3:21 and the end of chapter 5.

Paul, in actuality, believed in "costly grace." Dietrich Bonhoeffer, who paid for his Christianity with his life in resisting Hitler, helps us see that God's grace has a high price indeed. It is costly "because it cost God the life of his son." "Costly grace is the treasure hidden in the field; for the sake of it a man will gladly go and sell all that he has. . . . Costly grace confronts us as a gracious call to follow Jesus." As Bonhoeffer puts it: "When Christ calls a man, he bids him come and die." Following Jesus will change every aspect of our lives. Costly grace demands that we give up everything for Jesus as we respond to His love and devote our lives to doing God's will.

"Sinner" Means Everybody

What shall we conclude then? Are we any better?
Not at all! We have already made the charge that
Jews and Gentiles alike are all under sin. Rom. 3:9, NIV.

WELL, IT'S ABOUT TIME.

I thought Paul would never put an end to his extensive discussion of sin that begins in Romans 1:18. But now he tells us that he is ready to cap off his discussion with a conclusion.

Of course, he didn't actually talk about the topic of sin in Romans 3:1-8. Rather, he reacted to objections to his theology. Verse 9 really picks up where Romans 2:29 left off. In chapter 1, as we have repeatedly noted, Paul finds the wicked Gentiles to be sinners standing under condemnation, and in chapter 2 he came up with the same status for the Jews and other moral people. Thus he doesn't find the Jews to be any better than others. All are sinners, and all stand under God's condemnation.

Paul has spent a great deal of space demonstrating universal sinfulness and condemnation, because for him it is important that his readers are clear on those points. Leon Morris indicates the reason when he claims that "unless there is something to be saved from, there is no point in preaching salvation," or embracing it, for that matter.

The apostle's extensive treatment of universal sin and condemnation has paved the way for him to discuss God's great plan of salvation. And just as he has repeatedly stressed the fact that both Jews and Gentiles are sinners, so he will repeatedly emphasize that salvation is for everyone. God's great salvation has no racial, ethnic, or other barriers. His grace is free to all.

At first glance Paul might sound as if he is contradicting himself in Romans 3:9 when he says that the Jews are no better off than other people when he has already said in verse 1 that they had greater advantages. But in verse 1 he was referring to privileges and responsibilities, not favoritism, since even God's chosen people are not exempt from judgment.

Lord, help us as Your modern-day chosen people not to mistake our extra responsibilities as favoritism. Help us to learn the humility that comes from knowing how weak we are. Help us to realize just how much we need Your grace. Help us to be willing to accept that gift. And help us this day to keep our eyes fixed on Your strength rather than on our failings.

Paul's Dump Truck

*"There is no one righteous, not even one; there is
no one who understands, no one who seeks God. All have
turned away, they have together become worthless; there is
no one who does good, not even one" Rom. 3:10-12, NIV.*

PAUL NOW BACKS UP his dump truck as he begins to inundate the Jews with a flood of their own scripture. So, he asks in effect, you think you are God's special people because you have the Bible? Why don't you read it and see what it says about God's chosen ones?

And with that he lets them have it with a series of quotations, largely from the Psalms, that runs from Romans 3:10 through verse 18. He is using a Jewish method of listing one quotation after another that they referred to as "stringing pearls."

Each of his quotations drives home the point that the Jews aren't quite as good as they think they are. The first quotation is a paraphrase of Psalm 14:1-3. It lists six indictments.

First, "there is no one righteous, not even one" (Rom. 3:10, NIV). "Righteousness" is a key word in Romans. In its essence it means being right before God. Paul's point is that there is not a single person, apart from Jesus, who has lived a sinless life—not one.

Second, "there is no one who understands" (verse 11, NIV). Thus as humans we are not only morally evil, we are also spiritually ignorant.

Third, "there is . . . no one who seeks him" (verse 11, NIV). In addition to being universally evil and spiritually ignorant, Paul now claims that people are all rebellious. They avoid Him. Of course, they don't shirk the duties of religion. People like pageantry and they like to do things that make them feel religious. But seeking God with all one's heart is a bit more threatening than our human solutions.

Fourth, people not only fail to seek God, but they deliberately turn away from Him, like a soldier running the wrong way in the midst of battle.

Fifth, Paul charges that the natural person is "worthless" (verse 12, NIV). It is the same word used of milk when it has gone bad. Human nature without God is soured and useless.

Lastly, "no one . . . does good" (verse 12, NIV). That charge is both a repetition of the first one and a summary of the previous five charges.

Paul wants his readers to sense the depth of their need so that we will humble ourselves and bow to Him at the foot of the cross in humility.

MORE "PEARL STRINGING"

"Their throats are opened graves; they use their tongues
to deceive. The venom of vipers is under their lips. Their mouths
are full of cursing and bitterness." Rom. 3:13, 14, NRSV.

DWIGHT L. MOODY, the great evangelist, used to tell of being asked by the warden of a large prison in New York City to speak to the inmates. Since it had no chapel or other suitable place to preach, he spoke from the aisle at the end of a long row of cells. Throughout the sermon he couldn't see the face of a single prisoner.

After his message the warden granted Moody permission to speak face to face with some of the men through the bars of their cells. He soon found out that most of them hadn't even been listening.

The evangelist asked several of the inmates why they were in prison. The response was invariably one of innocence—there had been false witnesses, it was a case of mistaken identity, or the judge or jury had it in for him. No one admitted to their guilt.

Moody claims that he began to get discouraged. Then he came to an inmate with tears streaming down his cheeks. "What is your trouble?" asked the evangelist.

With despair and remorse the man looked up and said, "My sins are more than I can bear."

"Thank God for that," Moody replied.

Our sins are greater than we can bear. That is what Paul has been seeking to drum into our heads ever since halfway through Romans 1.

In today's lesson he continues to pound his message home through a continuation of his "pearl stringing" technique. In Romans 3:13, 14 he quotes from Psalms 5:9; 140:3; and 10:7. All three passages have to do with our mouths.

Jesus pointed out repeatedly that people's characters will inevitably manifest themselves in their conversation. "For the mouth speaks out of that which fills the heart," we read in Matthew 12:34 (NASB). On another occasion He taught them that "the things that proceed out of the mouth come from the heart" (Matt. 15:18, NASB). James implies that there is nothing more difficult to control than our tongues (James 3:8). Peter knew that. So do I.

Daily we stand condemned by our words. Our sins, like those of Moody's prisoner friend, are greater than we can bear. But that very realization is the very one that God wants us to have. He asks to bear them for us.

THE DOCTRINE OF TOTAL DEPRAVITY

"Their feet are swift to shed blood, in their paths are ruin and misery, and the way of peace they do not know." Rom. 3:15-17, RSV.

PAUL ISN'T FINISHED stringing pearls yet. Today's text is in effect a continuation of Romans 3:13 and 14. Paul systematically lists the various parts of the human body. Thus sinners' *throats* are as open graves, their *tongues* practice deceit, their *lips* spread snakelike poison, their *mouths* utter bitter curses, and their *feet* don't merely pursue violence, but are swift to do so. Verse 18 will deal with people's *eyes*.

Sin affects every part of our humanity. Not only the physical organs listed in Romans 3:13-18, but our minds, our emotions, our sexuality, our appetites, our conscience, and our will. The tragedy of the sin problem is that the bodily organs Paul listed God had originally created to be a blessing to those around us. He gave them to us that we might glorify Him and bless our fellow humans. Yet we use them to harm people and rebel against God. Such is the biblical teaching of total depravity.

Total depravity doesn't mean that we are as wicked as we could be. I heard on the news recently about a 20-year-old woman who had her car hijacked. Her abductors beat her brutally, shot her in the chest, ran over her with her own car, and then burned the car itself. Sick! Her attackers were about as evil as they could be.

But that is not what the Bible has in mind when it talks about total depravity. You don't have to be a Hitler to be totally depraved. To the contrary, Paul is telling us that sin affects every part of our life, every part of our body and mind. It affects us totally in all of our aspects.

That is why God wants to redeem us in our totality. He didn't come just to save our souls, but to renew our minds, transform our attitudes, and eventually resurrect our bodies. Just as sin affects us totally, so does salvation.

That salvation begins here on earth. He wants us to dedicate our lips, mouths, feet, and eyes to Him today, so that we can be a blessing to others and find the peace that He desires that we have.

Today, our Father, we give over our total selves to You for Your service. Help us to be the blessing that You made us to be to those around us. May Your transforming and empowering Spirit be our guide and protector. Amen.

FEARING GOD

"There is no fear of God before their eyes." Rom. 3:18, NRSV.

WHO DO YOU FEAR?

I used to fear my father. I can still remember his descending out of nowhere, grabbing me by the arm, and vigorously warming my backside as we went round and round in a circle for my having disrespected my mother. I always looked both directions before transgressing his rules. The last thing I wanted was to participate in one of those merry-go-round episodes with him. I had a healthy fear for his authority, power, and righteous indignation.

Fear toward God in the Bible has several meanings. Some are positive, while others are negative.

On the positive side, fear implies a reverence for God. That reverence includes an awareness of His power, His glory, and His holiness. True worship is an outgrowth of such reverential fear. It was so in the case of Isaiah. "Woe is me!" penned the prophet. "For I am lost; for I am a man of unclean lips, and I dwell in the midst of a people of unclean lips; for my eyes have seen the King, the Lord of hosts!" (Isa. 6:5, RSV).

When we see who God is we will not only realize His greatness, but also our own poverty. As in the case of Isaiah, awe of God will lead us to worship and serve Him.

In Proverbs 1:7 we read that "the fear of the Lord is the beginning of knowledge" (RSV). The people in today's text don't even fear God. Thus they not only lack wisdom, they don't even have wisdom's starting point.

Fear of God also has a negative meaning. As Leon Morris puts it, "evildoers would do well to have a healthy fear of him who will determine their eternal destiny."

It is unfortunate that most people in our culture fear their neighbor's opinion more than they do God. They fear their boss or financial destitution more than the Lord.

Lord, help me today to get my eyes open that I might experience life in proper proportion. Help me to realize that when I "fear" You in a healthy way then I will have no reason to fear anyone or anything else. Today, Lord, I want to rededicate my life to You. I want to be Your daughter, Your son, so that You can live out Your life through me. Help me to have the kind of "fear" that will give me both peace and spiritual power.

SLIPPERY CHURCH MEMBERS

*Now we know that whatever the law says it speaks to those
who are under the law, so that every mouth may be stopped, and
the whole world may be held accountable to God. Rom. 3:19, RSV.*

SO PAUL HAS FINISHED with his string of pearls. He has dumped his truckload of quotations on his readers in Romans 3:10-18.

Now in verse 19 he needs to anticipate a question from his Jewish readers because, as John Calvin points out, "whatever was said in the law unfavorably of mankind, they usually applied to the Gentiles, as though they [the Jews] were exempt from the common condition of men."

The apostle knows his people. And he knows us. Churchgoing people can be some of the slipperiest on earth. We are always trying to weasel out of our true condition. Condemnation is always for others. Even when we speak of the kingdom we tend to employ the first person, as if we were already on the inside. After all, don't I go to church every week? Don't I pay tithe? Don't I understand and keep God's true Sabbath? Don't I live a good clean life? Don't I read my Bible?

Things haven't changed much in the past 2,000 years. That is exactly the way the Jews felt. It must have been those nasty old Gentiles that Paul's dump truck of quotations applied to, rather than to those who are already in God's covenant.

That is just the logic Paul smashes in Romans 3:19. Listen up! he tells his readers. The law (in this case meaning the entire Old Testament) is aimed at those who are under it—that is, the Jews. Those quotations mean you, Mr. and Mrs. Jew, Mr. and Mrs. Churchgoer.

And what do those Bible texts in Romans 3:10-18 prove? That you are dead meat! That you stand condemned. Thus every mouth is stopped. C.E.B. Cranfield notes that "the reference to the stopped mouth evokes the image of the defendant in court, who, when given the opportunity to speak in his own defense, remains silent, overwhelmed by the weight of evidence against him." There is nothing to do but to wait for the pronouncement and execution of the sentence. "The whole world [both Jew and Gentile]," Paul concludes, will "be held accountable to God." None of us can rest on our spiritual pedigrees.

We can thank God that verse 19 is not the end of the book of Romans. It is rather the next text to the last in the beginning. With verse 21 Paul will begin to set forth God's solution to the sin problem.

WHAT THE LAW CAN'T DO

By the deeds of the law there shall be no flesh justified. Rom. 3:20.

HOW DO WE GET right with God? How do we escape the judgment of sin? How do we perfect character? These are perennial challenges that every human faces. Paul's audience, people who put their trust in the law and lawkeeping to get them right with God, also faced them.

Getting right with God by being good isn't a monopoly of the first-century Jews. It soon flowed over into Christianity. The early church had many ascetics. One was Simeon Stylites (c. 390-459). In his search for an escape from sin Simeon had himself buried in sand up to his neck. After that exercise he thought of a better one. His next way to holiness was to sit on top of a 60-foot pillar, where he would be removed from all temptation. For 36 years (until his death) Simeon remained atop his pole. Not only did his body "drip" with vermin, but he performed excruciating exercises far above the desert floor. Once, for example, he is said to have touched his feet with his forehead more than 1,244 times in succession.

Even in our time we find such "spiritual athletes." Jesuit William Doyle, for instance, inflicted upon himself great personal discomforts, including the wearing of a hair shirt next to his flesh, exposure to nettles and to freezing water at midnight, and lying on cold chapel stones. Of course, he had to deal with his vigorous appetite—a perennial area of behavioral concern across history. Doyle's notebook records in detail his many temptations with sugar, cake, honey, jam, and other delicacies: "Violent temptation to eat cake, resisted several times. Overcame the desire to take jam, honey, and sugar. Fierce temptation to take cake, etc." "God has been urging me strongly all during this retreat to give up butter entirely."

I can identify with Doyle, Stylites, and Paul's Jewish readers. I still remember as a 19-year-old convert to Christianity promising God out loud that I would be the first perfect Christian since Jesus. And how was I to accomplish such a feat? Through good behavior, of course.

That is just what Paul is telling us won't work. It is a well-beaten path, but it ends only in frustration. Humans might be able to distance themselves from temptation, but they are still sinners. Only God in His grace provides an adequate solution to the problem of sin and salvation.

UNLAWFUL USES OF THE LAW

By the law is the knowledge of sin. Rom. 3:20.

THE LAW IS VALUABLE for some things, but absolutely useless for others. In 1 Timothy 1:8 Paul writes that "the law is good, if any one uses it lawfully" (RSV). The astounding truth is that the law can be used either properly or improperly. One of the greatest temptations for "nice church-going people" like us is to use God's law unlawfully.

It cannot do one all-important thing—it can't save us. Paul tells us that the function of the law is not justification but telling us where we have gone wrong. As he says in Romans 7:7: "If it had not been for the law, I should not have known sin" (RSV).

James 1:23-25 compares the law to a mirror. Before I leave for work in the morning I go to the mirror to discover what is right and wrong with my face and hair. The mirror tells me that not all is quite ready for public exposure, that I have egg on my face or that my hair is only half combed.

Now, the function of the mirror is to point out things that need improvement. With that knowledge I can go to the soap, washcloth, and comb. But it won't do to rub the mirror on my face to get the egg off or to run the mirror through my hair to comb it. The purpose of the mirror is to remind me of needed improvements.

So it is with the law. When I compare myself with God's law I find that I have problems in my life. But the law cannot correct them. It has another function: to tell me that I am a sinner. The law shows me my problems and needs, but it does not solve them. The Phillips translation of Romans 3:20 graphically portrays the function of the law: "Indeed it is the straight-edge of the Law that shows us how crooked we are." The New Living Translation is also helpful: "For no one can ever be made right in God's sight by doing what his law commands. For the more we know God's law, the clearer it becomes that we aren't obeying it."

The law is not a ladder to heaven. But it makes us aware of such a ladder. The law points beyond itself to Jesus and the real solution to our problems. It is to that topic that Paul now turns as he moves beyond his extensive analysis of the sin problem to the good news about justification.

The Good News of Justification

Romans 3:21–5:21

TAKING A THIRD STEP WITH PAUL

*But now a righteousness from God, apart
from law, has been made known. Rom. 3:21, NIV.*

"BUT NOW."

With those two words we have arrived at the second great turning point in the book of Romans. During the first step, as you will recall, we met Paul and his gospel. At the second step he demonstrated, at times in excruciating detail, that every person is a sinner headed for judgment, the wrath of God, and eventual death.

Not a very bright future. That's where Paul's "but now" comes in. D. Martyn Lloyd Jones claims that "there are no more wonderful words in the whole of Scripture than just these two words 'but now.'"

Why make such an emphatic statement? The answer is in the context. Paul has left his readers in a state of hopelessness and helplessness. In Romans 3:19 he noted that every person stands under God's just condemnation. Then in verse 20 he emphatically stated that people couldn't get right with God even if they wanted to be good and zealously kept the law. At that very point Paul drops in his "but now."

"But now," he writes, "a righteousness from God, apart from law, has been made known." With those words Paul sets the agenda for step three in his tour through Romans.

This step picks up the righteousness by faith theme of Romans 1:16 and 17 and fills out its meaning in a mighty passage that runs from Romans 3:21 through 5:21. His initial treatment of the topic extends from Romans 3:21 through 3:31 in what Leon Morris claims might be "the most important single paragraph ever written."

The salvation that Paul exposes us to in that tightly packed paragraph will focus on three metaphors: (1) justification (an image from the law court), (2) redemption (an image from the slave market), and (3) propitiation (an image related to the sacrificial system).

The good news is that God has intervened in human affairs. He has done for us what we could not do through the law. "But then" reflects the fact that God's saving work through Christ has transformed the human predicament.

With Romans 3:21 we have come to the beginning of the heart of Paul's understanding of the gospel. From the apostle's perspective, sinful humanity may be weak, but God is powerful—powerful to justify, powerful to sanctify, powerful to glorify those who accept His grace.

GOD'S ETERNAL PLAN

The law and the prophets bear witness to it [i.e., God's righteousness revealed apart from law]. Rom. 3:21, RSV.

THE PLAN OF SALVATION through Christ was not an afterthought. Nor was it something new. Paul tells us that the law and the prophets (the Old Testament) "bear witness to it." *The Desire of Ages* speaks to the same point when it notes that Christ's life was the "fulfillment of the plan that had existed from the days of eternity" (p. 147).

The first glimmer of the Old Testament witness to righteousness apart from the law comes in Genesis 3:15, in which God tells us that Christ would bruise the head of the serpent. That glimmer becomes more open in the experience of Abraham, whom God counted righteous because he believed Him, an aspect that Paul treats extensively in Romans 4. But perhaps the most explicit showcase of the plan of salvation in the books of Moses is the sacrificial system. It is of interest that John the Baptist refers to Christ as the "Lamb of God, which taketh away the sin of the world" (John 1:29) and Paul describes Christ as "our passover" who was "sacrificed for us" (1 Cor. 5:7).

David speaks of the "righteousness from God, apart from law" (Rom. 3:21, NIV) when he relies on God's mercy to "blot out" his "transgressions" and to wash him from his iniquity (Ps. 51:1, 2). Isaiah 53 foretells the One who will justify many by bearing their "iniquities" (Isa. 53:5). Again, the same chapter notes that "he was wounded for our transgressions, he was bruised for our iniquities: the chastisement of our peace was upon him; and with his stripes we are healed" (verse 5).

Jeremiah wasn't backward on the topic. He refers to the coming Branch of David who would be called "THE LORD OUR RIGHTEOUSNESS" (Jer. 23:5, 6). And the great prophetic chapter of Daniel 9 notes: "Seventy weeks are determined upon thy people and upon thy holy city, to finish the transgression, and to make an end of sins, and to make reconciliation for iniquity, and to bring in everlasting righteousness" (Dan. 9:24).

Paul knew what he was talking about. God's plan for saving people by means other than obedience to the law is a theme that runs throughout the Old Testament. It is a theme to which Paul repeatedly turns in his various letters. And it is the theme to which he will now turn as he expounds upon righteousness by faith in Romans 3:21 through 5:21.

RIGHTEOUSNESS FROM GOD

*This righteousness from God comes
through faith in Jesus Christ. Rom. 3:22, NIV.*

WITH ROMANS 3:22 we have come to the beginning of an absolutely central part of Paul's argument in Romans. Verse 21 noted that God had a righteousness "apart from law" (NIV). That is the negative side, what righteousness is not. But with verse 22 we come to the positive explanation that Paul has been wanting to get to ever since Romans 1:16, 17.

In that passage Paul said that he was "not ashamed of the gospel, because it is the power of God for the salvation of everyone who believes: first for the Jew, then for the Gentile. For in the gospel a righteousness from God is revealed, a righteousness that is by faith from first to last" (NIV).

Paul did not stop to explain what he meant because he had a task that he had to accomplish first. He wanted to make clear that *everybody* needed God's righteousness, and that we could not obtain it by any human condition or achievement—not by birth into the covenant people, or by having or keeping the law.

Since the law's function was to point out sin (Rom. 3:20), it had no power to save, but could only condemn. Everybody—even the good churchgoing Jews—were under condemnation, with no way out.

Now that Paul has made those points he can pick up on his statement about the gospel of righteousness by faith that he had set forth in Romans 1:16, 17. He is now ready to explain what he meant by the phrase. After all, we should all be ready to listen, since we have no hope outside of God's gracious offer.

Righteousness is an important word in Romans, appearing more than 30 times. The next-highest usage is six times in 1 Corinthians and Matthew. The phrase "the righteousness of God," as found in today's text, shows up eight times in Romans, but only twice in all the rest of Paul's letters combined.

"God's righteousness" or "righteousness from God" can refer to either God's character or His gift. In the context of Romans 3:21, 22 it has in mind that righteousness which God has provided and offers to those who have faith in Christ. To Paul this righteousness is humanity's greatest need. Thus it stands at the very center of his presentation of the good news. It forms the very essence of his understanding of the gospel.

SALVATION'S ONE CONDITION

The righteousness of God . . . [is] for all who believe. Rom. 3:22, RSV.

SALVATION IS NOT AUTOMATIC. It must be accepted. It has a condition, and that condition, we read yesterday, is "faith in Jesus Christ." Today's reading reinforces that point. Righteousness is "for all who believe."

But what is faith? What is it that Paul is telling us that we so badly need? C. K. Barrett helps us to understand the meaning of faith in the context of Romans when he writes that faith "can hardly better be defined than as the opposite of man's self-confident or self-despairing attempt to establish a proper relationship between himself and God by legal (that is, by moral or religious) means. Instead of concentrating his hope upon himself he directs it towards God," particularly toward His saving act of grace through Jesus Christ.

I would like to suggest that biblical faith includes both believing and trusting, that it is a trust based on belief. Just as the first step in sin involved distrust in God (Gen. 3:1-6), so the first step toward Him is trusting faith. Faith is coming to grips with the fact that we must trust God because He has our best interests at heart, and because there is nothing else completely trustworthy.

Biblical faith, we should note, is always absolute; it is never moderate. James Denney can therefore write that faith is much more than accepting a legal arrangement; "it is *the abandonment of the soul,* which has no hope but in the Saviour, *to the Saviour. . . . It includes the absolute renunciation of everything else, to lay hold on Christ.*" Faith is a *"passion* in which the whole being of man is caught up and abandoned unconditionally to the love revealed in the Saviour."

Ellen White says much the same thing when she pens that "faith is trusting God—believing that He loves us and knows best what is for our good. Thus, instead of our own, it leads us to choose His way. In place of our ignorance, it accepts His wisdom; in place of our weakness, His strength; in place of our sinfulness, His righteousness" (*Education,* p. 253).

Lord, help me today to give up on my way and to accept Your way. Help me to abandon belief in myself and to put my faith in You. Help me to realize that Your way is the only way and that without You and Your gift in Christ I have no hope. And help me to accept the one condition for salvation. Thank You for that righteousness which You have provided "for all who believe."

NO DIFFERENCE BETWEEN WHAT?

*There is no difference, for all have sinned and fall
short of the glory of God. Rom. 3:22, 23, NIV.*

"THERE IS NO DIFFERENCE."

No difference in what? That every human being who has ever lived (except Jesus) has been a sinner and fallen short of what he or she should be.

But, you may be thinking, *I am better than some people.* Are you? Read Paul in his context. Oh, it's true that your sins aren't as open and visible as those of the most disgraceful and notorious lawbreakers, but you are just as hopelessly distant from "the glory of God" as they are.

As Handley Moule notes, God's "moral 'glory,' the inexorable perfectness of His character, with its inherent demand that you must perfectly correspond to Him in order to be at peace with Him—you are indeed 'short of' this. The harlot, the liar, the murderer, are short of it; but so are you. Perhaps they [from our faulty perspective] stand at the bottom of a mine, and you on the crest of an Alp; but you are as little able to touch the stars as they."

The verb tenses in today's verse may have a lesson for us. All "have sinned" is a Greek aorist that pictures sinning as being in humanity's past. But that doesn't mean that sin is merely universal in the past. The next verb, "fall short," is in the present tense, reflecting a continual process. Thus the sin problem is truly universal in both historic time and space.

A first reading of Romans 3:23 might make us think that the verse is out of place, an intrusion into the text, since Romans 3:21-31 is not talking about sin but about the way of salvation. It seems that verse 23 should have been a part of Paul's concluding statement on the sin problem that ran from Romans 1:18 through 3:20.

But a look at Romans 3:23 in its context makes the verse even more forceful than it would have been earlier. After all, Paul has embedded it right in the middle of his treatment of righteousness by grace through faith. It is the context that highlights the full meaning of "no difference." Just as we are all sinners, even so we all (every one of us) need God's grace. And only when we realize that in God's sight there is no difference between us and the wildest profligate can we be saved.

With that realization comes the first step in our salvation. Whether we like it or not, Paul is correct when he declares that there is "no difference."

AND WHAT IS JUSTIFICATION?

They are justified by his grace as a gift. Rom. 3:24, RSV.

MARTIN LUTHER VIEWED justification as the central scriptural doctrine. It is, he claimed, "the master and ruler, lord, governor and judge over all other doctrines." And it is the unique Christian doctrine that "distinguishes our religion from all others." Paul also put justification by faith at the center of his gospel (see, e.g., Rom. 1:16, 17; 3:24-26; Gal. 2:16-21).

Part of the reason Luther and Paul saw justification as central to the plan of salvation was undoubtedly the judgment theme that runs throughout the Bible (e.g., Eccl. 12:14; Dan. 7:10, 26; Matt. 25:31-46; Rom. 2:5; Rev. 14:7). But beyond the judgment imagery were the two men's own personal experiences. Early in their lives both were Pharisees at heart. Both hoped to win God's favor through amassing merits on the balance scale of judgment. But that attempt, as both learned, was an impossible task.

Paul and Luther in their Pharisaic days were not altogether wrong. After all, righteousness does demand perfect lawkeeping. And the automatic penalty for failure is condemnation and death (see Rom. 6:23; 4:15). They were also correct about their shortcomings on obeying the law as God demanded.

The great breakthrough for both of them came when they understood justification as God's free gift.

Justification, a legal term, is the opposite of condemnation. Both are pronouncements by a judge. Justification does not mean "to make righteous," but rather "to declare righteous." It is more than pardon, which is the remission of a penalty or debt. To the contrary, justification is a positive pronouncement of righteous status on the repentant sinner.

Luther referred to the transaction in which Christ becomes sin for us, while we receive His righteousness (2 Cor. 5:21), as the "wonderful exchange." Ellen White reflects on the same idea: "He died for us, and now He offers to take our sins and give us His righteousness. If you give yourself to Him, and accept Him as your Saviour, then, sinful as your life may have been, for His sake you are accounted righteous. Christ's character stands in place of your character, and you are accepted before God just as if you had not sinned" (*Steps to Christ*, p. 62).

Accepted as if I had not sinned! Not only pardoned but declared righteous. That is justification. That is God's incomparable gift to me.

THE REDEMPTION PRICE

All who believe . . . are justified freely . . . through the
redemption that came by Christ Jesus. Rom. 3:22-24, NIV.

TODAY WE WANT TO examine the word "redemption." What does it mean for Christ to redeem us? If justification, as we saw yesterday, is a metaphor of the law court, redemption comes from the language of the marketplace. Let me illustrate.

My mother used to be a great saver of S & H Green Stamps. For every dime she spent at participating stores she received a stamp, which she pasted into specially made booklets. She also had a catalogue that told her what gifts she could get for a given number of Green Stamp books. When she had enough books filled, she hauled them down to the Green Stamp store, where she could turn them in to "redeem" her gift. The Green Stamp store, interestingly enough, was called a "redemption center."

The most basic meaning of "redeem" is "to buy" or "to buy back." The use of "redemption" in the universal Greek culture of antiquity had its origin in the practice of warfare. After a battle, the victors would round up the vanquished and take them home to sell as slaves. Sometimes, however, they discovered that they had captured important people who were worth more to their native country than they were as slaves. On these occasions the victors let their enemies know of such valuable captives and offered to release them for a price. The other governments often accepted such offers. As a result, they would raise money to "buy back" (redeem) the special prisoners of war. The purchase price was called the "ransom."

The Old Testament used that same concept. Thus a slave in Israel could be redeemed by one who could pay the purchase price (Lev. 25:47-49).

The New Testament applies the redemption concept to Christ. Romans 6:16 speaks of sinners as being slaves of sin. But unlike the Old Testament Jew who might become rich and thus redeem himself (Lev. 25:49), Satan's captives struggle in vain against the bondage of sin.

It is in that context that Paul tells us that Christ became our redemption. As Jesus told His disciples, "the Son of man" came "to give his life as a ransom for many" (Mark 10:45, RSV). Paul notes that "Christ redeemed us from the curse of the law, having become a curse for us" (Gal. 3:13, RSV). And Peter reminds us that we weren't ransomed with silver or gold, "but with the precious blood of Christ, like that of a lamb without blemish or spot" (1 Peter 1:18, 19).

PROPITIATION IS A BIG WORD

God hath set forth [Jesus Christ] to be a propitiation. Rom. 3:25.

PROPITIATION IS A BIG WORD. With it Paul moves away from language of the court of law (justification, Rom. 3:24) and from the language of the marketplace (redemption, verse 25) to a third metaphor of salvation—propitiation, taken from the language of the sacrificial altar.

The basic meaning of propitiation is "turning away wrath." In the Greek world in which the New Testament arose, propitiation had the flavor of bribing the gods, demons, or the dead in an attempt to win their favor and get their blessing. Since the gods were "mad" they needed to be appeased. We find that type of propitiation in the Old Testament when the king of Moab, seeing the battle was going against him, offered "his eldest son who was to reign in his stead" as a "burnt offering" to Chemosh in the hope of winning his favor (2 Kings 3:26, 27, RSV).

But we must not confuse Paul's use of the word with that of the pagans. It is absolutely crucial to recognize that the Bible is clear that Christ did not shed His blood to appease God's wrath. To the contrary, according to Romans 3:25 God "put forward" (RSV) the propitiatory sacrifice. "Herein is love," writes John, "not that we loved God, but that he loved us, and sent his Son to be the propitiation for our sins" (1 John 4:10).

The cross, therefore, does not represent a change in God's attitude toward sinners. Rather, it is the supreme expression of His love. We read in *Steps to Christ* that "the Father loves us, not because of the great propitiation, but He provided the propitiation because He loves us" (p. 13).

The Bible usage of propitiation is not that of the pagan world. To the contrary, "God so loved the world, that he gave his only begotten Son, that whosoever believeth in him should not perish [because of sin], but have everlasting life" (John 3:16).

God has taken sin seriously. He could not just ignore its destructive results. It is destroying His beloved people. God's wrath is His judgment on sin. Paul's teaching in Romans 3 is that Christ's death removes the sentence of God's just condemnation from those who through faith accept His sacrifice.

The good news for today is that He died in our place. The good news is that Christ died for me personally. The good news is that God through Christ justifies, redeems, and propitiates. In short, God saves from sin those who cannot save themselves. That's you and me.

THE BIBLE'S
MOST IMPORTANT WORD

Blood. Rom. 3:25.

WHERE, YOU MAY BE asking, is our text for today? I didn't give you one. Why? Because I want your full attention. I need it because we are dealing with one of the most important words in the Bible, particularly when it speaks of Christ's blood "as a sacrifice of atonement" (Rom. 3:25, NIV).

A lot of people today don't want to talk about Christ's sacrifice for us or the necessity of His shedding His blood to solve the sin problem. That perspective is an ancient one. Cain didn't think much of the idea either (see Gen. 4:1-4; Heb. 11:4). Neither did the Greeks to whom Paul tried to preach. To them it was just plain "foolishness" (1 Cor. 1:18).

The Bible writers, however, had no such qualms on the topic. The substitutionary sacrifice of the lamb without blemish was the central object lesson of the Old Testament. And the New Testament writers leave us without the slightest doubt that the sacrificial lambs foreshadowed the death of Jesus as the Lamb of God.

Blood and the death of Christ for us are absolutely central to the New Testament understanding of salvation. Not only is the focal point of each of the four Gospels the death of Christ, but each of the major metaphors that Paul employs has an intimate relationship to Christ's shed blood. Thus "God hath set forth [Christ] to be a propitiation through faith in his blood" (Rom. 3:25); "in him we have redemption through his blood" (Eph. 1:7, RSV); we are "now justified by his blood" (Rom. 5:9); and God acted "to reconcile to himself all things, . . . making peace by the blood of his cross" (Col. 1:20, RSV).

Propitiation, redemption, justification, and reconciliation are all tied to and based upon the shed blood of Christ. John R. W. Stott concludes from the centrality of Christ's blood in those great salvific themes that sacrificial "substitution is not a 'theory of the atonement.' Nor is it even an additional image that takes its place as an option alongside the others. It is rather the essence of each image and the heart of the atonement itself. None of the four images could stand without it."

Thank You, Jesus, for dying for me. Thank You for dying the death that is mine that I might have the life that is Yours. No wonder Paul calls this good news. No wonder the great hymns of the Christian church uplift the blood of Christ.

JUSTICE RELATED TO BLOOD

*He did this [provide Christ's sacrifice] to
demonstrate His justice. Rom. 3:25, NIV.*

THE CROSS OF CHRIST was not only an accomplishment; it was also a demonstration. It not only supplied the propitiatory sacrifice, but also illustrated God's justice. In Romans 3:25 and 26 Paul has some extremely important things to say about divine justice.

The first thing we want to note is that the Bible especially stresses the theme of God's justice. That emphasis not only shows up in Romans 3, but is especially prominent in the songs in the book of Revelation. It is particularly interesting to see that Revelation ties God's justice and vindication to the death of Jesus on the cross and the fairness of His judgments.

The songs of Revelation 4 and 5 begin to build the theme when they repeatedly declare God's worthiness in the context of the heavenly throne room/sanctuary. "Worthy art thou, our Lord and God, to receive glory and honor and power" (Rev. 4:11, RSV). In chapter 5 John weeps because he can find no one "worthy" to unseal the mysterious scroll. Then the Lamb enters, and the heavenly beings sing "a new song, saying, *'Worthy* are thou to take the scroll and open its seals, *for thou wast slain and by thy blood* didst ransom men for God" (Rev. 5:9, RSV). The numberless host of heaven then proclaim "with a loud voice, *'Worthy is the Lamb who was slain,* to receive power and wealth and wisdom and might and honor and glory and blessing!" (verse 12, RSV).

We should note that those passages directly relate to the "worthiness" of Christ to unseal the scroll of salvation history to His propitiatory sacrifice. It was that sacrifice, Paul claims in Romans 3:24-26, that shows God's righteousness in justifying sinners.

A second major round of Revelation's worship doxologies appears in the judgment scene of the seven last plagues. "Just and true art thou in these thy judgments," the angel proclaims in Revelation 16:5 (RSV; see also Rev. 16:7; 15:3, 4).

The third round occurs at the Second Advent. Revelation 19 reads: "Hallelujah! *Salvation and glory and power belong to our God, for his judgments are true and just"* (Rev. 19:1, 2, RSV; cf. verse 11).

The justice of God is not at the edge of the great controversy between God and the devil—it is at the very center. He must truly demonstrate that He is love in everything He does.

WHAT ABOUT PEOPLE BORN BEFORE THE CROSS?

[God needed to demonstrate His justice] because in
His forbearance God had passed over the sins
that were previously committed. Rom. 3:25, NKJV.

THIS IS AN INTERESTING passage because no translation renders it in the same way as the King James Version, which reads that God would provide "his righteousness for the remission of sins that are past." Many nineteenth-century Adventists read those words and concluded that justification by faith was for past sins, but that present duty was theirs to perform. Their misunderstanding led them to conclude that they had justification by faith for all sins committed before their conversion, but since then they needed justification by works.

In its context the passage has no such meaning. Remember that it is dealing with God's justice. Paul is telling us that one thing the death of Christ accomplished was to demonstrate that God is just. Specifically, that He was just in not immediately punishing sinners in Old Testament times, an idea clearly reflected in every translation that I have examined except the King James Version. Thus the *New American Standard Bible* translates the passage to the effect that Christ's death on the cross "was to demonstrate His righteousness, because in the forbearance of God He passed over the sins previously committed."

Here is a beautiful truth. God had told Adam and Eve that in the very day that they ate the forbidden fruit they would die (Gen. 2:17). But they didn't perish immediately. God in His forbearance (patience) granted them full lives in which to discover His grace. In a similar manner, He put up with the Israelites of Moses' time, giving them the sacrificial system as an illustration of grace, showing that help was on its way in the Lamb who would die once for all. God didn't act against sin right away because He knew that He would send Christ, whose death alone would absorb the penalty for sin. That death would be not only for those born after the cross, but for the whole human race from the beginning of earthly time.

God hasn't changed. He still hasn't given sinners their just desserts. To the contrary, just as with Adam and Eve He is still reaching down to us in grace. The Lord is "longsuffering to us-ward, not willing that any should perish, but that all should come to repentance" (2 Peter 3:9).

GRACE ISN'T FAIR

He did it to demonstrate his justice at the present time. Rom. 3:26, NIV.

HOW CAN GOD TAKE some people to heaven while destroying others in the second death when the plain fact is that all have sinned and deserve death? Is that just?

I still remember reading the parable of the lost son in Luke 15 for the first time. It upset me. How could God the Father just forgive and restore His rebel son? I thought he should have put him on probation and made him prove himself through faithful and long-term service on the family farm. The son should have paid, at least to some extent, for his sins. But the father welcomed him back with open arms and fully restored him to sonship. Where is the justice? He didn't get what he deserved.

The problem intensifies in the light of the older brother's life. Now, here was a really *good* person. He made no trips over fool's hill to experiment with sin. To the contrary, he stayed at home and devoted his life to working hard for the father. The older brother did all the right things. And when he got upset at the father because the father restored his brother, so did I. After all, why rejoice because he came home? What choice did he have? He was destitute and reduced to eating pigs' food. That was as low as a Jew could get. *And now he came home,* the older brother thought, *so that he can spend my share of the inheritance after he has already thrown away his on foolish living. That is nothing to rejoice about.*

What a travesty of justice. Neither brother got what he deserved. How unjust can it get? Isn't getting what you deserve a basic principle of justice?

But that is where grace comes in. You see, we can define grace as getting what we don't deserve. Thus in His grace God gives those who accept Christ life when they really deserve death. He makes us sons and daughters when we really shouldn't be in the family. How can God do that and still be fair? How can we trust someone who doesn't play by the rules that He has set forth?

Those types of questions indicate the reality of God's problem. Tomorrow we will examine how God can offer people what they don't deserve but still be just or righteous.

But for today, let us just praise God that He doesn't give us what we deserve. If He did, we wouldn't be.

THE JUSTIFICATION OF GOD

*[God sent forth Christ as a sacrifice] to demonstrate
his justice at the present time, so as to be just and the one
who justifies those who have faith in Jesus. Rom. 3:26, NIV.*

THE CENTRAL ISSUE in the great controversy is not your or my individual justification, but God's. How, as we noted yesterday, can God be just and yet treat people as if they had never sinned?

The natural thing to say, notes William Barclay, "would be, 'God is just, and therefore, condemns the sinner as a criminal.'" Such reasoning is fully in harmony with the instruction that He gave to human judges, who were to "justify the righteous, and condemn the wicked" (Deut. 25:1). Anyone who justifies the wicked, we read in Proverbs, and "condemns the righteous" is "an abomination to the Lord" (Prov. 17:15, RSV).

How can God break the rules He set up for human judges and still be just? How can He justify sinners by grace and still be righteous? That is one of the questions Paul has been wrestling with in Romans 3:21-26.

God's unmerited forgiveness through grace demonstrates that God is merciful and compassionate. But, suggests Leon Morris, "some would be tempted to doubt His justice. 'Not anymore,' Paul is saying in Romans 3:24-26. 'The cross demonstrates the . . . justice of God. . . . It is not the fact that God forgives that shows him to be righteous, but the fact that he forgives in a certain way, the way of the cross. . . . God does not set aside the moral law when he forgives." Neither does He abolish the penalty (see Rom. 6:23) of the broken law. To the contrary, Christ not only kept God's law, but He became "sin for us" and died the death that was ours that we might have His righteousness (see 2 Cor. 5:21).

God had taken His law and the penalty for transgressing it seriously. At the cross the entire universe saw the outworking of the kingdoms of good and evil. On Calvary God demonstrated that He could be trusted, while Satan proved that he indeed was a liar and a murderer (John 8:44) when he took the life of the sinless Son of God, the one person in human history who was beyond sin's death penalty.

It was in the brutal fact of the cross that God demonstrated that He was both just and loving, and that we could trust His way, since He was willing to sacrifice of Himself for the good of the universe. It was at the cross that the Godhead laid the foundation for forgiveness and justification. Because of the cross God could justify sinners yet still be just Himself.

BOASTING'S END

Then what becomes of our boasting? It is excluded.
On what principle? On the principle of works?
No, but on the principle of faith. Rom. 3:27, RSV.

D. L. MOODY REPEATEDLY noted that if anyone ever got to heaven by what he or she had done, the rest of us would never hear the end of it.

One of the most disgusting things that I can think of is having to listen to Aunt Bertha or Uncle John explain how good they were for about 10,000 years. Such a rendition is repulsive for even 10 minutes. Having to hear such endless self-praise would be closer to hell than to heaven, and it would certainly remind us of some of the things we had to endure on earth.

We despise nothing in others as much as boasting. Yet we all do it ourselves and are oblivious to the fact. Boasting in a sinful world is quite natural.

But in today's text Paul warns us that no boasting will exist in the kingdom. I like the Phillips translation of Romans 3:27: "What happens now to human pride of achievement? There is no more room for it. Why, because failure to keep the Law has killed it? Not at all, but because the whole matter is now on a different plane—believing instead of achieving."

The saved, Paul has been telling us, have nothing to brag about. None will have made it to heaven because of their goodness. To the contrary, the apostle's gospel teaches that it is their acceptance of the goodness of Christ that gets them into the kingdom. But it isn't only accepting His goodness—it is accepting His death in our place. As we saw yesterday, that death provided the grounds for God to give each of those who receive Jesus what they don't deserve. Grace, life, forgiveness, justification: we aren't entitled to any of them. Yet God provides them to us as a gift. Thus all Christian boasting, claims Paul, is excluded on "the principle of faith." All we can do is come to God thanking Him for His mercy to us.

As a result, the saints in heaven will have boundless praise for God and the "Lamb that was slain" (Rev. 5:12), but none for themselves.

But why wait for heaven? When we cease to think so highly of ourselves, our churches will be more pleasant places to visit. And when we realize our total dependence on God, it will make us more gracious to others who aren't quite as "good" as we are. The implications of "no boasting" can transform our lives even here on earth.

THE CONSEQUENCES OF GOD'S PLAN

Therefore we conclude that a man is justified
by faith without the deeds of the law. Rom. 3:28.

SO FAR IN ROMANS we have seen a powerful argument. First, Paul demonstrated that every person who has ever lived (both Gentile and Jew) has been a sinner. Second, he showed us that neither birth as a part of the covenant people nor keeping the law can help individuals, because the function of the law is to point out sin rather than to be a ladder to heaven. And third, in a tightly packed paragraph running from Romans 3:21-26, Paul has revealed that God saves people through their faith in Jesus. Paul sums up God's salvation in the words "justification by grace through faith alone," without the works of law. His formula is grace + faith + nothing = justification.

The next five verses (Rom. 3:27-31) go on to present three implications or consequences of God's plan of salvation. The first, which we began to examine yesterday, is that God's way of salvation by grace through faith *excludes boasting.* It leaves the saved person with nothing to brag about or to claim as merit, since God did it all. God's way of salvation places us quite humbly at the foot of the cross. The old song puts it nicely: "Nothing in my hand I bring, simply to Thy cross I cling." Those who are truly saved in Christ realize that they have nothing to be proud of. They have fully accepted God's unmerited favor and rejoice in His loving kindness. When it comes to themselves they remain speechless.

The second consequence of God's great plan is, as we shall see in Romans 3:29 and 30, that *salvation has been provided for everybody.*

The third (Rom. 3:31) is that, far from providing a Christian with grounds for immorality or lawbreaking, as some suppose, God's way of salvation actually *upholds the law.* As we saw in our discussion of the justification of God related to Romans 3:25 and 26, the Lord took the law into consideration in His great plan. God's revealed plan of salvation in actuality shows how seriously He regards His own law. He couldn't just ignore its requirements or its penalties. Rather, Christ not only kept it, but He absorbed the death penalty of the broken law for each of us.

Thank You, Lord, for Your unparalleled provision for us. We know that we don't deserve what You have done for us. All we can do is rejoice and praise Your name for so great a salvation.

MONOTHEISM TO THE RESCUE

*There is only one God, who will justify the circumcised by faith
and the uncircumcised through that same faith. Rom. 3:30, NIV.*

I IMAGINE THAT PAUL caught his Jewish readers off guard with
Romans 3:29, 30. Here he tackles the issue of salvation from the perspective of monotheism.

One of the great texts of Judaism was Deuteronomy 6:4: "The Lord our
God is one Lord." Every day every male Jew recited that passage as part
of the Shema. They had no doubt in their minds on the topic of monotheism. Not only were they convinced that there was only one God, but that
that one God had only one people—Israel. The Canaanites had their gods,
and the Egyptians theirs, but Israel belonged to the only true God—
Yahweh, who had created heaven and earth and everything in them.

It is at that very point that Paul challenges them to think. If there is
only one true God, and if that Being created all that exists, isn't He also
God of the Gentiles? Or as Paul put it in verse 29: "Is God the God of Jews
only? Is he not the God of Gentiles too?" Then stating the only possible
conclusion, Paul adds, "Yes, of Gentiles too" (NIV).

Most Jews hadn't thought of it that way. But Paul's logic has a crushing forcefulness. What they had forgotten was that their special privilege
as God's chosen ones did not exclude the Gentiles, but was meant for their
inclusion, since all the peoples of the earth were to be blessed through
Abraham (see Gen. 12:3).

Having made his crucial point, the apostle goes on to note in Romans
3:30 that not only is God the God of the entire world, but that the plan of
salvation is for the entire world—both Jew and Gentile.

Not only is the plan of salvation for all humanity, but, Paul concludes,
it saves both Jews and Gentiles in the same way. All are saved through
faith—the exact same type of faith—without exception. None, as we saw
in verse 20, are saved by lawkeeping. Everyone who is ever saved will be
saved through faith.

Once again we see that there is no room for boasting. Yes, God still
has a special church with a special message, but that specialness represents a responsibility to preach the gospel. Instead of a status symbol of
superiority, it is rather an imperative to serve others.

FAITH ESTABLISHES LAW

Do we then overthrow the law by this faith? By no means!
On the contrary, we uphold the law. Rom. 3:31, RSV.

PAUL IN THE EYES of some of his readers might appear to have placed "law" and "faith" in opposition to each other. They might fear that his emphasis on faith actually "overthrew" or did away with the law.

Anticipating that response to his theology, the apostle quickly and firmly asserts that salvation by grace through faith, far from doing away with the law, actually establishes or upholds it.

What does Paul mean? The answer depends on how he uses the term *law* in our text. We can think of at least three possible interpretations. First, if Paul is referring to the Old Testament in general (the Jews often thought of the Old Testament as the Law and the Prophets) then his gospel of justification by faith in this context would be seen as upholding the law in the sense that the Old Testament itself taught the truth of justifying faith. He has already set forth that interpretation in Romans 3:21. If it is correct, it sets the stage for Romans 4, which asserts that both Abraham and David were justified by faith.

Second, if law refers to its more restricted meaning as related to the law of Moses, then Paul is saying that faith upholds the law by assigning to it its proper place in the plan of salvation. As he saw it, the law's role was to expose and condemn sin. Thus, as the apostle argues in Galatians 3:21-25, the function of the law is to keep sinners in their guilt until Christ comes to liberate them. In that way the gospel and the law are united in the sense that the gospel justifies those whom the law condemns.

Third, if we view the law as God's moral requirements (such as the Ten Commandments), some of his readers might have assumed that he was teaching antinomianism, that is, that Christians don't need any law, that they are free to live in sin since they are saved by grace. That charge, which Paul has already alluded to in Romans 3:8 and will deal with extensively in chapters 6–8, is the most likely problem undergirding Paul's statement in Romans 3:31. In this sense the saved-by-grace Christian will fulfill the "just requirement of the law" in their lives through the Holy Spirit (Rom. 8:4, RSV).

The last thing that Paul has in mind is to do away with the law. While it is not a means of salvation, the law holds a crucial place in God's universe. As such, faith reinforces the place of the law in its proper role.

THE MEANING OF ABRAHAM

*So what can we say that Abraham, the father
of our people, learned about faith? Rom. 4:1, NCV.*

PAUL HAS EXPOUNDED UPON his basic argument on how people are justified in Romans 3:21-26 and defended it against its critics in verses 27-31. In making his presentation he has been quite emphatic that justification by faith is an Old Testament understanding (see Rom. 1:2; 3:21, 31). The next step in his argument is to supply Old Testament illustrations.

His first example is Abraham. He couldn't have chosen a more important one. Abraham, after all, was the acknowledged father of the Jewish people, the most important figure in the Old Testament.

Think for a moment of other Old Testament heroes. Moses stands near the top. The Jews almost deified him as the lawgiver. He was the deliverer whom God had specifically chosen to lead His people out of bondage. And didn't God speak to him, as it were, face to face? Or consider David, the greatest of Israel's kings. Bringing his nation to the apex of its power in the ancient world, he gave his people some of their most impressive psalms and was the man through whom the Messiah was to come. Elijah, another of the greats, was foremost among the prophets. And who can forget Daniel? Not only a powerful statesman, he was God's prophet.

Yet all of those heroes of the faith were second to Abraham. All Jewish people knew that Abraham was the father of their race. The central man in their heritage, he was the one who received the covenant promises. He was the one whom God assured that he would be the father of many nations. Twice the Old Testament refers to him as God's "friend"—a title assigned to no one else.

Here is a test case for Paul's doctrine of salvation. If he can demonstrate that Abraham is in harmony with justification by faith, the apostle wins his case. But if Paul fails, he loses his argument.

As a result, he will give one of his 16 chapters in Romans to this all-important personage. It would be helpful if you could take a couple minutes to read Romans 4 through at least once right now. As you do, seek to follow Paul's argument paragraph by paragraph. And as you read, think about how the points he makes reinforce his argument in Romans 3:21-31.

ABRAHAM'S "BOASTING"

*For if Abraham was justified by works, he has something
to boast about, but not before God. Rom. 4:2, NRSV.*

PAUL BEGINS HIS TREATMENT of Abraham by alluding to the Jewish belief that the great patriarch had been justified by works, one widely held by Jewish teachers.

Basing their thoughts upon Genesis 26:5 (that God blessed Abraham because "Abraham obeyed my voice, and kept my charge, my commandments, my statutes, and my laws") the Jews reasoned that the patriarch "had performed the whole law before it was given" (Kiddushin 4:14). Again in the Jewish book of Jubilees we read that "Abraham was perfect in all of his actions with the Lord and was pleasing through righteousness all the days of his life" (Jubilees 23:10). The Prayer of Manasseh mentions that Abraham, Isaac, and Jacob didn't have to repent to God because they were righteous and "did not sin against you" (Prayer of Manasseh 8). Lastly, the Wisdom of Sirach states that "Abraham was the great father of a multitude of nations, and no one has been found equal to him in glory. He observed the law of the Most High, and entered into an agreement with Him. He certified the agreement in his flesh, and, when he was tested, he proved faithful" (Wisdom of Sirach 44:19, 20).

Abraham in the eyes of the Jews was the perfect man. He had kept the law. God therefore formed a covenant with him.

If all that is true, then Abraham certainly did have something to boast about. He would be able to take credit to himself for having accomplished his own justification and would have had a right to "toot his own horn."

Paul challenges that whole Jewish framework of thought. "If," he says, "Abraham was justified by works, he has something to boast about." Next he adds that he has no such grounds for boasting before God. Paul then proceeds in Romans 4:3 and the following verses to demonstrate why Abraham has no basis for bragging. The Jews, he will prove in effect, had misread their history. Abraham, in fact, had been justified by faith rather than works.

We find here a lesson for Christians of all stripes. It is all too easy to take the heroes of our faith, of our denomination, of our church, and put them up on a pedestal. But the plain truth is that all have sinned and are saved by grace. That is the only Christian reading of history. The gospel of grace is not just for the "weak." It is for everyone, even Abraham.

FAITH OR FAITHFULNESS?

What does the Scripture say? "Abraham believed God,
and it was credited to him as righteousness." Rom. 4:3, NIV.

PAUL, AS HE SO often does, goes to Scripture to prove his point that Abraham had nothing to boast about on the grounds of justification by works. His text is Genesis 15:6. The passage's context is that God had promised Abraham that in spite of his wife's age and barrenness he would have a son, and his personal offspring would be as the stars of heaven (verses 4, 5). Abraham believed God's promise, Scripture tells us, "and it was credited to him as righteousness."

Clearly Paul is using Genesis 15:6 to prove that Abraham was justified by faith rather than works. But that interpretation, interestingly enough, was not the one held by the Jews of Paul's day. In 1 Maccabees 2:52, for example, we find the following question: "Did not Abraham prove faithful under trial, and so win credit as a righteous man?" That passage changes the idea of faith into faithfulness or a meritoriousness that deserved a reward. Again Rabbi Shemaiah, who lived about 50 B.C., represents God as saying: "The faith with which their father Abraham believed in me merits that I should divide the [Red] sea for them, as it is written: 'And he believed in the Lord, and he counted it to him for righteousness.'"

Thus the Jews by the time of Christ had begun to consistently interpret Abraham's faith as a type of merit-earning faithfulness. In short, they saw Abraham's faith in terms of good works.

Paul knew that. Yet he deliberately chose Genesis 15:6 to prove just the opposite. That may seem strange to us, but Paul really couldn't avoid that well-established understanding of the text. He needed to meet it head-on and demonstrate that, rightly interpreted, Genesis 15:6 confirmed his contention that Abraham had nothing to boast about because he had been justified by dependent faith apart from good works. The apostle proceeds to make his demonstration in Romans 4:4-8.

Paul is fighting one of the most difficult battles ever waged. People don't like to feel dependent on others for anything. We like to believe that we can take care of ourselves. As a result, we will do everything before giving up our self-sufficiency. And yet in that surrender to our helplessness and God's graceful powerfulness lies the secret of salvation.

OF GIFTS AND WAGES

*Now if a man works his wages are not counted
as a gift but as a fair reward. Rom. 4:4, Phillips.*

A BIG DIFFERENCE EXISTS between a gift and wages. On Christmas morning I present my children with gifts. They never work for these gifts. Rather, I choose to give them something for free, something that they didn't work for or earn.

On the other hand, usually during Christmas week I receive a check from my employer for work that I have done. That check is not a gift. It is my wages. I earned every penny of it and consider it my just reward for service rendered.

In today's text Paul highlights the difference between a gift and wages. The word translated in Romans 4:4 as "gift" is actually "grace." Paul is in effect contrasting grace with works. One of the points that comes out is that grace is a free gift. It is not wages, or even a bargain—something that we get for half price, something that we worked for but was beyond our ability to pay for in full.

No! Grace is a gift pure and simple. We do nothing to deserve it. It is not God making up the shortfall between what we are and what we should be.

Well, you may be thinking, *how does this relate to Abraham?* As we noted yesterday, to say that Abraham exercised faith would not necessarily get Paul's point across, because the Jews interpreted faith in terms of faithfulness in doing God's commands. Thus to them Abraham's faith was a form of works. As a result, to say that Abraham was saved by his faith could be misinterpreted.

Paul in Romans 4:4 moves his argument beyond faith to grace. He is suggesting that Abraham was not saved by works of any sort, but by God's gracious gift. There was no way to misinterpret that statement. The apostle has removed all ambiguity about the method of Abraham's salvation.

Of course, the apostle could have gone on to say that Genesis says nothing about God owing Abraham anything, so that he could not have been saved by works. But Paul does not stop to make that point explicit. It must have seemed so obvious to him that it needed no fuller discussion.

Father, help me today to put aside my self-sufficiency. Help me to stop bargaining with You. Help me to learn how to accept Your gift for what it is—a gift.

IMPUTED RIGHTEOUSNESS

*To the man who does not work but trusts God who justifies
the wicked, his faith is credited as righteousness. Rom. 4:5, NIV.*

ONE OF THE KEY WORDS in Romans 4 is "credited." The King James
Version translates the word as "counts" or "imputes," while the Revised
Standard Version renders it as "reckon." Paul uses the word 10 times in
chapter 4 and five times alone in the six verses of Romans 4:3-8. When
employed in a financial or commercial context, it signifies to put something to somebody's account. Paul uses the word that way when he writes
to Philemon about Onesimus: "If he has wronged you at all, or owes you
anything, charge that to my account" (Philemon 18, RSV).

Paul couldn't make it plainer: God justifies the wicked not by what
they have done, but through their faith and trust in Him. Their faith is
counted as righteousness or imputed as righteousness. It is from this chapter that we get the phrase "imputed righteousness." Ellen White employed
it when she speaks of imputed righteousness or justification as "our title
to heaven" (*Messages to Young People,* p. 35). She also notes that the reception of imputed righteousness only takes a moment. In other words, at
the moment a person accepts God's grace by faith the Lord credits their
account in the books of heaven with Christ's righteousness. What happens
when we come to Jesus? "The Lord imputes unto the believer the righteousness of Christ and pronounces him righteous before the universe"
(*Selected Messages,* book 1, p. 392).

Romans 4:1-8 is one of Paul's clearest presentations on how Christ's
righteousness is transferred to a sinner who comes to Jesus. It comes not
by works of any type, but by faith in Jesus. At the very moment that a person accepts Jesus by faith, God accounts him or her righteous.

Righteousness by faith is one of the great wonders of God's universe.
It stands at the heart of Paul's gospel. Any attempt to water it down will
only pervert the apostle's teaching. Paul is adamant on this point. He admits no compromise, such as earning heaven by faith plus works. No, it is
all of grace; it is a gift and not a bargain. None of us can do anything to
earn it. It is this teaching that sets Christianity off from all of the other
world religions and from all human schemes of morality. Salvation is 100
percent God's gift.

DAVID'S TESTIMONY

David says the same thing when he speaks of the blessedness of the man to whom God credits righteousness apart from works. Rom. 4:6, NIV.

PAUL MUSTERS HIS BIG GUNS as he aims at his fellow Jews' objections to justification by faith. If Abraham was the most important person in Jewish history, David wasn't far behind. Next to Abraham and Moses, David was probably the most revered. Israel's foremost king, he was its most successful soldier, most prominent musician and poet, and a prophet.

Beyond that, the Messiah was to come through David's line. The Christ was to be a son of David. The very first verse of the New Testament highlights David's importance in Jewish thinking: "The book of the genealogy of Jesus Christ, the son of David, the son of Abraham" (Matt. 1:1, RSV). David, like Abraham, was a central figure in Israel's covenant history, God having made an everlasting covenant with the shepherd king.

Thus in Romans 4 Paul calls on the two most important witnesses available to prove his point that righteousness is by faith without works. We should note that when Paul summoned a second witness he was clearly following Deuteronomy 19:15, which explicitly states that "a matter must be established by the testimony of two or three witnesses" (NIV). As a former Pharisee and a student of the law, Paul was well acquainted with that principle. Thus he invokes David, who, he claims, agrees with Abraham.

The choice of David is interesting for another reason. While Abraham, though he had his faults, might possibly be thought of as a man who had enough goodness to merit salvation, there is no question of salvation by works with David. It is difficult to recall his name without thinking of his adulterous affair with Bathsheba, the murder committed to hide his guilt from her husband, and the disastrous effects both of those sins had on David's family.

In short, if David is saved, it will have to be by grace. Thus he presents an excellent case in Paul's argument.

That is good news. The turf is level in front of the cross. We all stand equal, no matter how sinful our life, no matter how tainted our past. There is a wideness in God's mercy. God is willing to save all who come to Him in faith. And He is not only willing, He is also able.

JUSTIFICATION'S NEGATIVE SIDE

"Blessed are they whose transgressions are forgiven,
whose sins are covered. Blessed is the man whose sin the
Lord will never count against him." Rom. 4:7, 8, NIV.

DAVID, AS WE NOTED yesterday, was hardly a shining example of justification by works. On the other hand, as Paul well knows, he offered an excellent illustration of grace and God's forgiveness.

David's most prominent sin was his affair with Bathsheba. To cover up his guilt, David arranged in cold blood for the murder of her husband. But such a maneuver was merely a cover-up. It solved nothing. In fact, it made things worse. The guilt was still there. David knew that only God could remove it.

David later wrote two penitential psalms to praise God for His forgiveness and to express his own joy in being forgiven. Psalms 51 and 32 have been a blessing down through the ages to those carrying a heavy burden of guilt.

In Romans 4 Paul quotes Psalm 32:1, 2. Interestingly enough, that passage does not even mention the word "righteousness." The reason for Paul's choice lies in the fact that it employs the word "credit" or "impute," a central word in Romans 4.

Yet that all-important word is used in a different sense with David than it was with Abraham. For the latter, Paul tells us that God credited his faith as righteousness. But for David we find that God *did not* credit or count his sin to his account.

Thus Paul in just a few short verses explains justification as having two aspects—a positive and a negative. First, God counts our faith as righteousness. Second, He does not count our sins against us. As a result, those who come to God through faith in Christ are truly "clean."

God did for David what the king could not do for himself. He forgave him, covered his sins, and did not impute his sins to his account. Paul in Romans 4 equates David's experience with righteousness and justification.

Thank You, Lord, for both the positive and the negative—for accounting our faith as righteousness and for not crediting our sins to our account when we humbly come to You in faith. Help me today to remember Your graciousness to me personally. Help me to tell others of what You are willing to do for them. Help me never to take the credit or the honor or the glory that belongs to You alone.

SALVATION THROUGH CIRCUMCISION

Is this blessedness only for the circumcised,
or alone for the uncircumcised? Rom. 4:9, NIV.

BLESSEDNESS! PAUL PICKS UP that word from the quotation from David in Romans 4:7 and 8: "Blessed are they whose transgressions are forgiven, whose sins are covered" (NIV). The apostle was undoubtedly aware of the fact that some Jewish teachers considered blessedness to be only for the circumcised Jew. Being a Gentile placed one outside the realm of God's blessing.

It is difficult to comprehend the importance that the ancient Jews placed on the rite of circumcision. It was so vital that it divided their world into two parts—the circumcised (Jews) and the uncircumcised (everybody who wasn't a Jew and was thus a Gentile).

As the Jews saw it, circumcision had a direct relationship to salvation. Thus we read in the apocryphal book of Jubilees that "anyone who is born whose own flesh is not circumcised on the eighth day is not from the sons of the covenant which the Lord made with Abraham since (he is) from the children of destruction. And there is therefore no sign upon him so that he might belong to the Lord because (he is destined) to be destroyed and annihilated from the earth" (Jubilees 15:25). On the other hand, Rabbi Menachem wrote, "Our Rabbins [rabbis] have said that no circumcised sons will ever see hell."

Such beliefs were so strong in Judaism that many Jewish converts carried them over into Christianity.

That whole set of beliefs will raise two questions that Paul will have to answer. First, what about Abraham? Wasn't he blessed because of his circumcision? Second, what about the Gentiles? Are they even candidates for God's blessing if they don't become Jews through circumcision? Paul will treat both of those questions in Romans 4:9-12.

Meanwhile, we should note how easy it is for us humans to rely on outward symbols of salvation rather than in God's revealed plan. The Jews put their trust in circumcision, but some Christians have done the same thing with baptism, Mass, Communion, or some other external. But, as Paul repeatedly asserts, salvation is not a matter of rites or externals but of the heart.

FAITH + NOTHING

*We have been saying: "Abraham's faith was counted as
righteousness." In what circumstances was it so counted?
Was he circumcised at the time, or not? He was not
yet circumcised, but uncircumcised. Rom. 4:9, 10, REB.*

IN TODAY'S PASSAGE Paul refers us back to his argument in Romans
4:3 that Abraham's faith was the ground for God's counting him as righteous. Then Paul asks two questions that do not seem to have occurred to
the Jews of his day.

The first question: "In what circumstances was it so counted?" And
the second: "Was it before or after his circumcision?"

Both questions were of the utmost importance to Paul and his Jewish
detractors. By this point they might be ready to argue with Paul that he
had proved his point that Abraham had been justified by faith. *But,* they
may have been thinking, *there must be more to it than that. The faith explanation is just too simple. There must be something that we have to do,
something that Abraham did. After all, Abraham had been circumcised.
That must have counted for something, since it is the sign of the covenant.*

It is all too easy to think that way—to assume that there must be
something we need to do in order to be justified. Faith is good, but faith
plus works would be even better. Faith + baptism, or faith + tithing, or
faith + Sabbathkeeping. There must be more. It just can't be that simple.

That is the exact attitude that Paul combats in Romans 4. He has
forcefully argued that justification is God's gift "apart from works" of any
kind (Rom. 4:6, RSV).

It was so in Abraham's case, Paul asserts. He only had to go back to
Genesis for that conclusion. Genesis 15:6 declared Abraham to be justified even though the circumcision command did not come until Genesis
17, 14 years later.

Therefore, Paul's case is proved. Circumcision is not the reason that
God counted Abraham righteous. He had been justified by faith alone
rather than faith + circumcision.

Paul's gospel is radical. It not only cuts across the way the Jews
thought but also across the way we think. Certainly there must be something we need to do before we can be justified. But Paul's answer is clear.
Our only requirement is to come to God in faith, accepting the cleansing
he made possible through Christ's sacrifice on Calvary.

OF SIGNS AND SEALS

[Abraham] received circumcision as a sign
or seal of the righteousness which he had by faith
while he was still uncircumcised. Rom. 4:11, RSV.

HERE WE HAVE ANOTHER important question. If circumcision doesn't contribute to our salvation, of what use is it? And if circumcision isn't necessary, why did God command it for the Jews?

Paul answers those questions with two words: circumcision was a "sign or seal" that Abraham had righteousness by faith.

A sign has two functions. The first is that it points beyond itself to something greater than itself. So if I am driving down the road and come to a sign that says "Chicago 100," I understand that Chicago is 100 miles ahead of me. The sign is not Chicago, but it directs us to that city. Even though the sign is less than the city, it still has value.

The second function of a sign is to indicate ownership. When I see a sign reading "Jill's Diner," I don't confuse it with a place to eat, but I know that it both guides us to a place to eat and designates Jill's ownership.

The sign of circumcision does much the same thing. First, it points beyond itself to the covenant promises God made with Abraham. Second, it indicates ownership in the sense of belonging to God.

For Christians, baptism has much the same meaning. Baptism, like circumcision, is an initiating rite that points to God's covenant promise through faith in Christ. Beyond that, baptism is a sign of God's ownership, that Christians are God's children and belong to Him.

A seal is a stamp or mark that guarantees authenticity. For example, certain important papers have to be taken to a notary public so that they can have a seal placed on them to certify that they are genuine. In the same way, circumcision for a Jew and baptism for a Christian is a guarantee that God's covenant promises will be fulfilled to those who accept them by faith.

Circumcision, baptism, and even the ordinance of the Lord's Supper are important because they are signs and seals of what has happened spiritually, but we must never regard them as a means of salvation. They are outward witnesses of that salvation obtainable only through faith in Christ's work for us.

FATHER ABRAHAM GETS MORE CHILDREN

So then, [Abraham] is the father of all who believe
but have not been circumcised, in order that
righteousness might be credited to them. Rom. 4:11, NIV.

THE JEWS LOVED TO TALK of "Father Abraham." Jesus picked up on that in the parable of the rich man and Lazarus, in which He has the rich man beg "Father Abraham" to send for Lazarus to place just a drop of cool water on his tongue. From that parable it seems quite evident that the Jews pictured Father Abraham as heaven's gatekeeper (Luke 16:19-31).

John the Baptist also utilized the Jewish understanding when he told them not to say "We have Abraham as our father," since "God is able from these stones to raise up children to Abraham" (Luke 3:8, RSV).

"Father Abraham!" How sweet the sound. It gave the Jewish people a sense of security. Yet how strange it must have seemed to hear Paul claim that Abraham was in fact the father of the uncircumcised because God had counted him righteous while he was still uncircumcised.

What Paul is really saying is that God's true children are not those by blood descent or those who took circumcision as a model, but those who received God's gift in faith as Abraham did. The apostle never tires of hammering home that point. "It is men of faith who are the sons of Abraham," we read in Galatians 3:7 (RSV). Paul goes on in that passage to say that it is through justification by faith that God fulfilled His promise to bless many nations through the patriarch. Again, in verse 29 Paul notes that "if you are Christ's, then you are Abraham's offspring, heirs according to promise" (RSV).

The case of Abraham is not the only time that the Bible uses "father" in a nonliteral way. Thus Jabal was the father of livestock breeders, while Jubal was the father of musicians (Gen. 4:20, 21). In both cases the Bible has in mind the characteristics of people rather than paternal descent.

It is the same, says Paul, in the spiritual realm. Those who live by faith in Christ are emulating Abraham and are therefore his spiritual children. Thus Father Abraham is also the father of all believing Gentiles. They belong to the family of God. When it comes to salvation, Paul is teaching the radical notion that Jews and Gentiles stand on an equal footing before God. Both, as they accept Christ, become Abraham's children.

THE PRICE OF BELONGING

*At the same time [Abraham] is the father of the circumcised,
provided they are not merely circumcised, but also follow
that path of faith which our father Abraham trod while
he was still uncircumcised. Rom. 4:12, REB.*

WILLIAM GLADSTONE, the great nineteenth-century British statesman, used to tell of an oil painting he discovered in an antique shop. The painting was exquisite. It pictured an aristocrat dressed in an old Spanish costume with a ruff, plumed hat, and lace cuffs. Gladstone wanted to buy it, but found it too expensive.

Some time later while visiting the home of a rich merchant he saw the same portrait hanging on his wall. The owner, noticing his interest, told Gladstone that it was a portrait of one of his ancestors who had been a minister at the court of Queen Elizabeth.

Gladstone, knowing that to be untrue, responded, "For three pounds he would have been my ancestor."

You may not know much about your ancestors. They may have been rich or quite undistinguished. But this much is certain. You can belong to the greatest family on earth, and it won't require a cent, though it will cost you your self-sufficiency, airs, and pretensions.

Romans 4:11, 12 tell us plainly that Abraham is not only the spiritual father of the uncircumcised, but also of the circumcised. For none, however, is sonship or daughtership automatic. Faith is the one condition of entrance into the family.

The circumcised are included, but it is not their circumcision that gets them in. It is not the circumcised as such who can enter in, but circumcised believers—those Jews who "follow that path of faith which our father Abraham trod while he was still uncircumcised."

Paul never ceases to hammer home the importance of faith. Circumcision or uncircumcision (Jew or Gentile) matters little, but faith is all-important.

The apostle's teaching transformed the place of Abraham in history. Anders Nygren notes that "the Jews looked upon Abraham as the great dividing point in the history of mankind. But according to Paul, Abraham through his faith became the great rallying point for all who believe."

We are all brothers and sisters in Christ. True Christianity puts race, caste, nationality, tribe, sexism, and all other discriminations behind it. All who have faith are children of Abraham.

THE PROMISE OF GOD

*It was not through law that Abraham and his offspring received
the promise that he would be heir of the world, but through
the righteousness that comes by faith. Rom. 4:13, NIV.*

WE HAVE ON OUR HANDS a very persistent apostle. Paul just won't
give up. He keeps pounding away at his thesis that justifying righteousness comes through faith alone. In Romans 4:1-8 he proves that Abraham
obtained his righteousness through faith *without works.* Then in verses 9-
12 he demonstrates that Abraham's righteousness resulted by faith *without regard to circumcision.* Now beginning in verse 13 he argues that the
patriarch's blessing came by faith *rather than by law.* Before his argument
is over Paul will have shown that grace and law are incompatible in terms
of obtaining God's promise and that grace is God's only method.

At first glance we might have expected Paul to continue to use the
chronological argument in this paragraph. After all, if Abraham's blessing
was not a result of circumcision, since he had received the promise 14
years before his circumcision, wouldn't it be equally valid that the blessing couldn't have come from his relation to the law, since God gave the
law 430 years after the promise? Paul uses that argument in Galatians 3.
But in Romans 4 he follows a line of thought that shows that God's
promise rests on grace rather than law.

The idea of promise is fundamental in Paul's thinking. The promise,
of course, was the one that God made to Abraham. It came in three in-
stallments. First, that Abraham would have a vast number of descendants
embracing many nations (Gen. 12:2; 13:16; 15:5; 17:4-6, 16-20). Second,
that he would possess the land of Canaan (Gen. 13:15-17; 15:12-21; 17:8),
and third, that Abraham would be the medium through whom God would
bless the world (Gen. 12:3; 18:18; 22:18).

Those promises have flown right into the Christian church. The greatest is that God's people will still inherit the earth. Jesus tells us that a day
will come when He will make "all things new" (Rev. 21:5, RSV). At that
time God "will wipe away every tear from [our] eyes, and death shall be
no more, neither shall there be mourning nor crying nor pain any more,
for the former things are passed away" (verse 4, RSV).

The church still awaits the complete fulfillment of the Abrahamic
promise as it prays "Even so, come, Lord Jesus" (Rev. 22:20).

PROMISE VERSUS LAW

For if those who live by the law are heirs, faith has no value and the promise is worthless, because law brings wrath. Rom. 4:14, 15, NIV.

LEGALISM DOESN'T WORK. No one will ever make it into God's kingdom by what they have done.

How come? Why can't we achieve God's kingdom and salvation through the law?

Paul provides us with two answers. One reason is that God never made the law to save anyone. He established it as a standard to be kept, but once it is broken, as Paul noted in Romans 3:20, it points out our sin. The law can witness against us that we have disobeyed it and thereby deserve the penalty of the violated law (Rom. 6:23), but nothing in the law can save us. It has no plan of salvation built into it. The broken law brings only wrath and death.

That's where Paul's second answer comes in. God's promise can do what the law cannot. His promises imply grace. Those to Abraham were based not on the fact that he was a perfect man, but upon the reality that he was a needy sinner who had faith. That faith runs all the way through the patriarch's life. Thus when he took Isaac to the land of Moriah for a sacrifice, Abraham had faith that God would provide a lamb for a burnt offering (Gen. 22:8). Alternately, "by faith Abraham, when he was tested, offered up Isaac, and he who had received the promises was ready to offer up his only son, of whom it was said, 'Through Isaac shall your descendants be named.' He considered that God was able to raise men even from the dead" (Heb. 11:17-19, RSV). The patriarch didn't know how God would fulfill His promises, but he believed that the Lord could and would. His faith transcended his sight. It is that dynamic faith expressed throughout his life that made Abraham the recipient of God's promise, that made him the father of those who live by faith.

The promise was not something he had earned. No, it was God's gift to him. It came not through law but by God's grace.

Paul is telling us that there are not two ways to the kingdom. There is only one—for us to rely on God's promise with all our strength. The way of law and the way of promise (grace) are incompatible. Of course, Paul is not against God's law, but he is opposed to its use as a means of salvation. He wants us to realize that only one way leads to righteousness—*through the Lamb that He has provided.*

LAW AS POLICE OFFICER

For where no law is, there is no transgression. Rom. 4:15.

ONCE AGAIN PAUL DEALS with the function of law. One role of law is to erect boundaries. "This is where you need to stand," says the law. "This is how you must act." Thus in the ten-commandment law we read that we should not steal or commit adultery, and that we must honor both God and our parents. Law sets standards of conduct or boundaries.

But not everybody is happy with boundaries. That brings us to the word "transgression." Transgression is sin, but of a particular type. We employ transgression to indicate the overstepping of a boundary line. Thus it can be used for when someone breaks a clearly defined commandment.

Today's text reads that "where no law is, there is no transgression." What does the passage mean in its context? Paul appears to be using a negative statement to confirm the truthfulness of the fact that where a law does exist it reveals transgression, with wrath as the final result.

Remember that he is speaking to those legalistic Jews who believed they could obtain God's promise through lawkeeping. He is telling them that it can offer no salvation. Why? Watch his logic: 1. They have God's law. 2. But they have all transgressed its requirements. 3. Consequently, they face the penalty of transgression. 4. Therefore, if they don't get help through accepting God's grace, they are certainly without hope.

Paul is not saying that places exist without law. After all, in Romans 1-3 he indicated that the Gentiles had a law in their conscience and that the Jews had God's revealed law. Everyone has some glimmer of His law in some form.

Neither is Paul suggesting that the law has anything wrong with it or that there is something wrong with lawkeeping. By no means. Rather, he came to teach the obedience of faith (Rom. 1:5; 16:26) and he claims that the law is good, just, and holy (Rom. 7:12).

What he means is that even though the law is good for some things, it is worthless as a way to earn salvation. It reveals our sin (transgression) and points us to our need of faith in God's mercy. The law ought to wake us up to the fact that we must have grace. The tragedy is that we sometimes try to make it a substitute for grace.

THE PROMISE GUARANTEED

Therefore, the promise comes by faith, so that it may be by grace and may be guaranteed to all Abraham's offspring. Rom. 4:16, NIV.

BECAUSE OBTAINING THE PROMISE of salvation or righteousness is impossible through a legalistic obedience to the law, Paul declares that we can get it only by faith. Since the law brings only condemnation, it offers no hope. Justification and salvation and promise come through faith, just as they did for Abraham.

In today's passage the apostle ties faith to grace. The sense seems to be that grace is the effective agent that provides the promise and faith is the way in which people accept God's gift. That is, grace is the gift, and faith is, so to speak, the hand by which we accept the gift.

Because the promise is through grace, Paul tells us that it is "guaranteed" or "made certain." Thus it is something that we can trust. Human performance and human promises are far from secure. But the fact that it is God's grace that makes His salvation available to us puts the gift beyond the realm of human untrustworthiness. That guarantee is for all "Abraham's offspring," all Christians, whether their heritage be Jewish or Gentile. Only one way of salvation exists for anybody.

That way ought to be near our hearts and on our tongues as we seek to share it with others. Ellen White writes: *"Lift up Jesus,* you that teach the people, lift Him up in sermon, in song, in prayer. Let all your powers be directed to pointing souls, confused, bewildered, lost, to 'the Lamb of God.' Lift Him up, the risen Saviour, and say to all who hear, Come to Him who 'hath loved us, and hath given Himself for us.' *Let the science of salvation be the burden of every sermon, the theme of every song.* Let it be poured forth in every supplication. Bring nothing into your preaching to supplement Christ, the wisdom and power of God. Hold forth the word of life, presenting Jesus as the hope of the penitent and the stronghold of every believer. Reveal the way of peace to the troubled and the despondent, and show forth the grace and completeness of the Saviour" (*Gospel Workers,* p. 160; italics supplied).

Praise God today for the guarantee of His promise to each of us who accepts Jesus as our Savior. God will bring us through if we hold on to His grace.

Father, please give me the grace to hang on to Your grace, no matter what trials and temptations come my way.

FROM ABRAM TO ABRAHAM

As it is written: "I have made [Abraham]
a father of many nations." Rom. 4:17, NIV.

IN ITS CONTEXT today's passage refers to the fact that everyone who is finally saved, both Jew and Gentile, will not only be a child of Abraham, but they will be saved in the same way he was—by placing faith in God's gracious promises. That, Paul has repeatedly asserted, is the only way to inherit the promise or to be justified.

We have in previous readings noted that Paul applies membership in Abraham's family to all those who have faith. Today we will go back to the Old Testament and examine some of God's promises to Abraham. The quotation in our text comes from Genesis 17:5. God made it at the very time that He changed Abram's name to Abraham.

The renaming is significant. His original name meant "exalted father," but God now calls him "father of a multitude." The New Living Translation of Genesis 17:4-6 is helpful in enabling us to see the extent of God's blessing on the patriarch: "This is my covenant with you: I will make you the father of not just one nation, but a multitude of nations! What's more, I am changing your name. It will no longer be Abram; now you will be known as Abraham, for you will be the father of many nations. I will give you millions of descendants who will represent many nations. Kings will be among them!"

All of us are recipients of that covenant promise to Abraham. Not only was he the bloodline father of the Jews, but also of the Midianites, the Edomites, the Ishmaelite Arabs, and other Arabic tribes. Beyond that are the multitude of Christians around the world who have accepted Christ by faith and are thus his spiritual descendants.

The great missionary outreach of the nineteenth and twentieth centuries did much to fulfill the promise God made to Abraham thousands of years ago. It is in that sense that Christians living in the twenty-first century are still involved in God's purpose. We not only have faith like Abraham, but we seek to send God's message to the most remote parts of earth, thereby making Abraham the father of still more nations and peoples. That process will go on until "this gospel of the kingdom shall be preached in all the world for a witness unto all nations; and then shall the end come" (Matt. 24:14).

BRINGING SOMETHING OUT OF NOTHING

Such a faith implies the presence of the God in whom [Abraham] believed, a God who makes the dead live and who calls into being what does not exist. Rom. 4:17, Moffatt.

TWO PHRASES JUMP OUT at us in this passage. The first is that Abraham placed his faith in a "God who makes the dead live." The second is that this God "calls into being what does not exist."

What does Paul mean by those phrases? The first could bring several allusions to mind. One is Ezekiel 37, in which the prophet finds himself in a valley of dry bones, and God asks him if those bones could live. The chapter moves on to a vision of resurrection. A second allusion might be to the resurrection of Jesus. The New Testament repeatedly speaks of giving life to the dead against the backdrop of the resurrection of Jesus.

Then again, Paul may have been alluding to the typical Jewish estimate of the Gentiles, and the fact that God could give even them life.

More to the point would be the fact that every person (both Jew and Gentile) outside of Christ is "dead" in "trespasses and sins" but is "made alive" in Jesus (Eph. 2:1, RSV). In that case Paul would be referring to justification as a sort of resurrection from spiritual death.

All of these concepts could have been in the back of Paul's mind. But there is yet another that is even closer to the context of today's verse. We see that interpretation reflected upon in Romans 4:19, in which we read that Abraham's body and Sarah's womb were "as good as dead" (NIV). God took their "dead" organs and brought life out of them and made them the parents of many nations.

That last interpretation also fits the fact that God "calls into being what does not exist." The reference once again in the context of the passage is that God brought many nations out of the seemingly barren union of Abraham and Sarah. That calling into being, of course, also reminds us of God's general power to create.

We, like Abraham, serve an awesome God. In our lives He can bring life out of spiritual death and will someday bring eternal life out of physical death. Every conversion to Jesus is just as much a miracle as is resurrection or creation. Abraham had his faith in a Being who had the power to shape his life. We are invited to share that same life-shaping faith.

HOPE AGAINST HOPE

*In hope [Abraham] believed against hope, that he should
become the father of many nations; as he had been told,
"So shall your descendants be." Rom. 4:18, RSV.*

"HOPE" IS AN IMPORTANT word for Paul. It appears 53 times in the
New Testament, 36 in Paul's writings. Romans, of all the New Testament
books, uses hope most often—some 13 times.

In Paul's letters hope has two very distinct flavors. On the one side are
those without hope. Ephesians 2:12, for example, speaks of those who are
"strangers from the covenants of promise, *having no hope,* and are *without God* in the world." Again, in 1 Thessalonians 4:13 Paul writes: "I
would not have you be ignorant, brethren, concerning them which are
asleep [dead], that ye sorrow not, even as others which have *no hope."* In
that passage, he comforts those who have faith in Christ by pointing to the
coming resurrection of the dead. After describing that event he urges his
readers to "comfort one another with these words" (1 Thess. 4:18).

For Paul, those without Christ have no hope. Thus throughout his
writing he connects hope with faith. If those without faith in Christ have
no hope, so those with faith do have hope.

In Romans we find several examples of Paul's positive use of hope.
Those who have faith can "rejoice in hope of the glory of God" (Rom 5:2).
"Hope maketh not ashamed" (verse 5). The Bible records God's dealing
with humanity so that we "might have hope" (Rom. 15:4). And "the God
of hope fill you with all joy and peace in believing, that ye may abound in
hope, through the power of the Holy Ghost" (verse 13).

Paul intimately tied hope to faith in God. It was the same with
Abraham, who "against hope . . . believed in hope" that God's promise
would be fulfilled. The meaning here is that Abraham's belief transcended
his sight. He believed God's promises in spite of his and Sarah's physical
condition. That is faith. And that is the faith of Abraham. Faith moves beyond what we can see to what God has promised.

It is the kind of faith that each of us needs as we await the "blessed
hope" at the second coming of Jesus (Titus 2:13).

*Father, help me today to have the hope of Abraham, hope that sees
beyond the visible.*

114

FAITH BEYOND CIRCUMSTANCES

Without weakening his faith, he faced the fact that his body
was as good as dead—since he was about a hundred years old
—and that Sarah's womb was also dead. Rom. 4:19, NIV.

TALK ABOUT A HOPELESS SITUATION!

A similar passage appears in Hebrews 11, the great faith chapter: "By faith Sarah herself received power to conceive, even when she was past the age, since she considered him faithful who had promised. Therefore from one man, and him as good as dead, were born descendants as many as the stars of heaven and as the innumerable grains of sand by the seashore" (Heb. 11:11, 12, RSV).

Two ideas jump out at us when we read Romans 4:19 and Hebrews 11:11, 12: deadness and faith.

Deadness in both potential parents. Deadness everywhere! Yet, Paul asserts, Abraham did not weaken in his faith, even though the promise of an heir looked impossible from a purely human perspective.

Faith does not close its eyes to life's realities. Abraham took full account of the impotence of his body as well as of his wife's condition. Those were the hard facts of the situation.

Yet faith is not limited by human estimates of what is possible, because as we read in Romans 4:17, God can make the dead live and call "into being what does not exist" (Moffatt). Abraham realized through faith that only God can give life where there is none now.

Leon Morris notes that "in view of all this deadness it was not possible for the couple to have a child in the normal human fashion, and to believe God's promise under those circumstances was more than a passive acquiescence in a conventional religious posture; it was the active exercise of a profound faith."

What, we might ask, does Abraham's experience signify for me? At the very least it means that I should not base my faith on the present realities that I see in the world around me. Does the church seem dead? Does it seem that Christ will never come? Does it seem that my feeble efforts are as nothing in a world of 6 billion people?

The answer is yes to all of the above. But faith—my faith—can transcend those realities to the ultimate reality that God will fulfill His promise in spite of what appears to be hopelessness. That's what the faith and hope of Abraham are all about.

THE "YET" OF ABRAHAM

*Yet, with respect to the promise of God, [Abraham] did not waver in
unbelief but grew strong in faith, giving glory to God. Rom. 4:20, NASB.*

"YET" IS A KEY WORD in this passage. It refers us back to the preceding
context. *The Message* paraphrase nicely brings it out: "Abraham didn't
focus on his own impotence and say, 'It's hopeless. This hundred-year-old
body could never father a child.' Nor did he survey Sarah's decades of in-
fertility and give up. He didn't tiptoe around God's promise asking cautiously skeptical questions. He plunged into the promise and came up
strong, ready for God, sure that God would make good on what he had
said" (Rom. 4:18-21).

"Yet!" Abraham went forth in spite of it all. How is it with us? Could
God say "yet" regarding my course of action? How is my relationship to
Him? Is my major focus on the spiritual and other problems before me or
on God's power and faithfulness? Can God say "yet" about me? If not,
why not? And if not, today is a good time to ask for God's power to
strengthen my faith so that I might be included in the "yet" of Abraham.

A second key word in today's text is "waver." Abraham wasn't like
the double-minded man in the book of James who was as unstable in his
ways as the waves of the sea and, as a result, received nothing from the
Lord (James 1:5-8). To the contrary, Paul is telling us that Abraham was
certain in whom he had believed, and that the constancy of his faith allowed God to make him strong.

A third key word is "grew." Our passage tells us that Abraham "grew
strong in faith." Faith is not static. Rather, it is a dynamic, expanding sort
of thing. New Christians have faith, but maturing Christians ought to day
by day be growing in faith as they come closer to God and experience His
watchcare over time. That appears to have been Abraham's experience in
the book of Genesis. Scripture pictures him as a man of many faults, but
he let God strengthen him through time—he grew in faith.

A last key word is "glory." Abraham gave glory to God for what He had
done and was doing in his life. Giving praise and glory to Him is the normal
response of those who realize who God is and how much He loves them.
Giving glory to God is to worship Him with all our heart, and mind, and soul.

*Today, dear Father, I want to glorify Your name for all that You have done
in my life. Keep me from wavering today. And enable me to grow in Christ.
In all of my weakness help me to become a part of the "yet" of Abraham.*

DID ABRAHAM REALLY BELIEVE?

*Abraham was] fully convinced that God was
able to do what he had promised. Rom. 4:21, RSV.*

PAUL DECLARES THAT Abraham was "fully convinced that God was able to do what he had promised," that He would give him a son through Sarah (see Gen. 17:16).

Well, Paul, what are you going to do about the book of Genesis? There we read that after the promise "Abraham fell on his face and laughed, and said to himself, 'Shall a child be born to a man who is a hundred years old? Shall Sarah, who is ninety years old, bear a child?'" Then the good patriarch offered to help God out of the scrape by substituting Ishmael (his son through Hagar) for the promise (Gen. 17:17, 18, RSV). After all, one shouldn't hold God to any foolishness. And then maybe he hadn't heard properly.

At that point God jumped back into the picture and said: "Sarah your wife shall bear you a son, and you shall call his name Isaac. I will establish my covenant with him as an everlasting covenant for his descendants after him" (verse 19, RSV).

As we noted yesterday, we need to see Abraham's faith as dynamic and growing. *At first he did the same thing most of us would have done—he laughed!* After all, from a human perspective the suggestion about Abraham and Sarah was quite laughable. I personally am not yet quite 100 years old and my wife is not quite 90, but I think I can understand why Abraham might have laughed. There are, you know, such things as the facts of life.

Abraham was like us. Faith apparently didn't come any easier for him than it does for the rest of humanity. It was not automatic for him. He knew the problems and realities that all of us face.

Yet his faith grew, as we see by the fact that he circumcised all the males of his household as a sign of the covenant before Isaac was conceived (verses 22-27). Years passed between the giving of the promise of Genesis 15:5 and its fulfillment in Genesis 21:2. During those long years Abraham must have struggled with doubt. But his faith grew, and God was able to strengthen him (Rom. 4:20, 21). When Paul tells us that Abraham was "fully convinced that God would be able to do what he had promised," he is talking about his mature faith, not his immediate reaction. As one author puts it: "The unbelief was momentary, the faith was constant."

RESURRECTION FAITH

The words "it was credited to him" were written not for him alone, but also for us, to whom God will credit righteousness—for us who believe in him who raised Jesus our Lord from the dead. Rom. 4:23, 24, NIV.

GOOD NEWS! We are saved in the same way that Abraham was. Not through works, or our church pedigree, or our baptism, or the law, but by faith in God's promise through Christ. Abraham had righteousness credited or imputed to him as a gift. God will give us righteousness in the same way *if* we are willing to accept it through faith.

Ellen White writes that "the thought that the righteousness of Christ is imputed to us, not because of any merit on our part, but as a free gift from God, is a precious thought. The enemy of God and man is not willing that this truth should be clearly presented; for he knows that if the people receive it fully, his power will be broken. If he can control minds so that doubt and unbelief and darkness shall compose the experience of those who claim to be children of God, he can overcome them with temptation. That simple faith which takes God at His word should be encouraged" (*Gospel Workers*, p. 161).

Paul explores in several places his claim that the Old Testament promises and lessons are for us. In Romans 15:4, for example, he declares that scripture is written for our instruction, and in 1 Corinthians 10:11 that the events in the history of Israel "were written for our admonition" (NKJV). In that vein the apostle tells us that "the words 'it was credited to him' were written . . . for us who believe in him who raised Jesus our Lord from the dead."

Please note that Paul ties saving faith to Jesus' resurrection from the dead. The importance of Christ's resurrection in the minds of the apostles and the early church is impossible to overestimate. The preaching in the book of the Acts of the Apostles centers on that event.

Christ's resurrection guarantees that God can indeed give life to those who are dead in their sins and trespasses (Rom. 4:17; Eph. 2:1). Beyond that, His resurrection guarantees the resurrection at the end of time of those who believe in Him. Thus Paul's firm belief in the resurrection is tied to both hope and faith. It is the accomplished resurrection of Christ that provides the basis of Christian hope and the foundation of our faith. Abraham saw that resurrection from afar, but we witness it in the New Testament and the early church.

JESUS DIED OUR DEATH

[Jesus] was delivered over to death for our sins. Rom. 4:25, NIV.

JESUS "WAS DELIVERED over to death for our sins." Peter makes a similar declaration at Pentecost: "This Jesus, delivered up according to the definite plan and foreknowledge of God, you crucified and killed by the hands of lawless men" (Acts 2:23, RSV).

As we look at those and similar passages, we should note two points. First, that Christ's death was part of God's plan. Today's text tells us that Jesus didn't merely die but that He was "delivered over" to that death. Who handed Him over? The Jewish leaders or the Romans? The New Testament implicates both parties. But the focus in the texts above is that it was a part of God's plan. Romans 8:32 is quite explicit in claiming that God "did not spare His own Son, but delivered Him over for us all" (NASB). It was part of His plan to accomplish human salvation through the death of Christ. That is why Revelation 13:8 refers to Jesus as "the Lamb that was slain from the creation of the world" (NIV). The death of Christ was no accident. It had been in God's plan from the beginning.

The second thing we should observe about today's text is that Jesus died "for our sins." Death is the penalty for sin (Gen. 2:17; Rom. 6:23). But Christ had not sinned and therefore did not deserve death. Rather, we find in today's text that He died "for our sins"—He died in our place.

That thought reminds me of Barabbas. Just imagine him sitting in his cell waiting for his death summons. He might have been looking at his hands, thinking of the nails soon to pierce them. Every loud noise begins to sound like a hammer to him. Then he hears the shout of "Crucify Him."

Imagine his surprise when the jailer comes to his door and tells him that he is a free man, that the crowd has asked for his release and the crucifixion of Jesus.

If he remained for the crucifixion he would have realized that Christ died in his place. Barabbas is the only man in the world who could say that Jesus took his physical place. But all of us can say that Jesus accepted our spiritual place. He died for our sins. He died the death that was ours that we might have the life that is His.

That message is at the very heart of the gospel. Of that the New Testament writers are both explicit and certain.

JUSTIFICATION AND RESURRECTION

[Jesus] was raised to life for our justification. Rom. 4:25, NIV.

THERE IS NOTHING MORE useless than a dead Savior! But the good news all through the New Testament is that Jesus triumphed over death. That is the reason Paul combines both the death and the resurrection in his "definition" of the gospel in 1 Corinthians 15:1-3.

But what does Paul mean when he claims that Jesus "was raised to life for our justification"? That question is especially important in light of the fact that he relates our justification to Christ's death in Romans 3:24 and 5:9.

The best explanation is that Christ's death had indeed taken care of the sin problem, with its penalty of death. He had died in our place, and His cry from the cross, "It is finished," signified the completion of His work as the Lamb slain from the foundation of the earth.

But, some have asked, was His death fully acceptable to God for the sins of others? Did God accept His atonement? For three days the question remained unanswered as Jesus rested in the tomb. But in raising Christ to life on resurrection morning God declared in full and clear tones to the universe that He approved of Christ's sacrifice and that His death had accomplished its function in providing for the redemption of those who received His sacrifice by faith.

Reuben A. Torrey puts it this way: "I look at the cross of Christ, and I know that atonement has been made for my sins; I look at the open sepulcher and the risen and ascended Lord, and I know that the atonement has been accepted. . . . My sins have been as high as mountains, but in the light of the resurrection the atonement that covers them is as high as heaven. My sins may have been as deep as the ocean, but in the light of the resurrection the atonement that swallows them up is as deep as eternity."

Reformer John Calvin makes the interesting suggestion regarding Christ's resurrection for our justification that it was not enough that Christ died. He also needed to be "received into celestial glory," so that by His "intercession" He might apply the fruits of His sacrifice on our behalf. Paul presents a similar thought in Romans 8:34 as he pictures the risen Christ at the right hand of God in His heavenly ministry of intercession.

Jesus "was delivered over to death for our sins and was raised to life for our justification."

WE HAVE PEACE

Therefore being justified by faith, we have peace
with God through our Lord Jesus Christ. Rom. 5:1.

SOME YEARS AGO *Look* magazine ran a feature entitled "Peace of Mind." It asked 16 prominent Americans how they found tranquillity. For best-selling author James Michener it was taking his dog for a walk. Former presidential candidate Barry Goldwater found it in his hobbies and in walking in the Grand Canyon, while for CBS anchor Walter Cronkite it was "going to sea by small boat." Sammy Davis, Jr., claimed he found peace by looking for "good" in other people.

As one reads those recipes for peace it is quite noticeable that they are subjective and based on favorable circumstances. But beyond that subjectivity is the shared assumption that pursuing peace of mind is important. In fact, such pursuit is a universal human quest, whether in the realm of the personal, international, domestic, or industrial. Everyone is interested in peace.

But beyond peace in general is peace with God. The world's great religions began with that goal in mind. Paul alluded in Romans 1 and 2 to a universal sense of guilt. How to atone for that guilt and/or make God happy motivates not only world religions, but also the various world literatures. Cultures and languages may differ, but the underlying needs of peace of mind and peace with God transcend those categories.

Romans 5:1 is Paul's answer to that universal human quest. He seems to be saying at least two things in that verse, which he connects to his presentation on justification by faith in Romans 3 and 4 by the word "therefore." First is the sense of assurance of salvation possessed by those who have accepted Christ by faith. We can have peace because we know that we are right with God. Such assured peace does not rest on our subjective feelings, but, as Paul has argued in chapters 3 and 4, on the objective reality of Christ's finished work on the cross and His resurrection from the dead (Rom. 4:25).

A second sense in which we have peace is that of the fruit of the Spirit, which Paul describes in Galatians 5. Thus some of the results of justification are joy and peace.

The Christian believer knows that real peace comes only from being in a right relationship to God.

WE HAVE ACCESS

*[Christ] has given us access to that grace
in which we now live. Rom. 5:2, REB.*

IF PEACE WITH GOD is a first consequence of our justification, then access to God and God's graciousness is a second. Translators have struggled over the word rendered "access." Some hold that "access" is the essential idea, while others favor "introduction." Actually both translations help us unpack Paul's meaning.

When we say that Christ provides us with an introduction to God, the idea is that of us being led into the audience chamber of a monarch. We cannot enter His presence on our own merits, but we need an introduction. Thus Christ is the active agent in providing us with our presentation to God. It is His merits and not ours that get us into the audience chamber of the King of kings.

On the other hand, the idea of "access" also seems to be important in the text. After all, a Christian is not merely introduced to God but has continuing access "to that grace in which we now live."

Christ has opened the way for His followers into the very throne room of God. As the book of Hebrews puts it, as Christ's followers we can "come boldly unto the throne of grace, that we may obtain mercy, and find grace to help in time of need" (Heb. 4:16).

Ephesians presents the same message. Those who are "no longer foreigners" "have access to the Father by one Spirit" (Eph. 2:18, 19, NIV). Again, in Christ "and through faith in him we may approach God with freedom and confidence" (Eph. 3:12, NIV).

Christians are privileged persons, because they have direct access to the Father through the Son. It was not so in the Old Testament services connected to the Temple. Only the priest could enter the Temple proper. And only the high priest once a year had access to God's throne room—the Holy of Holies.

But now through Jesus we not only have a standing introduction to the Father but we have continual access any time we desire it or need it.

Have I taken advantage of my privileged status? How often do I seek the Father's presence? Through Jesus we can come "boldly" to the Father whenever we need mercy or help. It is time that we took advantage of our privileges.

WE HAVE JOY

We rejoice in our hope of sharing the glory of God. Rom. 5:2, RSV.

WE ARE IN THE MIDST of a pack of "we haves." In Romans 5:1 we discovered that those who are justified by faith have peace. The first part of verse 2 declares that they have access, and in the second part we find that they have joy.

But note, I played a small trick on you. The apostle in chapter 5 is not talking about impersonal "they haves." No, he is really being quite specific and personal. We (those who have accepted God's way of salvation by faith) have peace, access, and joy. We—that means you and me—have something to rejoice about.

In actuality the word for "rejoice" in our passage for today is the same word translated as "boast" in Romans 3:27 and 4:2. But those passages tell us that no one has room for boasting in relation to their accomplishments in lawkeeping, and that even Abraham couldn't boast about his works. The fact that righteousness comes through God's gift rather than human accomplishment leaves us no room to brag about our spiritual condition.

But there is a difference now. *Romans 5:2 urges us to boast.* Why the change? Because Christians are not exalting their own accomplishments but rather what the Lord already has done for them and will do for them in Christ in the future. Christians boast in the goodness and graciousness of their Lord, who has given them peace with God and continual access to Him. That is worth boasting about.

It is that sense of the word that has led translators to seek to express the meaning implied by the word usually translated boasting as being an attitude of rejoicing. C. K. Barrett suggests that the word in the present context "means a triumphant, rejoicing confidence" in God.

The Christian's rejoicing derives from "our hope of sharing the glory of God." Left to ourselves, Paul has already told us in Romans 3:23, all of us have fallen short of God's glory. Christ prayed that His followers would see His glory (John 17:24), and the dying Stephen did glimpse it (Acts 7:55), but Paul tells us that the consummation of its fullness is still future (Rom. 8:18). But we have certainty of that future because of our acceptance of what God has done in Christ. No wonder as Christians we have joy.

Christians are those who have traded in boasting for rejoicing. Today and every day is an occasion for rejoicing for those who have accepted God's salvation.

WE HAVE SUFFERINGS

We also boast [or rejoice] in our sufferings. Rom. 5:3, NRSV.

SO, SOME MAY HAVE been thinking as they read Paul's argument, *you have peace with God, you have access to God, and you have joy. Then how come Christians have just as many troubles and sufferings as other people?* That was a live issue, since it wasn't always easy to be a Christian in the Roman Empire.

A desire to head off such potential criticism probably led Paul to take up the problem of suffering. His Jewish readers in particular would be critical at this point, since they in general believed that sickness and troubles resulted from sin. If Christians had "peace with God," how is it that they also faced illness, persecution, and other difficulties? Then again, such sufferings probably caused Christians to doubt the reality of their so-called blessings.

Paul in his usual manner took a positive approach to the topic by claiming that we should rejoice or boast in our sufferings. Now the word translated as "suffering" is a forceful word. It does not refer to minor inconveniences, but to real hardships. The Greek original is *thlipsis,* which literally means pressure. It is the word used of crushing olives in a press or of squeezing grapes to extract the juice.

In a similar manner, life's troubles pressure and squeeze Christians. The Bible itself makes it clear that Christians are not immune from suffering and tragedy. Take John the Baptist, for instance. Jesus taught that John was the greatest of the prophets, but he ended up with his head on a platter after languishing in prison. And during those sufferings even John questioned whether Jesus was the One who was to come.

The Romans apparently dipped the apostle John into boiling oil and imprisoned him on Patmos. And Paul himself was beaten to within an inch of his life more than once and had some sort of disease that even prayer hadn't removed.

Suffering, of course, can do one of two things to people. It can crush them as the olive in the press. Or they can view sufferings as instruments to open up new opportunities for growth and development. People who see them as chances for growth can indeed rejoice or boast in even life's pressures and tribulations.

A Side Lesson on Suffering

Sufferings. Romans 5:3, NRSV.

SUFFERINGS!

Disgusting things! But we all have them—even Christians seeking to walk with God. Yesterday we noted that Paul wrote that Christians "rejoice" in their sufferings.

Such a thought was not new with Paul. Jesus raised it in the Beatitudes: "Blessed are those who are persecuted for righteousness' sake, *for* theirs is the kingdom of heaven. Blessed are you when men revile you and persecute you and utter all kinds of evil against you falsely on my account. *Rejoice and be glad, for* your reward is great in heaven, for so men persecuted the prophets who were before you" (Matt. 5:10-12, RSV).

That was the only Beatitude that Jesus repeated. Perhaps He needed to do so because it is so hard to swallow. Why rejoice and be glad in the face of trouble? The twice-repeated "for" provides one explanation. Both times that preposition is followed by the fact that those who are Christ's will inherit the kingdom. This world is not the end. Our sufferings will cease someday.

In Luke 6:23 Jesus tells us that Christians should not only rejoice in the face of trouble but actually "leap for joy" (RSV). Try that one when you have been insulted or rejected or are seriously ill or just got robbed of $5,000.

It's not normal! That's true, but neither Paul nor Jesus is saying that born-again Christians are normal according to our world's standards. They are abnormal in the sense that they have a Savior as the focal point of their life. Thus they can rejoice in suffering because they know not only that it is temporary but that God can make good things come out of bad events.

In 2 Corinthians Paul declares in the face of his own suffering and seemingly unanswered prayer that Christ had told Him that His " 'grace is sufficient' " for his needs and that His power " 'is made perfect in weakness.' " The apostle concluded: "I will all the more gladly boast of my weaknesses, that the power of Christ may rest upon me. For the sake of Christ, then, I am content with weaknesses, insults, hardships, persecutions, and calamities; for *when I am weak, then I am strong*" (2 Cor. 12:9, 10, RSV).

Remember what Paul is talking about in Romans. It is easy to become proud and boast in our achievements. But afflictions have a ministry. They show us our helplessness and drive us to Christ, our source of both strength and righteousness. As a result, Christians can even rejoice in sufferings.

THE SCHOOL OF HARD KNOCKS

Because we know that suffering produces perseverance;
perseverance, character; and character, hope. Rom. 5:3, NIV.

"BECAUSE" IS AN IMPORTANT word in today's text. It points us back to the idea that Christians should not only rejoice in their hope (Rom. 5:2) but also in their sufferings (verse 3). The reason they should rejoice, Paul claims, is that sufferings or pressures set off a chain reaction in their lives that when fully understood can only lead to thanksgiving.

The first step in that chain is that sufferings produce perseverance. "Perseverance" represents two Greek words that literally mean to abide or stay under. The idea is that a person not only learns to abide in Christ when all is well, but also in troublesome times. It is all too easy to quit when life becomes difficult. But Christians discover through hard experiences that instead of sufferings being causes of quitting, they can be the means of utilizing their faith to enter a deeper relationship with Jesus. A Christian in a Communist country, pressured to give up his faith and conform, declared, "We are like nails: the harder you hit us the deeper you drive us." That is perseverance, that is "staying under" the rule of Christ.

But perseverance isn't an end in itself. It develops character. Character was the word used of testing precious metals to purify them and to demonstrate their purity. Just as the metalsmith uses intense heat to melt silver and gold in order to remove physical impurities, so God uses sufferings to rid His children of spiritual impurities. Those who persevere will be cleansed.

We do not achieve strength of character in the everyday world by whining and groveling in the face of difficulty. That is the road to weakness and flabbiness. Strength comes from meeting problems head-on in a faith relationship to God through Jesus. "Blessed is the man," James tells us, "that endureth temptation: for when he is tried, he shall receive the crown of life, which the Lord hath promised to them that love him" (James 1:12).

The final link in the chain is that character produces hope. That thought brings Paul full circle back to Romans 5:2, in which he noted that believers "rejoice in the hope of the glory of God" (NIV). He will continue in verse 5 with the thought that hope in God will never disappoint us. We can rejoice even in sufferings because our God will never let us down.

A NEW MEANING FOR HOPE

*Hope does not disappoint us, because God's love
has been poured into our hearts through the
Holy Spirit which has been given to us. Rom. 5:5, RSV.*

HOPE! WHAT DOES IT MEAN? I heard someone say the other day that she hoped that her cousin Fred would be able to visit next summer. The way we usually use the word lacks firmness. It is kind of like a wish.

But that is not the way Paul employs the word. For him "hope" is certitude. Hope implies not the slightest doubt. When he speaks of the "blessed hope" of the Second Advent, he is not suggesting that event is merely wishful thinking that might or might not take place. No! The Advent was a certainty. The question was not if it would take place, but when.

The apostle uses hope in the same way in today's text. That is why he can tell the Romans that hope will not disappoint them. Of course he is speaking of Christian hope rather than hope in general.

Wayne Hooper picked up on the certainty of Christian hope in his great hymn:
We have this hope that burns within our hearts,
    Hope in the coming of the Lord.
We have this faith that Christ alone imparts,
    Faith in the promise of His Word.
We believe the time is here, when the nations far and near
Shall awake, and shout, and sing Hallelujah! Christ is King!
We have this hope that burns within our hearts,
    Hope in the coming of the Lord.
Paul and Wayne are on the same wavelength. Those who have placed their faith in Christ will not be disappointed. They have certitude.

The apostle goes on to say that we have hope as Christians "because God has poured out his love into our hearts by the Holy Spirit" (Rom. 5:5, NIV). "Poured out" is not a moderate word. It means "to flood." God doesn't give us His love, so to speak, with an eyedropper, but in torrents.

Love, by the way, is an interesting word in Paul's writings. We often think of John as the apostle of love, but of the 116 appearances of the word in the New Testament, Paul is responsible for two thirds of them.

He knows that at the bottom of the entire plan of salvation is the love of God, who so cared about the world that He sent His Son. That love not only dispatched the Son, but it guarantees our salvation.

DYING FOR THE UNGODLY

*While we were still weak, at the right time
Christ died for the ungodly. Rom. 5:6, RSV.*

HAVING JUST MENTIONED in the previous verse the powerful influence of the love of God that the Holy Spirit floods into the hearts of believers, Paul now goes on in Romans 5:6-8 to explore the depths of that love as expressed by the cross of Christ. Douglas Moo summarizes the apostle's argument as follows:

    "a. Human love, at its best, will motivate a person to give his or her life for a truly 'good' person (v. 7);

    "b. Christ, sent by God, died, not for 'righteous' people, or even for 'good' people, but for rebellious and undeserving people (v. 6);

    "c. Therefore: God's love is far greater in its magnitude and dependability than even the greatest human love (v. 8)."

Thus the apostle provides further evidence that the Christian's hope cannot fail. A God that loved us enough to die for us while we were at war with Him will never let us go.

Today's verse tells us that Christ died for the weak and the ungodly. "Helpless" or "powerless" are synonymous for weak here. In chapters 1-4 he has already demonstrated how helpless human beings are to earn or achieve their own salvation. The Greek word used for weak frequently refers to the physically limited. The King James Version of Acts 4:9 translates it as "impotent." *The Seventh-day Adventist Bible Commentary* notes that impotent is not an "unsuitable description of the condition of a sinner before his acceptance of the saving grace and power of God. Paul's reference to the impotence and helplessness of the unregenerate sinner stands in contrast to his picture of the justified believer, now rejoicing [Romans 5:1-5] as he grows stronger in hope, in endurance, in character, and in the assurance of God's love."

Christ died not only for the weak, but for the ungodly. By ungodly he does not mean that Christ died for some people who were worse than others. To the contrary, all were ungodly and needed His grace. Ungodly does not necessarily equate with powerlessness. People may be powerless or weak to earn their salvation, but as both the Bible and the daily news demonstrate, they have plenty of energy to rebel against God.

Wonder of wonders that Christ would go to the cross for those powerful to do evil.

WHOM WOULD I DIE FOR?

Very rarely will anyone die for a righteous man, though for a good man someone might possibly dare to die. Rom. 5:7, NIV.

WE NEED TO SEE THIS verse in the context of the preceding one, which states that Christ died for the ungodly. That rather startling thought calls forth verses 7 and 8, in which the apostle explores the meaning of Christ's death.

In today's text we find ourselves glimpsing into the depths of God's love. It also raises a question in my own heart. Whom would I die for? Whom would I really sacrifice to help? I have to admit that I have never been asked to die for anyone physically. But sometimes I have received requests to aid a person, such as a student or older person who really needs my help if they are to live comfortably or accomplish their goals.

The first thing that runs through my mind when invited to make a major commitment of time or money to someone's well-being is whether they are worthy. Have they been good people? Will they make a positive contribution to society? Are they deserving of my sacrifice?

Yes, some of us might sacrifice something for another person, but it is a calculated sacrifice. It is that contrast that highlights the love of God. He sent Christ to die for the worthless, for the ungodly, for the ungrateful.

Closeness to someone might inspire an individual to give up their life for that person. A story tells of a tough young boy from the inner city whose only sister had been crippled and desperately needed an operation. Following the operation she needed a blood transfusion, and the physician asked her rather anxious brother to volunteer because he and his sister both had the same rare blood type.

When the transfusion was finished, the doctor put his arm around the young man and told him he had been very brave, but he didn't know how brave until the boy asked him a question. Totally ignorant about medical things, the brother looked up at the doctor and inquired, "How long before I croak?" He had somehow gotten the idea that he would have to die to save his sister, that the blood he gave to her would mean death for him just as it meant life for her. But he did it anyway!

Such stories reflect what we might call the best of human love—that one might possibly die for a loved family member or someone deemed "worthy." But in Romans 5 we read that Jesus died not for the worthy but for those in rebellion against Him and the Father. It is that kind of love that undergirds the Christian's hope.

THE GREATEST LOVE

But God proves his love for us in that while we still
were sinners Christ died for us. Rom. 5:8, NRSV.

CHRIST DIED FOR SINNERS! With that forceful truth Paul brings to a climax the line of thought he had begun in Romans 5:6.

God's love, he has shown, far surpasses human love. The cross demonstrates His love in the sense that He died for the ungodly, for sinners.

Now, a sinner is one who is not merely out of harmony with God's will. Rather, a sinner is in active rebellion against God. Sin is against God personally. "The mind that is set on the flesh" (unconverted human nature), Paul writes, "is hostile to God" (Rom. 8:7, RSV).

Beyond being personal, sin is moral. It is a deliberate act of the will to rebel against God. Sin is a choice, a rejection of God. Thus Herbert Douglass can correctly say that "sin is a created being's clenched fist in the face of his Creator; sin is the creature distrusting God, deposing Him as the Lord of his life." Emil Brunner puts it succinctly when he claims that sin "is the son who strikes his father's face in anger, . . . it is the bold self-assertion of the son's will above that of the father."

It is with those thoughts in mind that we can begin to see the heighth and depth and breadth of God's love. A small card with the 12 parts of John 3:16 in one column and descriptive phrases in a second column seeks to illustrate God's profound love for each of us. It goes like this:

God	the greatest lover
so loved	the greatest degree
the world	the greatest company
that he gave	the greatest act
his only begotten Son	the greatest gift
that whosoever	the greatest opportunity
believeth	the greatest simplicity
in him	the greatest attraction
should not perish	the greatest promise
but	the greatest difference
have	the greatest certainty
everlasting life	the greatest possession

Is it any wonder that the greatest hymns of the church down through the ages have focused on God's love? For Paul the greatest fact of the ages is God's love, and the greatest demonstration of that love is the cross of Christ.

THE BIBLE'S MOST DISGUSTING TEACHING

Much more then, being now justified by his blood,
we shall be saved from wrath through him. Rom. 5:9.

IT WAS 1:30 in the afternoon of April 15, 2000. I had just arrived home from church.

After a quick microwaved lunch I went out to the garage to get Scottie, my vibrant little cockapoo. As usual, his compliant little body responded to my call. Trustingly he looked up at me, hoping no doubt that I had a dog biscuit behind my back.

Picking the dog up gently, I took him to the basement, since my strange task for the day was not something I wanted the neighbors to see. Safely secluded, I let the dog lie beside me as I set up my apparatus and knelt in prayer.

Then, placing my right hand on his head, I confessed my sins. Meanwhile, my left hand ran a well-honed knife across Scottie's unsuspecting and trusting throat. It was all over by 1:50.

The experience devastated me. I hadn't killed anything for years, let alone with my bare hands. As I knelt in a semistupor, I could feel the dying dog's arteries pulsating out the remaining blood—every pulsation thundering out the message that "the wages of sin is death, the wages of sin is death." Nauseated beyond description, I stumbled over to the washbasin, where I sought to cleanse my sticky fingers from the reminder that innocent little Scottie had died for my sins.

Now, before you call the humane society, please realize that the above account is *entirely fictitious.* I made up the story so that you could get a "feel" for the Old Testament sacrificial system—the system that pointed forward to Christ the Lamb of God, who died for the sins of the world.

If the illustration disgusted you, I achieved my purpose—a purpose aimed at highlighting the costliness of sin and its ugly consequences in Christ's life. Remember, He died for my sins. He died in my place. He took the death penalty for me, that I might have His life.

The sacrifice of Christ for sinners may be the Bible's most disgusting teaching. But it is also the most important, because the entire plan of salvation rests upon the death of the Lamb of God. Through Christ's death God did for me what I could not do for myself.

ENEMIES WITH GOD NO MORE

When we were God's enemies, we were reconciled
to him through the death of his son. Rom. 5:10, NIV.

PAUL IN ROMANS 5 has had a mouthful of descriptions for those who haven't been saved. He has called them "powerless" (Rom. 5:6, NIV) in the sense that they are unable to save themselves; "ungodly" (verse 6), meaning that they possess a total incapacity for good; and "sinners" (verse 8) in that they break God's law.

To that rather impressive list he now adds that "we were God's enemies." The New Testament declares a number of times that sinners are God's enemies. Philippians 3:18 talks of those who "live as enemies of the cross of Christ" (RSV). Colossians 1:21 speaks of those who were "once estranged and hostile in mind, doing evil deeds" (RSV), and James 4:4 mentions that "friendship with the world is enmity with God" (RSV).

"Enemies" is a strong word. "An enemy," Leon Morris points out, "is not simply someone who falls a little short of being a good and faithful friend. He belongs in the opposite camp. He is opposed to what one is doing. Sinners are putting their effort into the opposite direction to that of God." An enemy is, as in the case of war, out to destroy the other.

Now, it is clear all through the Bible that sinners are God's enemies, that they oppose the principles of His kingdom. But, we need to ask, does the phrase "God's enemies" say anything about His attitude toward sinners? The contrast indicates a definite yes to our question. The fact that those who cling to their sins will eventually experience God's wrath (Rom. 5:9) indicates His hatred of the sin that destroys people's lives.

We must be aware of a fine line here, though. God hates sin but loves sinners. He loves them so much that He sent Jesus to heal the relationship, to reconcile them to Himself. To reconcile means to bring together two estranged parties. We speak of an estranged husband and wife being reconciled to each other. In the same way Paul claims that God "has reconciled you by Christ's physical body through death to present you holy in his sight, without blemish and free from accusation" (Col. 1:22, NIV).

Reconciliation is a two-sided affair. Paul makes it clear that God (in this case the wronged party) has taken all the necessary steps to heal the conflict between Himself and those at war with Him. The second part is for us to accept His offer of both peace and salvation. He wants us to let loose of our sin and take hold of Him.

"Half Saved"

How much more, having been reconciled,
shall we be saved through his life! Rom. 5:10, NIV.

"HOW MUCH MORE" than what?

Verse 10 in its entirety represents salvation as a two-step process in which we are presently "half saved" from the sin problem. The first step we examined yesterday: "We were reconciled to him through the death of his Son" (NIV). Paul uses the past tense in that half of Romans 5:10. Our reconciliation has already been accomplished. It is a present reality.

Then comes the "how much more." Based on the present reality of our reconciliation with God "how much more . . . shall we be saved through his life!" Here Paul is using the future tense. Christ's death has already reconciled us, but we will someday be fully saved through His life.

By the use of "how much more" Paul is arguing from the lesser to the greater. C.E.B. Cranfield helps us see the point when he writes that "since God has already done the much more difficult thing (in this case, reconciled us, when we were His enemies, to Himself), we can with absolute confidence expect that He will do what by comparison is but a little thing, namely, at the last save us who are now His friends."

In short, because of our justification (Rom. 5:9) and our reconciliation (verse 10), our full salvation at the end of time is guaranteed. Then God will not leave His people in their "half-saved" state. Those who are walking with Him as friends here on earth can look forward with full assurance to walking with Him in the earth made new.

We are saved by His life. Paul in various places provides more than one meaning to that phrase. Romans 8, as we saw earlier, is especially rich in themes related to our being saved by Christ's life. Verse 34, for example, highlights His ministry in the heavenly sanctuary. In that passage the apostle speaks of "Christ Jesus, who died, yes, who was raised from the dead, who is at the right hand of God, who indeed intercedes for us" (RSV). His heavenly ministry would have been impossible without His resurrected life.

Then again, saved by His life refers to His resurrection from the grave, a guarantee of the resurrection of each of His followers. We serve a Savior who has "the keys of hell and of death" (Rev. 1:18).

Christians long for the fulfillment of the "how much more."

DO WE REJOICE?

We also rejoice in our God through our Lord Jesus Christ, through whom we have now received the reconciliation. Rom. 5:11, NKJV.

CHRISTIANS "REJOICE"! Do they? I have seen some mighty miserable-looking Christians.

Rejoice is an important word in the first half of Romans 5. In Romans 5:2 Christians "rejoice in the hope of the glory of God" (NIV), in verse 3 they rejoice in their sufferings, and in today's passage they rejoice because they have already "received the reconciliation" and because the fullness of their salvation at the end of time is guaranteed (verse 10). If even their troubles are a cause of rejoicing, Christians must have a lot to rejoice about.

Joy is also a vital word in Romans. In Romans 14:17, for example, Paul tells us that "the kingdom of God is not food and drink but righteousness and peace and joy in the Holy Spirit" (RSV); in Romans 15:13 he prays that God will fill us "with all joy and peace" (RSV), and in verse 32 he writes that he hopes to visit the Romans in joy. Then in Romans 16:19 he tells the Roman church that he is "full of joy" (NIV) because of their obedience to God.

Joy and rejoicing are central to Paul's teaching. As he sees it, they are the natural response to our acceptance of the gospel, the good news of salvation in Christ. He even places joy second (right after love) in his listing of the fruit of the Spirit in Galatians 5:22, 23.

If Paul places such a large emphasis on joy and rejoicing, I wonder why so many Christians look so miserable. To look at some of them you would think that the sign of sanctification is appearing as if your face had been cured in a pickle jar.

And they certainly wouldn't be seen rejoicing in church. One of the sermons I like to preach the most is entitled "It's Not a Sin to Smile in Church."

Why is it that Christians—or perhaps so-called Christians—don't have more joy and rejoicing? Today's text implies that they will rejoice when they realize that they have already been saved in Christ. Perhaps those who aren't rejoicing haven't grasped what Paul has been so desperately trying to explain in Romans 3, 4, and 5—that those who have accepted Christ have already been justified, reconciled to God, and possess the guarantee of the resurrection as long as they remain in a faith relationship to God through Christ. Having already passed from death to life, Christians can't help but rejoice.

THERE IS ONE THING YOU DON'T NEED TO TEACH CHILDREN

Sin came into the world through one man and death through sin, and so death spread to all men because all men sinned. Rom. 5:12, RSV.

ONE THING YOU NEVER have to teach your children is how to sin! It seems to come naturally. Everyone does it. Thus Paul's conclusion in Romans 3:23 that all have sinned and fallen short of God's ideal.

Sin and its effects are universal. One commentary to its power and prevalence is that every state must have its army, police, judges, courts, and penal system. Reinhold Niebuhr phrased the issue succinctly when he wrote that "where there is history . . . there is sin."

But you don't have to be a theologian such as Niebuhr to reach that conclusion. Even if the Bible did not exist, we would still have a doctrine of sin. Written on the very fabric of existence, its universality is attested to by the pagan writers of antiquity as well as by the philosophical, literary, sociological, psychological, political, and other theorists of the present day.

Secular novelist John Steinbeck put it accurately when he penned: "I believe that there is one story in the world, and only one. . . . Humans are caught—in their lives, in their thoughts, in their hungers and ambitions, in their avarice and cruelty, and in their kindness and generosity too—in a net of good and evil."

In today's passage Paul explains the obvious universality of sin by the simple phrase that "sin came into the world through one man"—Adam. He goes on to add that sin resulted in death, and that "death spread to all men because all men sinned." The implication is clear that all people are sinners through some connection to Adam.

Please note that Paul, although he deals with the universality of sin and death, does not in any way seek to explain *how* sin and death spread to everyone. He just treats it as a fact.

Romans 5:12-21, rather than trying to explore how sin and death took over humanity, focuses on Adam and Christ as models of two types of life. John Brunt is quite correct when he writes that "what Paul is most interested in showing us . . . is that no matter how big a mess Adam got us into, Christ's solution not only cleaned up the mess but went far beyond. Yes, Adam got everyone into a mess. . . . But now Christ has a solution for everyone as well."

LAW AS CLARIFIER

Until the Law sin was in the world; but sin is not imputed
when there is no law. Nevertheless death reigned from Adam
until Moses, even over those who had not sinned in the
likeness of the offense of Adam. Rom. 5:13, 14, NASB.

ONE CAN ALMOST HEAR the working of some minds as they read
Paul's words in Romans 5:12. How can he say that all people have sinned
and are therefore subject to death? After all, they didn't have the law of
Moses. And didn't the apostle just mention in Romans 4:15 that "where
there is no law there is no transgression" (RSV)?

Paul, as usual, responds aggressively in verse 13: Of course sin was
in the world before the coming of the law. He could have pulled up some
illustrations. Sin and its results are major themes of the Bible throughout
the patriarchal period. The existence of sin before the giving of the law on
Sinai is a fact that none of Paul's readers would doubt.

At that point he notes that "sin is not counted where there is no law"
(Rom. 5:13, RSV). That's confusing. What does Paul mean? He can't be
suggesting that people weren't held responsible. After all, they *did* die. And
beyond that, as he noted in Romans 1 and 2, everybody through nature and
conscience has a knowledge of right and wrong. C.E.B. Cranfield's translation helps us see Paul's point: "in the absence of the law, sin is not regis-
tered *with full clarity.*" He added the three italicized words to indicate that
Paul is saying that "in the absence of the law sin is not the clearly defined
thing, starkly shown up in its true character, that it becomes when the law
is present." That interpretation builds upon Paul's previous comment in
Romans 3:20 that it is through the law that we know sin. Thus the command
"thou shalt not kill" is much clearer than merely having an uneasy conscience about such actions. The law makes God's will quite explicit.

Paul is now ready for verse 14, in which he reemphasizes that death
still reigned during the interval between Adam and Moses, even though
people living at that time didn't have a definite commandment in the same
sense that Adam did in Genesis 2:17 (not to eat of the tree) or that Israel
had after Moses received the Ten Commandments.

Once again Paul is driving home the purpose of the law. Clarifying
God's will, it holds people accountable. And breaking it means eternal
death. Paul never ceases to point out that it is from that dreary ending that
Christ wants to save us. All have sinned, and all need Christ's atonement.

THE ADAM WAY OR THE CHRIST WAY?

Adam . . . was a pattern of the one to come. Rom. 5:14, NIV.

NOW, THERE'S AN interesting thought: Adam the sinner is a pattern of Christ the sinless? How can that be? What is Paul talking about?

One way to get at the question is to ask ourselves what are the most important events in human history. How would you answer? Would it be the invention of the wheel? the discovery of fire? the introduction of printing? the development of the computer? the testing of atomic power?

Those are all important, but from Paul's point of view they pale into insignificance in the light of the two events he cites in Romans 5: the fall of the race through Adam and its redemption through Christ. The significance of what Christ and Adam did touches every human being who has ever lived. Adam is a type or pattern of Christ in the sense that both affected the entire race. They came to represent two ways of facing life. John Brunt has outlined the results of our relationship to Adam and to Christ in the following way:

Adam	*Christ*
Sin entered through him (verse 12)	
By his trespass many died (verse 15)	Through Him God's grace overflows (verse 15)
He brings condemnation (verse 16)	He brings justification (verse 16)
Through him death reigned (verse 17)	Through Him, we reign in life (verse 17)
He brings condemnation to all (verse 18)	He brings life to all (verse 18)
Through his disobedience the many were made sinners (verse 19)	Through His obedience, The many will be made righteous (verse 19)

Paul in Romans 5:12-21 is really writing about two ways of life—the Adam way and the Christ way. Beyond that, in the entire context of Romans with its emphasis on faith, he implies that all people choose whether they will align with Adam or Christ. In the end every person will either remain in Adam in the sin life and its inglorious ending or will unite by faith to Christ and receive both justification and life everlasting.

137

SIN IS A SMASHING SUCCESS

If the many died by the trespass of the one man, how much
more did God's grace and the gift that came by the grace of
the one man, Jesus Christ, overflow to the many! Rom. 5:15, NIV.

SIN IS A SMASHING SUCCESS!

Just look at Adam's sin. It succeeded in creating alienation and destruction in every part of Adam and Eve's life. First and foremost was the religious effects—they became separated from God. Whereas the innocent Adam had enjoyed fellowship with his Maker, the Bible tells us that after the entrance of sin he and his wife "hid themselves from the presence of the Lord God" and that they were "afraid" of Him (Gen. 3:8-10, RSV).

Such alienation is quite understandable on the human plane. For example, children who have violated their mother's will do not wish to meet her or look her in the face. They have something in their heart that they wish to hide. Likewise, guilt renders God's presence unbearable.

A second success of sin came to light in the universe's first family argument. When God asked Adam if he had eaten any of the forbidden fruit, he quickly blamed Eve. "The woman whom thou gavest to be with me, she gave me fruit of the tree, and I ate" (Gen. 3:12, RSV). It's her fault! So much for the world's only perfect marriage.

The great tragedy of the social effects of sin is that they didn't stop in Genesis 3. The message of Genesis 4 through 11 is one of the ever-widening social impact of sin. We view it daily in the news as neighbor destroys neighbor.

A third success of sin was to alienate a person from his or her "self." After God finished questioning Adam, he moved to Eve. "What," He asked her, "is this that you have done?" "The devil made me do it," she replied (Gen. 3:13, paraphrased). Here we come face to face with the problem of people being unwilling and, in most cases, unable to face up to themselves and to evaluate honestly their actions and underlying motives. As Jeremiah pointed out, "the heart is deceitful above all things" (Jer. 17:9, RSV).

The ultimate success of sin, of course, was to bring about both spiritual and physical death (Gen. 3:19).

Sin has been a smashing success in disrupting God's world and human lives. But, Paul claims in our text for today, God's grace is a "smashinger" success. We will turn to that success tomorrow.

GRACE IS A "SMASHINGER" SUCCESS

Nor is the effect of God's gift the same as the effect of that one man's sin. For in the one case one man's sin brought . . . condemnation. But, in the other, countless men's sins are met with . . . justification. Rom. 5:16, Phillips.

I AM NOT SURE "smashinger" is a word. But it is now. It means that God's success is more than smashing. His successes more than overcome the effects of sin.

That thought was primary in Romans 5:15, in which Paul claims that "the gift is not like the trespass" (NIV). In what way are they unlike? The gift of grace is greater than all the effects of sin. As *The Revised English Bible* puts it: "God's act of grace is out of all proportion to Adam's wrongdoing. For if the wrongdoing of that one man brought death upon so many, *its effect is vastly exceeded by the grace of God* and the gift that came to so many by of the grace of the one man, Jesus Christ."

The apostle continues to exhibit superiority of the gift of grace in verse 16: "Again, the gift of God is not to be compared in its effect with that one man's sin; for the judicial action, following on the one offence, resulted in a verdict of condemnation, but the act of grace, following on so many misdeeds, resulted in a verdict of acquittal" (REB).

If the effects of sin were smashing, the effects of God's gift is "smashinger." The gift more than conquers the sin problem.

Sin is not the last word, because, claims Paul, the gift changes the sinner's entire situation. The gift provides a way of escape. The gift opens up an avenue that releases the sinner from the penalty of judgment. And the gift provides for the justification of the sinner full and free.

The word "gift" is significant in Romans 5. It appears 5 times in verses 15 to 17 and Paul picks it up again in Romans 6:23, in which he tells us that eternal life is the gift of God.

"Gift" not only points to the freeness of salvation, but also to the fact that those who accept the gift do not have to strain heroically against Adam's legacy of sin as the price of acceptance. Acceptance does not come through struggle. Rather we receive it as a gift from God through Christ, who paid the redemption price.

Greater by far than sin and all its effects is God's gift to those willing to accept it. Our God isn't a halfway-measure God. He has provided for our needs in every way. The good news is that the gift is greater than the curse.

AFLOAT IN A SEA OF "HOW MUCH MORES"

How much more will those who receive God's abundant provision of grace and of the gift of righteousness reign in life through the one man, Jesus Christ. Rom. 5:17, NIV.

IF "GIFT" IS A central word in Romans 5, so is the phrase "how much more."

In Romans 5:9 we read that "since we have now been justified by his blood, *how much more* shall we be saved from God's wrath through him" (NIV).

Then verse 10 states: "If, when we were God's enemies, we were reconciled to him through the death of his Son, *how much more,* having been reconciled, shall we be saved through his life" (NIV).

Verse 15, as we noted yesterday, utilizes the *"how much more"* philosophy to emphasize the complete triumph of grace over the judgment on sin.

Finally, in today's text (verse 17), Paul employs the *"how much more"* formula once again to contrast the superior achievements of Christ with the penalty of death, the heritage of Adam that was the subject of verses 12 through 14. "For if, by the trespass of the one man, death reigned through that one man, *how much more* will those who receive God's abundant provision of grace and of the gift of righteousness reign in life through the one man, Jesus Christ."

Paul is telling us that we have a "how much more" kind of God. In each use of the term the apostle seeks to express the Father's extreme love and generosity for His children. It seems that Paul is trying to tell us that God wants to do more for us than we can even imagine. He not only intends to save us from the penalty of sin, but longs to give and give and give more and more to those who accept His gift through faith in Christ.

That overflowing generosity concept is especially evident in the "how much more" of verse 17, where Paul ties it to "God's abundant provision of grace." Translators have struggled with that phrase. Goodspeed renders it "God's overflowing mercy," Moffatt as "the overflowing grace and free gift of righteousness," and *The Message* as "this wildly extravagant life-gift."

No matter how we translate the phrase, Paul's idea is clear. Not only does grace defeat sin, but we have a "how much more" kind of God who wants to fill His children's every need. Today we can be thankful for the "how much more" of our God.

JUSTIFICATION FOR "ALL"

Therefore as by the offence of one judgment came upon all
men to condemnation; even so by the righteousness of one the
free gift came upon all men unto justification of life. Rom. 5:18.

WITH VERSES 18 and 19 Paul is ready to conclude the argument that he began in Romans 5:12. The word "therefore" signals that he is about to sharpen the point of what has gone before. He has not the slightest doubt in verse 18 that just as condemnation came upon all humanity because of Adam, so justification reaches all through Christ.

But what does he mean in each case by "all men"? There is not the slightest uncertainty that the judgment of condemnation has come upon every individual because all have sinned. That has been Paul's theme since Romans 1:18, and he explicitly states it in Romans 3:23.

But that is not the only theme in the first five chapters of Romans. A second theme follows from the fact that all have sinned (Rom. 3:23) and stand condemned. Immediately following in Romans 3:24 and 25 and into chapter 4 and beyond the apostle begins to emphasize justification by faith as a solution to universal sinfulness and condemnation. Paul couldn't be plainer that it is those who have faith who are justified. He sets forth faith as the condition of their justification. Without it they are not justified, but still remain under condemnation. Paul doesn't suddenly change that model in Romans 5:18. While Christ died to provide justification for all people, they still need to accept it before it is theirs.

Some are not happy with that explanation. They point out that it says that "the free gift came upon *all men* unto justification of life." But an interpretation that implies that Christ justifies all people not only removes verse 18 from its context in Romans 3 through 5, which sets forth faith as God's way of justifying people, but it also has to face the challenge of the parallel passage in 1 Corinthians 15:22.

That text claims, in the context of the resurrection of the righteous, that "as in Adam *all* die, so also in Christ shall *all* be made alive" (RSV). Thus to claim that the "alls" in Romans 5:18 and 1 Corinthians 15:22, 23 mean everybody would result in a universalism (everyone will be saved) that flatly contradicts the Bible, which tells us that some will reap eternal destruction.

Paul couldn't be clearer throughout his writings that salvation comes through faith in the merits of Jesus. Today is the day to reaffirm our personal decision and to thank Him for His gift.

"MANY" IS NOT "ALL"

For as by one man's disobedience many were made sinners, so by one man's obedience many will be made righteous. Rom. 5:19, RSV.

THE GOOD NEWS IS that Christ died for all. The bad news is that not everybody accepts His gift.

That brings us to the tension between the "all" of Romans 5:18 and the "many" of verse 19. Does verse 19 mean that "many" are sinners or that "all" are sinners? Paul already answered that question in Romans 1:18–3:20 and in 3:23, which plainly state that "all have sinned and fall short of the glory of God" (RSV). Thus in Romans 5:19 when he states that "many were made sinners" he means everybody.

That leads to an important question: If "many were made sinners" by "one man's disobedience" indicates everybody, doesn't it follow that "many will be made righteous" by "one man's obedience" implies that everyone is justified? In other words, aren't the two "ways" exact parallels? Once again, Paul has already answered that question in Romans 3:22-26 and 5:1, in which he plainly teaches that only those who have faith in Christ are justified, reconciled, and have peace with God. All others remain at enmity with Him and are dead in their trespasses and sins (see Eph. 2:1). Thus the "many" who "will be made righteous" is not everybody (or the all of Romans 5:18), but those who have accepted Christ's offer of free grace.

The true parallelism, therefore, is that "all people insofar as they relate to Adam are sinners and insofar as they relate to Christ are righteous." Many is not all. Being justified has a faith condition.

Having said that, however, it is absolutely crucial to realize that Christ died on the cross for all people in the sense of every human being who has ever lived. His sacrifice made provision for the justification of the entire human race. Beyond that, the gift is offered to all. But not all respond positively. Some decide to follow the Adam way rather than the Christ way.

Ellen White, speaking in a slightly different context, makes essentially the same point: "The *provisions* of redemption are free to all; the *results* of redemption will be enjoyed by those who have complied with the conditions" (*Patriarchs and Prophets*, p. 208). The condition of justification in Romans 3–5, of course, is acceptance by faith. Thus "many" is not "all" when it comes to salvation.

ABOUNDING GRACE

Moreover the law entered, that the offence might abound.
But where sin abounded, grace did much more abound. Rom. 5:20.

ROMANS 5:20 WAS John Bunyan's text. Most of us know him from his classic *Pilgrim's Progress,* but his devotional autobiography, *Grace Abounding to the Chief of Sinners,* best describes his life and spiritual progress. He based his title on today's text and 1 Timothy 1:13-16.

Bunyan had good reasons for his title. Born in 1628 to poor parents, he eventually took up his father's trade as a tinker—one who mended pots and pans and other things. He eventually became known as "the tinker of Bedford."

Living a rather loose life, Bunyan found himself justly troubled by a sense of personal sin. It was, as he put it, "as if the sun that shineth in the heaven did grudge to give light, and as if the very stones in the street, the tiles upon the houses, did bend themselves against me; methinks that they all combined together to banish me out of the world; I was abhorred of them, and unfit to dwell among them, or be partaker of their benefits, because I had sinned against God."

The good news is that God found Bunyan, saved him, and gave him great peace. *Grace Abounding to the Chief of Sinners* vividly expresses what he discovered. He had learned that no matter how great his sin was, God's grace was not only sufficient but superabundant.

Let's think about that superabundancy for a moment. The first part of today's text picks up one of Paul's themes throughout Romans—the law's role is to identify sin and condemn it. That function brings a sense of guilt in its train, and it is gnawing guilt that drives men and women to Jesus at the foot of the cross.

And what do they find? They discover a God willing to give them what they don't deserve (grace). But the good news is that He doesn't dole it out with an eyedropper. To the contrary, as Paul notes, He pours it out abundantly.

He does not withhold it because of our sin. If someone offends me, I am tempted to withdraw from that person and to restrain any natural generosity I might feel toward him or her. But not God. He never withholds grace because of sin. Rather, He pours out His grace to deal with that sin. Thus, as the New International Version translates Romans 5:20: "Where sin increased, grace increased all the more." His grace is not in short supply. It is there *for me today.*

A TALE OF TWO KINGS

*So that, just as sin reigned in death, so also grace might
reign through righteousness to bring eternal life
through Jesus Christ our Lord. Rom. 5:21, NIV.*

ONCE UPON A TIME there lived two kings. The first was despotic. He invaded Planet Earth, took control, and ruled with a ruthless efficiency. His goal was to control the life of every man, woman, and child. His kingdom resulted in destruction and death for everyone. The king's name is Sin.

The other king was bighearted and gracious. Wanting the best for His people, he came to earth to free the captives of His despotic adversary. His goal was to create a realm of eternal happiness. The king's name is Grace.

This "Tale of Two Kings" is the essential message of Romans 1 through 5, now summed up in Romans 5:21, the concluding verse of Paul's extended discussion of the problem of sin (Rom. 1:18–3:20) and God's solution through grace (Rom. 3:21–5:20).

James Montgomery Boice points out that Romans 5:21 tells us something about grace that we usually don't consider adequately. It indicates that grace is a power. We generally define grace as an attitude in which God provides unmerited favor to the undeserving. "But grace is more than an attitude. It is also a power that reaches out to save those who, apart from the power of grace, would perish."

Grace, in this sense, invades the kingdom of Sin in a struggle over a territory and people wrested away from God. We are dealing here with spiritual rather than physical warfare, but the issues are just as real. The attack is just as costly and decisive as was the D-day invasion of June 6, 1944. God has put everything He has into the galactic struggle with Sin, and Grace will prevail. The kingdom of Grace will someday be the only kingdom.

Paul closes out his extensive discussion of sin and its solution with a mention of "Jesus Christ our Lord." Since Jesus has made our salvation possible, Paul never tires of singing the praises of Christ, who died on a cross for our sins that we might live His life. To Paul the life, death, and resurrection of Christ are everything. Without those events the kingdom of Grace could never have overcome the usurper—Sin.

But as Paul so vividly points out, the objective victory of Grace over Sin will be fruitless unless those whom Christ died to save respond in faith. God's part in justification is accomplishment; our part is acceptance.

STEP 4
The Way of Godliness

Romans 6:1–8:39

TAKING A FOURTH STEP WITH PAUL

What are we to say, then? Shall we persist in sin,
so that there may be all the more grace? Rom. 6:1, REB.

THUS FAR IN OUR JOURNEY through Romans we have taken three steps with the great apostle. First, we met him and the Romans, and we glimpsed the reasons he wrote to them (Rom. 1:1-17). Second, Paul introduced us to the all-pervasive problem of sin among both Jews and Gentiles, and we discovered that all stand under the law's condemnation, which eventually results in death (Rom. 1:18–3:20). Third, Paul vigorously explored God's solution to the sin problem—justification by grace through faith. He left no stones unturned to demonstrate that salvation is a gift of God (Rom. 3:21–5:21).

We are now ready for a fourth step in our important journey. In chapters 6 through 8 Paul will describe the way the justified should live.

His teaching that salvation is a gift from God was not only revolutionary, but it raised all kinds of questions. One quite natural response was this: "If everything depends on what God has done, if our achievements don't bring about our justification or even aid God in granting it, then what does it matter how we live?" That question is inevitable once a person realizes that God has made full provision for our justification.

Sometimes the question comes from genuine believers who honestly want to know how they should live if they have been saved by grace. At other times those who desire to live a sinful life will raise it as an objection. And then others would like to show the irresponsibility of Paul's theology and how it leads to antinomianism (lawlessness).

It is the latter two groups that Paul probably has in mind in Romans 6:1. Their logic runs something like this: (1) Paul claimed in Romans 5:20 that the law identifies sin and thereby increases it; (2) more sin means more grace; (3) therefore, let's go on sinning so that grace may increase and God will be glorified all the more because of His ever more extensive gracefulness (Rom. 6:1; 3:8).

Such reasoning would invalidate Paul's theology among serious thinkers and provide a basis for profligate living among the irresponsible and insincere.

Paul, as we will see, violently rejects such a perversion of the gospel. In the process he will provide us with essential information about how the justified person will live.

146

A DISGUSTING THOUGHT

By no means! How can we who died
to sin still live in it? Rom. 6:2, RSV.

"BY NO MEANS!" (RSV). "May it never be!" (NASB). "God forbid!" (KJV). "What a terrible thought!" (Phillips). "Never!" (Moffat).

No matter how we translate the Greek words, they present the fact that Paul stands totally aghast at the idea that a Christian should go on living in a state of sin. The strongest idiom of repudiation in the Greek New Testament, it appears 14 times in Paul's letters. Thus far in Romans he has used it in Romans 3:4, 6, 31, and he will employ it another six times before he concludes the book (Rom. 6:15; 7:7, 13; 9:14; 11:1, 11). The phrase projects a sense of *outrage* that anyone could ever consider such a foolish idea as being true.

The very thought that sin could in any conceivable way be pleasing to God or be to His honor absolutely appalled the apostle. He doesn't even stop to reason with such stupidity. Rather than providing an argument against it, he asks a rhetorical question: "How can one who died to sin still live in it?"

The answer was obvious! It is impossible for one who has died to sin to continue to live in sin as a way of life. "Previously," notes Leon Morris, "they had been dead *in* sin (Eph. 2:1); now they were dead *to* sin." Only the most perverted logic would conclude that a life of sin was the way for Christians to exist.

"What is the business of Grace?" asks D. Martyn Lloyd-Jones. "Is it to allow us to continue to sin? No! It is to deliver us from the bondage and the reign of sin, and to put us under the reign of grace."

The verb "died" in today's text is in a verb tense that suggests a completed past action. It is referring to when we first accepted Christ and He gave us a new heart and a new mind so that the things we once hated we now love, and the things we once loved we now hate.

Paul is not saying that converted people never commit acts of sin. Rather, he means that they do not live a life oriented toward sin. When they do sin, of course, the condemning function of the law springs into action and forces them back to the cross, where they receive grace and power. They no longer love sin. Recognizing its destructive nature, they want to live the principles of God. But they also know that when they do sin they can turn to the Father, who has abundant grace.

BAPTISM IS VIOLENT

Don't you know that all of us who were baptized into
Christ Jesus were baptized into his death? Rom. 6:3, NIV.

PAUL, RATHER SURPRISINGLY, turns to the image of baptism to illustrate what it means to die to sin. Baptism, unlike so much of the vocabulary in Romans, isn't one of Paul's absorbing themes. Of the numerous times the term appears in the New Testament, Paul uses it only 13 times, three of them in Romans 6:3, 4.

But here the idea of baptism provides the perfect image for what Paul wants to illustrate. "Baptize" was not a nice warm fuzzy word in history. It means "to dip under," "to immerse," "to sink," "to drown." Writers in the ancient world used it to describe sinking ships or drowning people. Jesus picked up on that rather violent aspect of the word when He referred to His death as a baptism (Mark 10:38; Luke 12:50).

The apostle employs the term, as is particularly clear in Romans 6:4, in reference to death as a whole way of life. Then in verse 6 he will utilize crucifixion in relation to death in much the same way that Jesus did when He told His disciples that they would have to take up their cross and lay down their life for Him (Matt. 10:38, 39; 16:24, 25).

Becoming a Christian is a violent sort of thing. We enter it through baptism, a symbol of death to the old ways. Now Paul tells us in Romans 6:2, 3 that if a person has died to the old ways, it is ridiculous to claim that he or she would still want to live in them. No genuine Christian would want to continue a life of sin.

But his use of baptism contains something else as well. Baptism not only represents death to old ways of thinking and living, it also means "being baptized into Christ Jesus." As Paul phrases it in 1 Corinthians, "we were all baptized into one body" (12:13, RSV). Thus the baptized believer is incorporated into the body of Christ, represented on earth by the church.

One last thing that we should note in today's verse is that believers are "baptized into his death." Christ provided for our justification on the cross through His own death. We are incorporated into that event at the time that we accept Christ as our Savior, choose to die to the way of sin, and symbolize that change by being baptized into His death.

At that point we are *in Christ* rather than *in Adam,* having passed from death unto life. We have died to sin and are alive to God's will.

THE PERFECT SYMBOL

We were buried therefore with him by baptism into death,
so that as Christ was raised from the dead by the glory of
the Father, we too might walk in newness of life. Rom. 6:4, RSV.

BAPTISM IS THE PERFECT symbol of death to the old way and resurrection to a new way of life. C. H. Dodd aptly notes that baptism by "immersion is a sort of burial; emergence from the water as a sort of resurrection."

The present passage is one of the clearest on the meaning of baptism in the New Testament. Not only are those being baptized "buried with him" (NIV) in the watery grave, but they are "raised" out of the watery grave just as God raised Christ from the dead. Any other form of baptism would completely miss the meaning of Paul's symbols. In fact, if baptism in Paul's day were of any other form than immersion (such as sprinkling or dipping), Paul would never have used the illustration. He couldn't have employed it, since it would have made no sense. But immersion perfectly illustrates the death, burial, and resurrection process as reenacted by all new Christians when they become a part of the body of Christ.

If Romans 6:3 emphasizes baptism as an outward symbol of the death of the old way in a Christian's life, verse 4 moves the symbol beyond the negative into the positive realm. That is, baptism illustrates not only death to the old sinful way of life, but also resurrection to a new way of life based on God's principles.

Paul claims that just as Christ was raised, so are we that "we too might walk in newness of life." The word "walk" is important here, because it not only expresses a process of ongoing fellowship with God, but signifies directionality, since every walker has a goal, a thought especially clear in 1 John: "If we say we have fellowship with him while we *walk* in darkness, we lie and do not live according to the truth; but if we *walk* in the light, as he is in the light, we have fellowship with one another, and the blood of Jesus his Son cleanses us from all sin" (1 John 1:6, 7, RSV). Again, "He who says 'I know him' but disobeys his commandments is a liar, and the truth is not in him; but whoever keeps his word, in him truly love for God is perfected. By this we may be sure that we are in him: he who says he abides in him ought to *walk* in the same way in which he walked" (1 John 2:6, RSV). Christians, Paul emphasizes in Romans 6, will walk with God in newness of life—in God's way. It is impossible for them to tread the path of sin as a way of life.

UNITED TO CHRIST

If we have been united with him like this in his death, we will certainly also be united with him in his resurrection. Rom. 6:5, NIV.

UNITED WITH CHRIST! That is a powerful thought. The person who has accepted Christ by faith is joined to Him, not only in a death "like" His, but also in a life like His. Paul uses the word "like" or "likeness" (KJV) here because our experience is only similar to His rather than exactly like it. He, for example, died and resurrected physically, whereas we die spiritually to the way of sin and are spiritually resurrected to a walk with God.

Commenting on being "united" with Christ, William Sanday and Arthur Headlam note that "the word exactly expresses the process by which a graft becomes united with the life of the tree. So the Christian becomes 'grafted into' Christ." While the concept is broader than grafting, that metaphor is still a beautiful one that helps us understand the Christian's relationship to Christ. The union between the believer and Christ is of the closest sort. And just as the parent vine sends up sap and nutrients into a grafted branch, so Christ supplies the needs of those who have accepted His sacrifice by faith and given their lives to Him. Another way of saying it is that the spiritual life of the believer is not self-originated but derives from Christ. Thus the ongoing Christian life entirely depends on union with Christ, just as a grafted branch can survive only by remaining in union with the vine.

We need to let that thought sink in a bit. Branches lying next to a vine receive no nourishment. Branches merely in sight of the vine obtain none of the life-giving nutrients that only the vine can supply.

But some of us Christians who need to be united with Christ never quite get close enough to Him to be energized and enlivened. I need to ask myself, "Am I really united to the vine, or do I just kind of hang around the vine? How much time do I spend each day in some sort of intimate relationship with Christ through prayer, Bible reading, or meditation?"

It is little wonder that some of us look a little anemic spiritually.

Today, dear Lord, I want to rededicate myself to spending significant time with You. Today I will begin to set aside daily time for fellowship with You that I might truly experience the union of which Paul speaks.

CRUCIFIED WITH CHRIST

We know that our old self was crucified with Him. Rom. 6:6, NIV.

"WHEN CHRIST CALLS a man, he bids him come and die." Dietrich Bonhoeffer's words reflect the one essential test of Christian discipleship. He has good authority for his statement. You will recall that Peter played the role of the tempter to Christ at Caesarea Philippi by telling Him that He did not need to die. After turning on Peter and addressing him as Satan, Jesus gave the disciples one of His most frightful teachings. "If any man would come after me, let him deny himself and take up his cross and follow me. For whoever would save his life will lose it, and whoever loses his life for my sake will find it" (Matt. 16:24, 25, RSV).

Modern people miss the stark meaning that the passage had for the disciples. The idea of being crucified doesn't do much to our twenty-first-century imagination. We have never seen a crucifixion. To us the word is dead. But not for the disciples. When they saw a knot of Roman soldiers escorting a man through town carrying or dragging part of a cross, they knew it was a one-way trip. They considered the cross to be the cruelest and most humiliating of deaths—and one that the ruling Romans were more than willing to use to keep troublesome areas such as Palestine under control.

To Jesus and the disciples the cross meant crucifixion. It symbolized death and nothing else.

When Paul speaks of "our old self" being crucified, he is referring to that self-centered attitude and lifestyle that puts our self at the center of our life, that places our pleasures and desires ahead of God and concern for other people.

Christ had His cross, and we have ours. He died on His for our sins, in which He had no share; and we die on ours to all pride, self-reliance, and self-seeking, that we might partake of His life.

From Paul's perspective in Romans 6:6, people who have been crucified with Christ will have not the slightest desire to live the life of sin. Not only are they dead to sin, but, as Paul repeatedly asserts, they are alive to the ways of Christ. Such persons will never come up with the idea that they should sin that grace might abound (Rom. 6:1). Rather, they will want to do everything possible to live in the ways of God.

SLAVES TO SIN NO LONGER

We should no longer be slaves to sin. Rom. 6:6, NIV.

"SLAVERY" IS AN IMPORTANT word in the book of Romans. Paul uses it in the book's very first verse, when he announces that he is a slave to Christ. Slavery also dominates the last half of Romans 6, in which Paul contrasts those who are slaves to sin with those who are slaves to righteousness.

But here in Romans 6:6 the apostle claims that Christians are those who have voluntarily allowed God to crucify their "old self" so that they will no longer be dominated by the enslaving, despotic power of sin.

What does it mean to be a slave to sin? I think of the substance abuser who has to have a daily fix no matter how it damages mental or physical health or how much it costs and who has to be robbed to supply the money.

I think of the overachiever, the workaholic, who can't sit still, who must continue to push with everything available in the hope that someone will feed his or her ego through praise.

I think of the person enslaved to materialism. Busy, busy, busy. Busy for what? You can drive only so many cars, wear only so many dresses, eat only so much food, enjoy only so many houses.

Addictions stand at the heart of much human activity. Ask some people why they are doing something, and they will look at you blankly without an answer. They just know that they are "driven" to do this or that. Paul would use the word "enslaved."

Today's verse speaks to such situations and individuals. Those who have been crucified with Christ are those who are in union with Him, those who have broken their ties with Adam, those who have been justified and reconciled to God and are "no longer slaves to sin."

As he has done so often in Romans, Paul has personified sin in today's passage. He pictures it as a despotic ruler of slaves who assumes full control over those who have not died with Christ to its power.

That is a pretty accurate description of anyone addicted to various forms of self-destructive activities. But the good news is that the power (dynamite) of God's grace can release from bondage those who are crucified with Christ. They no longer need to be ruled by sin.

AM I DEAD TO SIN?

Whoever has died is freed from sin. Rom. 6:7, NRSV.

REALLY? ARE WE ACTUALLY free from sin after we accept Jesus by faith, give our lives to God, and are crucified with Christ? Do we no longer have any desire to do wrong? Are we no longer genuinely tempted? If so, I am in deep trouble, along with every other person I have ever known.

John Stott, in dealing with the confusion that this text brought into his life, writes that he was taught that "to die to sin was to be insensitive" to sin.

Dead things are totally unresponsive. Thus if one spots a dog lying in the road, it is impossible to tell if it is resting or dead until one gets close to it. At that point you can nudge it with your boot. If it is alive, it will immediately jump up, but if it is dead it will not react at all.

"Just so," claims Stott, "according to this popular view, having died to sin, we are as unresponsive to temptation as a corpse is to physical stimulus." Why? because our old nature was crucified with Christ, "it was nailed to the cross and killed, and our task (however much evidence we may have to the contrary) is to reckon it dead" (see verse 11).

Many Christians have picked up that interpretation. One recently stated that Christians, like those physically dead, are "insensible" and "immovable" in the presence of sin and temptation. "A dead man cannot sin."

Such an interpretation, though, faces at least three problems. First, in His life on earth Christ was genuinely tempted. His mind and body found going to the cross repulsive, and He felt Himself drawn toward some aspects of the wilderness temptation. Second, universal human experience identifies with Christ's reaction. Temptation is temptation because we are drawn to it. Third, Paul goes on to tell his readers in verse 12 that they should not let sin *"reign"* in their lives. It can't reign if Christians are really immune to it, since it should get no response.

In verse 12 we find the key to a proper understanding of today's text. Paul is not talking about being unable to respond to sin, but rather to being unable to live a life of sin. That same idea appears in verse 6, which tells us that Christians "should no longer be slaves to sin" (NIV). John Wesley captured the truth of what Paul is saying when he wrote that "sin *remains* but no longer *reigns.*" Christians no longer live lives characterized by sin, but when they do sin, John tells us, "we have an advocate with the Father, Jesus Christ the righteous" (1 John 2:1).

LIVING WITH CHRIST

*Now if we be dead with Christ, we believe
that we shall also live with him. Rom. 6:8.*

IN THE CONTEXT OF Romans 6 it is absolutely crucial to recognize that Christianity is not merely a way of dying, but also a way of living. Christianity is primarily a positive force, not a negative. The death of self as the center of existence opens the way and sets the stage for Christian living. Paul has been telling us that just as Christ's resurrection followed His death, so a parallel experience happens in each of His followers.

God's ideal for His people is not a moral void, but a new life of fullness with Christ. That life begins with the death of the old life that was marked by egocentric selfishness. Repentance is an abhorrence of one's sin, accompanied by a responding to God's love in Christ. The Christian life is not merely a turning *away* from something, but a turning to a new life based upon God's principles.

At the same time that God justifies a sinner, He also begins the process of sanctification. Paul teaches that through His grace God gives converted people new hearts and minds, new ways of looking at the world, and new motives for living in it (Col. 3:9, 10; Rom. 12:2; Eph. 4:22-24).

Ellen White reflects that same thought when she writes that "God's forgiveness is not merely a judicial act by which He sets us free from condemnation. It is not only forgiveness for sin, but reclaiming *from* sin. It is the outflow of redeeming love that transforms the heart. David had the true conception of forgiveness when he prayed, 'Create in me a clean heart, O God; and renew a right spirit within me' " (*Thoughts From the Mount of Blessing,* p. 114).

Paul refers to the person who accepts Christ's work as a "new creation"—one for whom the old way "has passed away" and "the new has come" (2 Cor. 5:17, RSV). Again, he writes: "I have been crucified with Christ; it is no longer I who live, but Christ who lives in me; and the life I now live in the flesh I live by faith in the Son of God, who loved me and gave himself for me" (Gal. 2:20, RSV).

"We shall live with him" is Paul's message all through Romans 6. Those who live *with* Him will live *like* Him and will daily pray to reflect His likeness more perfectly. Such is the way of godliness.

Too Bad for Lazarus

*For we know that Christ being raised from the dead will never die
again; death no longer has dominion over him. Rom. 6:9, RSV.*

"LAZARUS, COME FORTH."

Think about that one for a moment. Lazarus did come forth. Dead for
four days, with the stench of death upon him from the Palestinian heat.
Stumbling forth "bound hand and foot with graveclothes: and his face . . .
bound about with a napkin" (John 11:43, 44).

What a sight! At the sound of the voice of the Life-giver the insatiable
grave lets loose of its prey. Here was public witness that Jesus had power
over the material world and death itself. The corrupt corpse raised to life.

But there is a problem here. Jesus had raised Lazarus supernaturally,
but the man would die again. His deliverance was temporary, merely extending his life.

That, Paul tells us, is where Christ is different. Our belief that we will
live with Christ (Rom. 6:8) is not baseless. It rests upon our knowledge of
His resurrection life. As Paul puts it, "Christ being raised from the dead
will never die again." Unlike the resurrection of Lazarus, Christ's is irre-
versible. It can never be undone.

Why? Because "death no longer has dominion over him." To the contrary, He has permanent dominion over death. Thus His victory cry: "I am
alive for evermore, Amen; and have the keys of hell and of death"
(Rev. 1:18). Thus Paul's rejoicing in 1 Corinthians 15 regarding the
Savior who won the victory over the grave and will someday destroy the
"last enemy"—death.

Death is powerful. In fact, "death reigned from Adam to Moses"
(Rom. 5:14, RSV). But that is over now. Christ is supreme. True, He trod
the path to a death on the cross. But that is past. Christ's resurrection defeated death. We can walk with Him because "he ever liveth to make intercession" for His followers (Heb. 7:25).

Someday the Jesus we walk with will share the fullness of His victory
over death with each of us. The voice that called Lazarus forth will one
day pierce our tombs. "The trumpet shall sound, and the dead shall be
raised incorruptible" (1 Cor. 15:52). "Then we who are alive . . . shall be
caught up together with them in the clouds to meet the Lord in the air; and
so we shall always be with the Lord" (1 Thess. 4:17, RSV).

That is one appointment I don't want to miss.

AIRPLANE VIEW OF ROMANS 6:1-14

*The death he died he died to sin, once for all, but
the life he lives he lives to God. Rom. 6:10, RSV.*

TODAY'S VERSE FORMS a bridge between Romans 6:9 and 11. The
flow of the passage is as follows:
1. Christ has been raised from death and has victory over it (verse 9).
2. In His resurrected life He lives for God (verse 10).
3. Christians are to live just as Christ does—dead to sin but alive to
   God (verse 11).

Verse 11 brings us back to verse 8, in which Paul tells us that "if we
died with Christ, we believe that we will also live with him" (NIV). *In the
context of the entire first half of Romans 6, it is impossible to escape Paul's
meaning: No Christian will "go on sinning so that grace may increase,"*
so that God can use more of His grace in forgiveness (verse 1, NIV).
Christians can't live in sin, in rebellion against God and His principles
(verse 2). Why? Because they have died to the way of sin and been resurrected to a new way of life, symbolized by their baptism (verses 3, 4).

Then in verses 5 through 7 the apostle begins to expand on the parallels between Christ's crucifixion and resurrection and ours. Christians,
Paul emphasizes in verses 6 and 7, cannot live a life characterized by sin,
because they have let God crucify the self-centered existence.

Having taken care of the negative aspect of the parallel between
Christ and us in verses 5-7 (we have died to sin), Paul moves on in verses
8 through 10 to the positive: Christians have been spiritually resurrected
and will live with Christ, just as Christ lives with God.

That brings Paul in verses 11-14 to the ultimate conclusion to the
question he asked in verse 1 regarding whether Christians should go on
sinning. As in verse 2, Paul's answer is a definite no! Why? Because:
1. They are alive to God (and dead to sin) through Christ (verse 11).
2. Sin cannot reign in their lives, because Christ won the victory over
   sin (verse 12).
3. They are to give themselves to God as instruments of righteousness (verse 13).
4. They have a new master—grace (verse 14).

Involved though the argument may be, Paul's meaning in the first half
of Romans 6 is crystal clear: Christians will not choose to live sinful lives.
Rather, they will walk with Christ in the way of godliness.

THE CHRISTIAN DIFFERENCE

In the same way, count yourselves dead to sin
but alive to God in Christ Jesus. Rom. 6:11, NIV.

THIS VERSE GOES BACK to Romans 6:5 and picks up Paul's statement that those who die with Christ to a sinful way of life, symbolized by the watery grave of baptism, "will certainly also be united with him in his resurrection" (NIV). Verse 5 is not speaking of the future resurrection at the end of time, but rather present experience. That is exactly where verse 11 has brought us. Christians are not only dead to sin; they are also "alive to God in Christ Jesus."

What does that mean? What has happened to us? First, we have been reconciled to Christ. Whereas once we were His enemies and under condemnation, now through our acceptance of Christ we are a part of God's family. We are friends to God and He to us. We have a new relationship.

Second, we have become, as Paul puts it, "new creatures" (2 Cor. 5:17, 18). Jesus says it differently when He tells Nicodemus that we must "be born again" (John 3:7), but the idea is the same. As Christians we have something new and different about us. Once we had no interest in Bible study, but now we hear the voice of God in it. We enjoy its study. Once we believed that apologizing for our faults and serving others indicated weakness, but now we want to be in good relationship with and be a blessing to even those who irritate us. What has made the difference? God has changed us. Having become alive to Him, we are new creatures.

Third, no longer satisfied with the restricted view of a materialistic culture, we have new horizons and new goals. We are no longer satisfied with the "stuff" of this world. Of course, looking back, we realize that possessing things really never satisfied us anyway. But we tried to keep up the illusion. Christians, however, have been freed from illusionary living. We realize that beautiful homes and fancy cars will someday be gone; that diversionary entertainment will eventually pass away; that even our IRAs and 401(k)s will be relegated to insignificance. Knowing ourselves to be only pilgrims here, we, like Abraham, look forward to "a city which hath foundations, whose builder and maker is God" (Heb. 11:10). Being alive to God has made a difference in our life.

REIGNING VERSUS REMAINING

*Therefore do not let sin reign in your mortal
body that you should obey its lusts. Rom. 6:12, NASB.*

THIS PASSAGE IS VERY realistic in the sense that on one hand it holds in tension the fact that Christians do not need to let sin reign in (or control) their lives because of Christ's victory. But on the other hand it raises the issue that even born-again Christians still find themselves tempted by the lusts of the flesh.

Paul exhorts his readers not to let sin rule. That very exhortation assumes that sin is still there, that believers do not have a serene existence that excludes the possibility of sin. Even though they are "in Christ" they still remain "in the flesh." They still feel its "twitches."

Paul personifies sin in Romans 5 and 6 as a dethroned but still powerful monarch determined to reign in Christians' lives just as he did before their conversion. Thus the apostle exhorts believers not to let sin have its old place of superiority, because it no longer has a right to rule.

In fact, sin has no power to control a believer unless the believer chooses to "obey its lusts." Peter makes a similar appeal: "You are a chosen people, a royal priesthood, a holy nation, a people belonging to God. . . . I urge you, as aliens and strangers in the world, to abstain from sinful desires, which war against your soul" (1 Peter 2:9-11, NIV).

Christians become citizens of God's kingdom the moment they come to Christ. At that very time they turn into aliens and strangers to Satan's realm of sin and death. But, Paul tells us in today's text, sin is still a force even though it is no longer supreme.

John Wesley helps us understand this tension: He notes that sin *"remains* in our heart; . . . 'even in them that are regenerate'; although it does no longer *reign;* it has not dominion over them. It is a conviction of our proneness to evil, of a heart bent to backsliding, of the still continuing tendency of the flesh to lust against the spirit. Sometimes, unless we continually watch and pray, it lusteth to pride, sometimes to anger, sometimes to love of the world, love of ease, love of honour, or love of pleasures more than of God." It shows up "in a thousand ways, and under a thousand pretenses" to depart, "more or less, from the living God."

Within the ongoing tension our only safety is to maintain a conscious relationship to the God of victory.

WHO GETS MY WEAPONS?

*Do not go on presenting the members of your body to sin
as instruments of unrighteousness; but present yourselves
to God as those alive from the dead, and your members
as instruments of righteousness to God. Rom. 6:13, NASB.*

NOTICE THE "DO NOT." It is the second one in two verses. The imperative command in verse 12 was "Do not let sin reign" (NASB). Now Paul tells us "Do not go on presenting the members of your body to sin as instruments of unrighteousness."

That passage contains two words of special interest in their context. The first is "present," often translated as "offer"—a word used in reference to offering sacrifices. It is a serious problem when the servants of God present or offer their bodies to sin and Satan rather than to their God. The same word appears in Romans 12:1, 2, in which Paul exhorts the Romans "to present [offer] your bodies as a living sacrifice, holy and acceptable to God, which is your spiritual worship" (RSV). In Romans 6:13 he urges them not to get involved in the wrong type of "spiritual worship." "Do not go on presenting [offering] the members of your body to sin."

The second word that we need to examine is "instrument." In John 18:3, in which Judas guides the band of soldiers to arrest Jesus, the same word is translated as "weapon." The same rendering appears in 2 Corinthians 6:6, 7, in which Paul links love and truthful speech to "weapons of righteousness" (RSV).

The same understanding fits today's text. The underlying picture is one of sin and righteousness as respective rulers in opposing armies. Hence the warning not to offer members or bodies or bodily parts to the rule of unrighteousness. To do so would not only be false worship of the wrong sovereign (in the offering metaphor) but would also be the action of a traitor to the One who had become his or her rightful ruler.

Paul closes the verse with a third imperative, this time a "to do" rather than a "do not." Christians are to offer themselves and their weapons to righteousness.

It is the Christian's desire always to glorify God in everything. Paul couldn't have framed it better than when he said: "Whether you eat or drink, or whatever you do, do all to the glory of God" (1 Cor. 10:31, RSV). A Christian's entire life is a love offering to the God of righteousness. It is our privilege to be His "weapons" for good in a troubled world.

LAW VERSUS GRACE

For sin shall not be your master, because you
are not under law, but under grace. Rom. 6:14, NIV.

IN THE PREVIOUS VERSE Paul left us with the alternatives of offering ourselves as weapons in the hands of God, or as weapons in the hands of sin.

William Barclay points out that the alternatives may overwhelm some people. "A man," he suggests, "may well answer: 'Such a choice is too much for me. I am bound to fail.' Paul's answer is: 'Don't be discouraged and don't be despairing; sin will not lord it over you."

Why? Because grace won the victory over sin at the cross, when Christ triumphed over Satan. Because of that victory, sin is not our ruler. We are "dead to sin but alive to God" (Rom. 6:11, NIV). A change of lordship has already transpired in believers' lives. It is in the assurance of victory won that they can go forth confidently to wage war against sin. Christians don't walk in their own strength, but in that of their new Lord, Jesus Christ.

It is at that juncture that the law and grace issue becomes important. Paul makes it quite explicit that believers aren't under the dominion of sin, *because* they are under grace rather than the law.

The contrast between law and grace was a new thought to both Jews and Jewish Christians. They had traditionally seen the law as a gift of grace, but Paul puts the two in an adversarial relationship in the present context.

He sets forth law and grace as alternatives. Thus those who are under the one are not under the other. Why does he place them in opposition? He did so in this case because he had to combat those of his Jewish contemporaries who sought to use the law as a way of salvation, as a way of gaining God's favor.

He has argued forcefully throughout Romans that God never gave the law for deliverance, but to provide knowledge of sin (Rom. 3:20), to increase the amount of sin and wrath (Rom. 5:20; 4:15), and so on. Those seeking deliverance by the law will find that its condemning function will silence every mouth and make the "whole world . . . accountable to God" (Rom. 3:19, RSV).

The law has its purposes, but Paul never ceases to hammer home that it is not to rescue us from the rulership of sin. That, he can't seem to say often enough, is the role of grace. It is because of grace that sin is no longer our master.

TWO HOSTILE BROTHERS

*What then? Are we to sin because we are not
under law but under grace? Rom. 6:15, RSV.*

"WHAT THEN?" Paul's question sounds very much like the "What shall
we say, then?" of Romans 6:1, in which he pictures his detractors as saying "shall we go on sinning so that grace may increase?" (NIV).

Paul smashed that question flat in Romans 6:2-14. But now he sees a
new question on the horizon. He has just finished declaring in verse 14 that
believers are not under law but under grace. That statement has always
down through church history raised questions in the minds of two types of
people. Emil Brunner notes that as soon as some hear "Free from the Law,
the sinful flesh scents the morning breeze." Such unsanctified individuals
see in grace the opportunity to dump the law and to do what they want.

On the other hand, Brunner points out, "legal Pharisaism gets ready to
draw dangerous conclusions from the doctrine of grace in order to destroy
it." This latter group sees grace as the enemy that permits people to sin as
much as they please.

As a result, the "hostile brothers" of lawlessness and legalism always
surround the doctrine of grace. Both sides shout out "Freedom from the
law means a free and open path to sin."

Paul meets the hostile brothers in Romans 6:15-23. He will in his
usual thorough fashion nail shut the door that suggests "If it is grace that
saves, it doesn't matter how we live. Sin doesn't matter, since God has a
superabundance of grace and will forgive us 70 times seven." Paul comes
down hard on such a perverse understanding of salvation by grace.

Intimately related to the issue at hand is what I like to think of as the
minimalist and maximalist approaches to Christian living. The minimalist
likes to ask, "Can I do this and still be saved?" Like asking "How close
can I get to the edge of a cliff before falling off?" it is an unchristian question. Christians are not concerned with how little can be done, but how
much. They are maximalists, who want their lives to glorify God in the
fullest way possible. And while they realize that no law can save them,
they eagerly dedicate their lives to loving God and their neighbors in
every aspect of their existence. They don't live the law to be saved, but
live it because they are saved.

THE ILLUSION OF FREEDOM

*By no means! Do you not know that if you yield yourselves to
any one as obedient slaves, you are slaves of the one whom
you obey, either of sin, which leads to death, or of obedience,
which leads to righteousness. Rom. 6:15, 16, RSV.*

"BY NO MEANS!" As in Romans 6:2, Paul stands aghast that anyone
could even think that they could use grace as an excuse for sinning.

People aren't really free, he tells us. God made them for obedience.
The only question is whether they will be obedient to sin or to righteousness, to God's principles or to Satan's. Freedom in the abstract is an illusion, something impossible. The only choice we humans have is *whom* we
will obey.

Thus freedom from the law does not mean an abstract freedom. And
for Christians, freedom from the law as a way of salvation, as Brunner
notes, "does not mean freedom *from* God but freedom *for* God." Faith is
just the opposite of being loosed from God. Rather, it is an intimate relationship with Him. As Paul so often says, a Christian is one who is *"in
Christ."* Persons of faith know that they belong to God. For Paul, obedience is faith's natural result. As we noted earlier, the expression "the obedience of faith" frames the entire book of Romans (Rom. 1:5; 16:26,
RSV). Paul can't even begin to imagine genuine faith that does not lead
to obedience.

Of course, if some choose not to be obedient to God, that merely
proves that they are obedient to the other force in the world—sin. A
Christian is one who has stopped being obedient to sin and has opted for
obedience to God.

It is in the context of the two obediences that Paul talks about the two
destinations of the two paths. One leads to death, and we would expect
Paul to say that the other path has life as its goal. But he doesn't. Rather,
he says obedience to God "leads to righteousness."

Wait a minute! Has the great apostle gotten confused? Is he saying
after all his talk of righteousness by faith without works of law that people can achieve righteousness by obedience?

By no means! But he is telling us that obedience is an important part
of a life lived in grace. The grace-empowered obedience of the born-again
Christian leads to righteousness in the sense that it motivates conduct
pleasing to God, conduct in harmony with the principles of His kingdom.

A "FROM THE HEART" EXPERIENCE

But God be thanked, that ye were the servants of sin,
but ye have obeyed from the heart that form
of doctrine which was delivered to you. Rom. 6:17.

PAUL'S EXCITED AND THANKFUL for what God has done for the Roman Christians—they had changed masters. It is not the first time in Romans that he has expressed thanks for the Christians in Rome. "I thank my God through Jesus Christ," we read in the first chapter, "for all of you, because your faith is being reported all over the world" (Rom. 1:8, NIV).

Now in Romans 6:17 we find out a bit more about their faith. A faith that had responded in obedience to the teachings of the early church, it led them to "enslave" themselves to a new ruler. Paul, like Jesus in the Sermon on the Mount, is absolutely convinced that "no man can serve two masters" (Matt. 6:24). The Christians in Rome had realized the fruitlessness of serving their first master (sin) and had voluntarily linked up as did Paul (Rom. 1:1) to become slaves of God.

Today's text tells us that the Roman Christians "obeyed from the heart." Paul nowhere else uses that expression. But it is full of meaning. Their obedience wasn't just a casual thing, nor a passing fad. It came "from the heart." The verb form used indicates an action taken at a point of time. It points to the decisive act of obedience when they turned away from sin and toward God. The phrase "obeyed from the heart" expresses a deeply felt experience, one that, as Charles Hodge points out, was "voluntary and sincere." Now they were slaves of godliness.

One of the great teachings of the last half of Romans 6 is that faith and obedience are inseparable. As one author puts it, "There is no saving faith in God apart from obedience to God, and there can be no godly obedience without godly faith."

J. H. Sammis caught that connection in his popular hymn: "Trust and obey, for there's no other way to be happy in Jesus, but to trust and obey."

Father in heaven. Help me today to both trust and obey. Help me to be a witness to the principles of Your kingdom. Help me to know the victory that comes from walking with Jesus. Help me have that "from the heart" kind of experience that You want for each of Your children. Amen.

REAL SLAVERY

You have been set free from sin and have
become slaves to righteousness. Rom. 6:18, NIV.

ON JANUARY 1, 1863, President Abraham Lincoln released his Emancipation Proclamation, in which all slaves in those states warring against the United States government were "then, thenceforward, and forever free." "Forever free," but not free from poverty, discrimination, and racial prejudice.

Emancipation from sin provides a slightly different pattern. While Christ's followers had been delivered from the dominion and condemning power of sin, Paul was not naive enough to suggest that they would be absolutely free. He knew that freedom from the reign of sin did not release people to wander in an aimless moral vacuum. To the contrary, the apostle knew that freedom from sin meant enslavement to Christ and the right.

In order to understand Paul, we need to grasp the status of a slave in his society. In our culture, when we think of a servant, we imagine a person who gives an agreed amount of time to the boss or master. But when that time is up, servants can do whatever they want. Time during working hours belongs to the master, but afterward the servants can do as they please. They may clean the house by day and devote themselves to classical music in the evening.

But the status of slaves in Paul's day was quite different. They literally had no free time. All of their time belonged to the one who owned them. Thus they did not have a moment to do as they liked. It was impossible to serve two masters because all their time belonged exclusively to one master.

That picture is in Paul's mind. As William Barclay puts it: "At one time you were the slave of sin. Sin had exclusive possession of you. At that time you could not talk of anything else but sinning. But now you have God as your master. God has exclusive possession of you. And now you cannot even talk of sinning: you must talk about nothing but holiness."

With God, my friend, it is all or nothing. Persons who keep some little corner of life to themselves are not really Christians. Christians have surrendered complete control of their lives to Christ and His principles of life. They hold nothing back. And, as Barclay points out, "no man who has done that can even think of using grace as an excuse to sin."

DOCTRINE OF THE TWO PATHS

*Just as you once yielded your members to impurity and to
greater and greater iniquity, so now yield your members
to righteousness for sanctification. Rom. 6:19, RSV.*

SCRIPTURE IS CONSISTENTLY clear that neutrality is not an option. People either choose God and His ways or Satan and his. Psalm 1 is an excellent illustration of that point. The first three verses deal with the path of the godly, while the last three reflect on the way of the wicked.

"Blessed is the man
who walks not in the counsel of the wicked,
nor stands in the way of sinners, nor sits in the seat of scoffers;
but his delight is in the law of the Lord,
and on his law he meditates day and night.
He is like a tree planted by streams of water,
that yields its fruit in its season, and its leaf does not wither.
In all that he does, he prospers.
The wicked are not so,
but are like chaff which the wind drives away.
Therefore the wicked will not stand in the judgment,
nor sinners in the congregation of the righteous;
for the Lord knows the way of the righteous,
but the way of the wicked will perish" (Ps. 1:1-6, RSV).

The contrast we find in Psalm 1 is exactly the same as in Romans 6:19-23. Not only are there two quite distinct pathways (the ways of the righteous and the wicked), but the two paths lead to two quite different ends. The way of the God-fearing person becomes like a well-watered tree that bears fruit and prospers, whereas the end of the wicked is to perish. Paul would put it a little differently in Romans 6:23: "The wages of sin is death; but the gift of God is eternal life," yet the picture is the same.

Note also that in both Psalm 1 and Romans 6 the two paths are dynamic rather than static. Psalm 1 presents a progression from *walking* in the way of sin, to stopping and *standing* in it, to finally being so relaxed and comfortable that *sitting* in the way of sin is a viable option (verses 1, 2). Similarly, Paul speaks of those who yield themselves to "greater and greater iniquity."

The Bible presents the way of the righteous as dynamic also. The path of God's people is one of increasing holiness that Paul refers to with the word "sanctification."

TWO TYPES OF SHAME

*When you were slaves of sin, you weren't concerned with
doing what was right. And what was the result? It was not
good, since now you are ashamed of the things you used
to do, things that end in eternal doom. Rom. 6:20, 21, NLT.*

WHAT AM I ASHAMED about in my life? And what am I proud of? The answers to both questions say a great deal about who I am.

From my earliest days of becoming a Christian at the age of 19 I have been interested in what the Bible has to say about shame. Perhaps my concern was because, like most teenagers, I didn't want to be different, I wanted to belong to the group, and now all of a sudden I had become a Christian. I felt proud about my new status and could easily express it in my circle of Christian friends, but I wasn't quite sure how to "expose" my new belief and way of life to my old buddies. In fact, I found it easier to hide the new me. Thus I was stuck in the tension between my old and new identities. In my spiritual immaturity I wasn't completely settled in what I was ashamed of or proud of.

Two texts struck me with great force in those early days. The first was Mark 8:38, in which I heard Jesus telling me that He would be ashamed of those who were ashamed of Him when He returned to the earth. The second was Romans 1:16, in which Paul proclaimed that he was not ashamed of the gospel, for it was God's power to save. I found those texts fascinating because I *was* ashamed, so much so that I found it hard even to open my mouth in certain circles about my new faith.

God had begun to lead me down His path. But I hadn't gone very far yet. In fact, in looking back I realize that I wasn't fully ashamed of my previous sinful ways. At times I still looked back longingly over my shoulder at the "good times" I had had and of the people I had taken advantage of.

Then one day a few months after my baptism as I was "sizing up" a young woman while my wife finished the shopping, God spoke so loud that I couldn't avoid the message. "What are you looking at? And why?" was the message that drummed through my somewhat overheated brain.

That very moment I knew that God had another step for me to take in the path of holiness. He wanted me to be proud of my faith in Him and ashamed of those things I used to do that had led to so much misery.

God wants to guide each of us down the path that leads to life.

Help us, Father, this day to take Your hand and follow Your lead.

Two Freedoms

*But now that you have been freed from sin and
enslaved to God, the advantage you get is sanctification.
The end is eternal life. Rom. 6:22, NRSV.*

THE TWO FREEDOMS. You, my friend, are freer than you think. God gives you freedom to sin if you so desire, or freedom to walk the way of holiness. He forces no one. But neither does He protect us from the consequences of our actions. As a Christian you have the liberty to lay down in the middle of the Interstate freeway at rush hour if you so choose. But God won't create a miracle to keep you safe. The same applies to substance abuse. You are free to smoke 10 packs of cigarettes a day if you have the time and inclination, but God won't intervene to protect you from lung cancer or emphysema. We live in a moral universe in which people harvest what they sow.

The harvest we eventually reap depends on the type of seeds we plant throughout life. Those who sow seeds of destruction will eventually see the result. The same goes for those who nourish seeds of love and caring.

Now, we may be free to sin, but the good news is that Christians do not have to be enslaved to addictive habits that lead to destruction. In fact, Paul tells us in today's text, God has released Christians from their enslavement to sin. They have been set free. And just as they were totally dedicated to sin, now, Paul notes, they will be just as committed to God and His ways—they will be "enslaved to God."

Paul tells us that one of the advantages the Christian gets from serving God is "sanctification." That word means not only to be set apart for holy use but to walk progressively closer to God as through His grace we trod the path of holiness.

D. Martyn Lloyd-Jones caught the contrast inherent in the two freedoms when he wrote: "As you go on living this righteous life, and practicing it with all your might and energy, and all your time . . . you will find that the process that went on before, in which you went from bad to worse and became viler and viler, is entirely reversed. You will become cleaner and cleaner, and purer and purer, and holier and holier, and more and more conformed unto the image of the Son of God."

Thank You, Lord, for giving us the freedom to walk with You in the pathway of life. Thank You that through the process of sanctification You help us become more like You.

TWO DESTINATIONS

The wages of sin is death. Rom. 6:23.

THAT IS ABOUT as blunt as one can get. "The wages of sin is death." The text goes on to note that "the gift of God is eternal life through Jesus Christ our Lord." Just as there are two paths (Rom. 6:19), and two types of shame (verses 20, 21), and two different freedoms (verse 22), so there are also two quite distinct destinations (verse 23).

The Bible is quite explicit that the two destinations are clearly related to the two paths, the two shames, and the two freedoms. God is not arbitrary. All persons, in the face of the knowledge they possess (Romans 1 and 2), choose the path they want to walk through life, but each path has a specific destination. Every choice, every action in life leads somewhere. And God in His wisdom and greatness allows people to select the route that they will individually follow.

In today's text Paul warns us that the end of the line for the path of sin is death. And, you may be thinking, what does he mean by death? It can't be physical death, because everybody, all the way from the most sincere Christians to the most unrepentant sinners, dies physically.

The clue to the apostle's meaning appears in the last half of our passage, in which he contrasts death with the reward of the righteous—"eternal life." He does not have earthly life and death in mind here, but eternal life and death.

The Bible consistently speaks of the final end of the wicked as "death" rather than continual suffering in an eternally burning hell. Thus Scripture describes them as "consumed" (RSV) by the lake of fire at the end of time (Rev. 20:9). That passage goes on to refer to that event as the "second death" (verse 14). In a similar manner, Malachi says that hellfire at the end of time will "burn them up" (Mal. 4:1).

God is not an infinite Hitler who tortures people who have misused their freedom throughout the ceaseless ages of eternity. Neither does He deny them freedom to choose the addictive and destructive sins so much in today's headlines. Rather, in His wisdom, He allows individuals the freedom to become what they have chosen. And since His loving character can't let the destructive consequences of their lives go on forever and ever, He does the best thing possible in a bad situation. At the end of time He makes them as if they had never been. That is what Paul and John are speaking of when they refer to the second or eternal death.

ETERNAL LIFE IS NOW!

But the gift of God is eternal life
through Jesus Christ our Lord. Rom. 6:23.

SEVERAL THINGS JUMP out at us when we read today's verse. The first is that salvation is a gift pure and simple. Of course, that is nothing new to those who have stayed with Paul so far through Romans. From Romans 1:18 to 3:20 he showed us why it had to be a gift; because sinners had no way to earn it. Then between Romans 3:21 and 5:21 he set forth and expounded upon the gracious gift itself. And now in chapter 6 he has been reflecting upon its effects in human lives, telling us that those who have accepted the gift enter a new life in which their highest desire will be to walk with God in the principles of His kingdom. Here in Romans 6:23 he is merely reinforcing the fact that those who accept the gift and have chosen to walk in the way of holiness rather than in the way of sin will live with God throughout eternity.

At this point we should note that eternal life for Christians is not something completely new but rather a continuation of what they have begun with Christ here on earth. That is clear from John, who writes that "he who believes in the Son has eternal life" (John 3:36, RSV). Again, Jesus promised that "he who hears my word and believes him who sent me, has eternal life; he does not come into judgment [i.e., condemnation], but has passed from death to life" (John 5:24, RSV).

Part of the gospel is that Christians already have eternal life through Jesus Christ. Ellen White reflects upon that concept when she writes that "the life on earth is the beginning of the life in heaven. . . . What we now are, in character and holy service, is the sure foreshadowing of what we shall be" (*Education*, p. 307).

Of course, in that passage Ellen White moves a bit beyond what Paul is explicitly stating. She is reflecting on the continuation of eternal life in heaven, though it is a topic that Paul was fully in harmony with.

Both of them also agree about the two paths and the life choices that lead people to different destinations. And both of them would concur on who will be in heaven. It will be those who have so internalized the great principles of God's character that they will be happy to be with God throughout the ceaseless ages of eternity. God forces no one to be what they aren't.

WHOSE WIFE, CHRIST'S OR THE LAW'S?

The Law can only exercise authority over a
man so long as he is alive. Rom. 7:1, Phillips.

WITH ROMANS 7 WE come to a major shift in Paul's argument. In the last half of chapter 6 he stressed that the believer is not under the rule of sin. Now in chapter 7 he goes on to make the point that believers are not under the mastery of law either.

The parallels between chapters 6 and 7 are quite forceful. In Romans 6:2 Paul tells us that the believer has died to sin, in Romans 7:4 that they have died to law. In Romans 6:7, 18 he depicts believers as free from sin, and in Romans 7:4 they are free from law. Finally, in Romans 6:4 believers walk in newness of life, while in Romans 7:6 they serve in newness of Spirit.

In these two chapters Paul indicates that Christians look at things and experience life and even religion from a new perspective. Romans 7 in particular is an expansion of Paul's statement in Romans 6:14 that "ye are not under the law, but under grace."

In partial explanation of that statement the apostle has already used illustrations related to baptism and slavery. Now in Romans 7:1-6 he draws an analogy from marriage law.

In order to realize the force of the illustration we need to remember that keeping the law was the way that pious Jews expected to gain salvation. The rich young man who told Jesus that he had observed all the commandments was quite sincere in his desire for perfection (Matt. 19:16-30), and when Paul writes that as a Pharisee he had been blameless regarding the law (Phil. 3:6), he was speaking in terms of sober fact as far as the Pharisaic mind perceived things. Yet in Christ he found a new life, new power, new joy, and new peace that he had never known before.

In Romans 7:1-3, using the marriage relationship as an analogy, he notes that a wife is bound to her husband as long as he lives, but that after his death she is free to marry another. Paul's argument is complex, but his meaning is clear. As F. F. Bruce points out, "death—the believer's death-with-Christ—breaks the bond which formerly yoked him to the law, and now he is free to enter into union with Christ." The law proved to be fruitless as a way of salvation. Union with the law brought sin and death, but union with Christ brings life eternal.

WHOSE DEATH, MINE OR THE LAW'S?

So, my brothers, you also died to the law through the body of
Christ, that you might belong to another, to him who was raised
from the dead, in order that we might bear fruit to God. Rom. 7:4, NIV.

DEAD TO THE LAW! In Romans 7:1-3 we noted that death puts an end to the legal obligation of marriage. Now in verse 4 Paul applies that illustration to Christian experience, but with a slight shift in characters. The illustration of verses 1-3 had the death of the husband freeing the wife from the law. But in the application of verse 4 the death of sinful self releases believers from the condemnation and dominion of the law and frees them to join Christ.

And how is it that Christians have "died to the law"? That death took place when they allowed their old selves to be "crucified" with Christ as they entered the watery grave of baptism (see Romans 6:3-6). The believer's death with Christ is a death to the law as a way of salvation. Trusting to the grace of God means putting to death any trust in the law as the road to heaven.

Christians are those who know that they have nothing good in themselves, that God did not give the law to save people, and that faith in Jesus is the only way to life eternal. They have died to all forms of self-sufficiency and lawkeeping as the road to life.

At this point we should be careful. It is the believer who died, not the law. The law is still alive and well, and as Paul will point out a little further in the chapter, the law is holy, just, good, and spiritual (Rom. 7:12, 14). But God never gave it so that people could save themselves by keeping it.

The law is not dead. As John Calvin, the great Reformer, notes, "we ought carefully to remember that this is not a release from the righteousness which is taught in the law." The law still stands as God's great standard of righteousness, it still condemns the sin of those who break it, and it still pushes men and women to the foot of the cross for cleansing from guilt and sin. But it has no cleansing power in itself. When people become dead to the law as a way of salvation, then they can be resurrected and remarried to God's true plan of salvation in Christ.

And in that new union they will produce fruit for God's kingdom. That fruit, as Paul noted in Romans 6:22, would be fruit to "holiness."

LIFE "IN THE FLESH"

While we were living in the flesh, our sinful passions,
aroused by the law, were at work in our members
to bear fruit for death. Rom. 7:5, RSV.

WHAT DOES PAUL MEAN by "living in the flesh"? We need to take a look at Paul's use of that phrase in its context. "Flesh" is an important word for Paul. Of its nearly 150 appearances in the New Testament, he uses it more than 90 times. But he utilizes the word in many different ways. In Romans 6:19, for example, he employed flesh in the sense of bodily weakness that led to moral weakness. It has that sense in today's text.

Thus when Paul speaks in the past tense about Christians "living in the flesh" he refers to the time when they "were controlled by the sinful nature" (NIV). Sinful nature is characterized by "fleshly desires and outlook." In that sense Paul contrasts "living in the flesh" in Romans 7:5 to living in the Spirit in verse 6. The first he and other Christians had when they lived under the dominion of sin, while the second came with the dominion of righteousness.

We must not equate living in the flesh with living in an earthly body. Rather, Paul is speaking to the fact that when the Romans used to live according to their lower nature (their sinful nature) the law aroused their sinful passions and produced deadly fruit.

And how, you may be asking yourself, did something as good and holy as God's law arouse sinful passions and produce death in people? For the answer to that, we need to go back and look at what Paul has already said in Romans about the law. In Romans 3:20 he pointed out that the function of the law is to identify sin, in Romans 4:15 he added that the law brings wrath and condemnation, and in Romans 5:20 Paul went so far as to say that the law increased sin in the sense that it made the meaning of sin explicit. Those who have the law, in that sense, have grounds for defining more things as sin than those who have no law.

But here in Romans 7:5 Paul seems to be going a bit further by indicating that the law actually produces sin itself. How? Think for a moment of the small child to whom you say: "No, don't touch that!" What is the first thing he or she does? Often cautiously to reach out one finger to touch the forbidden object. In the same way, those "living in the flesh" are tempted to rebel against God. God's answer is spiritual rebirth so that people no longer "live in the flesh" but in the Spirit.

172

LIFE IN THE SPIRIT

But now we are discharged from the law, dead to that
which held us captive, so that we are slaves not under the
old written code but in the new life of the Spirit. Rom. 7:6, NRSV.

BOYS ARE STRANGE creatures. When they are young, parents often have to develop rules related to the brushing of teeth, the combing of hair, and the washing of necks. I still remember having read in a comic strip about a boy whose mother caught him lying about his bath because the soap wasn't wet. To my mind that was very useful information. Thereafter whenever an adult told me to take a bath I always made sure the soap was wet, even if I hadn't used it.

Then came the big turning point in my life. I overheard the girl I had fallen for describing to her friend a guy who grossed her out because he had green on his teeth and smelled like sweat. That did it. It was the turning point in my sanitary life. Toothbrushing and two showers a day of about 20 to 30 minutes each (with lots of soap and shampoo) became the order of the day. Now I had become a problem to the family in another way. With six of us sharing the same bathroom, I was hogging the shower.

Why the radical change? I had fallen in "love," and nothing could stop me. I was keeping clean because I wanted to, not because Mom was going to punish me if I disobeyed.

Something like that happens when we come to Christ. In the past, Paul tells the Romans, they had been held captive to the condemnation of the law. People may have done their best to keep it in order to escape punishment, but their best was never good enough. Slaves to the law, they had no security or genuine peace with God.

But things changed when they realized the fullness of the gospel, including what God had done for them through Christ. At that point obedience became a response to love. It was transforming love empowered by God's Holy Spirit.

Christians may be free from the bondage of the law, but that freedom does not mean liberty to do what the law forbids (see Rom. 6:1, 15; 3:31). Freedom from the law does not offer license to sin. Just the opposite. For the first time in their lives, those who have become Christians are truly able to keep the law, since they have been reborn by the Holy Spirit. Now they no longer face the law as a dour legalist, but as one who is in love and can say with David, "O how I love thy law" (Ps. 119:97, RSV).

A Third "What Then?"

What shall we say, then? Is the law sin? Certainly not! Rom. 7:7, NIV.

"WHAT SHALL WE SAY, then?" For the third time Paul uses this literary technique. It forms part of a dialogue triggered by his adversaries' claim that if sin increased it would multiply grace. Therefore sin might be a good thing.

Paul's first "What then" showed up in Romans 6:1, in which he pictured his detractors as saying "shall we go on sinning so that grace may increase?" (NIV). Violently rejecting the idea, he demonstrated that no true Christian could ever think that way because they had died to sin and been resurrected to a new life in Christ (Rom. 6:2-14).

His second "What then" came in verse 15, in which the apostle pictured his adversaries asking whether sin was appropriate because Christians were not under law but under grace. Once again he aggressively dismissed that suggestion by showing how grace leads to the obedience of faith (verses 15-23) and that even though Christians have died to law as a way of salvation they still serve God in the new and deeper way of the Spirit (Rom. 7:1-6).

In the process of his explanation, Paul has said some pretty unflattering things about the law: that it "was added so that the trespass might increase" (Rom. 5:20, NIV); that it "brings wrath" (Rom. 4:15, NIV); and that it aroused the "sinful passions" (Rom. 7:5, NIV).

He fears that some will conclude from what he has said that the law is evil in itself. Once again he will vigorously react to such a suggestion, using the same Greek words as in Romans 6:2 and 6:15, translated as "by no means!" The rest of chapter 7 he will spend defending the goodness, holiness, and spirituality of the law and helping his readers to see that it is not the law that is the problem but sinful humanity's misuse of it.

Paul here walks a tightrope in his discussion of the law. On the one hand, he desires to help his readers see that it is a disaster when employed as a way of salvation. On the other hand, he wants people to recognize that the law is a good gift from God and, if rightly used, is of great importance in the life of believers. In Romans 7 Paul provides us with one of his most significant discussions of the role of the law in the lives of Christians. One of the most important things we need to understand is the law's true place in our walk with God.

Sin's Deeper Meaning

On the contrary, I would not have come to know sin except through the Law; for I would not have known about coveting if the Law had not said, "You shall not covet." Rom. 7:7, NASB.

"ON THE CONTRARY." Taken in its context today's verse means "Of course the law isn't sin, because it is the law that defines sin."

In Romans 1:20 and 2:14, 15 Paul pointed out that even those without the revealed law have an idea of right and wrong. But those people without the law don't really see wrongdoing as being against God. As Leon Morris points out, "there is a great difference between the breaching of a human moral code and sin, that evil thing which God forbids. It takes the law to show wrongdoing to be sin." And to see wrongdoing as sin against God helps people feel sin's weight and their need of a Savior. Thus the law does have an *indirect* salvific function.

Paul illustrates his claim that he would never have known sin without the law by referring to the tenth commandment. That is an interesting and insightful choice because it is the only one of the Ten Commandments that explicitly moves beyond outward actions to the inward root that undergirds sinful acts. That is, worshipping an idol, keeping the Sabbath, stealing, and honoring one's parents are all external behaviors or outward actions. Because of that, most people, including many Pharisees in Paul's day, identify sin as a behavior.

Paul, in deliberately selecting the tenth commandment, goes behind the behavior to the lusting motivation that undergirds it. In other words, he is saying that sin is much deeper than our outward acts. Jesus did the same thing in the Sermon on the Mount when He illustrated the height and depth and width of sin in His discussion of murder and adultery in the heart. Again He raised the same point in Matthew 15:18, 19, in which He claimed that sinful actions proceed out of a corrupt heart.

The apostle's selection of the tenth commandment is an extremely important contribution to our understanding of the law and sin precisely because it goes beneath the surface and relates them to that sinful self-centeredness that leads people to commit acts of sin in the sense of the other nine commandments.

Thus Paul refuses to see sin and conversion to Christ as surface matters. With him both are issues of the heart. That is also true of both lawbreaking and lawkeeping. The law has a deeper level than mere behavior.

SIN USES THE LAW

*Sin, taking opportunity through the commandment,
produced in me coveting of every kind; for apart
from the Law sin is dead. Rom. 7:8, NASB.*

ONCE AGAIN PAUL personifies sin—this time as a military aggressor. The word used for "opportunity" originally meant a starting point or base of operations for an expedition, especially a military campaign. Thus he depicts sin as an aggressor to lead people astray.

And how does sin accomplish its task? Surprisingly, Paul suggests that sin uses the commandment for its evil task. Then, once again, he employs the tenth commandment to illustrate his point: "Sin, taking opportunity through the commandment, produced in me coveting of every kind."

How can evil use God's "good" commandment (Rom. 7:12) to produce sin? Paul had earlier alluded to this issue in verse 5, in which he claimed the law aroused our sinful passions. Here in verse 8 he takes his logic to its natural conclusion in stating that the law produces sin.

How? Think about it for a minute. Remember the illustration we used in discussing verse 5—that when you tell young children not to touch a certain object, they suddenly have an overwhelming desire to gingerly put out one finger to do the forbidden thing?

Our adult minds operate in much the same way. If I am driving out in the middle of the desert and suddenly come to a sign that reduces the speed limit to 45 miles per hour, my mind immediately asks "Why?" and I am not only a bit perturbed at an arbitrary restriction of my freedom but tempted not to slow down, since I see nothing to slow down for.

In a similar fashion, one of my friends illustrates the issue with the command not to think about pink elephants. Even if you haven't thought about a pink elephant for years, the very command not to think about them puts them vividly in your mind. Paul says something similar about coveting. The command not to covet awakens in him thoughts about doing so.

Thus even though the commandments are good, sin drives the unrenewed person to see them as a limitation on freedom, and thus a cause of resentment and opposition. Without something to rebel against there are no rebels.

The real culprit, Paul is telling us, is not the law but sin, which is hostile to the law (Rom. 8:7). Sin twists the function of the law from exposing sin to that of provoking it.

THE BIRTH OF SPIRITUAL BANKRUPTCY

I was once alive apart from the Law; but when the commandment came, sin became alive and I died. Rom. 7:9, NASB.

DO YOU REALLY BELIEVE that? How could any Jewish boy of Paul's day from a pious family ever be "apart from the law"?

In its context Paul's words don't so much claim that he had had no knowledge of the law, but rather that he had not realized the full force and full depth of the law's demands and therefore lacked personal conviction of his sin. In Philippians 3:6, for example, he recalls the days when he deemed himself to be "blameless" "as to righteousness under the law" (RSV). Like the rich young ruler, he congratulated himself for having kept the commandments from his youth up (Matt. 19:20). And like the praying Pharisee, he could be thankful that he was not a sinner like other people (Luke 18:11).

"But when the commandment came, sin became alive." When Paul finally felt the full meaning, the full force, of the law, when the law became alive to him, at that point he realized that he was indeed a sinner. If, for example, he has in mind the command not to covet, he suddenly realized that he was infected by self-centeredness. That he wasn't really as "blameless" as he thought he was.

At that point sin sprang to life in him. Sin had, of course, always been there, but in the full light of the commandment he could recognize it for the first time for what it was. No longer could he ignore its existence. Because he had come to see the full depth of the commandment he also had come to realize that he was indeed a sinner, in spite of his sinful pride in his righteousness.

The result? He died. That death is not the Christian's death to sin that he spoke of in Romans 6:2, but death to his spiritual pride, self-confidence, and self-reliance. He realized his hopelessness, that the law, when he really understood it, left him destitute.

Paul's experience is that of every person. All must come to the place where they die to their personal righteousness, their ability to keep the law on their own, their ability to earn their own salvation. It is at that point that they began to feel their need of Christ's righteousness to cover their barrenness. Thus the full light of the law points us to Christ as our only hope.

DECEPTIVE COMMANDMENT KEEPING

*The very commandment which promised life proved to be
death to me. For sin, finding opportunity in the commandment,
deceived me and by it killed me. Rom. 7:10, 11, RSV.*

PAUL IS RIGHT ON when he said that the commandment promised life.
God never meant His law for death. He created it as a standard of righteousness. It presents the principles that lead to life. The psalmist was
quite clear about the blessedness of those "who walk in the law of the
Lord" (Ps. 119:1, 2). And even Jesus told a Jewish lawyer that if he kept
the law he would live (Luke 10:28).

The trouble is that since Adam's fall it has been impossible for people to fully obey God's law. Ellen White makes that point explicit when
she writes that "it was possible for Adam, before the fall, to form a righteous character by obedience to God's law. But he failed to do this, and
because of his sin our natures are fallen and we cannot make ourselves
righteous. Since we are sinful, unholy, we cannot perfectly obey the holy
law" (*Steps to Christ,* p. 62).

But sin doesn't tell us that. Rather it assures us that if we try hard
enough we will become good enough, that we can even become sinlessly
perfect through obedience to the law. Or as Paul puts it, "sin, finding opportunity in the commandment," deceives us into believing a lie.

The lie is that we can do it on our own, that we can become good people by keeping the law, that we can even make God look good by doing
what He commanded. The deceptiveness that had trapped Paul and others
is that one does not expect God's commandment to be the occasion of
death. Since the law appears to be the way to life, when actually it isn't,
sin utilizes the misunderstanding to bring about death.

It is interesting that every false religion, including erroneous approaches
to Christianity, in one way or another builds on self-effort, self-righteousness, and self-trust. *The Desire of Ages* claims that "the principle that man
can save himself by his own works lay at the foundation of every heathen religion; it had . . . become the principle of the Jewish religion" (pp. 35, 36).

The law, for all of its good points, never sought to save from sin. To
believe that will only lead to our eternal death. I suppose that if Paul could
have only one motto it might be "Look Unto Jesus."

THE GOOD SIDE OF THE LAW

*Wherefore the law is holy, and the commandment
holy, and just, and good. Rom. 7:12.*

WITH TODAY'S VERSE the apostle has come full circle in the argument that he has been presenting since verse 7, in which he pictures his detractors asking if the law is sin. He blasted that suggestion with his usual "by no means" or "certainly not." But he supplies a second answer in today's verse: The law is not only not sin but to the contrary it is "holy, and the commandment holy, and just, and good."

Sin may have abused the law and sinners may have put it to wrong use, as Paul emphasized in Romans 7:8-11, but that is no reflection on the law itself. The apostle lets his readers know that it is sin that is the culprit and that the law itself is as good as things get. In fact, for the rest of the chapter he continues to uplift the law, calling it "spiritual" in verse 14 and "good" in verse 16, while claiming that his "inward man" delights in it in verse 22. There is not the slightest doubt that Paul the apostle has extremely positive feelings about the law. His expression of those positive feelings is just as definite as his negative ones toward the wrong use of the law.

Paul is quite in harmony with the great passages in the Old Testament that praise the law. In Psalm 19, for example, David claims that "the law of the Lord is perfect, reviving the soul; the testimony of the Lord is sure, making wise the simple; the precepts of the Lord are right, rejoicing the heart; the commandment of the Lord is pure, enlightening the eyes; the fear of the Lord is clean, enduring for ever; the ordinances of the Lord are true, and righteous altogether. More to be desired are they than gold, even much fine gold; sweeter also than honey and drippings of the honeycomb" (verses 7-10, RSV).

As one author puts it, "the fact that the law reveals, arouses, and condemns sin and brings death to the sinner does not make the law itself evil. When a person is justly convicted and sentenced for murder, there is no fault in the law or with those responsible for upholding it. The fault is in the one who broke the law."

Paul the converted Christian still loves God's law. Only now he sees how he and others had employed it for purposes for which God had never intended. But when it is rightly used it is indeed "holy, and just, and good."

THE UTTER SINFULNESS OF SIN

Did that which is good become a cause of death for me? May it never be! Rather it was sin, in order that it might be shown to be sin by effecting my death through that which is good, so that through the commandment sin would become utterly sinful. Rom. 7:13, NASB.

NOW, HERE IS A complicated verse. The New Living Translation helps us see the meaning a bit more clearly: "Did the law, which is good, cause my doom? Of course not! Sin used what was good to bring about my condemnation. So we can see how terrible sin really is. It uses God's good commandment for its own evil purposes."

Let's look at the three main parts of our text. First, Paul moves his argument forward again by the use of a question: Was the good law the agent of death? As with the three previous questions in chapters 6 and 7 he vigorously rejects that suggestion with the strong phrase "By no means!" It is not the law that causes death, but sin.

At that juncture Paul moves to his second point in verse 13: Sin uses the good law to bring about condemnation, a truth he had previously raised in verse 10. How is that? The law identifies sin not merely as evil but as willful rebellion against God and the principles of His kingdom. That rebellion results in the penalty of death. But it wasn't the law that caused the death; rather, the sin identified by the law. Going back to the analogy of a murder trial that we looked at yesterday, it is the act of murder that merits punishment rather than the law against murder. The law has the good and healthy function of pointing out what is wrong. We shouldn't blame the law for the crime. The blame belongs to the sin that motivated it.

That brings us to the apostle's third point: the "utterly" sinfulness of sin. William Barclay helps us grasp the "utterly" character of sin when he pens that "the awfulness of sin is shown by the fact that it could take a fine, and splendid and lovely thing, and make it a weapon of evil. That is what sin does. Sin can take the loveliness of love and turn it into lust. Sin can take the honourable desire for independence and turn it into the lust for money and for power. Sin can take the beauty of friendship and use it as a seduction to the wrong things. That is what Carlyle called 'the infinite damnability of sin.' The very fact that sin took the law and made the law a bridgehead to sin shows the supreme sinfulness of sin."

Help me today, Lord, to see the utter deceptiveness of sin. Help me to have clear eyes to see Your law in its truth and beauty.

CHRISTIANS IN TENSION

*We know that the law is spiritual; but I am
carnal, sold under sin. Rom. 7:14, RSV.*

WITH ROMANS 7:14 WE encounter a highly controversial part of the book of Romans. Most of the debate on Romans 7:14-25 centers on who the "I" is; whether it is Paul, whether it is referring to people before they become Christians, or to them after they have done so. But we need to recognize that Paul is not so much concerned with our questions about human nature as he is about the law.

Unfortunately, it is impossible to interpret his words without taking a position on what he is implying about human nature. That wouldn't be so bad, but he appears in these 12 verses to make statements that apply both to the converted and the unconverted. Thus he can use the "I" in verse 22 to describe someone who delights in God's law and in verse 14 to picture a carnal person. Whoever the "I" is, it is a person in tension between good and evil.

The most adequate solution is to see the "I" in the passage that runs from Romans 7:14 to 7:25 as a true Christian when he or she has fallen into sin. That condition is not the full picture of their Christian life, since the victory aspect of that life is so clear in chapter 8. But here are individuals who know the good but cry out in anguish about their wretchedness when they don't do what they should.

All Christians identify with this passage on a psychological level. No believer is completely without sin. We are all caught in the tension. Thus the "I" has an existential aspect that we all face in daily life. Paul illustrates that existential aspect by using insights from his own experience.

To grasp Paul's expressions we need to recall how we feel when we fall into doing what we know is wrong in spite of what we would like to be. I don't know about you, but my cry is "O wretched man that I am!" (Rom. 7:24). I feel like kicking myself.

Remember, the apostle is not describing the entirety of a Christian's life. But even if that life is generally victorious and Christians have the peace and joy of their faith, at other times they still identify with Isaiah, who declared "Woe is me! . . . For I am a man of unclean lips" (Isa. 6:5, RSV), and with Peter, who in the midst of a crisis fell at Jesus' feet, exclaiming, "Depart from me, for I am a sinful man, O Lord" (Luke 5:8, RSV).

THE TENSION BETWEEN DESIRE AND ACTION

*I cannot understand my own actions; I do not act as I desire to act;
on the contrary, I do what I detest. Rom. 7:15, Moffatt.*

HERE IS SOMETHING that we can identify with. Do you always do the right thing? This verse obviously has in mind somebody whose heart is right toward God. The person knows what is right and has a deep desire to do so, but commits actions that conflict with that desire.

Why? What is the problem here? The answer begins up in Romans 7:14, in which Paul speaks of the divided self: "We know that the law is spiritual: but I am carnal, sold under sin." The word "carnal" points to human nature in its creaturely weakness. The apostle contrasts it with being spiritual, thus implying an inclination to sinfulness or self-indulgence.

Paul concludes verse 14 by noting that he is not only carnal and weak but that he is "sold under sin." That phrase at the very least reflects a periodically recurring residue of the slavery to sin that once ruled him all the time, a slavery that led him at times to do what he knew to be wrong.

The tension between knowing and desiring the right but from time to time doing the wrong leads us to verse 15, in which Paul declares that sometimes he doesn't understand his own actions, since he does not always act as he desires but does what he detests. James Denney points out that only the idea of "slavery explains his acts."

It is absolutely imperative when reading these verses to realize that Paul is not talking about the better times in Christian living. He is not saying that he never does right, but rather that he isn't as free from error as he would like to be. Nor is he saying that he does evil habitually or never does good. Of course, he isn't here concerned with the good. The apostle desires that and expects to live that kind of life. The problem is that sometimes he doesn't. By using the slavery metaphor, he expresses the thought that he still finds sin to be a powerful force and that he hasn't managed to resist it every moment.

Paul's insights fit in quite well with those of Jesus, who tells us that God forgives repentant sinners 70 times seven times, and with John, who states that God's ideal is that we don't sin at all, but that if we do, as Christians we can confess and God will "forgive our sins and cleanse us from all unrighteousness" (1 John 1:9, RSV).

THE TENSION BETWEEN GOD'S LAW AND IMPERFECT HUMANITY

Now if I do what I do not want, I agree that the
law is good. But in fact it is no longer I that do it,
but sin that dwells within me. Rom. 7:16, 17, NRSV.

IN THESE TWO VERSES we come to the heart of what Paul is trying to tell us in Romans 7:14-20. His main point is that it is not the law that is the problem but us as less than perfect people.

In chapter 7 Paul responds to two questions about the law: First, was it sin? And second, did it bring death? (Rom. 7:7, 8). With his claim that the law is "good" in verse 16 he answers both questions.

All right then, if the law is so good, why does it create so much trouble for us? It is that very question that Paul answers in Romans 7:14-20.

As we look at his answer in today's text we need to recognize several things. First, as we noted above, Paul fully believed in the law's goodness. Thus Paul does not oppose the law. He agrees with it.

Beyond that, the very fact that Paul calls the law good when he has done what he did not want to do (broke the law or sinned) demonstrates that it is not the real Paul behind the action. That is, his new man, his Christian self, is wholeheartedly confessing the goodness and blamelessness of the law. As a redeemed person he longs to honor the depth of the law and fulfill it perfectly.

Every Christian is like Paul in that sense. Each has a sense of the law's moral excellence and a desire to be in harmony with it. Beyond that, the more mature Christians become, the more they perceive the holiness and glory and goodness of God's law of love, the greater will be their desire to be in harmony with it.

Paul knows that it is not the law that is at fault in the tension he experiences, but the "sin that dwells within" him. The apostle had discovered what each of us also learns. Sin, in the words of Leon Morris, is no longer the "honored guest" it used to be before conversion, "nor the paying tenant, but the 'squatter,' not legitimately there, but very difficult to eject." Wesley, as we noted earlier, said much the same thing when he commented that in a Christian's life sin no longer reigns, but it does remain.

Help us, Lord, to learn how to deal with both sin and law in a healthy manner.

THE ROOT OF THE TENSION

I know that nothing good dwells within me, that is, in my flesh.
I can will what is right, but I cannot do it. Rom. 7:18, NRSV.

THAT THE LAW IS GOOD Paul has not the slightest doubt. It is not the law that is the problem or the cause of his tension. Rather it is his "flesh." As for the flesh, Paul says that it has "nothing good" about it. Thus the contrast is crystal clear: "good" law but "nothing good" in him.

Is that really true? Is there nothing good in Paul? After all, hadn't he just said that he approved of the law and desired in his inmost being to keep it? Those are certainly good attributes.

We need to recognize that the apostle uses a qualifier when he speaks of the "nothing good." He alerts us to the fact that the "nothing good" in him really refers to his "flesh." Here Paul is using flesh to refer to his "sinful nature." Thus he in effect contrasts his lower nature (his fleshly self) with his higher nature (his spiritual self).

In the process of coming to an understanding of Paul's meaning of flesh, we need to realize that he did not agree with those Greek philosophers who taught that the flesh was evil in itself. To the contrary, he looked forward to the actual resurrection of the body—something unthinkable to those Greeks who saw bodily existence as evil. For Paul the problem was not that the flesh is inherently evil but that it is weak, prone to succumb to temptation, and unable to always do the good that he approved of. Ernst Käsemann is helpful here when he notes that "flesh is, terminologically, the workshop of sin." And, as we know, the devil is an expert in knowing how to manipulate that particular "workshop."

Before leaving verse 18, we need to recognize where it moves beyond verses 15 and 16 in speaking to the topic of human weakness. In the earlier verses Paul has told us that he cannot stop doing things of which he disapproves. But here he adds that he can't put into action the things that he does approve of.

The flesh is truly weak. As Käsemann puts it: "A human being is not seen as one who can fight against his destiny, and can change his fate, as the moral self tries to do." We need help outside of ourselves.

And it is to that help that this chapter inexorably heads. Our only hope is in Christ Jesus our Lord.

184

YOU AREN'T THE ONLY
ONE WITH UPS AND DOWNS

For I do not do the good I want, but the evil I do not want is
what I do. Now if I do what I do not want, it is no longer I that
do it, but sin which dwells within me. Rom. 7:19, RSV.

THE FRUSTRATION GOES ON! In these verses Paul sums up both his inability to do good and to totally avoid evil. As a Christian who knows the depth of his weakness he is in agony of soul. He feels that there is nothing commendable about himself.

Once again, note that he is not saying that he cannot do anything good at all. Rather, as a Christian he mourns the fact that he is incapable of completely fulfilling the requirements of the law. He expressed something similar to that desire to the Philippians: "Not that I . . . am already perfect; but I press on to make it my own, because Christ Jesus has made me his own. Brethren, I do not consider that I have made it my own; but one thing I do, forgetting what lies behind and straining forward to what lies ahead, I press on toward the goal for the prize of the upward call of God in Christ Jesus" (Phil. 3:12-14, RSV).

It is one thing for individuals to come to Jesus and give their life to Him, confess their sins, receive justification and a new heart and mind, and be set apart for holy use in God's service. Those things all happen in a moment. But just because people have become Christians does not mean that they are fully sanctified or holy. John Wesley, Ellen White, and others have quite correctly identified progressive sanctification (growth toward becoming more like God) to be the work of a lifetime.

The Christian walk is a continuous one, and it has its setbacks, challenges, and failures. But as believers grow in their spiritual life they inevitably develop an increased hatred of sin, an increased love for righteousness and God's law, and an increased sense of their own weaknesses. Those aspects of growth lead to an ever increasing reliance upon God.

In our daily lives we need not become discouraged. Sure we have our ups and downs. And when they are downers we feel that we are absolutely worthless, that we have nothing good in us. But when that happens we can take courage. The same overwhelming discouragement came to Paul and David. They had their times of praise, joy, and peace. But when they failed they knew that their only hope was in God's grace and power.

EVIL IS ALWAYS CLOSE AT HAND

I find it to be a law that when I want to do what
is good, evil lies close at hand. Rom. 7:21, NRSV.

"EVIL LIES CLOSE at hand."

You bet it does. It is everywhere. In fact, toying with and exhibiting evil is one of the prime accomplishments of the modern television and movie industries. If a product isn't filled with sex and violence, it generally won't sell.

Children's programming, believe it or not, is even worse than that created for adults. Because of the short attention span of young children, they need to be fed several violent scenes per minute. If not, they will become bored, drift away from the tube, and miss the advertisement. And if they miss the advertisement, then they won't be primed to beg and whine for their parents to buy the latest in breakfast cereals—sugar-coated air. What a tragedy!

Yes, evil does lie "close at hand." Not only in the media but closer yet—in our brains. Whether we like it or not and whether it is our fault or not, our minds are full of images of evil that the "flesh" (sinful nature) finds quite attractive (tempting), despite the fact that a Christian knows the difference between sin and righteousness and even desires the good.

Christians need to realize that being baptized and imbibing new loves and desires does not imply a miraculous physical brain transplant. No, the same old "hunk of meat" is still between your ears, and it started your new Christian life with a full library of alluring images stored in its memory banks. Evil certainly does lie close at hand.

Christians may still have the old images stored in their minds, but because they have had a transforming experience with Jesus they also know that many of those images should not be encouraged because of their destructive consequences.

Because of their conversion Christians desire to do right. But then again, evil is so very close at hand, and it does make the "flesh twitch" without a person even having to think about it.

We can thank God that He also is close at hand and that we can call on His help for strength (and forgiveness when we need it). The Christian life is one of growth and development in which we come to a greater and greater sense of the holiness of God's law and a greater and greater sense of our own weakness and need of Christ and His righteousness.

THE MARK OF THE CONVERTED

I delight in the law of God after the inward man. Rom. 7:22.

HERE IS THE MARK of the converted person—one who can "delight in the law of God." A stronger expression than "to agree with" or to claim goodness for, "delight" expresses a rejoicing in God's law that those in opposition to God don't have.

Here we have the "real" Paul. Here is Paul the man of God. Here is Paul the Christian who "delights," rejoices, and finds pleasure in God's law. Here is the Paul who stands over against that other Paul who is tempted and falls. Here is the preoccupation of Paul's "inner man" as opposed to the frailty of Paul's "flesh" or outer man.

And here is part of Paul's proof that sin no longer reigns as his master, that God has indeed redeemed him. He delights in God's law.

That same delight will be found in all individuals who have given their hearts to God and have been born from above. God's law is no more an enemy to them than it is to Paul. They will love the law of love with all their heart and mind and soul.

Delighting from the heart in God's law was not something new with Paul. God intended it from the beginning. Perhaps the psalms express the most consistent attitude of delight in God's law. We have already mentioned it in an earlier study, but we will take a more extended look here.

Psalm 1 begins the "delight parade" with "blessed is the man" whose "delight is in the law of the Lord, and on his law he meditates day and night" (Ps. 1:1, 2, RSV).

Psalm 19 joins the delight chorus by noting that "the law of the Lord is perfect, reviving the soul" (Ps. 19:7, RSV).

And of course Psalm 119 refuses to be left out of this praise session: "In the way of thy testimonies I delight as much as in all riches" (Ps. 119:14, RSV); "I find my delight in thy commandments, which I love" (verse 47, RSV); "thy law is my delight" (verse 77, RSV); and "if thy law had not been my delight, I should have perished in my affliction" (verse 92, RSV).

How, my friend, is it with your "inner man"? Does your heart also resonate with love for God's law as did that of Paul and the psalmists? If not, why not? Such questions are of crucial importance as we examine ourselves and with God's help chart our course into the future.

SPIRITUAL REALISM

But I see another law in my members, warring against
the law of my mind, and bringing me into captivity
to the law of sin which is in my members. Rom. 7:23.

PAUL WAS THE BATTLEFIELD of a great controversy or struggle between good and evil. He loved God's law, but he saw "another law," "the law of sin," warring against his spiritual self. In short, he was locked in deadly combat with the forces of evil. The fact that he is still fighting, that he hasn't given up, is important. The devil never gives up, and neither should we, even though we have disappointed ourselves and fallen short (again).

As Paul has repeatedly mentioned since Romans 7:14, his life hasn't been everything that he would have liked it to be, but he hasn't given up. On the other hand, he has come to a sense of realism that seems to escape some modern Christians. That "realism," suggests J. I. Parker, "has to do with our willingness or lack of willingness to face unpalatable truths about ourselves and to start making necessary changes."

With Romans 7:14-24 in mind, James Montgomery Boice has put forth four statements that lie at the foundation of spiritual realism. First, "when God called us to be Christian people he called us to lifetime struggles against sin." It is all too easy for us to want escape from that fact by declaring ourselves to be safe and sound from all temptation and struggle. But, as Paul so vividly puts it, Christians will in great controversy fashion have to battle evil for the rest of their lives. Such warfare is not easy, since it is waged against the residue of sin that resides in even converted men and women. "Realism calls for rigorous preparation, constant alertness, dogged determinism, and moment-by-moment trust in him alone who can give us victory."

Second, "although we are called to a lifetime struggle against sin, we are nevertheless never going to achieve victory by ourselves." Third, "even when we triumph over sin by the power of the Holy Spirit, which should be often, we are still unprofitable servants." Why? Because even a Christian's victories come only through the power of God's grace.

Fourth, "we are to go on fighting and struggling against sin, and we are to do so with the tools made available to us, chiefly prayer, Bible study, Christian fellowship, [and] service to others." The apostle commanded us in Ephesians 6 to "be strong in the Lord and in his mighty power" (verse 6, NIV) and to "put on the full armor of God so that you can take your stand against the devil's schemes" (verse 11, NIV).

THE MARK OF
THE REPENTANT SINNER

What a wretched man I am! Rom. 7:24, NIV.

MANY STUDENTS OF Romans 7 claim that Christians could never say such a thing about themselves. After all, they point out, the Christian life is one of joy, peace, and victory.

Really? Have you never fallen? Have you never disappointed yourself, God, and others by an unloving action or a hasty word that cut someone to the quick? Or perhaps you are one of those whom John speaks of who think themselves so good that they are beyond sin. Although the most wretched of all people, they don't know it. They suffer from the sin of "goodness." In the process, says John, they not only "deceive" themselves but "make him [God] a liar" (1 John 1:8, 10). How wretched can you get? Some of those better-than-thou individuals are meaner than the devil in defending their doctrinal or lifestyle ideas. They even give truth to the bumper sticker I saw some time ago: "Save us Jesus . . . from your followers."

But who are His followers? The Pharisees who put Him on the cross because He didn't keep the Sabbath like them, or converts such as Paul the ex-Pharisee who had come to grips with Christian realism and his own wretchedness when he fell?

The mark of converted Christians is that they see their shortcomings, repent of them, and cry out to God, "O wretched man that I am!" That was certainly Paul's experience, even though, as we pointed out earlier, he is talking in Romans 7 about those times when he fell rather than about the general trend of his life, which he sets forth in Romans 8.

David, a person who God claimed was a man after His own heart, shared Paul's experience. Listen to his wretchedness in the face of his sin:
"For my iniquities have gone over my head;
    they weigh like a burden too heavy for me. . . .
I confess my iniquity,
    I am sorry for my sin. . . .
Do not forsake me, O Lord! . . .
Make haste to help me,
    O Lord, my salvation!" (Ps. 38:4, 18, 21, 22, RSV).

That, my friend, is the cry of a converted person, an individual who knows God and how wretched it is to disappoint Him.

THE JOYFUL SHOUT

*Who will rescue me from this body of death? Thanks be
to God through Jesus Christ our Lord! Rom. 7:24, 25, NRSV.*

THE APOSTLE MOVES FROM discussing his wretchedness to a cry for
deliverance: "Who will rescue me from this body of death?"

His answer is the joyful shout: "Thanks be to God through Jesus
Christ our Lord!" He knows from experience that the sin problem has only
one solution. It is Christ who delivers us from the ongoing sin dilemma
and will eventually quite literally rescue His people from "this body of
death" at the Second Advent, when, Paul assures us, "the dead will be
raised imperishable, and we will be changed. For this perishable must put
on the imperishable, and this mortal must put on immortality" (1 Cor.
15:52, 53, NASB).

The joyful shout of Romans 7:25 will provide the subject matter for
chapter 8. Dealing with Christian victory, it is in many ways the high
point of the book of Romans. But before moving to the victorious themes
of chapter 8 Paul adds a bit of balance at the end of chapter 7. His concluding words are: "So then, I myself in my mind am a slave to God's law,
but in the sinful nature a slave to the law of sin" (Rom. 7:25, NIV).

Some have found that to be a strange saying after the victory cry in
the first part of Romans 7:25 and just before the tremendous statement of
Christian assurance in Romans 8:1. Several interpreters, such as Moffatt
and C. H. Dodd, even go so far as to treat the placement of the last part of
verse 25 as a mistake and attach it to verse 23, which has the same theme.

But it is no mistake. Paul may know that Christ is the victory, but he
is still a realist. Thus the ending of verse 25 is a reminder, claims D. Stuart
Briscoe, that "the war was not over and the battle will continue, but with
the certainty of victory instead of the inevitability of defeat."

The ongoing tension between the spirit and the flesh remain. But the
Christian does not fight the battle alone. Christ is on the side of each believer. And through the Holy Spirit (a major topic of Romans 8) the victory will be won. Paul told the Philippians something quite similar: "I am
sure that he who began a good work in you will bring it to completion at
the day of Jesus Christ" (Phil. 1:6, RSV).

Praise God for all His blessings. Praise God that we do not stand alone.
Praise God that He never forsakes us, not even when the going gets tough.

JOY FOR THOSE "IN CHRIST"

Therefore there is now no condemnation for
those who are in Christ Jesus. Rom. 8:1, NRSV.

WITH ROMANS 8 WE have arrived at one of the most loved chapters of the Bible. If chapter 7 dealt with tension, frustration, and temporary defeat, chapter 8 is one of victory. As Griffith Thomas has pointed out, the chapter opens with "no condemnation" and ends with "no separation," while in between it is characterized by "no defeat."

Romans 8 is a chapter about victory. But even more than that it is a chapter about assurance, the assurance of salvation to those who are in Christ. The chapter illustrates the new and wonderful life that opens for those who put their trust in Him.

Romans 8:1 has two absolutely central ideas. The first is that there is "no condemnation." That is good news, particularly for those fighting the power and persistence of sin in their lives brought out in Romans 7. They may live lives of struggle and even fall at times but there is "no condemnation for those who are in Christ Jesus."

Why is there no condemnation? That is what Paul has been explaining ever since Romans 3:21. Carefully outlining how salvation by grace works, he has made it very clear that salvation is by grace through faith alone.

The word "faith" brings us to the second idea in Romans 8:1. Everybody is not free from condemnation, but only those who are "in Christ Jesus." Paul is especially clear that a person is either "in Adam" or "in Christ" (1 Cor. 15:22; Rom. 5:12-21). "In Christ" occurs 164 times in Paul's writings, including 11 times (counting pronouns and synonyms) in one of the great opening sentences of Ephesians (1:3-14).

James Stewart points out that "the heart of Paul's religion is union with Christ. This, more than any other conception—more than justification, more than sanctification, more even than reconciliation—is the key which unlocks the secrets of his soul." For Paul, those who are "in Christ" are justified, sanctified, and are being progressively sanctified and perfected. And if they stay "in Christ" they have assurance of the kingdom when Christ comes again.

But, you may be thinking, how does one get "in Christ"? Not by birth. We are born in the way of Adam. For Paul people become "in Christ" when they consciously accept Christ by faith as Lord and Savior.

THE ARRIVAL OF THE HOLY SPIRIT

*For the law of the Spirit of life in Christ Jesus has
set me free from the law of sin and death. Rom. 8:2, RSV.*

THE WORD "FOR" IS important in today's text because it connects Romans 8:1 to verse 2 and thus helps us begin to understand why there is "no condemnation for those who are in Christ Jesus" (verse 1, NIV). Why? "For" or "because" (NIV) "the law of the Spirit of life in Christ has set me free from the law of sin and death."

Verse 3 takes up the basis of that freedom. But before moving on to that verse we should note that the Holy Spirit (here spoken of in connection with "the law of the Spirit of life") is central throughout Romans 8. The focus on the Spirit signals a major shift in the Epistle. That transition is especially forceful when we contrast chapters 7 and 8. Romans 7 mentions the law and its synonyms 31 times, but the Holy Spirit only once. Chapter 8, by way of contrast, speaks of the Holy Spirit at least 20 times.

"The essential contrast" between Romans 7 and 8, notes John Stott, "is between the weakness of the law and the power of the Spirit. For over against indwelling sin, which is the reason the law is unable to help us in our moral struggle (7:17, 20), Paul now sets the indwelling Spirit, who is both our liberator now from 'the law of sin and death' (8:2) and the guarantee of resurrection and eternal glory in the end (8:11, 17, 23)."

Romans 8 depicts the Christian life as life in the Holy Spirit. It is a life brought about, sustained, directed, and enriched by the Spirit. Without the Holy Spirit the Christian life would be impossible. It is little wonder that Ellen White suggests that the gift of the Holy Spirit brings "all other blessings in its train" (*The Desire of Ages*, p. 672).

Romans 8:2 claims that the Spirit through "the law of the Spirit of life in Christ Jesus" (that is, the gospel) sets us "free from the law of sin and death" (that is, the condemnation of the law). Thus we find here a second privilege. In verse 1 we learn that we are no longer under the law's condemnation, while in the second verse we discover a certain liberation that Christians have in the gospel. That release is not, however, from the law itself (which is good, holy, just, and spiritual), but from both bondage to sin and from the law's condemnation.

Thus Paul proclaims Christian liberty that frees Christians from the negative and opens them up to the positive through the Spirit's guidance and power.

CHRIST TO THE RESCUE

For God has done what the law, weakened by the flesh, could not do:
by sending his own Son in the likeness of sinful flesh. Rom. 8:3, NRSV.

THE "FOR," AS IT WAS in Romans 8:2, is quite important. It places the first two verses of Romans 8 (with their proclamation of "no condemnation" and the Spirit's role in freeing Christians from the "law of sin and death") firmly on the foundation of Christ's great work. It is Jesus and His life and death that have made salvation not only possible but a reality.

But behind Jesus stands God, the Father who sent "his own Son in the likeness of sinful flesh." That phrase is one pregnant with meaning about Jesus the God-man. First He was God's "own" Son. There is a sense in which we could describe every Christian as a son (or daughter) of God, but as A. M. Hunter put it, Christ is "the Son by nature" and "we are sons by grace." Christ is not exactly one of us. He is the Son of God. That is why the angel called Him "that holy thing" in speaking to Mary (Luke 1:35). The Bible says that of no other child, because Jesus in a very significant sense was different from other humans: He was God's own Son and had the direct heritage of the Holy Spirit as His Father.

On the other hand, Jesus came "in the likeness of sinful flesh." Please note how careful Paul had to be here. If he had said He came "in sinful flesh" he would have created a theological disaster, because he had already stated in chapter 7 that sinful flesh was incapable of overcoming sin. Thus to have spoken of Christ as having "sinful flesh" just like other humans would have logically led to the conclusion that He was a sinner like the rest of humanity. But, on the other hand, God needed to identify Christ with those He came to save. As a result, Paul very carefully selected the words "in the likeness of sinful flesh." Thus he indicates that Christ fully participated in humanity without being exactly like other people.

Romans 8:3 lines up with Ellen White's helpful insight when she noted that "it is not correct to say, as many writers have said, that Christ was like all children. . . . His inclination to right was a constant gratification to his parents" (*Youth's Instructor,* Sept. 8, 1898). By way of contrast, she pointed out that other children are born with a "bent" or natural inclination to evil, which of themselves they cannot overcome (*Education,* p. 29).

Romans 8:3 tells us that because Christ was both God and man He was able to deal successfully with the sin problem. Thus all humanity is in debt to the One whom God sent to "save his people from their sins" (Matt. 1:21).

CHRIST DEALS WITH SIN

[By God's sending His Son] to deal with sin,
he condemned sin in the flesh. Rom. 8:3, NRSV.

THE FATHER SENT CHRIST "in the likeness of sinful flesh . . . to deal with sin" (Rom. 8:3, NRSV). Paul leaves not the slightest doubt as to why God dispatched Him. The human race was messed up and unable to help itself out of the pit of sin and resulting condemnation.

Christ was sent, as the King James and many other versions put it, "for sin." He was sent to deal with it once and for all. What does Paul mean by saying that Christ came "for sin" or "to deal with sin"? Some translations, such as the *New American Standard Bible* and the New International Version, build upon the Greek version of the Old Testament's repeated and consistent translation of "for sin" as being "an offering for sin." Hebrews 10:6-8 correctly reflects that translation. But the context of Romans 8:3 seems to demand a broader interpretation. And, of course, it is true that Jesus did deal with sin on more than one level.

Paul's purpose in this passage is to explain how Christians can have victory over sin, since the law was powerless to provide it for them. For that reason God sent Jesus, who dealt with sin with finality. Christ came to bear the penalty of sin by His death but also to destroy its controlling power in the lives of those who accept Him by faith. The words "to deal with sin" sum up His mission to this world.

Romans 8:3 says that the way He dealt with sin was to condemn it "in the flesh."

And how did Jesus condemn sin in the flesh? First, as the One who was sent "in the likeness of sinful flesh," He lived a life of complete obedience to God and thus as the second Adam overcame where the first Adam had failed.

Second, He not only lived in complete harmony with the law, thus becoming the spotless Lamb of God, but He died "in the flesh" a sacrificial death "once for all" (Rom. 6:10, NIV) by becoming our "sin offering" (Rom. 8:3, NIV). What Jesus did "in the flesh" in both His life and His death condemned all sin.

By His life and death Christ not only removed the sentence of condemnation for those who accept His grace but He provided the basis for removing the powerful grip that sin has on even believers. Christ dealt with sin in such a manner as to open up the way to victory for His followers.

WALKING IN THE SPIRIT

[Christ dealt with sin] in order that the just requirement of
the law might be fulfilled in us, who walk not according to
the flesh but according to the Spirit. Rom. 8:4, RSV.

WE SAW IN DISCUSSING the previous verse that Christ dealt with sin by condemning it in the flesh through His sinless life and sacrificial death. One purpose of His work was that "the just requirement of the law might be fulfilled in us."

What does he mean by saying that the law "might be fulfilled in us"? Some claim that Paul is suggesting that since Christ kept the law perfectly, He is passing on His perfect obedience to us. Thus He not only died for us vicariously, but He also lived for us vicariously. From that perspective today's text would not be speaking about our personal performance as Christians.

While that reading is a possibility, it does not seem to be what Paul has in mind in Romans 8. He appears to be here referring to what happens to people who are in Christ. In the words of F. F. Bruce, "God's commands have now become God's enablings" for those under the power of the Holy Spirit.

That implies that the fruits of justification and those of sanctification do not exist separately in the lives of believers. God counts those who are "in Christ" as righteous (justified) and provides them with power through the Holy Spirit to live the principles of the law in their daily lives (sanctification).

That victorious living, however, as we noted in chapter 7, is not without problems. But it does provide for a kind of living that is of a totally different quality from that which we had when we were slaves to sin.

The metaphor of walking in today's verse is helpful here. Paul speaks of those "who walk not according to the flesh but according to the Spirit." Progress in the Christian life for most of us is more akin to walking rather than to flying. Our spiritual growth may not be spectacular on a day-to-day basis, but it is steady.

But even that progressive walk is possible only because of the enabling power of the Holy Spirit. Those who live "according to the Spirit" not only have power for victory, but also have their horizons broadened as to what is important and possible in life. Walking with the Spirit is truly a transforming experience. God not only wants to do something *for* those in Christ (justification); He also intends to do something *in* them (sanctification).

195

WHERE IS YOUR MIND?

*For those who live according to the flesh set their minds on
the things of the flesh, but those who live according to the Spirit
set their minds on the things of the Spirit. Rom. 8:5, NRSV.*

PETER WASN'T SUCH a bad man. He just had his mind in the wrong
place. Thus the strong rebuke of Jesus: "Get behind me, Satan! You are a
stumbling block to me; you do not have in mind the things of God, but the
things of men" (Matt. 16:23, NIV). The disciple wasn't being outwardly
wicked, but he was looking at things from a worldly perspective. And that
viewpoint threw his life off center.

James and John had a similar "mental illness" when they sent their
mother to request the two best places in the kingdom for them. They were,
in Paul's language, thinking "fleshly thoughts" about position and power,
and thus were out of tune with the spiritual realm. As a result, their lives
were out of harmony with God's will for them.

Setting one's mind on the "things of the flesh" does not necessarily
refer to those thoughts and actions that we consider as gross sensuality, a
fact demonstrated by Paul's list of the works of the flesh in Galatians
5:19-21. He includes such things are jealousy, selfish ambition, and envy.
Thus a disposition that we might define as "of the flesh" may manifest itself in many ways. Such people may have good intentions and might even
be church members or even church employees, but their frame of reference is shaped by the things of this life. And that perspective influences
the way they live. Thus the way of the flesh, in line with Paul's metaphor
in Romans 8:4, is a way of walking through life.

Opposed to that perspective and life is the way of the Spirit. "Those
who live according to the Spirit" do so because they have "set their minds
on the things of the Spirit." Once again, those who center their minds on
spiritual things are not only somewhat interested in them. To the contrary,
their minds and lives are focused on spiritual things, just as those who
have set their minds on the "fleshly things" have lives dominated by the
things of this world.

Paul has no doubt about it. Where your mind is, there will your life be
also. That is a challenging thought. Where is my mind? What do I like to
think about when I have free time? What do the answers to those questions say to me about my spiritual orientation?

THE NEED TO WAKE UP THE DEAD

The mind set on the flesh is death, but the mind
set on the Spirit is life and peace. Rom. 8:6, NASB.

THIS IS AN INTERESTING VERSE because it doesn't say that "the mind set on the flesh *leads to* death," but that it *"is* death." Another way of putting it is that unsaved people, those not "in Christ," are already spiritually dead. Thus, as one author points out, "the apostle is stating a spiritual equation, not a spiritual consequence."

If that is true, you may be thinking, *then how can anyone ever come to Christ?* The truth is that sinners don't go to Him; He comes to them. That was so in the case of the fallen Adam, whom God searched for in the garden; it was true of the lost coin, of Zacchaeus, and of every other person in history. God through His Holy Spirit speaks to the hearts of every person to wake them up to their need. John Wesley called that work "prevenient grace," or the grace of God that goes before saving grace. Before people can accept God's gift in Christ they need to be awakened from their state of spiritual death.

Even though our text today views spiritual death as being the actual state of those whose minds are "set on the flesh," rather than as being a consequence of their thinking, there is also a sense in which sin leads to death. Romans 6:23 declares that "the wages of sin is death." That death, of course, is not the spiritual death of today's text but eternal death at the end of time. But the two are related. Those who refuse to be wakened from spiritual death, those who have their mind on the flesh, are on the pathway that culminates in eternal death at the end of the age.

In the opposite camp from those whose "mind is set on the flesh" are those whose minds are "set on the Spirit." Once again such a mind-set does not *lead to* life and peace. Rather, "life and peace" is what born-again Christians already have. As we noted in an earlier study, those who are "in Christ" already have eternal life (John 3:36) and peace with God (Rom. 5:1).

We should not equate Paul's teaching those who have their minds set on the things of the Spirit with church membership. There are, unfortunately, church members and even ministers whose minds are in the realm of the flesh rather than in the realm of the Spirit. But God's prevenient grace is still active in their cases. God is always out to wake up sinners to the joys of true life and peace.

THINKING MAKES A DIFFERENCE

The mind that is set on the flesh is hostile to God; it does
not submit to God's law, indeed it cannot; and those
who are in the flesh cannot please God. Rom. 8:7, 8, RSV.

MIND-SET IS IMPORTANT. How we think is one of the most important aspects of our lives. Paul has been highlighting that truth ever since Romans 8:5, in which he noted that people's mind-set expressed their basic nature as Christians or non-Christians. Then in verse 6 he indicated that mind-set not only says something about us now but also has eternal consequences.

In verse 7 the apostle pushes his line of thought a bit further and tells us that "the mind that is set on the flesh," that is occupied with the affairs of this world, "is hostile to God." Now, "hostile" does not mean slightly uncooperative. Those with such an orientation are actually God's enemies, a topic Paul has already raised in Romans 5:10. Hostility to God expresses a deep-seated animosity. John Stott remarks that "it is antagonistic to his name, his kingdom and will, to his day, his people and his word, to his Son, his Spirit and his glory."

Paul goes out of his way to claim that the mind set on the things of this world especially dislikes God's moral standards expressed in His law. The fleshly mind not only "does not submit to God's law," it "cannot." That is why the Bible describes a person's becoming a Christian as getting a new mind and heart, as being born again, as a death and resurrection symbolized by baptism through immersion (Rom. 6:2-4).

Thus becoming a Christian is not just another step in becoming better. No! It is a radical discontinuity with the old way of thinking and living—a new life altogether. It is a life "in Christ," as opposed to one "in Adam."

The final consequence of having a fleshly or this-worldly mind-set is that such people "cannot please God."

Paul has been speaking for four verses about two alternative mind-sets (the mind of the flesh and the mind of the Spirit) that lead to two patterns of conduct (living according to the flesh or according to the Spirit), and that are directly related to two spiritual states (death or life and peace). Thus how we think, what we dwell on, and what we value all have a central function in both our present conduct and future destiny. No wonder Paul appealed to the Philippians to "let this mind be in you, which was also in Christ Jesus" (Phil. 2:5).

EVERY CHRISTIAN HAS THE SPIRIT

But you are not in the flesh, you are in the Spirit, if in fact the Spirit of God dwells in you. Any one who does not have the Spirit of Christ does not belong to him. Rom. 8:9, RSV.

"BUT!"

Paul has been speaking in the previous verses about those who were fleshly minded, those who had their minds focused on the present world. "But" not everybody is in that camp. Counterpoised to those in the flesh are those "in the Spirit." The apostle feels so strongly about this topic that he goes on to say that those who do not "have the Spirit of Christ" do not belong to Him, that they are not Christians.

We find two important truths about the Holy Spirit in this verse. First, every Christian (rather than church member) has the gift of the Holy Spirit. That is exactly what Jesus taught during His evening meeting with Nicodemus: "Truly, truly, I say to you, unless one is born of water *and the Spirit,* he cannot enter the kingdom of God. That which is born of the flesh is flesh, and that which is born of the Spirit is spirit" (John 3:5, 6, RSV).

According to Paul, indwelling sin characterizes those "in Adam" (Rom. 7:17, 20), but the indwelling of God's Holy Spirit is the mark of the Christian. Jesus' promise in John 14:16, 17 reflects that spiritual indwelling: "I will pray the Father" to send the Holy Spirit, "even the Spirit of truth, whom the world cannot receive, because it neither sees him nor knows him; you know him, for he dwells with you and is in you" (RSV). Because of that indwelling Paul refers to our bodies as the "temple of the Holy Spirit" (1 Cor. 6:19, RSV).

The Holy Spirit is God's gift to every true Christian. Of course, beyond the gift of the Spirit to all Christians are those special gifts or talents bestowed upon individuals for specialized ministries. But we must not confuse them with the Spirit's indwelling in every person who has faith in Christ.

The second important thing to note about Romans 8:9 as it relates to the Spirit is its implication for the doctrine of the Trinity. The passage not only refers to the Spirit interchangeably as "the Spirit of Christ" and "the Spirit of God," but it also links what Ellen White refers to as the "heavenly trio" or the three "eternal heavenly dignitaries" (*Evangelism*, pp. 615, 616) in the closest intimacy in their work for human beings. The good news is that each Person in the Trinity cooperates with each of the others for our salvation.

ALIVE IN CHRIST

But if Christ is in you, your body is dead because of sin, yet your
spirit is alive because of righteousness. Rom. 8:10, NIV.

WITH ROMANS 8:10 WE have arrived at a tension between a dead
body and a live spirit that doesn't find resolution until verse 11, in which
Paul speaks of the resurrection and the joining of our living spirit with a
living body.

That is clear enough, but here in verse 10 interpreters differ over
whether death refers to a believer's death to sin's dominion at baptism
(Rom. 6:2) or death of the physical body, which is mortal, subject to
death, and will eventually pass away. Both are true, but it seems from
verse 11 with its mention of the resurrection that Paul has in mind our
physical bodies.

Be that as it may, the apostle's real interest is in seeing us whole and
fully alive. In other words, his theme is not death, but rather life. He concludes verse 10 by saying that our "spirit is alive because of righteousness," because of what Christ has done for us in the gospel plan, because
of the death and resurrection that we went through symbolized by our baptism (Rom. 6:2, 3).

Alive in Christ! What a thought! What a reality!

But what does it mean to be alive in Christ? For one thing, it indicates
that we are alive to God and spiritual realities. Before we became genuine
Christians we may have had some dim view of God and "believed" in
Him, but that's not too significant, James tells us, because even the dev-
ils believe and tremble (James 2:19). God at that time was kind of like an
"oblong blur." He was there, but not in a personal sense. But when we
came to Christ as Savior, the Holy Spirit entered our lives and God became as real as life itself. It's not that Christians don't still have frustra-
tions and doubts, but they *know* that God loves them and will be there for
them in time of need.

A second thing implied in being alive in Christ is that the Bible is a
new book. It's no longer just another dusty, dry volume on the shelf, but
has become a vital reality in our daily life. It speaks to our daily needs.

A third thing is that Christians are alive to other Christians and to the
needs and hurts of their fellow beings. They not only enjoy fellowship
with others who love Jesus but they have a desire, in the spirit of Jesus, to
serve the world around them.

RESURRECTION REVISITED

But if the Spirit of Him who raised Jesus from the dead dwells in you,
He who raised Christ from the dead will also give life to your mortal
bodies through His Spirit who dwells in you. Rom. 8:11, NKJV.

PAUL JUST CAN'T STAY away from the topic of the resurrection. In earlier meditations we have quoted from his great resurrection passages in 1 Corinthians 15 and 1 Thessalonians 4, and we have explored several of his allusions to the blessed hope of the Second Advent earlier in Romans.

Resurrection was an important topic to Paul, and it came in two flavors. The first is Christ's resurrection, an event that he hammers home repeatedly in 1 Corinthians 15, that *guarantees* the resurrection of those who follow Him on earth.

The second step is the resurrection of the physical bodies of those who have already been alive in spirit in their earthly life (Rom. 8:10). But at this point we need to look carefully at Paul's wording. He said that God "raised Jesus from the dead" but that He will "give life" to our bodies.

The two resurrections have big differences. Jesus had life in Himself, and claimed the power to not only lay down His life but to take it up again (John 10:17, 18). We aren't self-existent. Thus God not only needs to raise us, but He must also give us life. And the life that He grants us according to 1 Corinthians 15 will be immortal life. It is significant that Romans 8:11 says that God will give life to our "mortal bodies," since at the present time humans do not possess immortality. It is a gift of God at the last day.

Paul isn't the only writer excited about the resurrection. Ellen White had a similar interest. "Amid the reeling of the earth, the flash of lightning, and the roar of thunder," she says in describing the event, "the Son of God calls forth the sleeping saints. He looks upon the graves of the righteous, then, raising His hands to heaven, He cries: 'Awake, awake, awake, ye that sleep in the dust, and arise!' Throughout the length and breadth of the earth the dead shall hear that voice, and they that hear shall live. And the whole earth shall ring with the tread of the exceeding great army of every nation, kindred, tongue, and people. From the prison house of death they come, clothed with immortal glory, crying: 'O death, where is thy sting? O grave, where is thy victory?' 1 Corinthians 15:55. And the living righteous and the risen saints unite their voices in a long, glad shout of victory" (*The Great Controversy,* p. 644).

As the old song puts it: "What a day of rejoicing that will be!"

GRACE BEFORE LAW

So then, brethren, we are under obligation, not to the flesh,
to live according to the flesh. Rom. 8:12, NASB.

"SO THEN" OR "therefore" (NIV) is an important part of today's verse. It links verse 12 with the previous 11 verses of Romans 8. And what did they tell us?

1. That believers are no longer under condemnation.
2. That they have been set free from the law of sin and death.
3. That they are no longer under sin's dominion.
4. That they walk by the Spirit.
5. That their minds are set on the Spirit.
6. That they have life and peace through the Spirit.
7. That the resurrection of their bodies is guaranteed.

That's quite a list to be thankful for. Paul tells the Romans in verse 12 that they are "under obligation" or are "debtors" because of all of God's gifts to them. Their debt is to live according to God's principles. After all, if the indwelling Spirit has given them life (Rom. 8:10), how can they continue to live in the way of death? They cannot be both dead and alive simultaneously. Having been rescued from death, they are obligated to live the principles of life through the power of the Holy Spirit.

At this point *it is absolutely crucial to recognize that we are not in God's debt unless He has already rescued us.* First comes salvation, then follows the response of faith empowered by the Spirit. The Ten Commandments reveal the same pattern. First comes grace: "I am the Lord your God, who brought you out of the land of Egypt, out of the house of bondage" (Ex. 20:2, RSV). Then follows the law. The Israelites were in debt to God because of His rescue. First came salvation and then the response. Law from a Christian perspective must always be seen from the viewpoint of grace.

With that in mind, it is a genuine disaster to see the Ten Commandments listed in a book or on the wall of a church without Exodus 20:2, the verse that supplies the reason that the Israelites were to keep the law or even had it in the first place. Without the grace of God's rescue there would have been no law or law keeping. Grace precedes obligation.

The same is true in Paul's letter to the Romans. They are in debt to God because of His grace. Their response—our response, when we realize that we have been rescued—will be to walk in God's will.

A LESSON IN MORTIFICATION

If ye live after the flesh, ye shall die: but if ye through the
Spirit do mortify the deeds of the body, ye shall live. Rom. 8:13.

ROMANS 8:13 SETS forth a pair of options that we have become quite familiar with in the book of Romans: The way of the flesh leads to death, but the way of the Spirit leads to life.

In today's passage, however, we have a new nuance: the mortification of the deeds of the body. The concept raises at least three questions.

First, what is mortification? As John Stott points out, "mortification is neither masochism (taking pleasure in self-inflicted pain), nor asceticism (resenting and rejecting the fact that we have bodies and natural bodily appetites)." Rather, it is a recognition of evil as evil, leading "to such a decisive and radical repudiation of it that no imagery can do it justice except 'putting to death.'" That concept also appears in Galatians 5:24, in which Paul writes of crucifying "the flesh with its passions and desires" (RSV).

Second, how does mortification take place? Interestingly, today's passage says that it is something that we do. The text doesn't speak of being put to death, but of putting to death. In that work we are active rather than passive. We have a responsibility in the process. We can't, however, "put to death the misdeeds of the body" (NIV) by ourselves. Our passage makes it clear that it is through the power of the Holy Spirit. The Spirit gives us the desire, determination, and discipline to reject evil. Our part is, on the positive side, to hand over our will to that of God.

On the negative side, mortification of the deeds of the body means to repudiate those things we know to be wrong. We need to come to the place where we do not even "think about how to gratify the desires of the sinful nature" (Rom. 13:14, NIV). When such temptations first rise we need to reject them in prayer. "Help me, Jesus, I don't want to even think about this garbage," must be our cry. The alternative is to "enjoy" the thoughts and perhaps the actions and to repent about them later. That latter course, as we saw in chapter 7, is a possibility, but it is not the full victory that God wants His children to have.

Third, why should we practice mortification? Because we have an obligation (Rom. 8:12), but also because those who do so "shall live" the rich life here on this earth reflected in verses 14 through 17. Those who walk the way of God, says Paul, are the children of God with all the rights and privileges thereof.

ADOPTED AT LAST

All who are led by the Spirit of God are sons of God. Rom. 8:14, RSV.

THE REASON THAT THOSE who mortify the flesh in Romans 8:13 "shall live" is not only because the Spirit leads them but because they have become "sons of God." Having received the "Spirit of adoption," they are a part of the family of God and have the privilege of addressing God as Father and their fellow believers as brother and sister.

But isn't everyone a child of God, Christian or not? queries J. I. Packer. "Emphatically no!" he replies. "The idea that all men are children of God is not found in the Bible anywhere. The Old Testament shows God as the Father, not of all men, but of His own people, the seed of Abraham." And the New Testament plainly states that we are of Abraham's seed if we have accepted Christ (Gal. 3:26-29). "Sonship is not, therefore, a universal status upon which everyone enters by natural birth, but a supernatural gift which one receives through receiving Jesus. . . . *'As many as received Him,* to *them* gave He power to become the sons of God, . . . which were born, not of blood, or of the will of the flesh, nor of the will of man, but of God' (John 1:12f.)."

Thus adoptive sonship or daughtership is a gift of grace. It comes as what Jesus referred to as the new birth in John 3. It comes when a person accepts Jesus as Savior by faith. And it comes when people through the power of God's Spirit decide to give up their "in Adam" status in which they were born and to accept the "in Christ" status made possible by Jesus on Calvary. Those who accept Christ by faith, says Paul, "receive adoption as sons" (Gal. 4:5; Eph. 1:5, RSV).

Too many Christians for too long have misunderstood the good news of adoption. It doesn't happen at physical birth but takes place at the new birth. And a beautiful truth it is. Believers, notes John, are "called children of God" (1 John 3:1, RSV).

Being adopted into God's family will change every aspect of our lives. Not only will we continue to live in the Spirit, but it will heal our relationships with other members in God's family. After all, it is impossible to love the Father without loving His other children. Or, as Ralph Earle describes true Christianity, "they not only belong to the family but act like it!"

Do we?

GOD AS ABBA

Ye have not received the spirit of bondage again to fear;
but ye have received the Spirit of adoption,
whereby we cry, Abba, Father. Rom. 8:15.

ADOPTED INTO THE household of God. What a privilege it is to be a Christian. That is especially true when we understand adoption's full impact in Paul's world. In the Roman world of the first century an adopted son had been deliberately chosen (often as an adult) by his adoptive father to perpetuate his name and estates. As such, society considered him equal to natural sons, and he might actually enjoy the father's affection even more than they did.

It was an honor to be adopted into an important family. And for Christians adopted into the family of God, there can be no greater honor than to perpetuate the values and name of the Father.

The whole process of adoption moves one away from fear and from bondage to sin and toward the freedom of sons and daughters. If sin and its entanglements lead to fear, the apostle John lets us know that adoption into God's family frees us from fear. "There is no fear in love; but perfect love casteth out fear" (1 John 4:18).

Being adopted into the family of God means that we need not fear the Father. In fact, we may address Him in not only the more formal manner as Father but also as *"Abba." Abba* is a more everyday word. Ordinarily when Jews called Him Father they quickly added "in heaven" to demonstrate God's transcendence and distance from them.

Many authors have claimed that *Abba* is similar to our "Papa" or "Daddy." Even if that is true, we should not use the word in a way that is light and irreverent. We need to remember that the father in a Roman household was an awe-inspiring person who quite literally had the right to put family members to death. Thus even though the title *Abba* suggests love and intimacy, it is still a title of reverence.

Jesus addressed God as *"Abba,* Father" in Gethsemane. And in today's verse we find we have the same privilege. The term itself reflects God's closeness to each of us. He is not somewhere out there, but with us and willing to help us in our time of need.

Thank You, God, for being both our Abba and our Father. Help us this day to know how to be better daughters and sons to You, to know how better to approach You in time of need and to represent the family name.

GOD'S SPECIAL LEADING

The Spirit of God affirms to our spirit
that we are God's children. Rom. 8:16, REB.

ONCE AGAIN WE FACE a text with two spirits. In this case there is no problem deciding what the two spirits refer to. The Holy Spirit "beareth witness" (KJV) to our spiritual nature that we are God's children in all certainty.

Romans 8:16 seems to contain a contrast with verse 15 in the sense that in the earlier verse we are the ones who affirm or testify to our new relationship to God by crying *"Abba* Father," while in verse 16 the Holy Spirit bears witness to us that we belong to the family of God.

What is that witness? It appears to have two aspects. The first, the objective element, is the one many people feel most comfortable with. They have read their Bibles, understand the plan of salvation, have accepted it, and have agreed to live a life in accord with God's principles. Intellectually they know the truth of what it means to be a Christian. And, of course, they believe that the Holy Spirit has guided them to their understanding and commitment. That understanding provides them with a basis for testing the more subjective aspects of Christianity.

We find, however, more than a merely objective element in relation to the teaching that the Holy Spirit affirms to our spirit that we are God's children. The second aspect is the subjective. Here we are talking about something intensely personal that takes place just between the Spirit and the believer. There is such a thing as a genuine spiritual experience of the Holy Spirit in a person's heart. Such individuals have an overwhelming awareness of God's presence or sense that God has come upon them in a special way. They have no doubt that what they are experiencing is from Him. I have had several such instances that have been extremely vivid to me. Often they involve some important choice in my life that I have been praying about, including the calling to my lifework, whether I should move to a new location, or, in a special sense, my choice of a wife.

These are special occurrences in the Christian's life. There is, however, a danger that subjective experiences may be false. Thus we need to test the spirits (1 Thess. 5:19-21). But on the other hand, God does want to guide our lives personally. That is why we pray. Do we listen for His answers? At times in our lives the Spirit bears witness with our spirit regarding our duty or the course of action that we should follow. After all, He is close to us. He is our *Abba.*

Heirs of the Immortal

*Now if we are children, then we are heirs—heirs of God and
co-heirs of Christ, if indeed we share in his sufferings in
order that we may share in his glory. Rom. 8:17, NIV.*

HOW CAN WE AS Christians be heirs of God? After all, we conventionally use the word to refer to those who receive property when another dies. But God doesn't die!

The Bible does not always employ words in the same sense that we do. "Heir" implies that as Christians we have a special relationship to God as His "children." Because of that relationship we already possess the Father's blessing, and are assured of further blessing at the end of time.

In the Old Testament the concept of inheritance implied possession of the Holy Land. It came to be seen as part of the Messianic blessing (Ps. 37:9, 11; Isa. 60:21; 61:7). That concept carried over to the New Testament. Thus Jesus could call the meek blessed, "for they shall inherit the earth" (Matt. 5:5, RSV). Again, in speaking to the disciples, Jesus noted that "every one who has left houses or brothers or sisters or father or mother or children or lands, for my name's sake, will receive a hundredfold, and inherit eternal life" (Matt. 19:29, RSV). And at the final judgment, Jesus tells His followers, "Come, O blessed of my Father, inherit the kingdom prepared for you from the foundation of the world" (Matt. 25:34, RSV).

The saints' inheritance is possession of the promised blessings of God in all their fullness. We receive them on two conditions. First, *"if* we are children." The "if" in today's verse does not mean possibility but fact. The "if" should not be translated as "we might be," but "because we are His children." Because of that certainty Christians will receive the blessing of heirship without fail.

Second, "if . . . we share in his sufferings" we will share "in his glory." Once again, the "if" means "because." No one ever said, least of all Christ and the apostles, that the Christian walk would be an easy one. In fact, it is generally just the opposite, because our earth is caught in the midst of a galactic struggle between good and evil. Christians have opted for a Lord and a set of principles contrary to those of the "prince of this world" (Satan). Thus they can expect the same sorts of conflict that cost Christ His life and caused the apostles so much trouble. But trouble isn't an end in itself. Those who "share in his sufferings" will "share in his glory."

Glory Beyond Suffering

For I reckon that the sufferings of this present time are not worthy to be compared with the glory which shall be revealed in us. Rom. 8:18.

PAUL, IN LINE WITH other Jews, characterized history as being divided into two ages or eras: the present age and the age to come. For him two words—"suffering" and "glory"—depicted the two ages.

The sufferings Paul speaks about not only include opposition from the world (those opposed to God's principles) but also our physical and moral frailty, which result from our half-saved condition. God has arranged for our salvation. He has transformed our hearts and minds to love His principles, but Christians still exist in a less than perfect world in less than perfect bodies. The result is tension and the "sufferings of this present time."

Those afflictions were intensely real to Paul and other first-century Christians. At the present time many of us who live in economically upscale places where a form of "Christianity" is popular don't seem to suffer much in either the physical or the spiritual realm.

Perhaps that fact has led to the rather passionless church life that surrounds us. Have we confused heaven as the age to come with our current comfort, acceptance, and high standard of living? What would happen to our Christianity if those artificial props suddenly collapsed? If we lost our job today, our house tomorrow, and our social standing on the third day? In other words, what if sufferings became real for us, just as they are for multitudes in less-fortunate circumstances around the earth?

Then we would probably be able really to see what Paul is getting at. We would long for the glory of the age to come in ways that we seldom do in our present situation with its sense of well-being. And we would desire the coming of God's kingdom with all our hearts and minds.

And that desire would move us to action. Transforming spiritual sluggishness into spiritual fervor, it would translate sick and dying churches into dynamic places of Christian fellowship and outreach. It would make them into lighthouses of hope for the glory to come.

Would to God that we could catch the vision and even now in our rather comfortable state dedicate our lives to Him who will come again. Today is a wonderful day for such a rededication. Today is the day that can change the rest of our life and the lives of those around us if we will let God take over our hearts for service to Him.

ALL CREATION ON TIPTOE

For creation is waiting with eager longing for
the sons of God to be disclosed. Rom. 8:19, Goodspeed.

TODAY'S VERSE IS INTERESTING in the sense that it moves away from the usual emphasis on human beings and focuses on the creation. Thus, Paul implies, it is not only people who wait for God's glory, but a suffering creation.

But, we might ask, what does Paul mean by "creation"? John Murray, after pointing out that we must interpret the word in the context of Romans 8:20-23, notes that good *"angels* are not included because they are not subjected to vanity and to the bondage of corruption. *Satan* and the *demons* are not included because they cannot be regarded as looking for the manifestation of the sons of God and they will not share in the liberty of the glory of the children of God. The *children of God* themselves are not included because they are distinguished from 'the creation' [in verses 22 and 23]. . . . [And] . . . *unbelieving* . . . mankind cannot be included because the earnest expectation does not characterize them."

Thus creation here denotes "subhuman" creation, which Paul pictures as standing "on tiptoe" (Phillips) or "eagerly waiting" (Jerusalem) for God to reveal His children. Then, like the psalmist and the prophets who picture the earth mourning and hills, pastures, and valleys as they "shout and sing together for joy" (Isa. 24:4; Ps. 65:12, 13, RSV), Paul personifies subhuman creation in order to convey to his readers "the cosmic significance of both humanity's fall into sin and [the] believers' restoration to glory." Sin, as Romans 8 makes clearer than perhaps anywhere else in the Bible, has affected all of creation. Thus it is more than just a human problem.

What is it that the subhuman creation is waiting for? The disclosure of God's children. Paul has made it clear in Romans 8:14-17 that Christians are already God's children. "But," as Douglas Moo points out, "experiencing suffering (v. 18) and weakness (v. 26) like all other people, Christians do not in this life 'appear' much like sons of God. The last day will publicly manifest our real status."

In other words, the full disclosure of God's children will take place at the Second Advent, when Christ will come to take them home as well as to put the finishing touches on them for their new status.

What a glorious day that will be. All of Scripture points forward to it.

THE END OF CHANGE AND DECAY

*In the end the whole of created life will be rescued from the
tyranny of change and decay, and have its share in that magnificent
liberty which can only belong to the children of God! Rom. 8:21, Phillips.*

"CHANGE AND DECAY" is the stuff of life on this earth. It is so with
people. Anyone older than 50 or even 40 is well aware of that fact. Once
I had perfect eyesight, but now I have glasses. Once I had a strong back;
now I have nightly back exercises. Once I had lots of blond, wavy hair;
now I am happy to have a few "hairs"—silver gray at that. And so it goes.
Change and decay is the lot of life.

Solomon recognized that fact. In the last chapter of Ecclesiastes he
writes, "Remember also your Creator in the days of your youth, before the
evil days come, and the years draw nigh, when you will say, 'I have no
pleasure in them'" (Eccl. 12:1, RSV).

It seems like just yesterday that I could hardly wait for my next birth-
day. But times have changed. As the wise man puts it, people's "grinders
[teeth] cease because they are few," their "windows [eyes] are dimmed,"
"and desire fails; because man goes to his eternal home . . . and the dust
returns to the earth as it was, and the spirit [or breath] returns to God who
gave it. Vanity of vanities, says the Preacher: all is vanity" (Eccl. 12:2-8,
RSV). Change and decay is the lot of life.

Paul tells us that it even affects the "whole of created life." One
doesn't have to be especially wise to see that something is wrong with
our planet. A few days ago a mighty earthquake in India took between
70,000 and 100,000 human lives. Tornadoes, forest fires, drought, hur-
ricanes, pestilence, and disease strike everywhere. We live in a world in
which the weeds come up by themselves, but not first-class tomatoes,
wheat, corn, or apples. The natural world trembles on the verge of col-
lapse. Change and decay is the order of life.

It is that very order that Paul says will itself come to an end. "In the
end the whole of created life will be rescued from the tyranny of change
and decay, and have its share in that magnificent liberty which can only
belong to the children of God!"

A new day is approaching in which change and decay will vanish forever. Peter helps us grasp that time when he writes that "according to his
promise we wait for new heavens and a new earth in which righteousness
dwells" (2 Peter 3:13, RSV).

BIRTH PANGS OF HOPE

We know that the whole creation has been groaning as in the pains of childbirth right up to the present time. Rom. 8:22, NIV.

THE CURSE FOLLOWING Adam's sin fell not only upon Adam and Eve and their offspring, but upon the natural world. As God told Adam:
"Cursed is the ground because of you;
    in toil you shall eat of it all the days of your life;
thorns and thistles it shall bring forth to you; . . .
In the sweat of your face
    you shall eat bread
till you return to the ground
    for out of it you were taken" (Gen. 3:17-19, RSV).

Paul has picked up and expanded upon that curse in Romans 8. That chapter in verses 20 through 22 captures the past, present, and future of nature's travail. In the past nature found itself subjected to "frustration" (Rom. 8:20, NIV), a term that means emptiness, futility, purposelessness, or transitoriness.

Then in verse 21 Paul projects nature into the future, with the idea that it will be "rescued from the tyranny of change and decay" (Phillips). But in our text for today (verse 22) the apostle adds the present, observing that "the whole creation has been groaning . . . right up to the present time." But the good news is that those groans are not meaningless, being "as in the pains of childbirth."

That very allusion points to the birth of a new order in which all "the former things are passed away" and there will be no more "groaning" or crying or pain (Rev. 21:4, 5). Jesus presented a similar word picture in Matthew 24 when He spoke of wars, famines, and earthquakes as "the beginning of the birth-pangs" of the end of the age (Matt. 24:8, RSV).

Paul has painted a picture of hope in spite of our world's troubles, in spite of the groanings of subhuman creation, in spite of the omnipresence of change and decay. The pains of childbirth point to the end of the Genesis curse; they point to the new earth; they announce Christ's return and the fulfillment of all God's promises in their completeness.

We can be thankful for a God who is not only persistent in pursuing us with His grace, but one who constantly sets before us the hope of better things as we tread life's pathway.

MOVING BEYOND
BEING HALF SAVED

*We ourselves, who have the first fruits of the Spirit, groan inwardly while
we wait for adoption, the redemption of our bodies. Rom. 8:23, NRSV.*

WHAT'S GOING ON HERE? Paul told the Romans back in Romans
8:14-16 that they had already been adopted when they accepted Christ.
And now in verse 23 he mentions that they are still waiting for the adoption. How can we reconcile those two statements?

The answer lies in the texts themselves, and goes back to what I earlier called "half saved." When we come to God by faith, we receive justification, He sets us apart for service (sanctification), and He gives us a
new heart and mind. Those are all part of our salvation. And they are
things already accomplished.

But as chapter 7 so graphically pointed out, our new hearts and minds
are still housed in the same old bodies, with all their "twitches" toward
temptation. Thus we are adopted into the family of God at our conversion
but do not receive the full benefits of our adoption until "the redemption
of our bodies." Paul places that step at the second coming of Christ, when
those who have died in Christ God now resurrects with bodies that are
both immortal and incorruptible (1 Cor. 15). At that point, according to
today's text, our adoption will be complete.

John pictures a similar scenario when he writes that "we are God's
children now; [but] it does not yet appear what we shall be, but we know
that when he appears we shall be like him" (1 John 3:2, RSV). Thus what
we have now is real salvation, even though it is not everything.

We must point out two things here. First, that we need to watch out
that we don't become one-text persons. I am always worried about someone who can nail down a truth with only one text. They too often leave out
the balancing passages. It takes both of Paul's adoption texts (Rom. 8:14-
16, 23) to come to a full understanding on the topic. If we had only one of
them we would have a distortion of God's teaching. The tragedy of the
Christian church is that too many are happier with distortions than with
balanced truth.

A second point to remember is that God is interested in saving the
whole person, rather than saving something like bodyless spirits or free-floating souls. Just as Jesus had a resurrection body, so will His followers.

MOVING TOWARD GLORIFICATION

In this hope we were saved. Now hope that is seen is not hope.
For who hopes for what he sees? Rom. 8:24, RSV.

TODAY'S TEXT COMES NEAR the end of a paragraph triggered by Romans 8:17, in which Paul stated that believers, fellow heirs of Christ, will suffer with Him. The thought of suffering raised a question. Since Christians are already children of God, because, as John puts it, they already have eternal life, why the trials and affliction?

Paul proceeds to answer that important query in verse 18, when he points out that any suffering that we have to undergo is as nothing compared with the good things God has prepared for His children. He then went on to say in verses 19 to 22 that it is not only humans that endure the ravages of the Fall, but also the subhuman creation. The apostle also claimed that creation itself groans in the hope of being set free. That groaning for the full redemption, we saw in verse 23, is not limited to creation but is shared by humans as they await the completion of their own redemption.

Today's passage (verse 24) carries forward the tension between being half saved and fully saved, between the past and the future. The words "were saved" reflect the past. The tense of the Greek verb points back to a decisive past liberation from the guilt and bondage of sin and from God's judgment upon it.

Yet, on the other hand, today's text looks to the future and a hope yet to be fulfilled, a hope whose fulfillment we haven't experienced as yet. The apostle undoubtedly has in mind verse 23's promise about the redemption of our bodies.

Yet verse 23 has another image of hope—the "firstfruits." In the Old Testament firstfruits refers to the Jewish custom of bringing the first of the harvest to God as an offering. That action consecrated the entire harvest and carried with it the thought of later fruits.

Paul has shifted the idea of firstfruits away from what we give to God and toward what He gives to us. Thus the apostle is saying in Romans 8 that the measure of the Holy Spirit that we already have is but a foretaste of the many other blessings that await us in the future.

It is that idea that Paul follows up with future hope in today's verse. And never forget that the concept of hope in his mind is not one of wishful thinking. Rather, it is a certainty. Someday the suffering will be over and God's children will be "glorified with" Christ (Rom. 8:17, RSV).

PERSEVERING IN HOPE

If we hope for what we do not see, we wait
for it with patience. Rom. 8:25, NRSV.

WAITING PATIENTLY IN THE hope of a completed salvation (Rom. 8:17), waiting patiently for glorification and the end of suffering (verse 23), waiting patiently for the end of "bondage to decay" (verse 21, RSV), waiting patiently through labor pains for the birth of the new world (verse 22), waiting patiently for the hope that we haven't seen yet (verse 25), waiting patiently for the advent of our Lord in the clouds of heaven, Christians know that they have a hope worth waiting for.

Interestingly enough, the word that Paul uses for "patiently" in today's text also appears in the third angel's message of Revelation 14:12: "Here is the patience of the saints: here are they that keep the commandments of God, and the faith of Jesus." Immediately following that text in verses 14-20 the revelator pictures the great Second Advent harvest. God will have an end-time people who are patiently waiting for Him to come. And what will they be doing until He returns? Keeping God's commandments and having faith in Jesus. It is significant that the various New Testament writers seem to reach the same conclusions despite the fact that they approach their subject matter in very different ways.

The *New American Standard Bible* translates the "patience" of Revelation 14:12 and Romans 8:25 as "perseverance." That rendering may be a better one in both Revelation and in Romans, since the context of each passage deals with suffering. The Greek word that Paul uses denotes positive and even aggressive endurance more than it does a quiet acceptance. It is the word employed to picture the attitude of a soldier who in the midst of battle does not pull back but fights on in spite of outward difficulties.

Those with that kind of patient endurance know what their hope or goal is. They not only wait for it (Rom. 8:25), but wait for it "eagerly" (verse 23, NIV). What are sufferings and discomforts in the face of such a hope, a hope beyond comparison with any possible sacrifices on our part.

Paul was a man under conviction. He knew what he had put his trust in. He had dedicated his entire life to that sure hope.

How is it with me? Do I have those same convictions? Do I have that same hope?

Lord, help me today to be like the apostle Paul, who knows that the "blessed hope" is what makes life worth living.

EFFECTIVE PRAYER IN SPITE OF OURSELVES

In the same way, the Spirit helps us in our weakness. We do not know what we ought to pray for, but the Spirit himself intercedes for us with groans that words cannot express. Rom. 8:26, NIV.

PRAYER STANDS AT THE very heart of our daily Christian experience, a fact nicely brought out in three quotations from *Steps to Christ:* (1) "Secret prayer . . . is the life of the soul" (p. 98); (2) "prayer is the key in the hand of faith to unlock heaven's storehouse" (p. 94); (3) "prayer is the opening of the heart to God as to a friend" (p. 93).

Those statements are true. Yet how ignorant we are when we come before God's throne. Moses shared that ignorance when he vainly prayed to God to allow him to enter the Promised Land (Deut. 3:25, 26). Paul showed it when he prayed three times for the removal of his "thorn . . . in the flesh," only to have God tell him that God's strength "is made perfect in weakness" (2 Cor. 12:7-9, RSV). John Knox highlights the problem when he writes that "our needs go far beyond the power of our speech to express them." In short, "we do not know what we ought to pray for."

For that reason God has sent the Holy Spirit. The Spirit not only encourages us while we await the consummation of redemption (Rom. 8:23), but He helps us in prayer because of our weakness and ignorance. God leaves no stone unturned in seeking to empower those who have accepted Him by faith and have become a part of His great family.

"The Spirit himself," our text tells us, "intercedes for us with groans that words cannot express."

What exactly is it that the Spirit is doing for us? J. B. Phillips seems to be on to the answer when he translates the passage as "his Spirit within us is actually praying for us in those agonising longings which cannot find words." When we lack the words to express our deepest needs, when we make sounds that are no better than inarticulate noise, the Spirit takes those sounds and makes them into effective intercession.

What a great God we have. Not only is salvation all of God. Not only is our faith a gift from Him. But even meaningful prayer is the Spirit working in spite of our manifold weaknesses.

We have plenty of room for humility. But we also have great reasons to rejoice in a heavenly Father who accepts us in all of our weaknesses.

PRAYER IS A MULTIPERSON OPERATION

He who searches the hearts of men knows what is the mind
of the Spirit, because the Spirit intercedes for the saints
according to the will of God. Rom. 8:27, RSV.

PRAYER INVOLVES AT LEAST three persons—an interesting fact, since most of us tend to think of prayer in terms of just two.

Romans 8:26 and 27 set forth those three as (1) we Christians, who in our weakness don't really know what to pray for, (2) the indwelling Spirit, who intercedes for us with inexpressible groans, and (3) God the Father (who knows our minds and hearts and also the mind of the Spirit), who hears and answers.

Perhaps we should add a fourth person as we think of the ministry of prayer. That is Christ, who is "at the right hand of God . . . interceding for us" (Rom. 8:34, NIV). When we pray, the Bible tells us that we are in contact with the entire Trinity. Prayer is as awesome as it is important.

Paul in Romans 8 helps us to see the Spirit's role in prayer clearer than in any other portion of the Bible. The apostle makes three statements about the Spirit's prayer ministry. First, because of our weak, half-saved condition, "the Spirit helps us" (verse 26, NIV). Second, the Spirit intercedes for us (verse 26) because of our ignorance in what to pray for. Third, the Spirit's intercession is according to God's will (verse 27).

Two points are of special interest in the Spirit's intercessory work. First, amazingly, the Spirit is said to "groan" for God's children as He prays with us (verse 26). Thus the Spirit's groaning joins that of creation (verse 22) and the church (verse 23). The idea of the Holy Spirit groaning has offended some, but the thought seems to be that the Spirit identifies with our groans, our attempts to express our frustration. He identifies with the pain of the world and the church, and, like true Christians, He longs for the final restitution of all things. Thus we and the Spirit groan together.

The second point of special interest is that today's text declares that the Spirit intercedes for us "according to the will of God." Thus the Spirit and Christ, who three times in Gethsemane prayed "Not My will but Thine be done," were in harmony that they should pray always according to the divine will. That pattern is also of special importance for the prayers of God's church. After all, true Christians want to be in God's will.

FIVE FIRM CONVICTIONS

*We know that God causes all things to work together
for good to those who love God, to those who are
called according to His purpose. Rom. 8:28, NASB.*

"WE KNOW"! With Romans 8:28 we have come not only to one of the best-known texts in the Bible, but to a section that runs to the end of a chapter that, in the words of one authority, "soars to sublime heights unequaled in the New Testament." The Christian doctrine of assurance raised in Romans 8:12-17 resurfaces in verses 28-39.

That comforting passage starts out with five firm convictions. First, "we know" that God is active in our lives. He is not indifferent to what happens to us, but is ceaselessly and energetically and purposefully active in the life of each believer. That, says Paul, "we know."

Second, we know that God is not merely at work for His people, but that He seeks their good. Of course, the highest good—the one that the book of Romans is primarily concerned with—is their final salvation. To Paul that is the ultimate good to which all else is subsidiary.

Third, we know that God is not merely guiding *some* things for good, but rather *"all things."* That does not mean that all things work out for the comfort of believers, or for their worldly interests, but that God directs all things with an eye on their eternal salvation. Thus even the sufferings of verse 17 and the groanings of verse 23 have a positive impact as they force believers to realize their own weaknesses and turn to their only source of help.

Fourth, we know that the beneficiaries of God's working for good in all things are those who love Him. Of course, that love is not freestanding. John and Paul in various places point out that we love Him because He first loved us. Our love is a responsive love; His is initiatory.

Fifth, we know that God has called us "according to His purpose"—our salvation.

We can know these five things about God. While we don't always understand why some particular thing is happening to us, we can still trust God that He knows what He is doing and will actively use events in our lives to His glory and our salvation. One of the best illustrations of that providence in individual lives is that of Joseph, who could tell his brothers: "You intended to harm me, but God intended it for good" (Gen. 50:20, NIV). God still "causes all things to work together for good to those who love" Him.

PREDESTINED TO SALVATION

For those whom he foreknew he also predestined to be
conformed to the image of his Son, in order that he might be
the first-born among many brethren. Rom. 8:29, RSV.

THE WORD "FOR" in this passage takes us back to Romans 8:28, in which we read that "God causes all things to work together for good to those who love God" (NASB). That text in turn we must interpret in the context of the topic of suffering that begins in verse 17 and in the additional context of the groanings for the end of sin and decay that characterize verses 19-25.

Then in verses 26 and 27 Paul begins to offer words of encouragement, including the fact that the Holy Spirit makes our prayer life effectual and that God actively is working for the good of His children (verse 28). That pastoral love extends over into verses 29 and 30, in which God tells us that He has known all about us from the beginning.

He not only foreknew each of us, but He predestined each to be saved. As Paul noted in 1 Timothy 2:4, God "desires all men to be saved and to come to the knowledge of the truth" (RSV). Christ made a similar statement when He said, "Come unto me, all ye that labour and are heavy laden, and I will give you rest" (Matt. 11:28). Again, "whosoever believeth in him should not perish, but have everlasting life" (John 3:16). "Whosoever will, let him take the water of life freely" (Rev. 22:17).

The biblical pattern is clear: God offers salvation to all freely, but it is up to each individual to accept the offer. He forces no one.

The purpose of our passage is pastoral and practical. Paul continues to comfort those "suffering" and "groaning" in their half-saved condition. He assures them that not only is the Spirit with them (Rom. 8:26, 27), that not only is He actively working on their behalf in each of their troubles, but also that their ultimate salvation rests in His hands. The hands of the very One who foreknew them as Father and who predestined or selected them for salvation also cradles their future. They have nothing to fear in spite of what may have been foreboding circumstances.

The Lord not only selected them for salvation; He also wants them "to be conformed to the image of his Son." He desires for each Christian to become more like Jesus. He seeks to re-create Christ's image in each of His children. If we think of justification as the beginning of personal salvation, growth in holiness is its continuation in each Christian's life.

THE ASSURANCE OF GLORIFICATION

Those whom he predestined he also called; and those whom he called he
also justified; and those whom he justified he also glorified. Rom. 8:30, RSV.

WITH TODAY'S TEXT PAUL continues the pastoral comfort he began
in Romans 8:18. Taking up where he stopped in the previous verse, the
apostle tells us that God also called those whom He predestinated. Those
who responded to the preaching of the gospel—or what we might think of
as the gospel call—God justified or counted as righteous. And those who
remain faithful are assured of glorification.

It is significant that Paul uses the past tense with glorification in the
sense that every Christian who remains in Christ will be glorified at the
Second Advent. Such glorification is not a maybe but a certainty. The believer's glorification is just as certain as Christ's, who was not only resurrected but ascended to heaven.

Where, you may be asking, is sanctification in this list of the steps in
salvation? Shouldn't it come right between justification and glorification?

The answer is a definite yes. The topic of sanctification (or growth in
grace) is certainly important to Paul. He has dealt with it extensively in
chapter 6 and earlier in chapter 8 and will devote chapters 12-15 to the
topic. In fact, he alluded to it in Romans 8:29 when he wrote of believers
becoming conformed to Christ's image. We don't know why it's missing
here. Paul may have felt that he had so adequately covered the topic that
its place in the plan of salvation would be obvious to his readers. But more
probable is the thought that he desired to present glorification as an accomplished fact for those who persevered through the sufferings and
groanings of their half-saved state. In other words, he wasn't nearly as interested in listing each and every step in the plan of salvation as he was in
comforting believers who had experienced the internal tensions of
Romans 7 and the external tensions of chapter 8.

Paul repeatedly in Romans returns to the topic of the glorification of
the saints at the end of time. And in Romans 8:30 this theme is all the
more beautiful because it is completely contexted in statements dealing
with the assurance of those who are in Christ. Not only are they the sons
of God through adoption, but the apostle will soon tell them that nothing
can separate them from God's love (verses 31-39). No wonder he so
firmly states that glorification is an accomplished reality for those who
maintain their faith in Christ.

UNANSWERABLE QUESTION NUMBER 1

*What shall we then say to these things? If God
be for us, who can be against us? Rom. 8:31.*

TODAY'S VERSE BEGINS what some have called the Christian's *triumph song.* Paul has completed the first half of his letter to the Romans. He has demonstrated the universality of sin and has set forth God's plan of salvation in terms of justification, sanctification, and glorification. But before he moves on, he decides to give the trumpet of assurance a blast of certainty.

Building on the themes of adoption and glorification for those who remain in the family of God, the apostle asks five questions for which there are no answers. As John Stott frames it, "he hurls" his questions "into space, as it were, in a spirit of bold defiance. He challenges anybody and everybody, in heaven, earth, or hell, to answer them and to deny the truth which they contain. But there is no answer."

The first question asks, "If God be for us, who can be against us?" The force of that question lies in the assertion that *God is for us.* That is one of the most important truths that we can ever understand. *God is for us* is the entire basis of the gospel as presented by the New Testament. The Lord so loved the world that He sent His Son to die in our place while we were still His enemies. That takes love, that takes a "for us" kind of God.

God not only sent Jesus, but He justifies those who by faith accept Christ's sacrifice for them, dispatches the Holy Spirit to empower their sanctification, and guarantees their glorification if they choose to remain in a faith relationship to Him. Truly He is "God for us."

"If God be for us," then "who can be against us?" The obvious answer is "nobody." That doesn't mean that Christians don't face any opposition. Paul's whole biography is one of persecution and resistance to his message. Also, as we noted in Romans 7, indwelling sin is an ongoing, powerful adversary. And death is still an enemy, defeated but not yet destroyed.

No, Christians still have forces against them, but nothing can defeat them, because God is on their side.

God for us is the center of the gospel itself. We must never forget that truth, no matter how bad things may get. *God for us* is the distilled essence of the good news. That realization will give us the courage to continue day by day.

Unanswerable Question Number 2

He who did not withhold even His own Son, but gave
Him up for all of us, will He not also with Him
freely give us all things. Rom. 8:32, Weymouth.

WILL GOD REALLY GIVE us all things? I remember as a young man asking for a sports car. But I never got it. As a college student I prayed for a little extra money so that I could provide my family with something besides the barest necessities. But we continued to exist on necessities.

In answering our question, we always need to remember the context. One of the greatest faults of some Christians is to remove God's promises from the context that provides their meaning. The promise of today's text about God freely giving His children all things appears within the framework of the plan of salvation. Paul is saying that we can be absolutely certain that the God who is "for us" will provide everything necessary for our salvation. Of that the apostle has not the slightest doubt.

How do we know? How can we be confident that God will freely offer us everything needed for salvation? Because, said Paul, He "did not withhold even His own Son, but gave Him up for all of us." That text reminds us of Genesis 22:16, in which God blesses Abraham because of his readiness to sacrifice Isaac. The blessing came, God told him, because you "have not withheld your son, your only son" (RSV).

The big difference between God and Abraham is that Abraham was praised for his readiness to offer his son, even though he didn't have to go through with the sacrifice. For Abraham it was a test of faith. But for God it was a reality. He did in fact give His only begotten Son for the sins of the world at Calvary.

God offered up Christ "for all of us." That phrase adds a personal touch to Christ's work. He never *just* died; He stood in my place as my substitute.

Paul argues in today's text from the greater to the lesser. That is, since He has already given the greatest gift imaginable (His own Son), "how can he fail to lavish every other gift upon us?" (Rom. 8:32, REB).

In the Son He gave everything. The cross is the guarantee of the continuing generosity of a God totally dedicated to completing what He has begun in the gift of Jesus Christ.

UNANSWERABLE
QUESTION NUMBER 3

Who shall bring any charge against God's elect?
It is God who justifies. Rom. 8:33, RSV.

THIS THIRD QUESTION TAKES us in our imagination into a court of law. The question "Who shall bring any charge against God's elect?" might have been phrased "Who can make a charge stick against God's elect?"

Obviously many lodge all kinds of charges against Christians. Internally we have the Christian conscience, since Christians still struggle with sin as they grow in Christ. Externally we find those both inside and outside the church who are more than happy to condemn sincere Christians. But the greatest adversary of all is Satan, "the accuser of our brethren" (Rev. 12:10), the prototype of all those inside the church who so piously denounce others.

The best biblical example of the dynamic taking place in today's verse appears in Zechariah 3:1-5. There we see Joshua the high priest standing in the Temple, undoubtedly to present an offering. Satan is also there, accusing Joshua, who wears filthy garments symbolizing his sins. The devil argues that Joshua is unfit for office because he is a sinner.

But the scene includes one more person—God. Through an angel He declares, "The Lord rebuke you, O Satan! The Lord who has chosen Jerusalem rebuke you! Is not this a brand plucked from the fire?" (Zech. 3:2, RSV). Scripture then tells us that God had Joshua's filthy garments removed and clothed him with clean ones. "Behold," said the angel, "I have taken your iniquity away from you, and I will clothe you with rich apparel" (verse 4, RSV). The clean clothes, of course, represented his justification. Who could accuse him now? No one, because God had justified him.

That Old Testament picture parallels Paul's third question. Some may seek to condemn those Christians who retain a living connection with God through faith, but their accusations fall flat. God has justified them. Acquitted at the highest level, they are safe in Christ.

As Christians we have nothing to fear. Today we need to praise God for His boundless assurance. We must become more and more conscious of that precious doctrine. It ought to encourage us every day, especially in times when old *diablos* is on our case.

UNANSWERABLE QUESTION NUMBER 4

Who is to condemn? It is Christ Jesus, who died, yes, who was raised, who is at the right hand of God, who indeed intercedes for us. Rom. 8:34, NRSV.

THIS VERSE IS CLOSELY related to Romans 8:33, which asked who will bring any charge against God's elect. And as with that question, the answer is that while many would like to condemn, none will be able to make their accusations stick.

Why? Because, Paul says, Christ is on our side. And remember that Christ told us while He was on earth that "the Father judgeth no man, but hath committed all judgment unto the Son" (John 5:22). Thus even though "we must all appear before the judgment seat of Christ" to answer for our lives (2 Cor. 5:10), Christians (those who have a continuing faith relationship with God through Jesus) have absolutely nothing to fear.

Why? Because He (1) died for them, (2) was raised from the dead, (3) is sitting at the right hand of God, and (4) is presently interceding for Christians as their heavenly high priest.

Let's look at each of those four reasons. First, Christ died for the very same sins that would otherwise condemn Christians. As Paul noted to the Corinthians, He was made "to be sin who knew no sin, so that in him we might become the righteousness of God" (2 Cor. 5:21, RSV). Christ gave His life for the sins of His followers. As a result, there is "now no condemnation for those who are in Christ Jesus" (Rom. 8:1, RSV). He will not turn around and pronounce judgment against His followers for the very sins that He died for. He absorbed the penalty for those "in Him."

Second, Christ not only died for Christians, but also "was raised." Note that the "was raised" is a passive verb, thus symbolizing not only that He rose, but that the Father resurrected Him as a demonstration of the acceptability of His sacrifice.

Third, Christ is "at the right hand of God," the place of honor in the heavenly realm. And fourth, Christ intercedes for us. He is our heavenly high priest, "able also to save them to the uttermost that come unto God by him, seeing he ever liveth to make intercession for them" (Heb. 7:25).

If the judge is on our side there is no way that we can come under condemnation. We are safe in Jesus.

UNANSWERABLE
QUESTION NUMBER 5

Who shall separate us from the love of Christ?
shall tribulation, or distress, or persecution,
or famine, or nakedness, or peril, or sword? Rom. 8:35.

THE FIRST HALF OF the triumph song that began in verse 31 demonstrated the impossibility of any charge against the believer being sustained before God. With today's passage we move into four verses that deal with the impossibility of a Christian's being separated from Christ's love.

With his fifth unanswerable question the apostle suggests seven candidates that might possibly create such a gulf. The first three—trouble, hardship, and persecution (NIV)—seem to denote the pressures and distresses produced by Christians simply living in an ungodly and hostile world.

The next two, famine and nakedness, represent essential material needs. Any lack along those lines might have raised questions about God's care in the believers' minds, since the Sermon on the Mount (see Matt. 6:25-34) seemed to promise both necessities to all of God's children.

Paul concludes his list of possible things that might sever Christians from Christ's love with physical threats—peril (or danger) and sword, including the risk of death.

The apostle's seven candidates were hardly of academic interest to his first readers. Paul had endured the first six himself, and would in the not too distant future suffer from the sword when the Roman authorities put him to death for his faith. The Roman Christians to whom he was writing undoubtedly shared similar problems and would also do so even more in the forthcoming reign of Nero, when some of their number would burn as living torches for the sadistic entertainment of the emperor and his guests.

But none of those problems could separate a Christian from Christ's love or the salvation they had through their faith relationship to Him. They had assurance of salvation in spite of the fact that they would share with Him in suffering (Rom. 8:17).

Paul, however, overlooked one candidate that can indeed come between a Christian and salvation. That is, persistent rejection of faith in Christ as Savior and an unwillingness to walk with Him in God's principles. But even that rejection of His love and His salvation would not isolate us from His love.

TROUBLE BECAUSE WE ARE CHRISTIANS

Just as it is written, "For Your sake we are being
put to death all day long; We were considered
as sheep to be slaughtered." Rom. 8:36, NASB.

SOMETIMES WE GET THE idea that as Christians we will always be safe as long as we remain faithful; that all we have to do is pray and God will send a squadron of angels to make sure no one hurts us.

Nothing could be further from the truth. The life of Christ Himself demonstrates that even God's own perfect Son suffered pain and death. Paul's experience reinforced that truth. Martyrdom is an important aspect of church history. The apostle's point isn't that Christians won't suffer, but that nothing outside of themselves can separate them from Christ's love and their salvation.

In order to illustrate his point that being a follower of God does not exempt one from trouble, Paul quotes Psalm 44:22, which pictures Israel's persecution by the nations. They were not suffering because they had forgotten God or turned to idols. Instead, they faced persecution and trial because of their loyalty to Him. "For your sake we face death all day long" (NIV). Paul would pass on a similar message to Timothy for those living in the Christian era: "Indeed all who desire to live a godly life in Christ Jesus will be persecuted" (2 Tim. 3:12, RSV).

The cost of serving God has historically been high. According to Hebrews 11, God's faithful people had suffered for centuries before the incarnation of Jesus, not only at the hands of Gentiles but also from their fellow believers. "Some were tortured, refusing to accept release, that they might rise again to a better life. Others suffered mocking and scourging, and even chains and imprisonment. They were stoned, they were sawn in two, they were killed with the sword; they went about in skins of sheep and goats, destitute, afflicted, ill-treated" (Heb. 11:35-37, RSV).

Yet none of those things were able to separate them from the love of Christ. That lesson was important for the Roman Christians because of the times in which they lived. It is also vital to us, because of what the Bible teaches will happen before the Second Advent. But we, like the Roman Christians of old, can rest in full assurance that even though troubles will come, *nothing* can separate us from God's love.

MORE THAN CONQUERORS

In all these things we are more than
conquerors through him that loved us. Rom. 8:37.

"MORE THAN CONQUERORS." The Bible has few phrases more memorable.

That is especially true when we take "more than conquerors" in the context of the previous verse, which spoke of the people of God "as sheep to be slaughtered."

Think about that one for a moment. A sheep that conquers. One might imagine conquering lions or bears or even swarms of ants. But conquering sheep sounds ludicrous. Sheep just aren't the conquering type. They are more noted for their helplessness than their aggression.

Of course, Paul's images are figurative, but they are not meaningless. When it comes right down to it, it is the sheeplike characteristics of Christians that make them more than conquerors. Never forget that we are more than conquerors "through him that loved us." We are not triumphant on our own but in the strength of Jesus Christ, who met the devil on his own turf and defeated him.

Our strength as Christians lies in a recognition of our helplessness, our recognition that we are sinners, our recognition that we have no righteousness of our own, our recognition that our salvation is totally by grace and that we can do nothing to earn or even supplement the value of God's gift. In short, a Christian's strength lies in his or her sheeplike characteristics, those traits that drive us to the foot of the cross.

We are more than conquerors because we realize that holding on to Christ by faith and letting Him direct our lives is the only thing that can enable us to face the troubles without and the tensions within caused by our less than perfect lives. Even our weakness and sinfulness points us back to our constant need of Jesus and His grace.

Christians are those who are more than conquerors through that other Lamb, "the Lamb that was slain from the creation of the world" (Rev. 13:8, NIV). As such, it is our primary task to maintain a relationship with the Lamb of Calvary. Therein is our hope, therein is our assurance in both this world and in the one to come. Let us rejoice with Paul that in all things "we are more than conquerors through him that loved us."

VICTORY'S CRESCENDO

For I am persuaded, that neither death, nor life,
nor angels, nor principalities, nor powers, nor things
present, nor things to come, . . . shall be able to separate us
from the love of God, which is in Christ Jesus our Lord. Rom. 8:38, 39.

I LOVE THAT PASSAGE. I love to hear it. I love to think about it. And I love to contemplate the depth of its meaning.

Romans 8 is the great assurance chapter. It starts out proclaiming that there is "no condemnation for those who are in Christ Jesus" (Rom. 8:1, RSV), and it ends up with the declaration that absolutely nothing can separate us from the God who provided the free gift of salvation that Paul expounded upon in the first 7 chapters.

In between, Romans 8 is packed with further assurance: Christians are God's children, they have the certain promise of future glory, God has given them the Holy Spirit, God works out all things for their good, nothing or no one can condemn them, nothing can come between them and God, and they are "more than conquerors."

What more could Paul have said? He has hammered home, pounded down, and fully exhibited one of the greatest teachings of the Bible—that those who choose to maintain a faith relationship with God through Jesus cannot lose. That is powerful. Praise God from whom all blessings flow.

And now at the end of the first half of Romans Paul supplies us with a victorious crescendo, stamping home anew the security of those safe in Jesus. Nothing, neither death or life (anything that can happen to us in life), nor angels or demons (any cosmic or superhuman agencies), nor anything in time (neither the present or the future) or space (neither height or depth), nor any other power, nor anything else whatever shall be able to come between us and our God. Paul leaves no stones unturned in exhibiting his certainty, his confidence in God.

Let us never forget that our confidence and assurance rests not in our love for God—which is frail, fickle, and halting—but in His love for us, which is steadfast and persevering. Our hope is to "hang in there" by faith, never to let go of the God who is more than willing to supply freely all our needs in relation to justification, sanctification, and final glorification. For those "in Christ" Paul has the utmost confidence in the final outcome. Nothing (except themselves) can block them from final victory.

Salvation for Everyone

Romans 9:1–11:36

Taking a Fifth Step With Paul

I am speaking the truth in Christ, I am not lying; my conscience bears me witness in the Holy Spirit. Rom. 9:1, RSV.

ROMANS 9:1 SIGNALS a major shift in Paul's subject matter.

So far we have taken four steps with the apostle on his guided tour through the book of Romans. In the first, 1:1-17, we met Paul and the Roman Christians and saw his themes. The second, 1:18–3:20, introduced us to the problem of sin and its universality among both Jews and Gentiles. The third, 3:21–5:21, revealed how God's gracious gift of justification met the sin problem for those willing to accept it by faith. Then in 6:1–8:39 Paul helped us see that those who were in a faith relationship with Jesus would walk with Him in the principles of God. The apostle climaxed his treatment with a great hymn of victory and assurance.

Now we are ready for a fifth step with Paul. In this one he will help the Jews see how they fit into God's plan. Some authorities see this chapter as "a kind of postscript" to the plan of salvation set forth in the first eight chapters, but we should view it as an integral part of that presentation. After all, in the keynote of Romans in 1:16 Paul noted that the gospel "is the power of God for salvation to every one who has faith, to the Jew first and also to the Greek" (RSV). He is now ready to show what the gospel means for the Jewish people.

The "Jewish question" is a big one for Paul. The Jews had been God's chosen people, but now seem to have been displaced by a largely Gentile church. If the Jews are the "elect," why are most of them outside the Christian community? What part do they have to play in the plan of salvation?

It is to such issues that Paul now turns. But he starts out his three chapters on the topic in a very strange way. Three times in Romans 9:1 he emphasizes the truthfulness and sincerity of what follows: (1) "I am speaking the truth in Christ," (2) "I am not lying," and (3) "My conscience bears me witness in the Holy Spirit."

The apostle feels that some of his readers will have grave doubts about various points of his presentation. He wants them to know that he is speaking with the utmost heartfelt sincerity.

There is a lesson for us here. All of us face difficult situations in which we may be mistrusted and misunderstood. In such situations we need to bend over backward in reaching people if we hope to communicate with them effectively.

PAUL'S "IMPOSSIBLE WISH"

*I have great sorrow and unceasing anguish in my heart. For I could
wish that I myself were cursed and cut off from Christ for the sake of my
brothers, those of my own race, the people of Israel. Rom. 9:2-4, NIV.*

PAUL IS DEEPLY CONCERNED for Israel, since the vast majority of
them had not accepted the gospel that he believed provided the only
means of salvation. His anguish reaches the point that he claims that he
"could wish" that he himself might become a sacrifice for them if that
would mean their salvation.

That desire reminds us of Moses. After Israel sinned in worshiping the
golden calf, Moses prayed to God for them, saying: "Alas, this people
have sinned a great sin; they have made for themselves gods of gold. But
now, if thou wilt forgive their sins—and if not, blot me, I pray thee, out
of thy book which thou hast written" (Ex. 32:31, 32, RSV).

Thus Paul in wrestling with his fellow Israelites selects a forceful illustration from the nation's past history. Yet his "could wish" represented
what Everett Harrison refers to as an "impossible wish." After all, Moses
had not been able to fulfill his request. God told him: "Whoever has
sinned against me, him will I blot out of my book. But now go, lead the
people" (verses 33, 34).

Paul had a parallel concern with Moses for his people. But, as James
Denney points out, their concerns were not exactly the same. Moses in his
identification with the Jews was willing to die *with* them, but Paul suggested
that he would die *for* them. Thus, as Denney phrases it, he was reflecting "a
spark from the fire of Christ's substitutionary sacrifice." The apostle, of
course, knew that his wish was truly impossible. After all, he had just finished writing about the fact that there is nothing except our unfaith that can
separate us from God's love. And Paul was expressing anything but unfaith.

Martin Luther, the great Reformer, caught the essence of the apostle's
anguish when he pointed out that the whole context of the passage indicates his deep desire for the salvation of the Jews. "He wants to bring
Christ to them. . . . He appealed to them with a sacred oath, because it
seems unbelievable that a man should want to be damned in order that the
damned might be saved."

Do I have that same burning anguish for the lost that Paul had?

*Lord, help me today to enter into Your concern for individuals still in
sin's grip. Amen.*

SUPERLATIVE BLESSINGS

They are Israelites, and to them belong the sonship,
the glory, the covenants, the giving of the law,
the [temple] worship, and the promises. Rom. 9:4, RSV.

ISRAEL WAS A PRIVILEGED people. Paul had no doubt as to Israel's uniqueness among nations and its special role in salvation history.

In today's verse he begins to list the very blessings that should have prepared them to receive Christ. First, "theirs is the adoption as sons" (NIV). The Old Testament repeatedly presents Israel as God's "firstborn son" (see, e.g., Ex. 4:22). In a similar manner it proclaims that God is the nation's father (Jer. 31:9). But Romans 9:4 is the only place that speaks of Israel as being adopted, a term that denotes God's graciousness in bringing the nation into the heavenly family.

Second, the nation not only had a special relationship to God, but it had "the glory." That undoubtedly refers to the shekinah that represented God's splendor and filled the Most Holy Place of the wilderness tabernacle and later the Temple. That glory symbolized God as being "enthroned between the cherubim that are on the ark" (2 Sam. 6:2, NIV).

Third, Israel had been the recipient of the covenants that God had made through Abraham, Moses, and David. Those covenants became the vehicle through which Israel entered into a singular relationship to God as both a people of unique privilege and special responsibility.

Fourth, Israel was the custodian of God's law. The Jews prided themselves in having God's special revelation of His will, spoken by His voice and written by His finger. Paul agreed with them that their possession of the law had indeed put them in a unique position.

Beyond those blessings, the Jews had both the Temple worship and the promises. The promises, in particular, related to the coming of the Messiah as God's prophet, priest, and king. And the Temple worship was so special to them that they forbade the Gentiles, on pain of death, to enter sectors of it open to all male Jews.

Truly the Jews in Paul's mind were a blessed people. But, we need to ask, what good are advantages if they don't lead to salvation? Some such idea must have been in Paul's mind. That question should be in our minds also as we meditate upon our own personal relationship to God.

ADVANTAGES DON'T SAVE

Theirs are the patriarchs, and from them is traced the human ancestry of Christ, who is God over all, forever praised! Amen. Rom. 9:5, NIV.

PAUL HAS NOT YET finished listing Israel's profound blessings. He cited six in Romans 9:4, and in today's reading he supplies us with two more. First, they had the patriarchs, especially Abraham, Isaac, and Jacob, through whom God's blessings came.

And second, the Israelite nation was the channel for the Messiah. All the way from the first hint of the Messiah in Genesis 3:15 through the promises to David, the hope of the nation had focused on God's special Anointed One, who would save His people. For that reason Matthew in his Gospel's first chapter goes to great pains to demonstrate that Jesus of Nazareth had the proper Jewish lineage and ancestry to qualify as the predicted Messiah.

Eight great blessings. Yet the nation was not saved. Many individual Jews, of course, had come to Christ, but not the bulk of the nation. We find a lesson here: Superb spiritual advantages save no one. They may help prepare people's hearts, but without the choice to accept Christ they are meaningless.

Paul had experienced that truth himself. In Philippians he tells us of his own background. He lists six advantages, four by birth and two that he had earned through his own zeal. The apostle (1) had been circumcised on the eighth day, (2) belonged to the people of Israel, (3) was a Hebrew of the Hebrews (had a clear bloodline), (4) was a member of the exclusive Pharisaic party, (5) had demonstrated his zeal for God by spearheading the persecution of Christians, and (6) was "blameless" in terms of law righteousness (Phil. 3:4-6).

A young man with everything going for him, Paul had all the advantages. Yet they didn't save him. That happened when he encountered Jesus on the road to Damascus. At that point he concluded that all his privileges were not enough. When he met Jesus he realized what true righteousness was, and that all his prerogatives were as "dung." Instantly he traded in all his human advantages and achievements for the righteousness of Christ (verses 7-9).

Paul wants the same thing for his fellow Israelites. And he holds out the same for you and me. He longs for us to trade in all our advantages, all our achievements, even all of our selves, for salvation in Christ Jesus.

NOT EVERY CHURCH MEMBER IS A CHRISTIAN

It is not as though the word of God had failed.
For not all Israelites truly belong to Israel. Rom. 9:6, NRSV.

A CHAMPION WOODCUTTER from central Europe discovered a piece of wood in the mouth of a grain sack. Remarkably enough, the wood was the same color as the wheat grains, so he decided to carve the wood into imitation wheat.

After preparing a handful of them, he mixed them with some real wheat and invited his friends to tell them apart. But he had done his work so well that no one could tell the real from the artificial. In fact, the woodcutter himself couldn't identify the imitations. In the end the only way to distinguish the true from the false kernels was to place all the grains in water. After a few days the real grain sprouted, while the imitations remained exactly what they had always been: dead wood.

We find a parallel here to those who claim to be God's people. To human eyes it is often impossible to tell the genuine believers from those who have chosen to behave as if they were Christians. They may all belong to the same congregation, but a difference still exists nevertheless. Those who truly have a faith relationship with Christ will demonstrate that connection across time by their spiritual growth.

The distinction between those who only seem to be spiritual children and those who actually are is critical as Paul moves into the next section of Romans.

Paul here deals with the problematic issue of why so few Israelites had accepted the gospel. After all, God's promises had been made to Israel, yet the nation as a whole seemed unresponsive. Did that mean that the promises had failed? Or that God Himself had failed? Could one no longer trust the promises?

Not at all, Paul would answer. God's promises had nothing wrong with them. The problem resided in the recipients. The fact of the matter was that not all Israelites were spiritually connected to God by faith (cf. 2:25-29).

The same is true of church members. Not everyone who belongs to the church is a Christian. But those who truly have chosen to have a living relationship with God will demonstrate over time Christ's life within them.

ELECTED FOR RESPONSIBILITY

*It is not the children of Abraham by natural descent who are children
of God; it is the children born through God's promise who
are reckoned as Abraham's descendants. For the
promise runs: ". . . Sarah shall have a son." Rom. 9:8, 9, REB.*

IN ROMANS 9:6 PAUL noted that not all those descended from Israel actually belonged to Israel. He continues that thought in verses 7-9, illustrating his point from Abraham's family. He writes that not all of Abraham's children were true descendants of Abraham in the sense that they were included in the promises. In the process Paul quotes Genesis 21:12: "It is through Isaac that your offspring will be reckoned" (NIV). In other words, the promise came through Isaac's line and did not include Ishmael and the sons of Keturah (Abraham's wife after Sarah's death). All of Paul's Jewish readers would have quickly agreed with him. They were quite proud of their religious and family pedigree.

But Paul's Jewish readers would have denied his interpretation of the meaning of God's selection of Isaac. They would have seen the choice of Isaac as God binding Himself to Isaac's descendants and that the Lord therefore owed something to them as the true children of Abraham. It is a logic that made it almost impossible for them to see themselves as Jews on the outside of the heavenly kingdom. God would save them *because* they were the true children of Abraham. But that is not what Paul meant. He insisted that *God was free to choose* Isaac and reject Esau.

But at this point it is absolutely crucial to see *why* God picked Isaac. *He selected him for service rather than eternal salvation.* After all, Ishmael and Esau were included in the covenant, and at God's command were circumcised. Both received His blessing (see Gen. 17:20).

But while Ishmael and Esau might have had God's blessing, the nations they represented were not the people to whom God would give His revelation or through whom He would send the Messiah.

Thus God is God. He is free to choose whom He will honor with the responsibility of preserving and spreading His message on earth. But having been selected does not mean that they are better than others or will be automatically saved. God has given them a responsibility to uphold His name, but not a guarantee of personal or corporate salvation. That is the very point that the Jews had a difficult time grasping. Some Christians struggle with the same issue. Spiritual pride has a blinding effect on the soul.

THE DOCTRINE OF ELECTION

*Again, a word of promise came to Rebecca. . . . It came
before the children were born . . . , showing that God's act
of choice has nothing to do with achievements, good or bad,
but is entirely a matter of his will. Rom. 9:10-12, Phillips.*

THE DOCTRINE OF ELECTION! Some people don't like it. Others prefer to avoid it. But Paul lays it out just as firmly as words can state it.

In Romans 9 Paul has thus far told his Jewish readers that God had chosen and blessed them above every other people. But that very blessing raised a question. If they were the children of the promise, why hadn't they responded to Jesus? Why were they being passed by? Had God's word to them failed?

No! Paul replied. There was nothing wrong with God's word or the promises. The fault was rather in the Jews themselves and in their misunderstanding of how the Lord operates. God has a perfect right to call whom He wants to serve Him.

How do we know that He is not obligated to the Jews alone? Hadn't they been His people? On what basis can the Gentiles share in the promises?

Romans 9 seeks to answer those very questions. The apostle's first tactic is to demonstrate that God's election of a people for responsibility is not based on their goodness or merit, but according to His choice.

Paul illustrates his premise by appealing to Jewish history. How did the Jews become God's special people? First, God deliberately chose Isaac over Ishmael. That is clear enough, but some might not have seen the issue, since those two had different mothers and God had made the promise to Abraham and Sarah to the exclusion of Hagar.

With that thought in mind, Paul pushes his logic further. He takes up Esau and Jacob, who not only had the same mother but the same pregnancy. Yet God selected Jacob rather than Esau even before they were born, even before they could do good or evil.

What is the point? That God unilaterally elected or chose those to whom He gave the responsibility of fulfilling His mission on the earth.

The argument thus far in Romans is that since all are guilty, no one has an exclusive claim on grace. If God extends His grace to someone outside a given circle, its members have no ground to protest, because the only reason they are inside is past grace. God elects whom He will. That's good news. Christ died for everybody and wants to save all.

God "Hates" Esau

As it is written, "Jacob I loved, Esau I hated." Rom. 9:13, RSV.

IS THAT TEXT REALLY in the Bible? Yes, twice. Once here in Romans 9:13 and once in Malachi 1:2, 3, the source for Paul's quotation.

OK, you may be thinking, *it's in the Bible, but do we have to use it as a worship text? I don't like it. Why not just read our Bible as if the passage doesn't exist?*

Too often we just skip over those parts of the Bible we don't like. I would suggest that it is better to understand what God meant. Who knows, there might even be a blessing in this passage for us.

We need first to remember that the Bible doesn't always use words in the same sense we do. For example, Jesus claimed that we must "hate" our father and mother and wife if we are to be His followers (Luke 14:26). How do you line up that injunction with the fifth commandment, which tells us that we must honor our parents? The obvious implication is that we are not to hate our parents in the modern sense of the term but to choose to put Christ first in our life.

The same applies to Jesus' saying that His followers needed to "hate" their own life if they wanted life eternal (John 12:25). "Hate" in the Bible does not necessarily imply aggressive hostility. As in the case of Jacob's relationship to Rachel, whom he loved, and Leah, whom he "hated" (Gen. 29:30, 31), Scripture often employed the term to express a preference for one thing or person over another, both of whom one could feel affection for.

That biblical usage lines up with statements that claim that God is love (1 John 4:8), that He so loved the world that He sent Jesus (John 3:16), and that He loves sinners (Rom. 5:8).

The plain fact is that God *chose* the nation (both passages dealing with loving Jacob and hating Esau refer not to individuals but nations) flowing from Jacob (Israel) over the nation issuing from Esau (Edom). It was His choice to send the Messiah through one and not the other.

In the same way, when Jacob's offspring (the Jews of Christ's day) rejected Jesus, God felt compelled to give Israel's blessing to another nation—the church (Matt. 21:33-43). Thus, Paul states in Romans 9:1-13, God hasn't changed. He still operates on the principle He did when He chose Jacob over Esau. The Lord is not captive to any religious group. His promises have not failed. But because of Israel's rejection of Jesus, He has selected a new people to carry out His mission on earth.

"THERE'S A WIDENESS IN GOD'S MERCY"

Now do we conclude that God is unjust? Never! God says long ago to Moses: "I will have mercy on whom I will have mercy, and I will have compassion on whom I have compassion." Rom. 9:14, 15, Phillips.

IN ROMANS 9:6-13 Paul has answered the question of whether God's promises to the Jews had failed, since they were no longer His kingdom people. His answer was that the Lord could now work through a largely Gentile church just as He had originally chosen to use Israel. God Himself had made Israel's selection, independent of any merit on their part.

That answer raises a second question that Paul answers in verses 14-18. Is God unjust in being so arbitrary?

Absolutely not! is Paul's reply. Why? Because the question is framed wrong. God does not base His selection (or election or predestination) upon justice but mercy. The apostle proves his point by quoting Exodus 33:19: "I will have mercy on whom I will have mercy, and I will have compassion on whom I have compassion" (NIV). His Jewish detractors might argue with him, but they won't contradict Scripture.

God's election is always according to mercy. If He had given the Israelites what they deserved (justice), they would have been obliterated. The same applies to the Jews of Paul's day, or even to Christians living in the twenty-first century. We are totally dependent on God's mercy.

Given the nature of justice, John Stott points out that "the wonder is not that some are saved and others not, but that anybody is saved at all." If God, therefore, chooses to have mercy on some who are not of "our group," who are we to challenge Him? We must never forget that it is His mercy that is our salvation, not our worthiness.

We must keep a vital point in mind as we read the rather difficult (from the perspective of modern minds) portions of Romans 9. We must remember that Paul is not answering *our* questions about free will. He doesn't even address the issue in Romans 9. Rather, Paul is highlighting that God is merciful. So merciful that He elects not only Jews for salvation but also Gentiles.

As the old hymn puts it: "There's a wideness in God's mercy, like the wideness of the sea." We can praise God for that. Without His sovereign mercy we would not be.

ALL DEPENDS ON MERCY

So then it does not depend on the man who wills or the
man who runs, but on God who has mercy. Rom. 9:16, NASB.

"MERCY" IS THE KEY word in Romans 9–11. In fact, the entire section climaxes with the idea that "God has consigned all men to disobedience, that he may have mercy upon all" (Rom. 11:32, RSV). Mercy in relation to God appears nine times in these three chapters, but only twice in the rest of Romans.

But even though Romans 1–8 does not contain the word "mercy," the idea itself undergirds those chapters. After all, Paul had demonstrated that all human beings had sinned and deserved to die. Yet God opened up for them the plan of righteousness by faith, if they would only accept it.

Thus at the very foundation of the concepts of grace and justification by faith lies the bedrock of God's mercy. It is because God is merciful that salvation is possible. He chose to treat men and women with mercy. As a result, as Paul demonstrated in Romans 9:6-13, not only is God free to elect or predestine, but He has chosen to predestine to salvation on the basis of mercy. Everything involved in God's mission and the plan of salvation directly derives from His mercy.

Today's text is especially clear that everything depends on God's mercy. Humans might desire God to be merciful rather than a person of letter-of-the-law justice, but no matter how much they wanted it to be, or how much wishful thinking they did, they could not bring it about or force God to be that way.

Mercy rather than human effort leads to salvation. God is merciful by choice. Paul employs a picturesque word in the passage that literally means running. It was the word used of foot races in a stadium, and implies exerting oneself to the limit of one's powers in an attempt to advance. But, Paul reminds us, all our effort—even our most strenuous effort—cannot free us from condemnation. Everything depends on God's choosing to be merciful to those who have sinned. Even, in the context of Romans 9:6-13, God's dealings with Abraham, Isaac, and Jacob must be seen in terms of His mercy, since each of them was a sinner.

Thus mercy is not only the central word of Romans 9 through 11, but of the entire book and the entire plan of salvation. We can be thankful that the God who revealed Himself to Moses (and Paul) was "a God merciful and gracious, slow to anger, and abounding in steadfast love" (Ex. 34:6, RSV).

A PHARAOH LESSON

Scripture says to Pharaoh: "I raised you up . . . that I might display my power in you. . . ." Therefore God has mercy on whom he wants to have mercy, and he hardens whom he wants to harden. Rom. 9:17, 18, NIV.

DID GOD REALLY "HARDEN" Pharaoh's heart so that He could demonstrate His power? That is not what the text says if one reads it carefully. But that doesn't let God off the hook, because the Old Testament leaves us in no doubt that "the Lord hardened the heart of Pharaoh" (Ex. 9:12, RSV). That is not an isolated statement. Similar sayings appear in Exodus 10:1, 20, 27; 11:10; and 14:8.

But that's not the whole story. The Bible repeatedly asserts that it was Pharaoh who hardened his own heart (see Ex. 8:15, 32; 9:34) after the various plagues. How can it be that the Bible says both that God hardened Pharaoh's heart and that he hardened his own heart?

To answer, we need to look at what actually happened in Exodus. First God sent Moses and Aaron to talk to Pharaoh in an attempt to get freedom for the Israelites. Not having any success along that line, God sent a series of plagues to wake the king up. But the only result was that Pharaoh resisted, hardened his heart, after each one. In other words, Pharaoh's stubbornness resulted from his rebellion against God's divine revelation to him. Paul described such hardening in his first letter to Timothy as a searing of the conscience, as with a hot iron (1 Tim. 4:2). According to Romans 1:24, 26, 28 God leaves those who rebel against Him to the consequences of their actions. In that sense God is responsible, since, as the apostle put it, God "gave them up" to those consequences. But the consequences came as a result of their rebellion and sin. God could have intervened so that the consequences never happened. But He didn't. In that sense He was responsible for them.

It is in that sense that God hardened Pharaoh's heart. Hardened people are those who refuse to repent when God offers them grace. But since He allows them to continue living in their hardened state He does bear some responsibility for their condition.

How do we respond in the face of the Holy Spirit's convicting of our heart? Do we stiffen our necks and resist, or do we fall on our knees, repentant, and ask for forgiveness and restitution? The hardening of Pharaoh's heart is not a lesson in ancient history. It is for me individually today. God wants me to learn from Pharaoh and apply the lesson to my life.

IRREVERENT CLAY

*But who are you, a man, to answer back to God? Will what is
molded say to its molder, "Why have you made me thus?" Has
the potter no right over the clay . . . ? Rom. 9:20, 21, RSV.*

SO YOU DON'T LIKE the way God does things? And you want to talk
back to Him?

Just who, Paul challenges, do you think you are? Don't you know that
you are wax, while God is the molder? Don't you realize that you are mere
clay, and that God is the potter?

In his illustration of the potter and the clay Paul cites Isaiah 29:16 and
45:9, two passages in which the clay questions the rights of the potter to
do his will. The passages are especially appropriate in Paul's context in
Romans because they deal with God's formation of Israel as a nation and
His unquestioning right to treat that nation as He deems best.

God's prerogative to deal with people with perfect freedom and on
His own conditions is precisely the issue the apostle has in mind in
Romans 9. God is in charge, not Israel or anyone else. He is the potter and
they are the clay. If He chooses to have mercy on the Gentiles, that is His
business. And if He decides to include them in His blessings, that is His
privilege. No humans, no matter what their religious or racial pedigree,
have authority over God. Nor can the Jews or anyone else escape the results of rebellion. If they choose the way of sin, they also can become dishonorable vessels. People are not automatically honorable because of
their birth as Jews. Nor are they automatically dishonorable because they
are Gentiles. God is sovereign, and He sets the rules and conditions.

That doesn't mean that we can never ask God questions. Paul, after
all, has been raising them throughout the whole letter. F. F. Bruce notes
that it is "the God-defying rebel and not the bewildered seeker after God
whose mouth [Paul] so peremptorily shuts."

Romans 9 has never been the easiest chapter in the Bible for Christians
to understand. But when we read it in the context of whom Paul is dealing
with and what their objections were, the chapter helps us see the greatness
of our God, a God who spreads His mercy further than some church members would have Him. We "know" that we deserve His favor, but do those
"other people"? To all such questions Paul has one answer: Leave the judgment to God. Just as an infinite distance separates the potter and the clay,
so we find an infinite distance between us and our Creator.

GOD'S BOUNDLESS LOVE

*May it not be that God, though he must sooner or later expose
his wrath against sin and show his controlling hand,
has yet most patiently endured the presence in his world
of things that cry out to be destroyed? Rom. 9:22, Phillips.*

THAT IS A LONG VERSE. But Paul isn't finished with his thought. It continues in Romans 9:23 and 24: "Can we not see, in this [not destroying the wicked immediately], his purpose in demonstrating the boundless resources of his glory upon those whom he considers fit to receive his mercy, and whom he long ago planned to raise to glorious life? And by these chosen people I mean you and me, whom he has called out from both Jews and gentiles?" (Phillips).

Commentators recognize those three verses to be some of the most obscure in all of Paul's writings. But be that as it may, several ideas jump out at us. The first is God's seemingly boundless patience with rebels whose behavior, so to speak, demands their destruction. He could have already annihilated them. But even here He chooses to have mercy, as Peter puts it, "not wishing that any should perish, but that all should reach repentance" (2 Peter 3:9, RSV). It is a part of God's very character to be as longsuffering as possible. Nevertheless, as Paul and other New Testament writers note, there will come a time when God will have to destroy sin and those who cling to it. But even the timing of that event is still God's choice alone.

A second idea that leaps out at us in Romans 9:22-24 is that God has in His mercy willed to expend His "boundless resources . . . upon those whom he considers fit to receive his mercy." The Lord leaves no stone unturned in His desire to save humanity. He has done everything He can to prepare as many people as possible for glory, even though some cling to ways of life, habits, and attitudes that can only doom them for destruction. If He has to eradicate them in the end, it will not be because He has not done everything He can to save them.

A third obvious point is that the chosen people whom God plans "to raise to glorious life" will consist of both Jews and Gentiles. That point, of course, is the one that has been Paul's primary thesis in Romans 9.

The chapter centers on the Lord's right to be God and elect whom He will to salvation. The focal point of Romans 9 through 11 in its entirety is that God desires to have mercy on all—both Jews and Gentiles. He even wants to have mercy on you, my friend, if you will allow Him to do so.

GOD INCLUDES THE GENTILES

*"Those who were not my people I will call my people,
and the unloved I will call beloved. In the very
place where they were told, 'You are no people of mine,'
they shall be called sons of the living God." Rom. 9:25, 26, REB.*

IN THE VERSES PRECEDING Paul's quotation from Hosea, he had summed up the focal point of his argument in Romans 9. That is, God would call "not only from the Jews but also from the Gentiles" the "objects of his mercy" (Rom. 9:24, 23, NIV). The Lord's promises hadn't failed (verse 6). He had summoned the Jews to salvation. That call still remained open. But it wasn't restricted exclusively to them. The God who had chosen to show mercy on Abraham and Jacob also intends to display mercy toward the Gentiles.

Paul then launches into a series of quotations from the Old Testament to establish his point. They fall into two groups. The first (verses 25, 26) is from Hosea, which the apostle uses to ground the acceptability of the Gentiles. The second (verses 27-29) comes from Isaiah and proves that the call does not include all the Israelites, but only a remnant.

The first set of quotations cites Hosea 2:23 and 1:10. The background of the Hosea texts is that of the 10 northern tribes of Israel, which had apostatized into the crudest forms of idolatry, including child sacrifice and gross sensuality. In that context Hosea was a prophet of judgment against a nation that had all but closed its probation. Because Israel had spurned God, He had rejected them, and they would soon enter into the brutal Assyrian captivity beginning in 722 B.C.

God illustrates the unfaithfulness of Israel through the prophet's prostitute wife, Gomer, and their offspring: Lo-Ruhamah (a name meaning "not loved") and Lo-Ammi ("not my people").

Yet God went on to promise that He would reverse the rejection implicit in the children's names. In His grace He would take them back, just as Hosea accepted Gomer back. At that time those who were not His people would become His people and those not loved would become His loved ones.

Hosea had applied that lesson to Israel, but Paul takes it a step further and applies it to the Gentiles, who had not been His people. Through His mercy God would adopt and love them so that they would become "sons of the living God." Truly there is a broadness in God's mercy.

THE REMNANT OF ISRAEL

Isaiah makes this proclamation about Israel: "Though the Israelites be countless as the sands of the sea, only a remnant shall be saved; for the Lord's sentence on the land will be summary and final." Rom. 9:27, 28, NEB.

WITH TODAY'S TEXT PAUL turns from the *inclusion* of the Gentiles in the kingdom (demonstrated by the quotations from Hosea) to the *exclusion* of many of the Jews. In evaluating the apostle's argument, we need to remember that most of the Jews of his day had not accepted Christ. Thus they might have concluded that Paul must be wrong. If Jesus were the Christ, they could have reasoned, then God's people—the Jewish nation—would have gladly embraced Him. Because that hadn't happened, Paul was obviously wrong. That argument, of course, is the timeless one that implies that a religious majority establishes truth.

It is that very logic that the apostle sets out to smash. He does so by going back to Jewish Scripture itself, taking two quotations from Isaiah.

The first (today's passage) is from Isaiah 10:22. The passage states that Israel had become a large nation. That represented the direct fulfillment of God's promise to Abraham that his seed would be as numerous as the stars. The people of Israel, of course, loved to have their chosenness confirmed. Truly, they had come to believe they were God's special people and that their specialness guaranteed them a place in His kingdom.

Not so! says Paul. He backs up his assertion with the fact that only a "remnant" of the nation would be saved. While the passage in Isaiah 10 refers to the Assyrian captivity, Paul applies it to the nation's current rejection of Christ.

Paul's second quotation (Rom. 9:29) comes from Isaiah 1:9, in which the prophet stated that if the Lord hadn't left some remnant of Israel, the nation would have become like Sodom and Gomorrah, two cities that had ceased to exist. It would not be so with Israel. There would be, Paul implies, a remnant who had accepted Jesus' lordship by faith.

Christians will also find a lesson here. It is all too easy to think that because we belong to a church or have outward obedience we are right with God. Not so! Anybody can belong to a church. But to be a part of God's timeless remnant one must have a living faith relationship with Him.

Today, dear Lord, I want to rededicate myself to membership in Your modern remnant.

TOPSY-TURVY RIGHTEOUSNESS

What shall we say, then? That Gentiles who did
not pursue righteousness have obtained it . . . through faith;
but that Israel who pursued the righteousness which
is based on law did not succeed. Rom. 9:30, 31, RSV.

VERSES 30-32 ARE ABSOLUTELY crucial for understanding Romans 9, a chapter that has put the emphasis on divine initiative, on predestination, on election, on God's will, on His choosing of people such as Abraham as well as His "hardening" of Pharaoh. Many have incorrectly assumed from Paul here that everything is up to God and that humans are so much passive clay in His hands, that even before their birth God has predestined some to heaven and others to hell regardless of any choices they might make in life.

Paul puts all such theorizing to rest in these three verses. Here he shows us the human part in God's plan. As Emil Brunner puts it, the answer does not lie "in the mysterious decree of God, who prepares some to salvation and others to damnation," but in the human response to Christ.

The apostle presents a topsy-turvy picture. On the one hand are the Gentiles who didn't even have any interest in righteousness but who found it in spite of themselves. On the other hand are the Jews who earnestly pursued righteousness but failed, in spite of their zeal, to obtain it.

Why? With this question we have come back to the heart of Paul's argument in Romans 1 through 8. The reason the Gentiles obtained righteousness was that they had accepted Jesus by faith. And the Jews failed because they had sought to attain it by works of law, but they "did not succeed in fulfilling that law" (Rom. 9:31, RSV).

Human beings do have a part in salvation. It is not in striving to be perfect in lawkeeping but in surrendering to Jesus Christ in faith, in trusting in His sacrifice on their behalf, and in accepting the reality of their own weakness and the sufficiency of God's grace.

The Jewish tragedy is not that they loved God's law. Paul himself prized it. Their real problem was that they sought to make the law a ladder to heaven, something God never created it to be. If they would have seen it for what it is—God's holy ideal—they could still have loved it, but when they failed in obeying it, it would have driven them to Christ for grace and forgiveness. After all, the only kind of righteousness there is at all is righteousness by faith, a phrase that Paul uses repeatedly throughout Romans.

OF FAITH AND STUMBLING STONES

[Israel] stumbled at that stumbling stone. As it is written: "Behold,
I lay in Zion a stumbling stone and rock of offense, and whoever
believes on Him will not be put to shame." Rom. 9:32, 33, NKJV.

PAUL HAS COME TO the end of an extremely forceful chapter in which he demonstrates that God has opted to have mercy on everyone—both Jews and Gentiles. That does not mean that God's promises to Israel have failed (Rom. 9:6). To the contrary, it means that His mercy is broader than the "church members" (Jews) thought, and that God had made a decision to save all who chose to put their faith in Christ.

But not everybody in the "church" was comfortable with that solution. Some thought that the only righteousness really worth anything was that represented by human achievement in relation to the law (verses 31, 32).

It is just that group that Paul has in his sights in today's passage. They have "stumbled at that stumbling stone." In order to make his point more forceful the apostle utilizes four short quotations from Isaiah. The first and last quotations come from Isaiah 28:16: "I lay a stone in Zion" and "the one who trusts will never be dismayed" (NIV). The middle two are derived from Isaiah 8:14: "A stone that causes men to stumble" and "a rock that makes them fall" (NIV).

Paul uses those four phrases from Isaiah to affirm that God Himself has laid down a solid rock. That stone, of course, he saw as none other than Jesus Christ. As he noted to the Corinthians, "no one can lay any foundation other than the one already laid, which is Jesus Christ" (1 Cor. 3:11, NIV). And Jesus had boldly applied Psalm 118:22 to Himself: "The stone the builders rejected has become the capstone" (Matt. 21:42, NIV).

In today's text Paul claims that some would take "offence" at Christ. The word "offence" is the Greek word *skandalon,* from which we get our word "scandal." Paul employs it in 1 Corinthians 1:23 to tell us that it is "Christ crucified" that was a "stumbling block" to the Jews.

The plain fact is that when we meet Christ He will mean one of two things to us. Faith in His substitutionary sacrifice becomes either the foundation of saving faith or it becomes an offensive teaching that we end up rejecting. Humans like to do it on their own or at least have a part in their salvation. But to accept that teaching is to stumble over God's clear teaching on grace through faith. "Whoever believes on Him," claims Paul, "will not be put to shame."

Praying as God Prays

My brothers, from the bottom of my heart I long
and pray to God that Israel may be saved! Rom. 10:1, Phillips.

HOW WOULD YOU FEEL if you were Paul? The Jewish leaders had plagued his work practically from the time he had become a Christian. They not only hindered his efforts, but also had made sure that he got more than his share of physical pain and imprisonment. Some of them would eventually seek his life. His enemies meant him harm.

How would you deal with such people? Perhaps the best way to answer that question is to examine how we have treated those who have rejected us—those who have, so to speak, spit on us when we tried to give them a hand. I don't know how it is with you, but I am tempted just to write such people off. After all, I might say, "I've done all I can to help them. They just seem to like error, or the gutter. I guess they will have to learn the hard way." Or you might find yourself thinking that the old "blankety blanks" deserve whatever happens to them. (And, of course, they really do deserve it—and a whole lot more.)

Paul certainly could have felt that way about the Jewish leaders of his day. But the point of today's text is that he didn't—or if he did, he didn't let those emotions overwhelm his Christianity. Instead, he told them that he prayed from the bottom of his heart that they might be saved.

That's love. It is the same kind of love that Jesus said we must have if we are to be perfect as our heavenly Father is perfect (Matt. 5:43-48). And it is the same kind of love that God had for us when He sent Jesus to die for us while we were still His enemies (Rom. 5:8, 10).

That's powerful. That's Christianity. That's what God is like. And remember, He wants us to be like Him.

Instead of consigning his enemies to hell, Paul prayed for their eternal salvation. He prayed, in effect, that he might live next door to them in heaven.

How is it with you today, my friend? Do you have that kind of love? We hear a lot about character perfection in some circles, but Paul's action is central to what character perfection is all about.

Father, help me today to have a desire to be more like You. Help me to love, especially those who I believe have abused me or taken advantage of me. Amen.

A Fanatic Is . . .

For I testify about them that they have a zeal for God, but not in accordance with knowledge. Rom. 10:2, NASB.

ZEAL FOR GOD WITHOUT knowledge equals fanaticism. And the church has been full of such types down through the ages. Paul, in fact, had himself succumbed to the disease. "I myself," he claims, "was convinced that I ought to do many things in opposing the name of Jesus of Nazareth. And I did so in Jerusalem; I not only shut up many of the saints in prison, by authority from the chief priests, but when they were put to death I cast my vote against them. And I punished them often in all the synagogues and tried to make them blaspheme; and in raging fury against them, I persecuted them even to foreign cities" (Acts 26:9-11, RSV). Again, "I advanced in Judaism beyond many of my own age among my people, so extremely zealous was I for the traditions of my fathers" (Gal. 1:14, RSV).

Paul knew what it meant to be superlative in devotion among a fervent people. As C. K. Barrett has pointed out, "no nation had given itself to God with such devoted and courageous zeal as Israel." Rabbi Judah ben Tema nicely phrased that mentality when he said, " 'Be strong as a leopard, fast as an eagle, fleet as a gazelle, and brave as a lion, to carry out the will of your Father who is in heaven' " (Aboth 5:20).

But all the zeal in the world is of no good without knowledge to guide it. John Calvin points out that "it is better, as Augustine says, to go limping in the right way than to run with all your might" in the wrong direction.

To have zeal without knowledge is a vice, not a virtue. Every congregation seems to have a few of this type. Like the proverbial bull in the china cabinet they imitate the early Paul with their self-righteousness.

And what knowledge are they missing? The same as that absent during Paul's early experience: the knowledge that we are not self-sufficient but totally dependent upon the saving merits of Jesus Christ. Such understanding brings with it a humble zeal that recognizes both our weaknesses and the power of sin, but even more the awesome power of God.

Those who think they know, notes Martin Luther, cause endless problems, but "one who knows that he does not know is gentle and willing to be directed."

God wants us to have zeal. But it is to be an ardor filled with knowledge—a knowledge of our frailty, of our tendency to seek to be God to others, and most of all, of our need of His softening and informing grace.

BRAIN-DAMAGED RIGHTEOUSNESS

Since they did not know the righteousness that comes
from God and sought to establish their own, they
did not submit to God's righteousness. Rom. 10:3, NIV.

A STORY TELLS OF A company of American soldiers captured and incarcerated in a prisoner-of-war camp. Having no money, they resorted to bartering when one soldier had what another one desired. It was a less-than-satisfactory system, however.

But then one day a Care package arrived containing some Monopoly games. The soldiers were overjoyed, not because of the games, but because of the money they contained. They soon divided it up, with each man receiving an equal number of $500, $100, $50, $20, $10, $5, and $1 bills. That made trading simpler.

But any group usually has at least one with a strong capitalistic drive. Before long one soldier had accumulated nearly all the money in the camp.

About that time a prisoner-of-war exchange took place, and the POWs were airlifted back to Los Angeles. One of the first things our capitalist friend did was to go down to the local bank to open up an account. After filling out the proper forms, he plopped down $2,325,413. The teller took one look at the Monopoly money and called the manager. It was obvious to her that the soldier was suffering from some sort of brain damage.

The moral of the story is that Monopoly money may be good for playing games or in a prison camp, but is of not much use in world commerce.

So it is with righteousness. Too many people in the church are playing at righteousness but are either too ignorant or just plain "brain-damaged" to know that their righteousness is not the real thing, in spite of the fact that it may make them feel superior to other people.

Paul is concerned about his fellow Jews for two reasons: (1) they were ignorant of God's righteousness and were seeking to get by with their own, and (2) they did not submit to God's righteousness.

Those two things, Paul claims, stood at the heart of the problem of why the church now largely consisted of Gentiles. The problem wasn't in God's promises (Rom. 9:6) or in God's mercy, but in Israel's own ignorance. Perhaps there is no ignorance as deep as a spiritual one. And yet that very ignorance tends toward spiritual pride.

Help me, Father, to truly see the depth of my need and the greatness of Your mercy.

CHRIST, THE END OF THE LAW

*For Christ is the end of the law for righteousness
to every one that believeth. Rom. 10:4.*

CHRIST IS THE END of the law? What does that mean? This text has had many interpretations. One is that it proclaims the abolition of God's law so that Christians are now free to do as they please.

Paul headed off that understanding in Romans 3:31 when he pointed out that faith actually established the law instead of voiding it. Then again, he reminded his readers in Romans 7 that the law was holy, just, good, and spiritual (Rom. 7:12, 14), and he will return to the Christian's obligation to the law again in Romans 12:8-10. Jesus seemed to be on the same wavelength as Paul when He noted that He had not come to abolish the law but to fill out its meaning, and that not a dot or an iota would pass from the law "till heaven and earth pass away" (Matt. 5:17, 18, RSV).

A second possible interpretation, and one that certainly fits into the context of Romans 10, is that "Christ is the end [termination] of the law for righteousness." That is most certainly true. Paul has pounded home the fact that righteousness comes by faith rather than through lawkeeping. Recognition of that fact means the death of all legalisms in genuine Christianity. Thus he noted in Romans 10:3 that Christians gain righteousness by submitting to God's righteousness. There is no other way to achieve righteousness.

While that interpretation is certainly true, it may not be the full meaning of Romans 10:4. The word translated as "end" also means "goal" or "fulfillment." Thus, notes F. F. Bruce, "Christ is the goal at which the law aimed, in that he embodies the perfect righteousness which it prescribes. . . . Since Christ is the goal of the law, since in him the law has found its perfect fulfillment, a righteous status before God is available to everyone who believes in him and that implies the termination of the law's function (real or imagined) as a means of acquiring such a righteous status." John Ziesler is thinking of Christ as the goal of the law when he writes that Jesus fulfilled "the promises to Abraham" and thus "opened up the people of God to all who had faith in him."

No matter which way a person looks at our text for today, Christians are those who have righteousness through Christ, who truly did fulfill the law and made His righteousness available to all who have faith in Him.

A SALVATIONAL DEAD END

Moses describes in this way the righteousness that is by the law:
"The man who does these things will live by them." Rom. 10:5, NIV.

PAUL IS DEMONSTRATING in today's verse and the next few verses
that his view of justification by faith is not something new, but has always
been God's way of accepting people. He makes his point by assembling a
series of Old Testament passages.

His first is a quotation from Leviticus 18:5, which means to him that
the person who desires to establish righteousness by keeping the law must
live up to all the aspects and details of the law. That is, it must be obeyed
to the very letter. Anything less than that means no salvation, since the
law contains no inherent grace or mercy.

James said something similar when he claimed that "whoever keeps
the whole law but fails in one point has become guilty of all of it" (James
2:10, RSV). Thus if a person is somehow able to honor all of it except one
minor detail, he or she would still stand condemned and would be just as
lost as the one who had failed in every aspect of the law.

With that in mind, we need to remember that Paul has already demonstrated from the Jewish Scriptures themselves that all have sinned and
fallen short of God's glory (Rom. 3:9-20, 23). Thus at their very best,
even the most diligent human beings have been able to produce only imperfect and unacceptable righteousness according to the law. And in
God's sight such "righteousness" is entirely unrighteous.

Some of the Jews, of course, had deceived themselves into thinking
that they were perfect or almost so. The rich young ruler, for example, had
no qualms in claiming that he had kept all of God's commandments from
the time of his youth (Matt. 19:20). But Jesus soon exploded that deception
when He put His finger on the man's lack of concern for his neighbors.

Throughout the book of Romans Paul has set forth a series of propo-
sitions regarding law righteousness: (1) the person who pursues salvation
by keeping the law will be judged on the basis of that effort; (2) not one
person, outside of Christ, has kept it flawlessly; (3) as a result, all stand
under condemnation.

Paul has also consistently and repeatedly set forth God's plan of salvation by grace through faith as the only alternative to salvation by human
effort. The amount of time he has spent on the topic indicates how deeply
ingrained works-righteousness is in the human psyche.

A LESSON IN FAR AND NEAR

You need not say, . . . "Who could go up to Heaven to bring Christ down to us, or who could descend into the depths to bring him up from the dead?" No, the word is very near you, . . . in your own heart. Rom. 10:6-8, Phillips.

HUMAN BEINGS HAVE A wonderful perversity! All of us want what we can't have and despise anything that seems too easy or even free. We like a bit of struggle to obtain those things we deem valuable.

I remember when I was in graduate school and somewhat poorer than the proverbial church mouse. One of my great joys was to walk down to the used book store near my house and "drool" over those tomes that were outside of my budgetary possibilities. Of course, once in a while I would be able to dredge up a $10 bill and indulge my prevailing vice. But most of the time I had to merely content myself with gazing at that which lay beyond my reach.

Then one day the crisis hit. Forced to shut down, the book store offered its remaining stock at 25 cents per book. Suddenly the books were within my reach. But just as suddenly they had lost their value in my eyes. Now they were "junk."

That human trait of highly valuing the expensive or those things that need to be struggled for leaps over the fence from the material to the spiritual realm. How enthralled people are to go on religious pilgrimages or to participate in a crusade, or to give up all their possessions to achieve a spiritual goal. Such exploits fill history.

Tell us to climb to heaven itself or to descend into the depths, or to do some other great feat of human accomplishment, and we get all excited. That's sacrifice—something to be proud about, something I could write a book about, something that would make for an excellent testimony to share before the church. Such accomplishments have value in our perverted eyes.

In contrast, merely accepting Christ by faith sounds so pedestrian, so valueless, so void of anything I can brag about.

But it is that very unglamorous road to salvation that Paul is telling us is the only way. We don't have to climb Mount Everest or swim the English Channel for it. All we have to do is accept God's gift. What we need we already potentially have. It is near our hearts and minds. All we have to do is to accept it—today.

INWARD AND OUTWARD RELIGION

If thou shalt confess with thy mouth the Lord Jesus, and shalt believe in thine heart that God hath raised him from the dead, thou shalt be saved. Rom. 10:9.

CONFESSING AND BELIEVING. The outward and the inward. The combination of those two ideas is absolutely central in Christianity. The New Testament leaves not the slightest doubt that true religion is a matter of the heart. A surface religion is what the hypocrites or play actors have. Jesus accused the Pharisees of having such a religion when He called them "whitewashed tombs, which outwardly appear beautiful, but within . . . are full of dead men's bones and all uncleanness" (Matt. 23:27, RSV).

The inward is primary, but in New Testament Christianity the inward experience never stands alone. The inner state reveals itself in outward conduct; inward belief stimulates outward action.

Confessing Christ is a solemn religious act for the apostle. Early Christians may have used a confession similar to the one we find in today's verse in their baptismal services despite the fact that saying it could put them at risk. Confessions like this one were also of importance when Christians found themselves brought before legal authorities, such as the Jewish Sanhedrin. Of course, in such situations one always faces the temptation not to confess.

The content of the confession is enlightening. Acknowledging that Jesus is Lord meant a radical break with their past for both Gentile and Jewish converts, because it pointed to the deity of Christ. That was extremely clear for Jewish Christians, since the Greek version of the New Testament (the Septuagint) uses the word "Lord" more than 6,000 times for the name of God. Beyond that, in the Gentile world it was the word used to refer to a deity or for the emperor when worshiped as a god. Thus to confess Christ as Lord was to declare Him as God the Son.

The second aspect of the confession, dealing with Christ's resurrection from the dead, Paul also considered extremely important. The Resurrection placed the seal of God's approval on Christ's life and death. As Leon Morris puts it, "the resurrection is of critical importance. It is at the cross that God did his saving work, but Paul does not believe in a dead martyr but in a living Savior."

That living Savior, Paul tells us in other places, will return and bring the full blessings of salvation with Him. The one who has both an inward and an outward experience with Christ "shall be saved."

SECRET DISCIPLESHIP: AN IMPOSSIBILITY

It is with your heart that you believe and are justified, and it is with your mouth that you confess and are saved. Rom. 10:10, NIV.

YESTERDAY WE NOTED that genuine Christianity combines both an inward religious experience and its outward expression. It is not only believing that Jesus is the resurrected Lord, but confessing that faith. We saw that the inward naturally gives expression in outward forms. Today's verse continues that thought.

With that in mind it is important to ask if it is possible to be a secret believer in Christ. That issue is raised by such passages as John 12:42, 43, which states that many of the Jewish "authorities believed in [Christ], but for fear of the Pharisees they *did not* confess it, lest they should be put out of the synagogue: for they loved the praise of men more than the praise of God" (RSV).

You can feel the tension as you read the text. Perhaps most of us have shared it ourselves. To believe is one thing, but to let people know about it is something else—especially in social contexts in which it might not be popular or in which it might cost us our position and so on.

So in John we apparently have some secret disciples. In relation to Romans 10:10 the Jewish leaders in John make an interesting case study. Eventually they each faced the impossibility of secret discipleship. For some secrecy killed the discipleship, while for others the discipleship killed the secrecy. But the two could not remain in tension in perpetuity, because secret discipleship is a contradiction in terms.

Nicodemus discovered that contradiction. At first he came "to Jesus by night" (John 3:2). But that meeting had nourished the beginnings of belief in his heart. The next time we meet him he defends Jesus in a hidden way that lets no one know that he has begun to believe in Him. But he paid for even that cautious defense, since some jabbed at him with the accusation that he too must be some kind of follower (John 7:50-52). Then, at the death of Christ, the discipleship finally got the victory over the secrecy, and Nicodemus openly confessed his faith in Christ. Other Pharisees, however, let their secrecy crowd out their discipleship.

How is it with me this morning? As the young people say it, "Do I have my act together?" Is my outward lined up with my inward?

ONE IN CHRIST

*The scripture says, "No one who believes in him will be put
to shame." For there is no distinction between Jew and Greek;
the same Lord is Lord of all and bestows his riches upon
all who call upon him. Rom. 10:11, 12, RSV.*

PAUL IS A LOVER of God's Word. He not only loves it and knows it, but
he regularly cites it as authority as he makes his various points. The scripture
used in Romans 10:11 he also cited in 9:33, but now the apostle has made a
small addition that has a large meaning. He added the words "no one" when
he wrote about those not being put to shame. It underlines the universality of
God's people. When it comes to salvation there is no distinction between Jew
and Gentile. All who have faith will see God's salvation.

Paul recognizes only one way to salvation—faith. Just as he demonstrated that there was no difference in sin between Jew and Gentile (Rom.
3:22), he now says that there is no difference in salvation. And with that
thought he has returned to the major theme of chapters 9 through 11—that
God has chosen to have mercy on all.

The unity of Jews and Gentiles has been a theme all through Romans.
In Romans 1:16 Paul set the keynote to the entire Epistle by noting that
salvation comes to everyone through faith, "to the Jew first and also to the
Greek" (RSV). Then in Romans 2:9 he pointed out that individuals in both
groups would receive tribulation and distress for doing evil. In verse 10
he goes on to say that members of both groups would share in glory and
honor and peace if they did good, "for God shows no partiality" (verse 11,
RSV). Again in Romans 3:9 Paul points out that "all men, both Jews and
Greeks, are under the power of sin" (RSV).

Thus when he returns to the equality of Jews and Gentiles in the plan
of salvation in Romans 10:12, he indicates that Jews and Greeks must
have one way of salvation because there is one Lord over them both.

We find a lesson here for our day. Racial and ethical differences have
torn both the world and the church throughout history. That is understandable in the world at large, which still remains under the reign of the
divisive one. But for the church it is a betrayal of its faith, just as it was
in the struggle between the Jews and the Gentiles in Paul's day.

Let's face it—we all have the same sin problem, God has the same solution for all of us, and we share one Lord. Today God wants us to learn
how to better live like the brothers and sisters that we are in Christ.

ALL WHO CALL ON THE NAME

Anyone who calls upon the name
of the Lord will be saved. Rom. 10:13, TLB.

DO YOU BELIEVE THAT "every one" (RSV) and "anyone who calls upon the name of the Lord will be saved"?

What about those misguided souls that Jesus talked about in the Sermon on the Mount? Certainly they had been calling on the name of the Lord, yet they won't be saved. Listen to Jesus Himself on the topic: "Not every one who says to me, 'Lord, Lord,' shall enter the kingdom of heaven" (Matt. 7:21, RSV).

Do we find a conflict between what Paul and Jesus tell us? Not really, if we examine the contexts of the two passages. Jesus goes on to plainly state that it is only those who do the will of God who will be in the kingdom, no matter how many miracles or other signs they might have performed. In other words, they had to have faith that He was Lord and also outward compliance with His will.

The context in Romans has already made that same point. We noted a few days ago that both inward belief and outward confession (Rom. 10:9) go hand in hand and that people really can't have one for an extended period of time without the other.

The "everyone who calls on the name of the Lord" who "will be saved" in Romans 10:13 (NIV) is those who fit into the teaching of Paul in Romans 10. In fact, they are those who have accepted Paul's teaching throughout the Epistle. They recognize that they stand under the law's condemnation, that they can do nothing to rescue themselves, that Christ's death for them paid the redemption price, that Christ's resurrection guarantees their resurrection, that their baptism symbolizes an end to the old way of life and the beginning of walking with Jesus in God's will, that they have been totally saved by grace through faith, and that they have a burning desire to confess Christ as Lord and Savior. In its context the "anyone" and the "everyone" of Romans 10:13 are those who have both inward and outward faith in Christ.

All such "will be saved" without exception because they have called on the name of the Lord with all their heart, mind, and soul. The phrase "calls upon the name of the Lord" is an important one. It is so important to what a Christian is that Paul uses it in 1 Corinthians 1:2 to describe Christians. Christians are those "who in every place call on the name of our Lord Jesus Christ" (RSV).

THE EVANGELISTIC IMPERATIVE

How then will they call on Him in whom they have not believed?
And how will they believe in Him whom they have not heard?
And how will they hear without a preacher? How will
they preach unless they are sent? Rom. 10:14, 15, NASB.

THE FOUR QUESTIONS in today's passage refer us back to the previous verse, which noted that "everyone who calls on the name of the Lord will be saved" (Rom. 10:13, NIV). Thus, Paul appears to be saying, sinners must call on the Lord if they are to be saved. But that raises a series of questions that the apostle fires off in rapid sequence.

Question 1: "How then will they call on Him in whom they have not believed?" The very act presupposes a prior knowledge of God.

Question 2: But "how will they believe in Him whom they have not heard?" People need to hear about God before they can believe in Him.

Question 3: "How will they hear without a preacher?" Before the days of mass media the role of the herald (translated "preacher" above) was vital. In ancient times the major means of transmitting news was the herald's public proclamation in the city square or other public place. It is obvious that there could be no hearers without a herald.

Question 4: "How will they preach unless they are sent?" The word "sent" derives from the same word as "apostle." A true herald or preacher of God's message is one commissioned by God. The preacher's function is to pass on the message God has for His people.

John Stott suggests that "the essence of Paul's argument is seen if we put his six verbs in the opposite order: Christ sends heralds; heralds preach; people hear; hearers believe; believers call; and those who call are saved." With that line of logic the apostle lays the foundation for Christian evangelism.

And who is to be evangelized? Both Jews and Gentiles. But, given the context of Romans 9–11, Paul undoubtedly aimed these verses at the Jews. In fact, Romans 10:16 makes that clear. Paul will demonstrate in the rest of chapter 10 that the Jews have indeed heard the gospel message, even if most have chosen to reject it.

But still another side of the issue applies to all time. God is still sending men and women to preach the message. They also need to hear His call to evangelism if they are to go. Perhaps God, even this day, has a message that you personally need to deliver to someone. He might be calling you at this very moment.

BEAUTIFUL FEET

As it is written, "How beautiful are the feet of those who bring good news!" Rom. 10:15, NIV.

PAUL'S QUOTATION IS a rather loose paraphrase of Isaiah 52:7, which reads:
"How beautiful upon the mountains
    are the feet of him who brings good tidings,
  who publishes peace, who brings good tidings of good,
    who publishes salvation" (RSV).

In its original setting that comforting passage refers to the certainty of Israel's return from the Babylonian captivity. The apostle now applies it to his gospel of freedom from the captivity of sin. Implied in his usage of the passage is the idea that if people rejoiced at the good news of release from the Babylonian exile, they should rejoice much more in the light of the gospel message.

Before the days of e-mail, telephones, and other modern means of communication, a trusted courier generally hand-delivered messages. People vied for the honor of being the first one to deliver the announcement of victory to their ruler after a great battle. On the other hand, no one wanted the "honor" of delivering bad news to an Oriental potentate. Bad news could cost people their head.

But "how beautiful are the feet of those who bring good news!" We moderns might wonder as to why the prophet chose the feet for special mention. The phrase would not have stumped a person of Paul's time. Good news traveled by the feet of the messengers themselves. After a run of many miles the runner himself might be dirty, smelly, and ragged, but to those awaiting good news the sight of his feet moving rapidly across the fields was always a welcome sight. Everybody loves good news.

And what better news could there be than the gospel of salvation?

Have you thought much lately about the "feet" that brought you the good news of salvation? Perhaps it was an evangelist, a layperson, a family member, a teacher, a pastor, or maybe people in several of those categories. Whoever it was, they brought you good news. Whoever they were, why not return the blessing today? Write them a card or give them a call expressing how much you have appreciated their ministry in your life. Who knows, your card or call may prove to be a blessing to them just when they need it most. Then your feet will be beautiful too.

NOT EVERYBODY
LIKES GOOD NEWS

But not all the Israelites accepted the good news. For Isaiah says, "Lord, who has believed our message?" Rom. 10:16, NIV.

TWO THOUSAND YEARS AGO a man chose to follow a great leader of outstanding ability. His student for three years, he was part of a small group who not only learned from their master, but lived with him.

But over time this student became disillusioned with his teacher and betrayed him to his enemies. Shortly thereafter he became disillusioned with himself over what he had done. Disillusionment led to depression, depression to desperation, desperation to despair, and despair to suicide.

The student's name was Judas. His teacher was Jesus Christ.

Not everybody accepts the glad tidings of the gospel. Even Jesus had failures. In fact, most of the people He preached to never became His followers. They liked the miracles and the loaves and the fishes, but when the going got tough, they got going. They slipped right back into their comfort zone and out of a life dedicated to Christ.

That scenario hasn't changed much in 2,000 years. "Not all" accept the good news, whether they be Gentile or Jewish. But then Jesus told us it would be like that in His parables of the kingdom.

Jesus taught in Matthew 13 that the root of the problem in evangelism does not lie with God. After all, He has made provision for the gospel to be preached to all types of people (soils), but not all respond in the same way. Some allow the evil one to snatch the seeds of truth out of their heart (Matt. 13:19, the seed that fell in the path), others receive it with joy but give it up when they see the cost (verse 21, the shallow soil), some hear receptively but let the cares of this life strangle their interest in the life to come (verse 22, the seed that fell among weeds), while still others receive the word and bear Christian fruit (verse 23, the seed that bore from 30 to 100 fold).

The parable leaves us with two conclusions: (1) that only a minority who receive the word remain faithful, and (2) that the mixed reception of the gospel is not God's fault. He provides opportunities, but fruition depends upon human response. It was so in Christ's day and in ours.

Our job is not that of sitting down and worrying about the responses, but to shoe our feet with the gospel of peace (Eph. 6:15) so that we might be God's agents in preparing the way for faith in Him.

A UNIVERSAL MISSION

So faith comes from what is heard, and what is heard
comes by the preaching of Christ. Rom. 10:17, RSV.

DID PAUL'S FELLOW JEWS really have a fair chance to listen to the gospel message? Perhaps the reason that not many of them accepted it (see Rom. 10:16) is that they never really heard it in the first place. And not hearing is a serious problem because "faith comes from what is heard," and that results from the preaching of the gospel (verse 17). Maybe the problem with the Jews' response is that they were just ignorant on the topic of salvation through Christ.

Paul faces that issue in Romans 10:18, in which he asks, "Did they hear?" His answer is categorical: "Of course they did." He then goes on to quote Psalm 19:4 as proof. "Their voice goes out into all the earth, their words to the ends of the world" (NIV).

The apostle's choice of the passage at first seems surprising, since Psalm 19 celebrates the universal witness of the heavens to the Creator, rather than the worldwide spread of the gospel. Paul was well aware of that fact. He selected the psalm because it spoke of worldwide witness to God. What he did was to transfer the forceful language about global witness from the Creation to the church, viewing the former as symbolic of the latter.

The plain fact is that the message of the gospel had spread to the far corners of the Jewish world. Jewish pilgrims from all over the world filled Jerusalem both at the Passover crucifixion and the day of Pentecost. Certainly a fair percentage of them heard the big news (or the juicy gossip) and took reports home with them. Thus the gospel story had gone "into all the earth, . . . to the ends of the world."

Of course not every Jew had heard the gospel story, but enough had for Paul to make his claim and for them to respond. The gospel seed had been sown but had largely failed to germinate and multiply.

Thus response is important. But so is mission. If faith comes by hearing, and hearing from the preaching of the gospel, then each Christian has a responsibility in both personal witness to the gospel and in supporting mission to the more difficult places of the earth (such as the large cities), so that people will continue to have the opportunity to respond to God's grace.

WATCH OUT FOR YOUR CANDLESTICK!

*Then I said to myself: "Did Israel not know?" And my answer
must be that they did. For Moses says: "I will provoke you to
jealousy with that which is no nation, With a nation void
of understanding will I anger you." Rom. 10:19, Phillips.*

"OK," WE HEAR PAUL'S readers mutter to themselves, "we agree that
the Jews had at least heard the gospel. But maybe they didn't understand.
Wouldn't that explain the reason for their unbelief?"

Once again Paul rejects the claims of his detractors. He not only asserts that the Jews understood, but he presents two texts to prove it.

The first comes from Deuteronomy 32:21, in which God says that because of Israel's rebellion and disobedience, He will transfer His favor to
another people. That will force the Jewish nation to become jealous of a
nation that was "no nation" and lacked understanding.

The idea in the Deuteronomy passage is that when Israel saw what
was happening among the Gentiles it would provoke them into securing
some of the blessing for itself. If that is true in the political realm, it also
applies to the spiritual realm.

After all, the Jewish people did not lack knowledge. The Gentiles may
be described as "a nation void of understanding," but the Jews had the
law, the covenant, and a knowledge of God's ways. Given their spiritual
advantages, they should have been angry that they were losing the blessing. And it should have aroused them to their need.

Not only did the Jews have a superior knowledge of God, they were
also *the nation*—the chosen nation—that God originally had elected to be
His special people. They should have responded in jealousy to the "no nation" (the Gentiles) that in spite of its ignorance had found the gospel.

Here is a lesson that often needs reinforcing. It is all too easy for those
who belong to a church—especially one that thinks it has a special calling
or views itself as God's remnant—to become smug in its "superior"
knowledge and calling. All such churches are in danger, as John puts it,
of having their candlestick removed (Rev. 2:5) and given to another.
Christians need, collectively and individually, to remember that although
they may feel rich and increased with spiritual goods, they are really
"poor, and blind, and naked" and in constant need of grace (Rev. 3:17).

A History Lesson

Isaiah, more daring still, puts these words into the mouth
of God: "I was found by them that sought me not. I became
manifest unto them that asked not of me." Rom. 10:20, Phillips.

PAUL IS NOT YET finished with the excuse that possibly the reason the Jews had not accepted the gospel was that they hadn't understood it. He had just used Moses as a witness against that argument (Rom. 10:19). Now he summons Isaiah, who is "more daring still" in making Paul's point. If Moses had cut off any valid plea for ignorance on the part of the Jews and set the stage for the inclusion of the Gentiles, Isaiah is bolder yet for incorporating them into the covenant promises.

From Isaiah 65:1, Paul quotes:

"I was found by those who did not seek me:

I revealed myself to those who did not ask for me" (NIV).

Those Jews who knew the Isaiah passage recognized that the next clause is just as pertinent:

"To a nation that did not call on my name,

I said, Here am I, here am I" (verse 1, NIV).

The verses immediately following those two clauses contrast God's active seeking after the Gentiles to the failure of the Jews to respond to His grace, so much so that they "provoke" Him with their rebellion in religious things (verses 2, 3, NIV).

Paul is telling the Jews that they don't know their history. If they think that they are the only people that God cares for because they are Abraham's children, then they had better go back and read Isaiah 65.

The rejection of the gospel by the Jews in Paul's day wasn't the first time they had spurned God. Neither is the Gentile acceptance of the gospel the first time that God has sought to include them. In Isaiah's day He had revealed Himself to those who did not seek Him. Paul warns his fellow Jews that they need to go back and study their history. Then they would see things more clearly and could better understand God's current actions.

That is good advice even for twenty-first-century Christians. Ellen White has insightfully written that "we have nothing to fear for the future, except as we shall forget the way the Lord has led us, and His teaching in our past history" (*Life Sketches,* p. 196). God's people in every age can learn much about their present situation by reviewing how God has dealt with His people and His church in its past history.

THE GOD WHO HOLDS OUT HIS HANDS

But concerning Israel [God] says, "All day long I have held out my hands to a disobedient and obstinate people." Rom. 10:21, NIV.

WITH TODAY'S TEXT PAUL concludes the issue he raised in Romans 10:16 as to why not all the Israelites accepted the gospel. It wasn't because they hadn't heard, because they certainly had (verse 18). Nor was it because they didn't understand (verses 19, 20). Their real problem was that they were "disobedient and obstinate" (verse 21).

Today's passage tells us that God had repeatedly opened His hands to the Israelites. That is, He took the initiative toward them. He didn't just wait for them to find Him, but held out His hands to them "like a parent," suggests John Stott, "inviting a child to come home, offering a hug and a kiss, and promising a welcome."

God not only extended His hands to Israel, but He did so "all day long," symbolizing the persistent nature of His care for them.

But, Isaiah points out, the Israelites had been just as determined to reject God's repeated overtures as He had been in caring for them. He defines them as an "obstinate people,"

"Who walk in ways not good, pursuing their own imaginations—
a people who continually provoke me to my very face,
offering sacrifices in gardens. . . .
Such people are smoke in my nostrils" (Isa. 65:2-5, NIV).

We need to take the passages that we have been studying in the second half of Romans 10 in their context. In Romans' first eight chapters the apostle set forth his gospel as being for both Jews and Gentiles. But not many Jews had accepted it. That led Paul into a major discussion of why the Jews had failed and, on the other hand, how the Gentiles had found entrance into the covenant promises. Chapter 9 set forth the answer to those issues in terms of God's mercy. He chose to offer mercy to all who would accept it. Chapter 10 then examined the issue in terms of Israel's response to the gospel. By and large, it had not been positive.

But there was still hope, because Paul firmly believed that "everyone [Jew and Gentile] who calls on the name of the Lord will be saved" (Rom. 10:13, NIV). The good news is that the promise is not bounded by race, ethnicity, or time. It is as good today as it was 2,000 years ago.

GOD DOESN'T PLAY TIT FOR TAT

I ask, then, has God rejected his people? By no means! I myself am an Israelite, a descendant of Abraham, a member of the tribe of Benjamin. God has not rejected his people whom he foreknew. Rom. 11:1, 2, RSV.

IN TODAY'S PASSAGE PAUL picks up the thread that he had begun in Romans 9:6, in which he asked if God's promises to Israel had failed in light of the fact that most of the Jewish people and their leaders had not accepted the gospel.

He had ended chapter 10 by stating that the problem hadn't been with God, who had stood before them with open arms, but with the people who had rejected Him out of rebellion. Well, one might ask, if they had spurned Him, perhaps God had done the same for them—tit for tat.

Paul violently rejects that suggestion. "By no means!" is the strongest exclamation that he could use. God does not go back on His promises. Paul may have had Psalm 94 in mind in that firm exclamation. It speaks of God's judgment and of His disciplining those He loves. Yet it also says regarding Israel: "The Lord will not forsake his people; he will not abandon his heritage" (Ps. 94:14, RSV).

The apostle then sets forth four pieces of evidence to back up his claims. Today's passage contains two of them. The first is that Paul is himself a Jew and God has not rejected him. That is especially significant in the apostle's case. He had been a prominent persecutor of Christians, yet God had still welcomed him into the gospel with outstretched arms. That's grace. If the Lord hadn't rejected Paul, the way was certainly open for other Jews to follow the path to the gospel that he had traveled. No, God had not rejected "his people."

Paul's second evidence regarding God's nonrejection of the Jews was that He "foreknew" them. To foreknow in the sense that Paul here employs it means to choose. God had elected Israel to be His people in a special way. They had been the recipients of His revelation, the law, and many blessings. Certainly He would not shut them out of the blessing of the gospel.

God's nonrejection of Israel, even after they had persistently spurned Him, is important. It means that hope still exists for those of us today who have, so to speak, "spit in God's face." So had Israel. So had Paul. Yet God never rejected them. Those who fear that they have committed the unpardonable sin need to remember the lesson of God's relation to Israel. He does not reject us just because we have rebuffed Him.

So You Think
You're the Only One Left

And what was God's answer to [Elijah]? "I have reserved for myself seven thousand who have not bowed the knee to Baal." Rom. 11:4, NIV.

PAUL CONTINUES TO DEAL with his assertion that God had not rejected Israel (Rom. 11:1). As we saw yesterday, he supplied two reasons for God's nonrejection in verses 1 and 2. Then in verses 2 through 4 he provides a third, this time from history.

"Don't you know," the apostle asks, "what the Scripture says in the passage about Elijah—how he appealed to God against Israel: 'Lord, they have killed your prophets and torn down your altars; I am the only one left, and they are trying to kill me'?" (verse 3, NIV).

The context of Elijah's complaint to God is the victory he had just had over the prophets of Baal on Mount Carmel. Immediately afterward he had fled from Queen Jezebel in a state of absolute panic. Eventually he took refuge in a cave on Mount Horeb. God found the prophet there and asked why he was hiding. That is when he reminded the Lord of Israel's apostasy and that he was the only faithful one left (1 Kings 19:1-14).

God told Elijah that the prophet didn't know much about arithmetic. "And," asks Paul, "what was God's answer to him? 'I have reserved for myself seven thousand who have not bowed the knee to Baal.'"

So Israel's apostasy had not been complete. God had a remnant still faithful to Him. He had not rejected His people. To the contrary, He had "reserved" for Himself those who were faithful.

Yet Elijah felt all alone and discouraged. I can identify with that. At times it seems as though the church is a real mess. Why, did you hear about pastor so-and-so? Or do you know what the church voted to do? Such rumors fill the very air all too often. The real problem, though, is that they are not always rumors but sometimes realities.

In such times it is easy to despair. We identify with Elijah and think we are the only one left who is truly faithful to God. But at such times we need to recognize that we don't see the big picture that God does. Just as in Elijah's day God has a remnant in every situation, even though we might not be able to identify them from our limited and often discouraged situation. God is alive and at work in the church in spite of its problems.

GOD'S REMNANT

*In the same way then, there has also come to be at the present
time a remnant according to God's gracious choice. Rom. 11:5, NASB.*

SO FAR IN ROMANS 11 Paul has presented three evidences of why he
knows that God has not rejected Israel: (1) that he himself was an Israelite,
(2) that God had chosen Israel, and (3) the historical illustration of Elijah.

Now the apostle presents a fourth evidence: that there is "at the present time . . . a remnant chosen by grace" (NIV). Just as there had been a
remnant of 7,000 in Elijah's day, so there still existed one in Paul's. Such
a remnant was neither a figment of his imagination nor wishful thinking.
Even though the Jewish leadership and the majority of the Jewish people
had not accepted the gospel, James was able to tell Paul during one of his
visits to Jerusalem that "many thousands of Jews" had believed. It appears
that James referred to Jews in and around Judea (Acts 21:20). God had not
rejected His people.

One of the more interesting words in today's verse is "remnant." The
Old Testament pictures the remnant of Israel as those Israelites who had remained faithful to God. Thus there was, so to speak, an Israel within Israel.
We can say the same of the church down through the ages. There has always been a church within the church. Luther put it somewhat differently
when he spoke of the visible and the invisible church. Those who hold
membership in the organization represent the visible church. The invisible
church consists of those who have a living, "by faith," connection with God.
It is the invisible church that makes up God's remnant at any given time.

Gerhard Hasel points out that the Bible uses the idea of remnant in
three ways. First, the Bible sometimes speaks of a *historical* remnant made
up of survivors of a catastrophe, such as an invasion. Second, there is the
"faithful remnant," distinguished from the former group by their genuine
spirituality and true faith relationship with God. Here is the remnant Paul
has in mind in Romans 11. Then we find the *eschatological* remnant, con-
sisting of those who pass through the apocalyptic crises of the end-time
"and emerge victoriously . . . as the recipients of the everlasting kingdom."

God speaks of that faithful, eschatological remnant in Revelation
12:17: "The dragon was wroth with the woman, and went to make war
with the remnant of her seed, which keep the commandments of God, and
have the testimony of Jesus Christ."

The Lord will have a remnant up to the end of time.

THE GREAT INCOMPATIBLES: GRACE AND WORKS

[The remnant was] selected by grace, and therefore not
for anything they have done; otherwise grace would
cease to be grace. Rom. 11:6, Moffatt.

"WELL," YOU CAN IMAGINE some of Paul's readers saying, "we Jews are not such bad people. After all, at least 7,000 overcame in the days of Elijah. It is wonderful that they had such backbone and courage in a difficult age. There have always been Jews who have been faithful. Thank God that we have the strong spiritual character that we do."

It seems to be that kind of thought that Paul attacks in today's verse. Otherwise he would have absolutely no reason to include it. Paul has already expressed the concept several times in Romans. The most natural thing for him to have done would have been to move on to the material in Romans 11:7-10.

But the apostle refuses to allow the slightest misunderstanding on this most important point. In verse 5 he had noted that the remnant was chosen by grace. Today's text expands upon that concept and once again defines grace and works as mutually exclusive. It has to be one or the other.

Thus if a person is saved by grace, it cannot be by works, or else grace is no longer a free gift but an earned commodity or a bargain. On the other hand, some Greek manuscripts of lesser reliability add a second part to the verse: If being a part of God's people is on the basis of works, then grace must be excluded. The King James Version reflects the extended reading of Romans 11:6. But the meaning is clear in both the shorter and longer readings. Grace and works are totally incompatible.

Paul loved the doctrine of grace because of what it had meant in his personal life. He knew that even though as a Pharisee he thought he was better than most people because of his accomplishments, he had failed to realize that he had a depth of sin that not only made him self-righteous, but ready to kill anybody who disagreed with him on religion. It was the extent of his sin problem that he had had to face on the road to Damascus.

Paul knew that he had been saved totally by grace. Thus his emphasis. It is only as we see the depth of our sinful nature that we will be able to appreciate grace as the apostle did. Those without any sense of the magnitude of the sin problem tend to remain where Paul was in his Pharisaic days.

HARDENING VERSUS REDEMPTION

What then? What Israel sought so earnestly it did not obtain, but the elect did. The others were hardened. Rom. 11:7, NIV.

PAUL HAS COME TO the place where he needs to summarize what he has said. What conclusion can we draw about the position of the Jewish people in the light of what he has discussed thus far in Romans 9-11? Since God has not rejected His people (Rom. 11:1), what exactly is their position?

His answer is that the bulk of the nation had not obtained true righteousness. It's not, he notes, that they didn't try. No other people "sought [it] so earnestly." Their lawkeeping was truly a wonder. They had developed hundreds of rules and regulations related to the law. On Sabbathkeeping alone they had formulated some 1,520 rules. By anyone's count that constitutes earnest seeking. They wanted righteousness, Paul argues, but they chose the wrong route.

But not all of them, the apostle points out, fell into that pit. Some of them—whom he calls the elect—found the proper way to righteousness.

And what separates the elect from the majority of their fellow Jews? The context supplies the answer in the preceding verse (verse 6): the mutually exclusive avenues of grace and works. The elect were those who, realizing their helplessness in the face of sin, accepted Christ through faith. The others sought righteousness through human effort and failed.

That latter group, Paul tells us, "were hardened." How did they get that way? The same way Pharaoh did in Exodus, as Paul has reflected on in Romans 9. They had become resistant, not because God had cast them away—which He had not done, according to Romans 11:1—but because they did not submit to the righteousness of God. As *The Seventh-day Adventist Bible Commentary* on Romans 11:8 puts it: "When man persistently resists . . . grace, God, who will not force anyone against his will, . . . leaves man to the natural consequences of his stubborn resistance."

One of those consequences is hardening. With that in mind, Moffatt translates "were hardened" as "have been rendered insensible" and Goodspeed as "became callous." Paul points out other consequences in verses 8-10, such as a spirit of unresponsiveness, having their blessings turn into a snare, having their spiritual eyesight dimmed, and having their backs bent under the burden of ceaseless attempts to attain righteousness by the law. In the light of those consequences, it is little wonder that Paul ceaselessly offers grace not only to the Jews but to all.

STUMBLING BUT NOT FALLEN

Again I ask: Did they stumble so as to fall beyond recovery?
Not at all! Rather, because of their transgression, salvation
has come to the Gentiles to make Israel envious. Rom. 11:11, NIV.

BY THIS TIME IN our study of Romans it has become obvious that Paul moves the discussion along through a series of questions that he first raises and then answers.

With today's text we come to a new question, the second major one in Romans 11. In verse 1 he asked whether God had rejected Israel. His answer was that the Jews hadn't been cast off but that most had been hardened through their persistent rebuff of God's grace. Of course, not all had been hardened—a remnant had accepted the gospel.

But the hardened condition of the majority of the Jews raises a new question in Paul's mind: "Did they stumble so as to fall beyond recovery?" The word picture here seems to be one between two alternatives. The first is a stumble after which they regain their footing, dust themselves off, and again move toward the goal. The second leads to a serious fall from which one does not get up, such as falling over a cliff.

In the rest of Romans 11 Paul will illustrate that Israel has not stumbled beyond recovery. Hope still remains for his fellow Jews. They have stumbled but have not fallen irrevocably.

Meanwhile, the God who makes all things work together for the good of those who love Him (Rom. 8:28) has made something good come out of the Jewish failure to accept the gospel. Because of their failure, the gospel went to the Gentiles, who accepted it more readily.

The book of Acts repeatedly reflects Paul's assertion in today's verse. There the apostles first preached to the Jews in new locations. But when the Jews rejected Paul's message he went to the Gentiles, who often accepted it. That of course stirred up the Jews. Paul's hope in today's verse is that they will stay stirred up ("envious"), look into the blessings the Gentiles have found in the gospel, and in turn come to accept it themselves.

But that's not the way things have worked out in church history. Leon Morris points out that all too often Christians, instead of demonstrating the attractions of the gospel to the Jews, have treated them with prejudice, hatred, persecution, and malice. He concludes that "Christians should not take this passage (11:11) lightly." We as Christians need to work *with* God for the blessing of the Jews and others, not against Him.

THE CHAIN OF BLESSING

For if [Israel's] failure has so enriched the world, and their defection proved such a benefit to the gentiles, think what tremendous advantages their fulfilling of God's plan could mean! Rom. 11:12, Phillips.

IN ROMANS 11:11, 12 Paul pictures a chain of blessings with three links: (1) because of Israel's stumbling, salvation has come to the Gentiles (verse 11); (2) the salvation of the Gentiles would, hopefully, make Israel envious or jealous (verse 11); (3) if that jealousy led the Jews to accept the gospel, their inclusion would mean an even greater blessing to the world than if the Gentiles alone accepted it (verse 12).

Paul hopes that all people will accept the gospel—both Jews and Gentiles. For him it would be a major loss for anybody to be left out, since Christ died "once for all" (Rom. 6:10, NIV).

Of course in Romans 9–11 his primary concern is for the Jews rather than the Gentiles, a group in which he has had some significant evangelistic successes. He sees even greater days for the spread of the gospel message if the Jews would participate in the evangelistic outreach of the Christian community. The terms Paul employs in Romans 11:12 bring this out. If the Jewish defection proved to be a "benefit" to the world because it led to the preaching of the gospel to the Gentiles, he asserts, then the Jewish inclusion would be a "tremendous advantage." Thus Paul proposes a chain of blessing that runs from arithmatic riches or advantages because of the failure of the Jews to geometric increase in riches or advantages if both the Jews and Gentiles link their energies to further the gospel kingdom.

Have you ever thought much about chains of blessings or geometric increase? Most of us are content if our local church holds its own in terms of membership. Of course, we are happy if "our pastor" brings in a few extra members. But what if an entire congregation covenanted together to reach out to its community? What if 10 people each brought one to Christ this month, and those 20 each brought one to Him the next month, and those 40 did the same the third month, and those 80 . . . and so on?

Do you have the picture? A chain of blessing with geometric blessing is not something that only Paul could dream about. It is a sad commentary on the church when most of its congregations are located at Deadwood Junction.

Remember, a chain of blessing can begin with one person. That one person just might be you.

CREATING HOLY JEALOUSY

Now I am speaking to you Gentiles. Inasmuch then
as I am an apostle to the Gentiles, I magnify my ministry
in order to make my fellow Jews jealous [envious],
and thus save some of them. Rom. 11:13, 14, RSV.

AT FIRST GLANCE IT might seem strange that the apostle to the Gentiles spends so much time writing about ministry to the Jews. In fact, his readers may have wondered the same thing. This apostle, who identified himself as a messenger to the Gentiles in Romans' first chapter, has now addressed the Jews specifically in two and a half chapters. So at the point of today's passage Paul once again turns to the Gentiles and tells them why he has spent so much time speaking to the Jews. His basic answer is that he wants to provoke the Jews into following the example of the Gentiles, so that the Jews in turn might bless the Gentiles.

For Paul ministry is a unit. He deplores the Gentile-Jew division and in several places states that the division is really artificial, since God saves all people in the same way—through faith in Christ.

Yet racial struggles continued to tear apart the church in Paul's day, sickening the apostle's heart. But he isn't one just to sit down and cry about problems or, worse yet, say that the church is going to pot, so why do anything for it or even remain faithful to it. No! To the contrary, he concludes that even the divisions in the church can be put to productive use.

He hopes that his ministry to the Gentiles will make the Jews envious or jealous. Is that good? Is making someone envious a Christian motivation? Won't such an activity only stimulate unworthy motives in them?

Not necessarily. It depends on what they are becoming envious about. We may define envy as "the desire to have for oneself something possessed by another." Whether envy is good or evil depends on what people desire and on whether they have a right to possess it.

If the something desired is good, such as the blessing of God, then having envy and even coveting such a thing is also good. One can say that there is such a thing as holy envy.

God wants in our day so to bless each of His children (us) that all the world will be envious and jealous. He longs for us to live in Christ so intently that we are constantly doing evangelism by creating envy, jealousy, and covetousness for the joy, peace, and wholeness that we have as Christians.

270

REJECTED OR NOT REJECTED

*For if [the Jews'] rejection means the reconciliation of the world,
what will their acceptance be but life from the dead? . . . If the
root is holy, so are the branches. Rom. 11:15, 16, RSV.*

WELL, PAUL, PLEASE MAKE UP your mind. Up in Romans 11:1 you told
us that God had not rejected the Jews. Now in today's text you tell us that He
has abandoned them. Are you mixed up, or am I? How can such a logical
writer say such apparently contradictory things in the same half chapter?

Both statements are true. God had cast away Israel as His chosen
agency for evangelizing the world. But a remnant had responded in faith
to the Messiah (Rom. 11:5, 6), and the missionary outreach of the church
was constantly expanding their number.

As Paul noted in verse 12, the turning away of the majority of the
Jews from the gospel had opened up the way for Paul and others to bring
their ministry of reconciliation to the Gentile world. Thus their rejection
had been a blessing in disguise.

But Paul has an unwavering concern for his fellow Jews. He looks
forward to the possibility of many of them responding to the gospel message. When they do so it will be like a spiritual resurrection from the dead.

The apostle then moves on to two parallel illustrations in Romans
11:16. The first he takes from Numbers 15:17-21. Paul notes that when
the people offer flour as a holy firstfruit offering from their grain crop, the
bread made from that holy flour will also be sacred. The second illustration comes from agriculture and compares Israel to a tree. If the tree's root
is holy, then so will be any shoots from that tree.

In both illustrations he appears to be referring to the patriarchs, especially Abraham. If they were holy, that would have an effect on the latest
branches in the Jewish line of descent.

Paul's heart was never far from missions—missions both to the
Gentiles and to his own kin. He longed for the salvation of his people, the
Jews. Ellen White expressed that same concern when she wrote that "in
the closing proclamation of the gospel, when special work is to be done
for classes of people hitherto neglected, God expects His messengers to
take particular interest in the Jewish people whom they find in all parts of
the earth" (*The Acts of the Apostles,* p. 381).

Here is another focal point for our daily prayer, another area of world
evangelism to which we need to respond.

271

A LESSON IN REMEMBERING

Don't let yourself feel superior to the former branches.
If you feel inclined that way, remind yourself that you do
not support the root, the root supports you. Rom. 11:18, Phillips.

IN ROMANS 11:17-24 Paul expands on the metaphor of the holy tree that he alluded to in verse 16. Here, however, he identifies it as an olive tree. The olive tree was not only one of the most common and the most useful trees in the Near East, but the Old Testament had repeatedly employed it as a symbol of Israel. Jeremiah 11:16, for example, notes that God had once called Israel "a green olive tree, fair with goodly fruit." For the purposes of Paul's illustration in Romans 11, it is of interest that the Jeremiah passage goes on to predict that God would send a great tempest and set fire to that tree, "and its branches will be consumed" (RSV).

Paul uses the olive tree illustration to make the point that some of the natural branches (Jews by birth) had been broken off and that some wild olive shoots (Gentiles) had been grafted in to share the richness of the root that originated with the patriarchs (see Rom. 11:16, 17). Thus, as he points out in other places, some of the Gentiles had become part of God's Israel through faith in Christ (see Gal. 3:26-29).

It is at that point that Paul utters the stern warning found in today's text: "Do not boast over those branches" (NIV) that had been cut off. It would have been all too easy for the Gentiles to feel superior to the Jews and develop an attitude of contempt toward them. Not only were Jews despised in some areas of the Roman Empire, but they had largely as a people been "cast away" by God (Rom. 11:15, NKJV).

Such an attitude, Paul exhorts, is completely out of place, since without the Jewish root there would be no grafted-in branches. Or as William Barclay points out, *"there would have been no such thing as Christianity unless there had been Judaism first."* The Christian church has an unpayable debt to the Judaism from which it sprang.

Paul's warning about not feeling superior to others is just as meaningful today as it was 2,000 years ago. The church has too many divisions caused by such superior airs. Some may not be anti-Jew, but they may be anti-Black, anti-White, anti-Hispanic, anti-Asian, or anti-everyone else who doesn't believe like them or appreciate the same music as they do. The "antis" continue to tear apart Christ's church. The only solution for those with superior thoughts of themselves is to meet Jesus at the cross.

HOW TO GET CUT OFF

You will say then, "Branches were broken off so that I might be grafted in." Quite right, they were broken off for their unbelief, but you stand by your faith. Do not be conceited, but fear. Rom. 11:19, 20, NASB.

TODAY'S PASSAGE HITS AT the heart of the matter of who can belong to the olive tree of the kingdom and who cannot. We should note that no article appears before the word "branches" in Romans 11:19. That signifies that not all of the Israelites had been broken off but just some of them so that some Gentiles might be grafted in.

The crucial questions are: On what basis are some Israelites broken off while others remain in the tree? On what basis are some Gentiles grafted in while others remain in their natural state?

The answers to these questions take us to the very heart of Paul's gospel and to the very secret for the revival of Israel as being like a resurrection from the dead (verse 15) that Paul so fervently hopes for in Romans 11. Paul doesn't beat around the bush. According to verse 20, those on the olive tree (whether they be Jews or Gentiles) are those who have faith. Those not on the tree, either because they have not been grafted in (Gentiles) or because they were broken off (Jews), Paul characterized as having "unbelief."

Thus Paul pushes home the same lesson that He did in the first few chapters of Romans. That is, there is only one way to be saved—to have faith in Jesus Christ as Savior and Lord.

That thought brings us to the last two words in Romans 11:20—"but fear." Fear what? we might ask. Fear the result of spiritual pride and arrogance, because we have been saved but others have not.

Not only the Gentiles of Rome to whom Paul spoke, but all of us need to be on guard against spiritual conceit or arrogance. C. K. Barrett hits the nail on the head when he writes that "the proper attitude for the Gentile Christian, as indeed for any Christian, is 'reverent fear,' for he must recognize that there is in himself absolutely nothing which can secure his position with God. The moment he begins to grow boastful he ceases to have faith (humble dependence upon God), and therefore himself becomes a candidate for 'cutting off.'"

Jesus knew what He was talking about when He said, "Blessed are the poor in spirit: for theirs is the kingdom of heaven" (Matt. 5:3).

STAYING IN THE TREE

If God spared not the natural branches,
take heed lest he also spare not thee. Rom. 11:21.

THE BIBLE HARDLY TEACHES once saved always saved. In today's text Paul firmly warns the Gentiles that if they become as arrogant and boastful about their spiritual privileges as the Jews had (see Rom. 2:17-29), they will suffer the same fate. That is, even though they had been grafted in, they could be cut off.

In commenting on God's not sparing the natural branches, John Calvin writes: "This is a most powerful reason to beat down all self-confidence: for the rejection of the Jews should never come across our minds without striking us and shaking us with dread. For what ruined them, but that through . . . dependence on the dignity which they had obtained, they despised what God has appointed? They were not spared, though they were natural branches; what then shall be done to us, who are the wild olive and alien, if we become beyond measure arrogant? *But this thought, as it leads us to distrust ourselves, so it tends to make us to cleave more firmly and steadfastly to the goodness of God"* (italics supplied).

Realizing our weaknesses is a continuing must in the Christian life. Paul repeatedly teaches that none of us can have any hope, peace, or security except as we maintain a faith connection to God through Christ.

Thus the apostle has provided his readers with a clear and unmistakable warning not to presume on God's mercy. While God loves us and will do anything for us, we also need to remember His hatred of sin, because it is sin and its results that destroy the peace, happiness, and lives of His created beings here on earth. The God who justifies must of necessity also be the God who judges. He wants to put an end to the sin problem. With that in mind, Paul had excellent reasons to point out in Romans 11:20 that Christians ought to stand in fear of God. We should have a holy awe because of who He is and His responsibility in the end to judge sin and to bring an end to the sin problem.

God may be a deity of love, but His love is not that of a toothless old grandfather who lets everything go by. The God who truly loves must judge sin as being destructive. He urges us, if we desire to remain in the olive tree, to put away all arrogant sin from our lives.

BALANCING MERCY AND JUSTICE

*Consider therefore the kindness and sternness of God: sternness
to those who fell, but kindness to you, provided that you continue in
his kindness. Otherwise, you also will be cut off. Rom. 11:22, NIV.*

IN MANY WAYS THE church seems to consist of two kinds of Christians.
On the one hand it has those who seem to always want to talk about God's
mercy or kindness. On the other hand we find the judgment types.

Those who see God's primary characteristic as being linked to judgment picture Him as kind of a grand executioner, just waiting for someone to step over the line so that He can let 'em have it. Those on the love
side see God as being perfectly harmless.

Where is the balance? Paul seeks to establish it in today's verse. He
presents God as being both stern and kind. But the apostle also puts that
sternness and kindness in a context. God always extends His kindness to
those willing to accept it. He wants nothing more than to share the kindness of His grace with those on earth, both Gentiles and Jews. As one author put it, "His goodness will always be shown toward those who trust in
Him rather than in their own merits or the privileged position they enjoy."
Those who "continue in his kindness" or grace have nothing to fear.

But those who trust in themselves, reject His grace, and rebel against
God can expect to see the stern side of God. It is not that God wants to hurt
anyone, but that He desires to wake them up to their plight, so that they
might turn to His kindness and accept the life He wants to bestow on them.

Those who persistently refuse God's kindness, however, He will
eventually "cut off." Those are hard words. They are judgment words,
both in terms of the olive tree here on earth and of the future kingdom that
will come to fruition when Christ returns.

Today's text clearly teaches the possibility of falling from grace, of
Christians who separate themselves from God, despise and reject His
goodness and mercy, and then find themselves outside of the kingdom.
C.E.B. Cranfield suggests that the clause about being cut off "is a warning against a false and unevangelical sense of security."

Our hope, as the old song places it, is in Jesus Christ and His righteousness. Day by day our most important task is to stay connected to Him
and His kindness. Only then will we never be "cut off."

SALVATION IS FROM GOD

And as for the fallen branches, unless they are obstinate in their unbelief, they will be grafted in again. Such a restoration is by no means beyond the power of God. Rom. 11:23, Phillips.

THERE IS HOPE! Hope for the Jews of Paul's day! Hope for the backslidden! Hope for those who have never believed! Hope for both Jews and Gentiles in all ages! And there is even hope for those who have been "obstinate in their unbelief."

Paul in today's verse, of course, has in mind the Jews of his day. If they came to believe, they could be grafted back into the tree from which they had been pruned. In spite of their rebellion, in spite of their obstinacy, in spite of their rejection of Christ, they were still not beyond God's grace.

Part of Paul's hope for his fellow Jews lay not merely in the fact that God was willing to forgive them, but that He was actually seeking them out through His Holy Spirit and through preachers of the gospel. He was pursuing them with His Spirit and His Word just as He had the rebellious Adam and Eve in the Garden of Eden.

Salvation comes from God. Paul has not the slightest doubt of that fact. But he is also just as certain that it must be received by faith. Thus he says of the Jews, "if they do not persist in unbelief, they will be grafted in, for God is able to graft them in again" (Rom. 11:23, NIV). He then goes on to claim that if those branches grafted into the tree from a wild tree had prospered, "how much more readily will these, the natural branches" flourish if restored to the parent stock from which they came in the first place (verse 24, NIV).

Paul is full of hope for his people. Salvation comes from God. If they will only respond in faith, they can be saved.

God still works the same way in the twenty-first century. Salvation is still from the Lord. It comes through the preaching of the gospel and is something we enter when we turn from rebellion (sin) against God and place our trust in Jesus Christ as Savior and Lord. Although salvation is from God, He saves by bringing sinners to faith in Christ.

Today the door of God's grace still stands open, and the promise of the Bible is that "whoever calls on the name of the Lord shall be saved" (Acts 2:21, RSV).

"ALL ISRAEL WILL BE SAVED"

I do not want you to be ignorant . . . , so that you may
not be conceited: Israel has experienced a hardening in
part until the full number of the Gentiles has come in.
And so all Israel will be saved. Rom. 11:25, 26, NIV.

PAUL IS STILL SPEAKING to the Gentiles in Romans 11:25. Apparently some of them had concluded that the Jews were beyond hope. They had rejected the gospel, and it had passed to the Gentiles. Thus God had cast off the Jewish people and chosen the Gentiles. That is exactly the kind of pride Paul is opposing.

He is quite straightforward that a part (actually most) of Israel had become hardened by unbelief. But that did not mean that God had closed the door to them. Paul personally, in fact, had great hopes for Israel. It was true that at the present time Gentiles were predominant in the church, but no one should count the Jewish people out. The apostle then went on to suggest that "all Israel will be saved."

That last phrase has caused a great deal of discussion. What did Paul mean when he said that "all Israel will be saved"? One thing is certain— God will never force anyone to be saved. Paul has been arguing all the way through Romans that salvation is a choice that requires accepting God's gift of grace, and that it is against God's nature to impose His gifts on anyone. The apostle is not teaching universalism.

Already he has expressed his hope that "some" of the Jewish people might be saved (verse 14). It seems evident that he believed that many would continue to reject all efforts to save them. In verse 5 Paul had raised the concept of a faithful remnant of Jews from within the nation who had accepted the gospel. Building on the remnant idea and the realization that even though salvation comes from God it still needs a faith response, all those Jews who will have accepted Christ throughout the Christian Era will constitute the "all Israel" who will be saved.

Paul had a burden for the Jewish people. Modern Christians should also. "Among the Jews," pens Ellen White, "are some who, like Saul of Tarsus, are mighty in the Scriptures, and these will proclaim with wonderful power the immutability of the law of God. The God of Israel will bring this to pass in our day. His arm is not shortened that it cannot save. As His servants labor in faith for those who have long been neglected and despised, His salvation will be revealed" (*The Acts of the Apostles,* p. 381).

GOD IS FAITHFUL

Never does God repent of His free gifts
or of His call. Rom. 11:29, Weymouth.

GOD IS FAITHFUL TO His promises. Just because the bulk of the Jewish nation had spurned His gospel offer through Jesus does not mean that the Lord had rejected them (Rom. 11:1). Those Jews who had rebuffed His offer of grace may have become His enemies, but God still loved them and wanted their best good, especially their salvation. After all, "they are loved on account of the patriarchs" (verse 28, NIV). He hasn't forgotten the gifts (such as sonship, the covenants, and the law [Rom. 9:4, 5]) that He gave them, nor of His call to make them His special people (Rom. 11:29). God hasn't backed away from His promises to them. And He still, as verses 30 to 32 point out, offers them mercy.

That's grace. In spite of all the problems the Jews had caused Christianity, in spite of all the roadblocks that they had thrown up to the spread of the gospel, in spite of their part in crucifying Christ, God was still pleading with their hearts and begging them to accept mercy. Such an attitude is beyond the human imagination. God isn't giving them what they deserve. Rather, He is offering them what they need. That's grace.

It is a love that will not let go. God loves rebellious people in spite of their destructive selves. He remains faithful, even though every person might be faithless and reject His gifts.

The Lord yearns that we as humans might respond to that faithfulness. He desires that we might choose not only to accept His grace but to pass it on to those we deal with every day even though they might not deserve anything better than a sock in the face. God longs for us to become like Him. He dreams of our not only becoming absorbers of mercy but dispensers of the greatest resource that exists anywhere.

We can be thankful that God is faithful in His love and His calling. If He were like us, it would all have been over long ago, our planet smashed to smithereens by an indignant deity. In all justice He could have said, "It is enough. This mess has gone far enough, and it is time to put an end to the 'human problem.' "

But that isn't God's way. His faithfulness to His promises has given new depth of meaning to the term long-suffering. He has not repented of "His free gifts or of His call." The way of life is still open to all who will receive it.

MERCY FOR ALL

*God has imprisoned all men in their own disobedience
only to show mercy to all mankind. Rom. 11:32, Jerusalem.*

"MERCY TO ALL MANKIND"! And who is the all? Texts such as this one have led some to conclude that eventually God will have mercy on "all," meaning every person who has ever lived. But such an interpretation fails to take in the context of the New Testament. In Romans Paul has taught that there will come a day of "wrath and fury" against the obstinate (Rom. 2:5, 8, 9, RSV). His position is in tune with that of Jesus, who repeatedly distinguished between those who would be taken to the kingdom and those who would be left in outer darkness (Matt. 25:31-46; 7:13-27). Thus the saving of "all men" is not a doctrine of universal mercy.

As in so many passages, it is the immediate context that supplies the answer to what Paul meant by "all mankind." From Romans 1:16 on he has been arguing that all, both Jew and Gentile, had sinned and that both could be justified through faith in the gospel. Then, beginning in chapter 9, Paul relates in a highly detailed way how God would have mercy on both groups because of His sovereign choice to do so. Now in Romans 11:30-32 he sums up his argument of chapters 9–11. God's mercy will save both groups. He does not have in mind every individual when he says "all mankind," but rather the sense of both Jews and Gentiles. The only way to salvation for either group is through God's undeserved mercy (grace).

In painting his picture of mercy for all, the apostle compares disobedience to a dungeon in which all people have been incarcerated. This prison is so secure that, notes C.E.B. Cranfield, "they have no possibility of escape except as God's mercy releases them."

It is no accident that Paul uses the word "disobedient" four times in Romans 11:30-32. The apostle spent the first three chapters of Romans demonstrating the universal nature of disobedience among both Jews and Gentiles.

But for Paul disobedience is never the last word. He also mentions the word "mercy" four times in verses 30-32. That topic has been at the forefront of Paul's discussion from Romans 3:21 up through the present summary. *Mercy for all* is the central theme in the book of Romans. *Mercy for all* is the triumph of God's grace over the prison house of sin. *Mercy for all* is open to every man, woman, or child who has ever lived. And *mercy for all* is our only hope.

RICHES FOR THE DESPERATE

O the depth of the riches and wisdom and knowledge
of God! How unsearchable are his judgments and
how inscrutable his ways! Rom. 11:33, RSV.

FOR 11 CHAPTERS PAUL has been providing his readers with a comprehensive account of the human situation and God's solution to that problem—"the gospel," which "is the power of God for salvation to every one who has faith, to the Jew first and also to the Greek" (Rom. 1:16, RSV).

Step by step he has guided his readers through the universality of sin, God's solution in justification by faith, the way in which Christians should live their lives, and how both Jews and Gentiles are on equal ground when it comes to God's mercy.

Paul has covered a great deal of territory. Now he has reached the mountaintop. As the Swiss commentator F. L. Godet notes: "Like a traveller who has reached the summit of an alpine ascent, the apostle turns and contemplates. Depths are at his feet; but waves of light illumine them, and there spreads all around an immense horizon which his eye commands."

As Paul views the plan of salvation, he sets forth a mighty doxology in Romans 11:33-36. All he can do is praise God for all that He has done. Ordinary speech won't do. The majesty of what God has done leaves the apostle awestruck. "O the depths of the riches and wisdom and knowledge of God! How unsearchable are his judgments and how inscrutable his ways!"

"Riches" is an important word to Paul. In Romans 2:4 he spoke of "the riches of [God's] goodness and forbearance and longsuffering," in Romans 9:23 of "the riches of his glory," and in Romans 10:12 of the Lord who is "rich unto all that call upon him." Elsewhere, in Ephesians 2:4 he talks of "God, who is rich in mercy" and in Ephesians 3:8 about "the unsearchable riches of Christ."

The dominant thought in Paul's theology is that God, who has riches undreamed of, has chosen to pour out His treasures on human beings who have not the slightest legal claim on them. The wonder of God's generosity never ceases to amaze the apostle. How God could take a miserable persecutor of the church such as himself and shower him with blessings, including the blessing of salvation, left him with nothing but praise and wonderment. He didn't understand why God would do such a thing, but he was desperate enough to accept it and appreciate it. For Paul, one could even think of Christianity as a religion of the desperate.

A LESSON IN HUMAN SMALLNESS

"Who has known the mind of the Lord? Or who has
been his counselor?" "Who has ever given to God,
that God should repay him?" Rom. 11:34, 35, NIV.

BIOLOGIST WILLIAM BEEBE (1877-1962) used to like to tell the story
of his visits to ex-president Theodore Roosevelt's home on Long Island,
New York. Both men enjoyed talking, and both loved nature. Before turning in for the evening they would go outside, search the sky until they
found a faint spot of light beyond the lower left corner of the great square
of Pegasus. Then one of them would recite: "That is the Spiral Galaxy in
Andromeda. It is as large as the Milky Way. It is one of 100 million galax-
ies. It consists of 100 billion suns, each larger than our own."

At that point in their ritual, the other would respond by saying, "Now
I think we are small enough! Let's go to bed."

That story brings to my mind Psalm 8:

"When I look at thy heavens, the work of thy fingers,
  the moon and the stars which thou hast established;
 what is man that thou are mindful of him,
   and the son of man that thou dost care for him?" (Ps. 8:3, 4, RSV).

What is a person but an almost invisible speck on an almost invisible
speck (the Planet Earth) in an almost invisible speck in galactic terms (the
Milky Way Galaxy)? And yet God poured out the riches of heaven for
each of us. He sent His only begotten Son to rescue the planet in rebellion.
Why? Because of His love! But who can understand such love?

"No one" is Paul's answer. We can glimpse its depths and its majesty,
but we have no way to fully comprehend it.

That conclusion places each person in a rather humble position. Most
of us from time to time would like to tell God how to run things on earth
and just how to carry out the plan of salvation and the final judgment. But
in the final analysis we have to back off and let God be God.

Likewise, we can't contribute to His riches, no matter how hard we
work at it. As Paul has repeatedly noted, nothing we can do will buy our
salvation or even add to its value. All we can do is humbly accept God's
riches and pray daily that we might learn to walk with Him more perfectly
as we seek to let Him change us in such a way that we will become progressively more like Him. The wonder of wonders is that even though
God is beyond us, He has agreed to live out His life within us.

PRAISE UNLIMITED

From Him and through Him and to Him are all things.
To Him be the glory forever. Amen. Rom. 11:36, NASB.

HERE IS THE CONCLUSION of the doxology that began in Romans 11:33.

It has two parts. The first is a theological affirmation of why we are dependent upon God. "All things" are "from Him and through Him and to Him." Whether the "all things" refers to creation or salvation makes no difference, because both of them—along with everything else—are "from God." As John Stott puts it: "If we ask *where* all things came from in the beginning, and still come from today, the answer must be, 'From God.' If we ask *how* all things came into being and remain in being, our answer is, 'Through God.' If we ask *why* everything came into being, and where everything is going, our answer must be, 'For and to God.' . . . God is the creator, sustainer and heir of everything, its source, means and goal. He is the Alpha and the Omega, and every letter of the alphabet in between." Moffatt's translation captures the meaning of today's passage nicely: "All comes from him, all lives by him, all ends in him. Glory to him for ever, Amen!"

Paul concludes chapter 11 with one final ascription to God: "To Him be the glory forever. Amen." It is because God is the source of everything that all glory belongs to Him alone.

Human pride seeks to ascribe glory to itself. Thus Nebuchadnezzar was out of line when he exulted, "Is not this the great Babylon I have built as the royal residence, by my mighty power and for the glory of my majesty?" (Dan. 4:30, NIV).

Pride is behaving as if we were God, or, as one author puts it, "strutting around the earth as if we owned the place, repudiating our due dependence on God, pretending instead that all things depend on us, and thus abrogating to ourselves the glory which belongs to God alone." Thus pride is the apex of the anti-God approach to life.

With that truth in mind, it is easy to see why Paul has been so concerned with boasting thus far in Romans: both the wrongness of boasting in our human efforts at salvation, and the rightness of boasting in what God has done for us in Christ on the cross.

All glory belongs to God alone. That is the theological conclusion that flows out of Romans 1–11. But it is also the devotional conclusion. We praise God because we know the truth of what He has done for us.

STEP 6
Living God's Love

Romans 12:1–15:13

TAKING A SIXTH STEP WITH PAUL

"Therefore." Rom. 12:1, REB.

"THEREFORE" IS AN important word. Paul here signals that he is not only changing topics but that the new topic is directly related to his previous discussion in the first 11 chapters of Romans.

Thus far in Romans we have spent nearly nine months taking five important steps with Paul. The first (Rom. 1:1-17) acquainted us with Paul, his mission, and the recipients of his letter. The second step (Rom. 1:18–3:20) put us into contact with the depth and the breadth of the problem of sin. In the process Paul told us that all—both Jews and Gentiles—have sinned and are under condemnation.

Step three (Rom. 3:21–5:21) provided a grand tour of God's remedy for the sin problem through the cross of Christ and our acceptance of Christ's righteousness by faith. The fourth step (Rom. 6:1–8:39) took us through the way of godliness, what it means to walk with Jesus in the principles of God. Step five (Rom. 9:1–11:36) showed us how both Jews and Gentiles fit into God's program of "mercy upon all" (Rom. 11:32).

"Therefore" (Rom. 12:1) signals the beginning of step six. Paul has set forth his theology. Now he is ready for its ethical implications. *The "therefore" indicates that the issue of how we live is dependent upon what we believe.* First comes salvation, then the response to that salvation.

Thus in a sense the apostle is still concerned with justification by faith, because it is fundamental with him that it is impossible for a justified person to live in the same way as an unrepentant sinner. Paul raised that issue in chapters 6 through 8, but now he is ready to devote three chapters almost exclusively to the topic.

He is ready to talk about the great subtheme with which he brackets the entire letter: *"the obedience that comes from faith" (Rom. 1:5; 16:26, NIV). The legalist exclaims, "Do these things and you will live," but Paul tells us, "Live and you will do these things."* For Paul theology precedes ethics, salvation goes before behavior. People walk with Christ in God's law because they have already been saved. To the apostle, the order is fundamental. All too many people seek to obey without being saved first. The end result is legalism, meanness, spiritual pride, and lostness.

LIVING SACRIFICES

I appeal to you therefore, brothers and sisters, by the mercies
of God, to present your bodies as a living sacrifice, holy and
acceptable to God, which is your spiritual worship. Rom. 12:1, NRSV.

THIS PASSAGE CONTAINS several key words and phrases. The first is "brothers and sisters." Paul now moves beyond the distinction of Jews and Gentiles—of natural branches and grafted branches—that has occupied him for the previous three chapters. He will address all believers as a part of the family of God. All, no matter what their race or ethnic origin, have a duty to be holy, committed, humble, loving, and conscientious. All have the duty of living God's love and of treating one another as brothers and sisters.

The second key word is "mercies," one that takes us back to Romans 1–11. God expects us to live His love because of His mercies that have united us in one faith.

The third word, surprisingly to some, is "bodies." No Greek would have put it that way. To them the body was a prison to leave behind for a spiritual/mental existence. But not so with Christianity. A Christian's body is important. The temple of the Holy Spirit (1 Cor. 6:19), it will be resurrected at the last day (1 Cor. 15). Holy living includes both how we live as physical beings (Rom. 12:1) and in the mental/spiritual realm (verse 2).

The fourth key phrase is "living sacrifice." At first it sounds like a contradiction in terms. After all, a sacrifice was something that people in Paul's day took to a temple to be slain in a ritual manner. To suggest that Christians should be living sacrifices is a vivid piece of imagery.

I have often thought that it might be easier to die for Christ than to live for Him. After all, as difficult as dying might be, it is only necessary to wind up your courage once. Then it's all over. But being a living sacrifice means dedication to Christ every day for the rest of my life. And that, according to Paul and Jesus, means a continuous crucifixion of my willful self. It calls for a continuous offering of all that I am and all that I have to God. We must have daily grace to live the life of a living sacrifice.

But that kind of life, Paul hastens to add, is both a "spiritual act of worship" (Rom. 12:1, NIV) and our "reasonable service" (KJV) when we realize what Christ has done for us.

BECOMING A BUTTERFLY

*And be not conformed to this world: but be ye transformed
by the renewing of your mind, that ye may prove what is that
good, and acceptable, and perfect, will of God. Rom. 12:2.*

"TRANSFORMED."

An interesting word. It comes from two Greek words, the first
meaning "across" and the second "form." Thus to be transformed means
to change across from one form to another. We use the word in English
as "metamorphosis."

And what is "metamorphosis"? It is the process by which a sluglike
caterpillar becomes a butterfly. To me, that is one of the most graphic illustrations of what happens to a person when he or she meets Jesus.

God finds us in our self-centered, proud, and self-serving ways, and
then takes us and transforms us. Now, that's a miracle! Perhaps it's the
greatest of all miracles.

God wants to take a slug like me and teach me to fly. The Lord seeks
to take drab crawlers and paint them in beautiful hues and give them wings.

And the good thing is that He can do it. Praise God, He wants to transform me. He wants to make me like Him in character; He wants to make
me into something I am not. He longs to make me into a new creature after
the image of Jesus.

Paul isn't the only one to speak of this idea of transformation. Jesus
described it as being born again (John 3:3, 5). Then again, Paul tells us in
2 Corinthians 5:17 that Christians are new creatures. They refuse to be
"conformed to this world." J. B. Phillips translates today's passage,
"Don't let the world around you squeeze you into its own mould, but let
God re-make you so that your whole attitude of mind is changed. Thus
you will prove in practice that the will of God . . . is good."

Karl Barth refers to becoming a Christian as "a great disturbance,"
since "human behavior must inevitably be disturbed by the thought of
God." Becoming a Christian changes every aspect of people's lives. The
Christian value system opposes that of the world. Thus it is impossible for
the Christian to conform to the values and lifestyles of the present age.
God has transformed a Christian's mind, and he or she lets that new mind
guide each and every activity. It is to the various realms of Christian activity that Paul turns to in Romans 12:3–15:13 as he applies the gospel of
transformation to everyday living.

286

LESSON NUMBER ONE IN TRANSFORMED LIVING

In virtue of the gift that God in his grace has given me I say to everyone among you: do not . . . think too highly of yourself; but think your way to a sober estimate based on the measure of faith that God has dealt to each of you. Rom. 12:3, NEB.

THINKING TOO HIGHLY of ourselves seems to come with the baggage of being human. As James Denney notes, everybody in the church needs the counsel in today's verse, because "to himself, every man is in a sense the most important person in the world, and it always [takes] much grace to see what other people are, and to keep a sense of moral proportion" between ourselves and them.

Romans 12:3-8 deals with lesson number one in living the transformed life, the living sacrifice kind of life. Part of that transformed living involves having a correct estimate of ourselves in the context of the church and its ministries. According to Paul, Christians can no longer think of themselves in the proud way they did before they came to Christ. They can no longer conform to that worldly pattern, but must let God through His Spirit transform them to a genuine Christian humility.

Today's verse reminds us of Philippians 2:5-7, in which Paul urges the church members at Philippi to "have this mind among yourselves, which is yours in Christ Jesus, who, though he was in the form of God, did not count equality with God a thing to be grasped, but emptied himself, taking the form of a servant" (RSV). Having the mind of Christ frees us from self-conceit and allows us soberly to evaluate ourselves from the perspective of our total dependence upon God and the ministry of service for which He has equipped each of us.

Paul had the gift of apostleship, and, as he tells us in Romans 12:4-8, other church members also have gifts for ministry. "The danger," notes Ernest Best, "is that they will be so thrilled with [those gifts] that they will become *conceited* and not use them for the good of all, but to gather the admiration of others. So, taking up the idea of the renewal of their 'minds' (verse 2), Paul warns them to *think* soberly about themselves."

It never ceases to amaze me how disgusting I find pride to be in other people, yet how easy I am on myself when it comes to that particular vice. Today's admonition is one that each of us needs every day.

UNITY IN DIVERSITY

Just as each of us has one body with many members, and these members
do not all have the same function, so in Christ we who are many form
one body, and each member belongs to all the others. Rom. 12:4, 5, NIV.

MARTIN LUTHER ONCE noted that it is just as impossible to be a solitary Christian as it is to be a solitary adulterer.

Being a Christian means becoming a part of the body of Christ, the church. When we become related to Christ we also have a relationship to one another. When believers become heirs of God, they become fellow heirs with each other. That is why Christians often refer to each other as brother and sister. They have all been adopted into the family of God.

The immediate environment in which the "family" operates is the church. Paul in such letters as the one to the Ephesians characterized the church as the body of Christ. The church is that unity that we can describe as a functional body.

Romans 12:4, 5 highlights the truth that not all the members or parts of the body have the same role. Thus Paul is not only speaking to the unity of the church, but also to its diversity. The church is one in purpose, but the various members each make a different contribution, depending upon their special gifts.

Thus the plurality of the members leads to the health of the church as a body. Both unity and diversity are important at every level of the church. A church in which everyone had my temperament and talents would be a pretty boring place. It would also be quite ineffective. As Christians we need to value more both the unity we share as brothers and sisters in Christ and the diversity that makes us effective. In fact, we can define the effective church as one of unity in its diversity. Of course, that unity, if it is to be healthy, must be in Christ.

Unity in diversity was an important message to the Romans. After all, being located at the crossroads of the empire, the church in Rome comprised many ethnicities and races beyond the major Jewish and Gentile categories. The members needed to learn both how to work together and at the same time how to utilize their differences to increase their effectiveness in reaching out to the community around them.

The same challenges face the church in the twenty-first century. One of its greatest needs today is to maximize the beneficial effects of both its diversity and its unity.

THE CHURCH NEEDS ME

Through the grace of God we have different gifts. Rom. 12:6, Phillips.

PRAISE THE LORD! He needs us all! The church doesn't require just my gifts or only your talents; it needs each of us and all of us if it is to have wholeness.

Paul provides some wonderful insight on today's verse and its context in 1 Corinthians 12, in which he writes: "As the human body, which has many parts, is a unity, and those parts, despite their multiplicity, constitute one single body, so it is with Christ. For we were all baptised by the one Spirit into one body, whether we were Jews, Greeks, slaves or free men, and we have all had experience of the same Spirit.

"Now the body is not one part but many. If the foot should say, 'Because I am not a hand I don't belong to the body,' does that alter the fact that the foot *is* a part of the body? Or if the ear should say, 'Because I am not an eye I don't belong to the body,' does that mean that the ear really is no part of the body? After all, if the body were all one eye, for example, where would be the sense of hearing? Or if it were all one ear, where would be the sense of smell? But God has arranged all the parts in the one body according to his design. For if everything were concentrated in one part, how could there be a body at all? The fact is there are many parts, but only one body. So that the eye cannot say to the hand, 'I don't need you!' nor, again, can the hand say to the feet, 'I don't need you!' On the contrary, those parts of the body which seem to have less strength are more essential to health: and to those parts of the body which seem to us to be less admirable we have to allow the highest honour of function. The parts which do not look beautiful have a deeper beauty in the work they do, while the parts which look beautiful may not be at all essential to life! But God has harmonised the whole body by giving importance of function to the parts which lack apparent importance, that the body should work together as a whole with all members in sympathetic relationship with one another. So it happens that if one member suffers all the other members suffer with it, and if one member is honoured all the members share a common joy" (1 Cor. 12:12-26, Phillips).

The moral of the story: The church needs me and my special talents.

Today, Father, help me to discover more fully the spiritual gifts that You have given me. Beyond that, help me to dedicate them to You and find avenues to put them to use for service to others. Thank You.

GET OFF OF YOUR GIFT

If a man's gift is prophesying, let him use it in proportion to his faith.
If it is serving, let him serve; if it is teaching, let him teach; . . . if it
is in showing mercy, let him do it cheerfully. Rom. 12:6-8, NIV.

EARLY IN WORLD WAR II Winston Churchill said to President Franklin Roosevelt, "Give us the tools, and we will finish the job."

Churchill, of course, was speaking about the materials of war. But the role of spiritual gifts in the church finds a parallel to the British leader's needs. The church is also in a fight to the finish against the kingdom of evil. The spiritual gifts that Paul lists in Romans 12 and other places are tools for the church to use in its cosmic struggle. It's as if God has cabled us from the throne room of heaven and said: "I give you the tools (the gifts of the Spirit); now finish the job."

Romans 12:6-8 lists seven gifts. Some, such as prophesying, seem more glamorous than others. Others have less prestige but are equally important. But given the way people get puffed up about who they think they are, it is no wonder that Paul included an admonition for persons not to think more highly than they ought of themselves when he discussed the gifts. As Jesus told us, the sad fact is that people even get proud about giving or how well they think they have prayed (Matt. 6:1-8).

The problem of people in the church comparing their gifts with others also came up in 1 Corinthians 13, in which Paul told them that nothing really mattered if they didn't have true love for each other.

Beyond prophecy, Paul lists six other gifts: serving, teaching, encouraging, contributing to the needs of others, leadership, and mercy. Most of those gifts find their meaning in the everyday life of the church and its surrounding community. They are not exotic but regular duties.

The great danger is that we as Christians will not utilize the gifts that God has given us. That is why Paul specifically urges the use of each one. It is too easy to be a spectator in the great controversy rather than a participant and, so to speak, sit on our gifts. God's command to you today is to get off of your gift and let God use both it and you to His glory.

Perhaps it is not an accident that the last word in today's passage is "cheerfully." Nothing is as unappealing as cheerless, dour persons who are just "doing their duty." While the word "cheerfulness" (RSV) in Romans 12:8 refers specifically to showing mercy, it is important in the use of all the gifts. God wants us to serve Him with a smile on our face.

LESSON NUMBER TWO IN TRANSFORMED LIVING

Let your love be sincere. Regard evil with horror;
cling to the right. Rom. 12:9, Weymouth.

IN ROMANS 12:1, 2 Paul tells his readers that as Christ's saved children they need to live transformed lives as living sacrifices. He next provides lesson number one in transformed living. It involves the humility that each needs as he or she utilizes God's gifts in the church.

With verse 9 we come to lesson number two. It places one of the most important Pauline words on the table—love. Just as in 1 Corinthians 12 and 13, Paul moves from the topic of spiritual gifts to that of love. Again, in Galatians 5:22 the apostle puts "love" first in his list of the fruit of the Spirit. Beginning with today's verse Paul begins to spell out what it means to live the life of love. That task will carry him up through Romans 15:13.

Up to the present passage in Romans we have seen *agapē* (love) demonstrated on the cross (Rom. 5:8), poured into our hearts (verse 5), and persistently refusing to let us go (Rom. 8:35, 39). But now Paul begins to spell out the meaning of *agapē* for Christian discipleship. As John Stott notes: "Romans 12-15 are a sustained exhortation to let love govern and shape all our relationships."

Paul highlights three characteristics of Christian love in today's text. First, it must be completely "sincere." That is not exactly what the original Greek says. The actual word means "without hypocrisy." But hypocrites in Greek were play actors who wore masks to cover their true identity. That is, they were not sincere. But love, as Paul points out, is always sincere and transparent. It is a love cleansed of self, whose aim is to give more than it receives.

Second, love by its very nature hates evil. It regards it with horror. And it is a passionate word, because love is a passionate attribute based on the principle of wanting the very best for others. Thus it also must hate or be repulsed by those things that destroy the quality of human life.

Third, love clings to the right. The word here is the one used for glue. It implies that those who have God's *agapē* will be cemented to those things and principles that bring life and healthiness.

When our lives are infused with God's *agapē* they will be not just partially but totally transformed. So will our homes and churches.

A RADICAL ETHIC

Love one another with brotherly affection; outdo
one another in showing honor. Rom. 12:10, RSV.

I RECENTLY CAME ACROSS two other interesting variants of the so-called golden rule of Matthew 7:12. The first was "Do unto others before they do unto you." The second proclaimed, "He with the gold rules."

Well, maybe those golden rules aren't really new or unique. The plain truth is that they have been in control of earth's inhabitants ever since Adam and Eve headed east of Eden (Gen. 3:24).

Christianity has come to change all that. The Christian life, as Paul noted in Romans 12:2, is a transformed life. And living the transformed life means refocusing our love from ourselves to God and other people. And with that transformation the real golden rule comes into play as the dominant feature of our lives: "All things whatsoever ye would that men should do to you, do ye even so to them" (Matt. 7:12).

That is radical ethic. But it is the ethic of the kingdom. Paul is also telling us in today's verse that it must be the ethic of the church. Church members are to have "brotherly affection" for each other. In selecting those words he chose family words. Christians love each other because they belong to one family. They have God as their Father and are thereby brothers and sisters in the Lord. Christians are not strangers to each other. They are family members. As William Barclay notes, "the Christian Church is not a collection of acquaintances; it is not even a gathering of friends; it is a family in God."

That being so, the church's members need to live out their family love, lest they fall into that insincere "love" that Paul spoke of in Romans 12:9. Part of living out that love is to outdo one another in showing honor.

A story tells of an important yet humble man who arrived at a gathering only to encounter thunderous applause when he entered. Immediately he stepped back, let the next man pass, and began clapping himself, never dreaming that the applause was for him. He assumed it to be for another.

It is that spirit that the church so desperately needs. A spirit that esteems others above himself or herself. Too many hard feelings have surfaced because people have not been thanked properly or shown proper honor. It is time for us to begin to live like Christians in honoring others and to leave off our own petty hurts and sensitivities. God wants us to begin to live His love.

THREE MORE AGAPĒ CHARACTERISTICS

*Do not lag in zeal, be ardent in spirit,
serve the Lord. Rom. 12:11, NRSV.*

IN TODAY'S TEXT WE find Paul in the midst of a list of 18 rules for ordinary, everyday life. They all seem to be predicated on the first rule: "Love must be sincere" (Rom. 12:9, NIV).

Love will not only (1) be sincere, but it will (2) hate evil, (3) cling to the good, (4) be devoted to fellow Christians in brotherly love, and (5) honor others above itself.

Those five characteristics we have looked at the past two days. Today's text offers three more characteristics of genuine Christian love. First, it will not lag in zeal. Love is enthusiastic rather than sluggish. That is true even of human love. I remember courting my wife. I had a hard time just walking in her direction. I wanted to run and shout and give her a big hug. Love even on the human level is an exuberant experience. It is difficult to contain it.

That enthusiastic zeal leads to a second characteristic of genuine love in today's verse. It is ardent in spirit. "Ardent" comes from a word meaning to boil, seethe, or bubble. A zealous love boils over and is irrepressible. Christianity is no back burner affair. The Holy Spirit infuses the human spirit with fervent zeal. As William Barclay writes, "the one man whom the Risen Christ could not stand was the man who was neither hot nor cold" (Rev. 3:15, 16). Or as Ernst Käsemann puts it: "according to Revelation 3:15 lukewarmness is the worst offense. If nothing burns, there can be no light." The person indwelt by the Spirit of God is one desperately in earnest. A fire in the bones leads such people to be aflame for Christ.

The third characteristic of love in today's passage is that it serves the Lord. The word "serve" (actually, "slave") takes us back to the second word in the Greek text of Romans, which tells us that Paul was God's slave. So is every Christian. We are not slaves from fear, but from love; a love that impels us to serve the One who has given everything for us, a love that burns within and is shaped by zeal.

For a Christian, serving Christ is not an irksome duty but a joyful privilege. It is a privilege with implications for both one's brothers and sisters in Christ and, as we shall soon see, one's enemies.

STILL MORE AGAPĒ CHARACTERISTICS

*Rejoice in your hope, be patient in tribulation,
be constant in prayer. Rom. 12:12, RSV.*

THUS FAR IN ROMANS 12:9-11 we have seen eight characteristics of Christian love. Paul now provides us with three more.

The first is that love rejoices in hope. One writer has noted that "there are no hopeless situations in life; there are only men who have grown hopeless about them." But to grow hopeless is not the Christian way, because our hope is not in ourselves or our powers or our friends or our circumstances, but in God, who is more than able to fulfill all our needs.

The early Christians may, in terms of outward appearances, have had little to be hopeful about. But they could "rejoice in the Lord always" (Phil. 4:4, RSV). Joy and hope go hand in hand in the Christian experience. Both, along with love, have a central place in Paul's writings. He associates joy with love as the first and second items he listed as fruit of the Spirit (Gal. 5:22), and he intimately links hope with love as two of the three great things of 1 Corinthians 13. A Christian by definition is one characterized by genuine love and its outflowing in hope and joy.

A second characteristic of Christian love in Romans 12:12 is that it is patient in tribulation or adversity. A Christian's relationship to God will buoy him or her up and carry a believer through life's troubles. And troubles there will be. One man noted that suffering colors all of life. But the Christians can choose the color. They meet tribulation with a patience supported by hope and joy.

The book of Daniel tells the story of Shadrach, Meshach, and Abednego being cast into the fiery furnace. It surprised Nebuchadnezzar that they did not seem harmed. Noting to his retainers that they had cast three men into the furnace, he claimed that he saw a fourth in the flames, "like the Son of God" (Dan. 3:24, 25). William Barclay in relating that story remarks that "a man can meet anything when he meets it with Christ."

A final characteristic of genuine love set forth in today's verse is that it is "constant in prayer." Persistent prayer was a staple in Paul's personal life and ministry. It must be for anyone who seeks to live a life of genuine love, who rejoices in hope in spite of circumstances, and who is patient in tribulation. Such characteristics are sustained by prayer.

HOSPITALITY CHRISTIAN STYLE

Contribute to the needs of God's people,
and practise hospitality. Rom. 12:13, REB.

IN TODAY'S PASSAGE PAUL continues the characteristics of the out-flowing of Christian love. The New Living Translation renders the verse in the very personal way that the apostle intended: "When God's children are in need, be the one to help them out. And get into the habit of inviting guests home for dinner or, if they need lodging, for the night."

The first thing we should note is that Christians should provide for the needs of fellow church members. It is not to be a look-down-your-nose type of almsgiving but a genuine expression of love (Rom. 12:9).

The apostle, in other places, points out that Christian care for others should include parents and other relatives. He was so adamant on that obligation that he declared that "if any one does not provide for his rela-tives, and especially for his own family, he has disowned the faith and is worse than an unbeliever" (1 Tim. 5:8, RSV). Those are strong words, but they seem to be needed. Even today we find people who call themselves Christian yet overlook the genuine needs (both emotional and financial) of their parents and other relatives.

Beyond relatives, Paul in 1 Timothy, in the tradition of the Old Testa-ment, also pointed to the duty of Christians to support those who were "wid-ows indeed" (1 Tim. 5:3). In specifying the "indeed," he was reflecting on the fact that Christians should be careful not to create unhealthy dependen-cies. There is a fine balance here. It is a Christian duty to give people what they really need. With some it is immediate financial help. With others it is knowledge and encouragement to start on the road to self-sufficiency.

Paul demonstrated his concern for the poor by his collections for the poor in Judea. Do I—does my local congregation—reflect that same care?

The second admonition in today's text has to do with hospitality, an especially important issue when many Christians had to flee persecution in a world often without convenient motels (or at least safe ones) to house them. The world has changed, but the need to share our table and some-times our homes with others hasn't.

It is all too easy not to reach out to others. But what a blessing is in store for us and our guests when we do. Take something as simple as an invita-tion to Sabbath lunch, for example. How many strangers or lonely members have been neglected in this rather pedestrian aspect of Christian love?

CHRISTIANS REJECT "NORMALITY"

Bless them which persecute you: bless, and curse not. Rom. 12:14.

THAT'S NOT NORMAL! Our first thought is to hope the dirty so-and-so's get exactly what they deserve. Then they will know not to mistreat us again.

But whoever said Christianity was normal? Not Paul! Not Jesus! Both of them put forth a highly unnormal ethic of love. Jesus even tied being unnormal to being like God.

All of us are familiar with Jesus' admonition in Matthew 5:48 that Christians must be perfect, just as their Father in heaven is perfect. Most of us take that text out of context and supply our own definition of perfection and our own list of do's and don'ts that we think should help us to be perfect.

But that's a sick way to read the Bible. The only healthy way is to start with a passage in context. For Matthew 5:48, begin with verse 43: "You have heard that it was said, 'You shall love your neighbor and hate your enemy.' But I say to you, Love your enemies and *pray for those who persecute you, so that you may be sons of your Father who is in heaven;* for he makes his sun rise on the evil and on the good, and sends rain on the just and on the unjust. For if you love those who love you, what reward have you? Do not even the tax collectors [bad people] do the same?" (Matt. 5:43-46, RSV).

Did you read carefully what Jesus said? To be like the Father is to bless and pray for those persecuting us. That is the significance of the "so that you may be sons of your Father" in Matthew 5:45. The Bible defines the perfection of Matthew 5:48 not as some sort of itemized sinless living, but as loving even our enemies (cf. Luke 6:36).

As He hung on the cross Jesus prayed for those killing Him. Stephen died praying for forgiveness for those who stoned him to death (Acts 7:60). One of them was a man named Saul, who afterward became Paul, the apostle to the Gentiles. Without doubt Stephen's prayer was one of the things that turned Paul to Christ. As Augustine noted: "The church owes Paul to the prayer of Stephen."

Have you prayed for your enemies lately? If not, why not? This is a perfect time to do something that's not normal. Right now we can kneel and ask God to bless those who least deserve it.

UNLOCKING THE PRISON OF SELFISHNESS

Rejoice with them that do rejoice, and
weep with them that weep. Rom. 12:15.

P. STUART BRISCOE points out that "human beings are equipped with a great capacity for giving and receiving love. Even the hardest heart melts before the innocent smile of a child or the antics of puppies and lambs. But this capacity for love, sympathy, and empathy is often strangely locked up in the confines of selfishness."

We too often get so caught up in our own selves, our own things, our own achievements, our own gains and losses, that we find it inconvenient if not downright troublesome to "rejoice with those who rejoice" and "mourn with those who mourn" (NIV).

But, strangely enough, most of us find it easier to "mourn with those who mourn" than to "rejoice with those who rejoice." Centuries ago the early church father Chrysostom commented on this passage that "it requires more of a high Christian temper to rejoice with them that do rejoice than to weep with them that weep. For this nature itself fulfils perfectly; and there is none so hard-hearted as not to weep over him that is in calamity; but the other requires a very noble soul, so as not only to keep from envying, but even to feel pleasure with the person who is in esteem."

In short, it is generally more difficult to congratulate others on their successes, especially if that success involves disappointment for us, than it is to sympathize with others on their sorrows and losses. It is only when our "self" is dead, when it is freed from the "confines of selfishness," that we can take as much joy in the successes of others as we do in our own.

Today's verse spells out one more of the many ways that genuine love (Rom. 12:9) expresses itself. To empathize with others costs us in terms of our time and emotional energies, but it reflects the way God relates to each of us. God is not a distant "Other." Rather, He partakes of our joys and sorrows. In so doing, He shows us that we are important—that we count.

God has a ministry for each of us along this line. Today He is going to put someone in my path with whom I can weep or with whom I can rejoice. I can in a small sense be "God" to them as I help them to see that they are not alone, that someone cares, that their joys and sorrows are important.

Help me today, Father, to live Your love more fully.

THE GROUND BEFORE THE CROSS IS LEVEL

Live in harmony with one another; do not be haughty, but associate with the lowly; never be conceited. Rom. 12:16, RSV.

WE HAVE FINALLY COME to the end of Paul's list of how a Christian ought to express genuine love. Thus far he has given 15 elements. He will add three more in today's passage.

The first item in today's verse is for Christians to "live in harmony with one another." The basic idea is that Christians should be of the same mind. Since all true Christians (as opposed to all church members) have transformed minds, they share a common core of basic convictions, values, and concerns. The renewed mind, informed and guided by love, as Paul has defined it, will help Christians to "live in harmony with one another." Would to God that all church members were also Christians in Paul's sense of the word.

Second, Christians should not be haughty and proud. Their humility should lead them to be at ease with church members of every social class. Before the cross we all stand on flat ground. All of us have been saved by grace alone. A proud Christian is a contradiction in terms.

James illustrates the principle that Paul has outlined. "My brethren," he writes, "show no partiality as you hold the faith of our Lord Jesus Christ, the Lord of glory. For if a man with gold rings and in fine clothing comes into your assembly, and a poor man in shabby clothing also comes in, and you pay attention to the one who wears the fine clothing and say, 'Have a seat here, please,' while you say to the poor man, 'Stand there,' or, 'Sit at my feet,' have you not made distinctions among yourselves. . . . If you show partiality, you commit sin, and are convicted by the law as transgressors" (James 2:1-4, 9, RSV).

Paul's final injunction is that Christians must not be conceited. Come to think of it, there is nothing more pathetic than a conceited "Christian."

What a wonderful place the church would be if all of its members practiced the 18 qualities of genuine love presented in Romans 12:9-16.

The good news is that you don't have to wait for the rest of the church. You can start today. Paul has only one final bit of advice for you. If you "succeed," don't become conceited or haughty, but give all the glory to God.

LESSON NUMBER THREE IN TRANSFORMED LIVING

Do not repay anyone evil for evil, but take thought for what is noble in the sight of all. Rom. 12:17, NRSV.

WITH ROMANS 12:17 we have come to a third lesson in how to live the transformed life, the "living sacrifice" of verses 1 and 2. The first lesson (verses 3-8) had to do with the humility that each Christian needs as he or she works in the church and utilizes God's gifts. The second lesson (verses 9-16) concerned the characteristics of genuine love.

Paul's third lesson (verses 17-21) focuses on how Christians deal with those who mistreat them. Given the instinct for self-protection that every person has, it is only natural that thoughts of revenge surface in every human heart. Paul has already touched on the topic in verse 14, in which he said that Christians are to bless, rather than curse, those who persecute them. But that is easier said than done. As a result, Paul returns to the topic in verses 17-21.

His first injunction is that Christians should not repay evil for evil. There are several reasons for that. One of them is that revenge is a costly business.

Dale Carnegie tells of a visit to Yellowstone National Park back in the days when tourists could watch the rangers feed the massive grizzly bears. The grizzlies allowed no competition. They drove away with threatening growls any animal that threatened to get their food. That is, all competition except one small animal—the skunk! Though it was obvious that the big bears resented the skunk for its impudence and would have loved to take revenge on the small striped creature, they didn't. And why? The cost of getting even was just too high.

"Smart grizzly!" remarks Stan Mooneyham. "Smarter than a lot of us humans who spend frustrating days and sleepless nights brooding over resentments and plotting ways to get even. Those feelings of resentment, bitterness, and revenge exact a heavy toll in your body, soul, and emotions. . . . The cost is outrageously high and damaging."

The bottom line is that Christians live the life of love, even when treated with evil. That takes grace. You see, grace is not merely for forgiveness. It is also for transforming our attitudes and for empowering us to demonstrate love. I don't know about you, but in the light of today's text I need to pray for an extra outpouring of grace—right now.

299

THE ALLIGATOR WITHIN

If it is possible, as far as it depends on you,
live at peace with everyone. Rom. 12:18, NIV.

"LIVE AT PEACE with everyone" is a wonderful ideal. But is it possible? How does it work?

The plain truth is that it can't always be done. Our text has two conditions: (1) "if it is possible" and (2) "as far as it depends on you."

Let's face it, in a sinful world cantankerous people can make it impossible for others to live in peace with them. That's why Paul adds "as far as it depends on you." While we can't control other people, we are responsible for ourselves. That is where our responsibility lies—being a peacemaker in whatever situation we find ourselves.

Unfortunately, as we noted in Paul's treatment in Romans 7, Christians aren't completely sanctified. A story tells of a family moving to a new town. The young son, being lonely, decided to take his pet for a walk. He had hoped to meet a friend, but instead he ran across the local gang.

The gang bully, wishing to establish his authority over the newcomer, began to threaten the boy that he would have problems if he didn't join his gang. Then he noticed the boy's pet, saying, "That's the ugliest dog I've ever seen! Yellow, beady-eyed, long-nosed, short-tailed, and stumpy-legged! If you don't join our gang by tomorrow, I'm going to sic my dog Killer on yours."

The next day they met again, and the new boy refused to join the gang. At that point the bully unleashed his huge Doberman pinscher, and shouted, "Kill that ugly, yellow, beady-eyed, short-tailed, long-nosed, stumpy-legged mutt!" The huge dog circled the smaller pet a couple of times and then lunged for it. But the new kid's pet opened its large mouth and swallowed Killer in one gulp.

The gang members were horrified. Finally the leader asked the new boy, "What kind of dog is that, anyway?"

The boy responded, "I don't know, but before we cut off his tail and painted him yellow, he was an alligator."

Whether we like it or not, we Christians have still a bit of alligator left in us. That is why if we are to live peaceably with everybody we need to ask God to come into our lives to show us our faults, to calm us down, and to give us the grace to live God's love. There is nothing worse than a yellow, short-tailed, beady-eyed, long-nosed alligator masquerading as a Christian.

VENGEANCE IS GOD'S

My dear friends, do not seek revenge, but leave a place
for divine retribution; for there is a text which reads,
"Justice is mine, says the Lord, I will repay." Rom. 12:19, NEB.

OH HOW EASY IT is to feel that old payback urge. C. S. Lewis caught that point when he wrote that "everyone says forgiveness is a lovely idea, until they have something to forgive." It is the having something to forgive that brings the blood to our eyes.

Pastor Martin Niemöller tells of his experience in the Nazi concentration camp at Dachau, where he served as a political prisoner. The gallows stood just outside his window. He saw thousands go to their deaths. Some, he noted, cursed, others whimpered, and some prayed.

"What will happen," Niemöller asked himself, "on the day they lead you there and put you to the test? When they put that rope around your neck, what will be your last words? Will you then cry out, 'You criminals, scum! There's a God in heaven! You'll get yours!'

"What if Jesus had said that?" he queried, "if He had taken His last breath to cry out to the soldiers and the Sanhedrin, 'Criminals! Scum! This is My Father's world. You'll get yours!'?

"What would have happened? Nothing! One more poor sinner would have died there, lonely and forgotten, and nothing would have happened."

If Jesus, Stan Mooneyham comments, had cursed His executioners, demanded justice, or pleaded for His rights, no one would have been surprised. "He would have died as just one more sorry spectacle of broken, flawed, self-centered humanity. His name would not have been remembered beyond His generation."

Jesus understood that vengeance does not belong to us, that it is God's responsibility. He realized that justice in the end would be done in the Lord's good time. At the end of time, Paul now tells us, God will make all things right. Not in the way of senseless vengeance that requires a pound of suffering for a pound of sin, but in a manner that will be just to everyone.

We as Christians need to learn the lesson that Jesus practiced and Paul taught. It is not one of the easiest to absorb. After all, that short-tailed alligator still lurks below the surface of our consciousness. But in the end, unleashed alligators destroy not only others, but the person who houses them. God has a better way for us to deal with those who have done us evil. He turns to that better way in the next verse.

301

THE ALTERNATIVE TO "SWEET REVENGE"

If thine enemy hunger, feed him; if he thirst, give him drink: for in so doing thou shalt heap coals of fire on his head. Rom. 12:20.

WE HAVE ONLY THREE ways to relate to a person who has done us some malicious evil. The first, to ignore the person, solves nothing.

The second, and most natural way from a "normal" human perspective, is to let the person "have it" with all we've got. Revenge seems so sweet. Yet it is counterproductive. It merely generates more revenge as both sides up the payback ante.

America's longest and most savage family feud illustrates the point. No one knows how it began, but we have no doubts about the results.

Some authorities claim that the Hatfield-McCoy family feud in the mountains of Kentucky and West Virginia ignited during the 1860s, and was kept burning by disputes over a stray hog and a fiddle valued at $1.75. The problem exploded in 1882 when three of the McCoy brothers killed Ellison Hatfield because he had insulted them.

The head of the Hatfield clan had the three McCoys tied to bushes within sight of their family cabin, and then pumped 50 bullets into them. After that it was a life for a life, and sometimes two or three for a life.

After nearly a half century of bitterness, the record counts nearly 30 known deaths. It was a high price to pay for "sweet revenge."

If neither ignoring a situation nor revenge is helpful, what should we do when someone has wronged us? Paul suggests the unlikely third way of doing them good. To feed them when they are hungry, to give them water when they are thirsty, and so on. That, he says, will be the same as heaping "coals of fire" on their heads. Moffatt catches the symbolism in the "coals of fire" metaphor by translating the passage as "in this way you will make him feel a burning sense of shame."

The third way may not always win an enemy over, but it is the only approach that stands a chance. So "unnormal" that it catches people off guard, it makes them ask, "What kind of person is this who repays my evil with good?" The answer is that such a person is a Christian who is showing genuine love (Rom. 12:9) in the same way that God demonstrated it for us by sending Jesus to die for us while we were still His enemies (Rom. 5:8, 10).

OVERCOMING EVIL WITH GOOD

Don't allow yourself to be overpowered by evil. Take the offensive—overpower evil with good! Rom. 12:21, Phillips.

BUT SHE HAS IT COMING! I'll show her! If she can hit hard, she will find that I can hit twice as hard! I will teach her a lesson she won't forget!

Such thoughts naturally pass through our minds when someone has hurt us. We don't even have to generate them. They are just there—a part of sinful human nature.

But Paul tells us that to be a Christian is to be "unnormal." It is to be born again with a different set of values. A set of values that even wants the very best for one's enemies (see Matt. 5:43-48).

Early in the last century a hired union thug blew up—murdered—the governor of Idaho in the official's own front yard. Harry Orchard, a man with a string of murders to his record, was a hard man in a hard battle between capital and labor.

How would you feel if you were the late governor's wife? Would you desire "sweet revenge" as your natural right?

We happen to know how she felt. As a Seventh-day Adventist Christian she prayed *for* Orchard. But she did more than pray for him. She prayed *with* him in prison. She actually went to the prison and pleaded with her husband's killer to give his heart to God.

That caught Harry off guard. He was expecting a fist in his face—he knew how to handle that. And he knew how to escalate a fight by retaliation. But he didn't know what to do with love.

Eventually, overcome by goodness, he gave his life to God. For the rest of his days he served others for Christ in prison, even refusing an eventual pardon.

"Don't allow yourself to be overpowered by evil. Take the offensive— overpower evil with good!" That is what God has done for us in Christ. He didn't retaliate and give us what we deserve. Rather, He offered us what we don't deserve—grace, forgiveness, life everlasting. And those who realize the value of that gift will pass it on to others. Only those who have been justified freely by God's grace know the power of love, and only they can pass on that love as God uses them to overcome evil with good.

Today is as good a day as any to start being "unnormal."

Help me, Lord, through Your grace, to learn how to "overpower evil with good." Amen.

LESSON NUMBER FOUR
IN TRANSFORMED LIVING

*Let every person be subject to the governing authorities; for there
is no authority except from God, and those authorities that
exist have been instituted by God. Rom. 13:1, NRSV.*

SINCE ROMANS 12:1, 2 Paul has been discussing the Christian's transformed life in the real world of everyday living.

Thus far the apostle has discussed the faithful yet humble use of
God's gifts (verses 3-8), the characteristics of genuine love (verses 9-16),
and Christians' relationships with those who have mistreated them (verses
17-21). Paul has been presenting a radical way of life that repays evil with
good and honors others more than self. Such attitudes are kingdom attitudes. They reflect the transformation that has taken place in a born-again
Christian's heart, mind, and life. The apostle wasn't joking or using a figure of speech when he talked of a Christian being a "living sacrifice."
Quite specific in describing what it means to be a Christian in difficult situations, he speaks to those who have been justified by grace and thus have
a new set of principles that lead to a new way of life.

With Romans 13:1-7 Paul provides us with a fourth lesson on living
the transformed life. This time it involves a Christian's relationship to the
civil government.

One of the most obvious lessons in today's text is that Christians are
duty-bound to obey civil government because God established it in the
first place. From this passage it appears that Paul would hold the position
that even a bad government is better than none at all.

That very point seems to be a main lesson in the book of Judges.
Judges 19 through 21 contains one of the worst stories in the Bible. The
tale of a "cleric" gone wrong, it records murder, sexual misconduct, and a
vast catalogue of perversions. Read it if you have time. But when you do,
note that the passage is bracketed by the same thought: "In those days there
was no king in Israel" (Judges 21:25; 19:1, RSV). Judges 21:25 goes on to
add the punch line for the book when, after reporting that Israel had no
king, it claims that "every man did what was right in his own eyes" (RSV).

Civil government may not be perfect, but it is better than anarchy.
God established it for humanity's own good. Without civil government
life exists only by the law of the jungle.

SHOULD I ALWAYS OBEY?

He who resists the [civil] authorities resists what God has
appointed, and those who resist will incur judgment. Rom. 13:2, RSV.

PAUL IS CLEAR ENOUGH. Those who disobey the civil government
are rebels by definition and deserve to be punished, because God has ordained such government. *The Revised English Bible* says it about as
plainly as words can express it: "It follows that anyone who rebels against
authority is resisting a divine institution, and those who resist have themselves to thank for the punishment they will receive."

Does that mean that it is always wrong to oppose the civil government? What about my teacher who during World War II stole typewriters
from the Nazis?

At the time he helped edit the Norwegian *Signs of the Times*. Before
the war the Adventist publishing house had purchased six new typewriters to prepare God's message for His people. But after the invasion the oc-
cupying forces "traded" those typewriters for six old beat-up ones so that
they could type out their reports and send them to Berlin.

As the war went on my teacher and his colleagues at the Adventist
publishing house became part of the civil defense. During air raids everybody had to go underground except for those operating the antiaircraft
guns and the civil defense personnel.

At the height of one raid six of the men from the publishing house
took three stretchers and three blankets and went on a rescue mission.
They "rescued" six nice new typewriters from a German office building
(two on each covered stretcher). For the rest of the war the machines produced spiritual messages.

But where did they get paper in wartime? Simple. During blackouts
trucks had to move without lights. Sometimes vehicles carrying government paper went off the road. And sometimes the drivers contacted my
friend. Naturally he and his colleagues were more than willing to "help"
the Germans move their paper. They, of course, used the "liberated" paper
to print Christian messages.

Is it ever appropriate to resist the government? If so, on what basis?

Those are not academic questions. For much of world history they
have been at the center of daily living for a significant part of the world's
population. Perhaps you have never lived in such a situation. But you may
someday. How should you then serve both God and the civil government?

305

A Closer Look at the State

For rulers hold no terror for those who do right, but for those who do wrong. Do you want to be free from fear of the one in authority? Then do what is right and he will commend you. Rom. 13:3, NIV.

IS THAT REALLY SO? Do those who do right never have to fear the civil ruler? Will the government always commend them?

What about Daniel's three friends? They did what was right when they refused to worship Nebuchadnezzar's golden image. And what did the king do? Commend them? No, he threw them into the fiery furnace. How can Paul say that "rulers hold no terror for those who do right"?

And what about those early Christian martyrs who lost their lives to the Roman emperors Decius and Diocletian? The emperors had commanded Roman citizens to worship them on pain of death. All that a Christian had to do was to bow down to the emperor's image and curse Christ. Such was the direct order of the Roman government. After all, weren't religion and patriotism one and the same? The caesars had come to believe that a population's allegiance to the government was central to the health of the state. Is that such a bad theory? What government can stand if the people are not patriotic?

We need to say two things about today's verse. The first is that Paul is not seeking to cover every situation involving every government. After all, hadn't the Jewish and Roman governments persecuted Paul himself for his faith? And hadn't he also been the agent of the Jewish authorities to kill Christians before his own conversion?

Rather than speaking to every possible situation, the apostle presents the case of a healthy situation in which a legitimate authority makes a legitimate demand on its citizens. In healthy times the apostle is correct. The government rewards people for doing right and punishes those who do wrong. Thus the Christians to whom Paul is writing should obey the government in its legitimate demands.

That brings up a second issue. What is legitimate? Who defines what is right or wrong? Who decides what should be commended and what actions should be punished? Is Paul saying that the state has absolute authority?

Absolutely not! But he does remind us that every Christian has a definite responsibility to the government under which he or she lives. Obedience to the state for a Christian is not an option. As T. W. Manson puts it, "resistance to legitimate authority legitimately exercised is wrong."

HITLER'S FAVORITE TEXT

*For he [the ruler] is God's servant to do you good. But if
you do wrong, be afraid, for he does not bear the sword
for nothing. He is God's servant, an agent of wrath to
bring punishment on the wrongdoer. Rom. 13:4, NIV.*

ADOLF HITLER HAD TWO Bible passages that he was especially fond
of. The first was Romans 13:1-7 and the second 1 Peter 2:13, 14: "Be subject for the Lord's sake to every human institution, whether it be to the
emperor as supreme, or to governors as sent by him to punish those who
do wrong and to praise those who do right" (RSV).

One of those two texts had to be preached on every year in every
church in the Third Reich. And "observers" made sure that the texts were
"interpreted properly."

Hitler as God's "minister" (KJV) or "servant" (RSV) is an interesting
thought. He wanted all to know that he had authority direct from God to
take up the sword, that God had appointed him, and that he was God's
agent. Therefore, so the theory went, whatever he did was right.

That may sound convincing, but it is not what the text says. Paul is
saying that God has appointed civil authority (Rom. 13:1) to be *His servant*. Thus earthly rulers are not supreme but operate under delegated authority. They are to be God's servants and nothing more, in spite of
whatever exalted views they may have of themselves. Heads of state from
the Pauline perspective are not free agents. And their function is to bring
about good. That "good," of course, must fit God's perspective rather than
that of Nebuchadnezzar, Caesar, Napoleon, Hitler, Stalin, or Bush.

The ruler is God's servant (literally "deacon"), suggests Leon Morris,
"to enable God's other servants to get on with the job of doing God's
will." Thus it is incumbent upon such leaders to act responsibly. It is in
that spirit that Paul writes to Timothy: "I urge that supplication, prayers,
intercessions, and thanksgivings be made for all men, for kings and all
who are in high positions, that we may lead a quiet and peaceable life,
godly and respectful in every way. This is good, and it is acceptable in the
sight of God our Savior, who desires all men to be saved and to come to
the knowledge of the truth" (1 Tim. 2:1-4, RSV).

One of the functions of governments as God's servants is to establish
and maintain law and order so that the gospel might be preached. As
Christians we need to pray for our rulers every day.

WHEN GOD AND GOVERNMENT DISAGREE

Therefore, it is necessary to submit to authorities, not only because of possible punishment but also because of conscience. Rom. 13:5, NIV.

ONE OF CHRIST'S MOST remarkable teachings appears in Matthew 22:21: "Render therefore unto Caesar the things which are Caesar's; and unto God the things that are God's."

While that passage does not demand the separation of church and state, it did set the basis for it. Up to that time in world history, society always united religion and patriotism. The Jews had had no problem with that understanding as long as they lived in a Jewish state. But now they were under Rome. How should they relate to a pagan state?

Here is where Christ became revolutionary. He claimed that even Rome had rights as a government, and that Christians had a responsibility to the state, even if the government was wrong in its religious views. Paul picks up Jesus' teaching in Romans 13. Every Christian, the apostle reminds us, has a responsibility to his or her government.

But Christ also pointed out in Matthew 22, as did Paul in Romans 13, that the government's authority was not absolute. There was a realm that belonged to God outside the jurisdiction of earthly governments.

Christ taught that church and state are two spheres and that a Christian has a responsibility to both. But He did not say that the two realms were equal. Nor did He in Matthew 22 tell us which was the most important. But He did establish that Christians had a responsibility to Rome—a real issue to the people Paul was writing to.

But, you may be thinking, *if I have a duty to both God and the government, what do I do when their commands conflict?* The disciples early faced that issue. After Pentecost their preaching had spread throughout Jerusalem. The Jewish authorities had become so upset that they imprisoned the leading apostles and forbade them to preach.

The next day, however, found them again proclaiming Christ. Once more they found themselves hauled before the Jewish rulers, who asked them why they continued to cause a disturbance when they had received explicit commands not to do so. Peter's answer was that "we ought to obey God rather than men" (Acts 5:29). When the government's laws conflict with God's, the duty of Christians is plain.

CITIZENS OF TWO KINGDOMS

It is right, too, for you to pay taxes for the civil authorities are appointed by God for the constant maintenance of public order. Rom. 13:6, Phillips.

CHRISTIANS ARE TO BE good citizens of the country in which they live.

That might not sound revolutionary or profound to you. But it was to some of those to whom Paul was writing.

It was extremely important for him to emphasize civil obedience because the Jews as a people had been notoriously rebellious. Palestine was in a constant state of rebellion in the first century. The eventual leaders were the party of the Zealots, who were convinced that the Jews should have no king but God.

The Zealots refused to pay taxes to the Roman government and advocated its violent overthrow. They were anything but passive. Known as the dagger-bearers, they dedicated themselves to terrorism, even going so far as assassinating fellow Jews who paid tribute to the Roman government.

Paul, following Christ's command to render Caesar his due, had a totally different view of the Roman state. For him the Roman Empire had a divinely ordained function of saving the world from chaos. Without the empire the Mediterranean world would disintegrate into fragments. It was, in fact, the *pax Romana* (the Roman peace) that had enabled Paul and the other early Christian missionaries to move freely from one region to another so that within a few decades much of the empire had been evangelized. The Roman state in that sense had functioned as God's servant for the furtherance of the gospel.

Civil governments are not perfect (and some are worse than others), but they are better than the law of the jungle. They not only provide stability, but also many other services (such as sewage treatment, water, police protection, and so on) that would be impossible if every person were self-sufficient. Paul has not the slightest doubt that government (even the pagan Roman government that had crucified Christ and that would eventually put him to death) is a good thing, and that Christians have a duty to respect civil authority.

Those of us who live in the twenty-first century can find our own lesson here. We are citizens of two kingdoms—God's and the land in which we live. We therefore have a responsibility not only to tolerate civil government but to make a positive contribution whenever possible toward its health.

Paying Taxes Revisited

Render to all what is due them: tax to whom tax is due; custom to whom custom; fear to whom fear; honor to whom honor. Rom. 13:7, NASB.

IT IS ALMOST IMPOSSIBLE to read today's text without thinking about Christ's encounter with the Jewish rulers regarding the payment of taxes to Rome. Matthew tells us that the Pharisees were hoping "to entangle him in his talk." With that in mind, they engineered a loaded question: "Is it lawful to pay taxes to Caesar, or not?" (Matt. 22:15-17, RSV).

That question presented Jesus with a genuine dilemma. After all, if He said it was unlawful to pay taxes to Caesar, they could promptly report Him to the Roman authorities, and His arrest would quickly follow. On the other hand, if He approved the lawfulness of paying taxes to Caesar, He would lose influence in the eyes of His people. The Jews held that God alone was king and that to pay taxes to any earthly ruler was to admit the validity of that kingship and thus insult God. As a result, whatever answer Jesus gave to His detractors would open Him to trouble.

We see the difficulty of the situation also from the fact that the Pharisees and the Herodians had collaborated in the question. The two groups stood on opposite sides of the Jewish political fence and generally were in bitter opposition to each other. The vigorously orthodox Pharisees resented the taxes demanded by the Roman authorities, while the Herodians worked with the Roman government.

Jesus' answer is both unique and wise. He asks to see one of their coins, and after getting them to admit that it has Caesar's portrait on it, He sets forth the maxim that both Caesar and God should receive their due. That remarkable answer ends the attack. The Jewish leaders quickly see that Jesus has avoided the trap they have so carefully laid for Him.

Jesus not only escaped the trap but set forth a teaching that has shaped Christian attitudes toward civil government for two millennia. That teaching, picked up and expanded upon by Paul in Romans 13, has made respectful citizenship and honest taxpaying a religious obligation among Christians.

Such a perspective is not always easy to live by. It is all too easy, for example, for Christians to hedge a bit on their taxes—until they remember the words of Jesus and Paul. Then everything falls into place when they realize that even civil government has a role in God's providence.

LESSON NUMBER FIVE IN TRANSFORMED LIVING

*Let no debt remain outstanding, except the continuing
debt to love one another. Rom. 13:8, NIV.*

WITH ROMANS 13:8 WE come to a fifth lesson in transformed living. In fact, in verses 8 to 10 we find what we might regard as the very foundation of transformed living. That foundation is the core meaning of God's law—the Christian attribute of love.

Romans 12:20 earlier told us to love our enemies and let God handle the vengeance. Here in Romans 13:8-10 Paul moves back to the love theme, with his emphasis on loving our neighbors.

In between the end of chapter 12 and today's passage, the apostle dealt with the role of civil government as one of God's agents for administering vengeance on those who do wrong (Rom. 12:19-21; 13:4). He ends his discussion of the state with a Christian's duty to pay taxes (Rom. 13:6, 7).

The idea of debt has arisen several times in Romans. Romans 1:14 spoke of the debt to share the gospel, Romans 8:12-17 alluded to the debt Christians owe to the Holy Spirit to live a holy life, and Romans 13:6, 7 pointed out that we are in debt to pay taxes to the state.

From that debt to the state he immediately shifts to our debt to our fellow human beings. Here Paul moves from official debt to private debt. A major difference exists between the two. Taxes are finite. We receive a tax bill, and when we pay, we take care of it in full. That is the end of it until the next billing.

But the debt of love is infinite. We can never repay it fully. Christians can never stop loving somebody and say "I have loved enough." As Paul puts it, love will always be an outstanding debt.

That makes me uncomfortable. I want to eliminate my debts so that I can relax and be my real self. I like to know the limits. It would be very nice to know, for example, when I have fulfilled my quota of love to that truly obnoxious church member so that I can let him or her have it.

Paul's answer to that wish is the same as the one that Jesus gave to Peter when he asked when he could quit forgiving his neighbor. The answer is never. Just as God's love is infinite for me, so is my love and care for those around me to be without end.

God, please give me grace to live Your love. Amen.

311

THE LAW BEHIND THE LAWS

He who loves his neighbor has fulfilled the law. Rom. 13:8, RSV.

I WILL NEVER FORGET the shock I experienced when I discovered that the Ten Commandments were not the real *law*. In fact, in the context of universal history throughout eternity, we might view the Ten Commandments as a late development. Take, for example, the fourth commandment. It plainly states that God gave the Sabbath as a memorial of the creation of Planet Earth. The seven-day cycle of 24 hours points to the creation of our planet and our solar system as determinants of the Sabbath law found in the Decalogue.

Do you think God had to tell the angels not to commit adultery with any of their neighbors or to honor their fathers and mothers? Did they even have fathers and mothers?

Ellen White has suggested that "the law of God existed before man was created. The angels were governed by it. . . . After Adam's sin and fall nothing was taken from the law of God. *The principles of the ten commandments existed before the fall, and were of a character suited to the condition of a holy order of beings*" (*Spiritual Gifts,* vol. 3, p. 295; italics supplied). In another place she points out that after Adam's transgression the principles of the law *"were definitely arranged and expressed to meet man in his fallen condition"* (*Selected Messages,* book 1, p. 230; italics supplied).

It was apparently at the time of the fall of Adam that God first stated the law in its negative form as we now have it. The Lord had to tell sinful, selfish humans specifically what was wrong. Because of their fallen natures He had to instruct them not to lust after their neighbor's spouse, not to steal anyone else's belongings, and to respect their parents. Those things were not issues for the unfallen angels. But the principles of the law were just as important for them as they are for us.

And what are those universal principles? Jesus made them plain when He was asked about the greatest commandment of the law. He replied: "You shall love the Lord your God with all your heart, and with all your soul, and with all your mind. This is the great and first commandment. And a second is like it, You shall love your neighbor as yourself. On these two commandments depend all the law and the prophets" (Matt. 22:37-40, RSV). With Jesus we get a glimpse of the *law* behind the laws, the *law* that gives meaning and shape to the Ten Commandments.

312

THE RELATION OF THE TEN COMMANDMENTS TO THE LAW

The commandments, "You shall not commit adultery;
You shall not murder; You shall not steal; You shall not covet";
and any other commandment, are summed up in this word,
"Love your neighbor as yourself." Rom. 13:9, NRSV.

CHRISTIANITY IS NOT JUST an improvement of the old life. It is a total transformation of a person's way of thinking, acting, and living. Not only is the Christian in Christ; Christ is *in him or her* through the softening power of the Holy Spirit. We can know that we are safe in Jesus when His principle of love becomes the guiding motivation in our lives.

One of my favorite texts on the topic is John 13:35: "By this," said Jesus, "all men will know that you are my disciples, if you keep the Sabbath."

I preached on that text (using the above distortion to illustrate my point) one time and had a brand-new Adventist come up to me. "My Bible doesn't read that way in John 13!" he exclaimed. "Where can I find that text?" He was after the ultimate Adventist proof text. In his exuberance he had missed my emphasis on the actual reading: "By this all men will know that you are my disciples, if you have love for one another" (RSV). How I treat my neighbor is the acid test of Christianity.

It is because I love God that I love my neighbor. And that love to God and neighbor, Paul tells us, has a direct relationship to the Ten Commandments.

- Because I love God, I don't want to dishonor His name.
- Because I love God, I love my fellow beings.
- Because I love my neighbor, I will not steal from him or her.
- Because I love my neighbor, I cannot use him or her as a sexual object for my own pleasure.
- Because I love my neighbor, I will want him or her to share the delights of the Sabbath.

Love to God and neighbor is the centerpiece of Christianity. It reflects the *law* that undergirds God's many laws.

A real tragedy takes place when individuals try to keep the laws without having the *law* of God in their hearts. I have seen, for example, some Sabbathkeepers who are meaner than the devil. Such behavior happens when people have the laws without the principle of love that gives them meaning.

Perfection and the Law

Love does no wrong to a neighbor; therefore,
love is the fulfilling of the law. Rom. 13:10, NASB.

"LOVE DOES NO WRONG to a neighbor." That sounds about as good as good can get. The person who lives by this principle has indeed fulfilled the law and seems perfect to me.

Interestingly, the uniting of perfection with love to one's neighbor is a major New Testament teaching. Take, for example, Jesus' command for each of us to be as perfect as the Father in heaven in Matthew 5:48. People have gotten all kinds of strange ideas about perfection by taking that passage out of context. I remember my own case. When I first became a Christian I promised God that I would be the first perfect Christian since Christ. And I meant it. I knew what was wrong with the rest of the church members. They just hadn't tried hard enough. But I would. As a result of my promise to God I had soon amassed an enormous list of things I couldn't do, couldn't eat, couldn't think. In the process I had crawled into the cave of medieval perfectionism.

Unfortunately, the more I tried to become perfect by not doing all those things, the more disgusting it made me. I became self-centered, proud of my achievements, and difficult to live with. After all, if I was perfect, wasn't everybody else wrong? And if they were wrong, it was my God-given duty to tell them so. I became "perfectly delightful" to be around.

Only later did I discover what Jesus meant when He said we should be perfect like the Father. The context to that admonition begins in Matthew 5:43, in which Jesus told His hearers that in past times they had been told to love their neighbors but to hate their enemies. "But," He went on, "I say to you, Love your enemies, and pray for those who persecute you, *so that* you may be sons of your Father who is in heaven" (RSV). And what is God like? He blesses the land of both those who love Him and those who don't.

Biblical perfection is living God's love because "love . . . is the fulfilling of the law." "But why is it," I need to ask myself, "that I find it easier to love the people of Mongolia than those around me?" Perhaps it's because I don't have to live with them.

Help me, Lord, to learn how to truly love as You do. Help me to let Your love continue to grow in my heart and life right now. Help me do so today right here in my own family, church, workplace, and neighborhood.

LESSON NUMBER SIX IN TRANSFORMED LIVING

*And do this, understanding the present time. The hour has come
for you to wake up from your slumber, because our salvation
is nearer now than when we first believed. Rom. 13:11, NIV.*

UP TO THIS POINT in Romans 12 and 13 Paul has been writing of how
justified people should live. They should demonstrate the transformed life
of a living sacrifice (Rom. 12:1, 2) in humbly using their gifts for God, in
respectful harmony with the civil government, and in Christian love.

But why? First, because they have been justified freely by God's grace
(Rom. 1–11). Second, because Christ will come again. Phillips' translation
of today's text brings out that connection nicely: "Why all this stress on
behaviour? Because . . . every day brings God's salvation nearer." Lesson
number six for the transformed life has to do with living in the hope of the
Second Advent. Thus we might think of Romans 13:11-14 as motivational.
We need to wake up, because this life is not all there is.

When Romans speaks of salvation, it does so in three different aspects. One of them, justification, is past. Another, glorification, is future.
And the third, sanctification, is a present reality. Whereas people often
think of Romans as a book about justification, Paul devotes a tremendous
amount of space (chapters 6–8 and 12–15) to sanctification—living the
crucified life (Rom. 6:1-4), the transformed life (Rom. 12:1, 2).

Sanctified living in Romans takes place on the basis of a person's having been justified and in the certainty of eventual glorification. Emil
Brunner phrases it nicely when he writes that "the remembrance of what
God's mercy in Jesus Christ has done for us is one powerful impulse of
the new life; the other, which is inseparably linked with it, is the sure expectation of what he will do. Where faith in Christ looks at the future, it
turns into hope. . . . The future is already in process of happening. . . .
Faith is indeed nothing but living in the light of that which is to come."

Thus Christians live between two great events. The first is the beginning of the kingdom of God, which Christ asserted He had inaugurated
when He began His earthly ministry (Matt. 4:17). The second is the consummation of the kingdom, when Christ comes again, redeems our bodies (Rom. 8:23), and takes believers home to be with Him. That event,
claims Paul, ought to motivate us to live the transformed life.

EXCITEMENT OR DUTY?

The night is nearly over; the day is almost here. So let us put aside the deeds of darkness and put on the armor of light. Rom. 13:12, NIV.

WAKE UP! PAUL has told us in Romans 13:11. James Denney notes that the Christian's life is not a sleep, but a battle. As the apostle Peter puts it: "Be sober, be watchful. Your adversary the devil prowls around like a roaring lion, seeking some one to devour" (1 Peter 5:8, RSV). The apostle realized that our world is in the midst of a battle between good and evil and that each individual's heart and mind is the scene of a microcosmic great controversy, an individual manifestation of the macrocosmic struggle between Christ and Satan.

One of the great fears of Christ and Paul was that Christians wouldn't keep awake, but would rather slumber and sleep and therefore get caught unawares at the Second Advent (Matt. 25:1-13; 1 Thess. 5:1-11).

Being ready for that event is not watching the news only to get excited when we see the "signs of the times" being fulfilled. No! That is one of the devil's tricks. Christ repeatedly asserted that because no one knows the time of the Advent, His followers must not only watch (Matt. 24:42; 25:13), but use their talents as they wait (Matt. 25:14-30). They were especially to care for those less fortunate than themselves (verses 31-46).

It is living the Christian life during the waiting period that Christ and Paul emphasized, rather than some breathless excitement because of what we see on the news. Christ will come at a time we think not. And when He does He will find many of His so-called followers napping between two great excitements rather than doing what He told them to do in Matthew 24:32–25:46.

How many Christians looking for the Advent get their excitement from the signs of the times rather than from service—the service of living God's love that Paul talks about in Romans 13 and that Christ repeatedly emphasized? It is no accident that the discussions of the Second Advent in Matthew 24 and Romans 13 both stress the Christian's responsibility to live the life of love. Living His love will be the great dividing line in the judgment (Matt. 25:31-46; *The Desire of Ages,* p. 637).

It is time to wake up, put on God's armor, and get busy so that He might find us faithful servants when He returns. If I were the devil I would get Christians interested in the Advent to live on excitement rather than duty. With that one stroke I could accomplish my purpose of distracting them.

TRADING THE CESSPOOLS OF SIN FOR GOD'S BANQUET

Let us behave decently, as in the daytime, not in orgies and drunkenness, not in sexual immorality and debauchery, not in dissension and jealousy. Rather, clothe yourselves with the Lord Jesus Christ. Rom. 13:13, 14, NIV.

PAUL COULD HAVE WRITTEN that passage this morning. The prevailing sins of the world haven't changed much. It is only the people who have. Same sins, different people doing them.

Of course, you (as a Christian) may be piously thinking, *I don't do such things.* That may be true. But is it really true? Think about it. I know many people who wouldn't actually participate in orgies, drunkenness, or jealousy.

No, ma'am! No, sir! They wouldn't touch such sins with a 10-foot pole. They are clean and ready for Jesus. Just ask them and they can tell you how good they are. Of course they wouldn't do such things. They merely watch them on television and in the videos that they drag into their homes.

"Yes, ma'am, yes, sir, I am clean," they say. "I don't do those nasty things. I get my kicks vicariously and call it entertainment." But what kind of culture would call murder, torture, perversion, unfaithfulness, and dysfunctional lost people in soap operas entertainment? Only a sick society, a world needing the return of Christ to clean up the mess it has made.

We "good" church members, Paul warns us, must wake up. We need to put away the sickness that we classify as entertainment and put on the armor of salvation. One of the most serious problems in modern Christianity is that the devil has indeed invaded our homes and mesmerized us with the cheap, the brutal, and the worthless.

We need to commit ourselves to a change through God's grace this very day. We need to commit ourselves to mental, moral, and spiritual health. And we need to put off the garbage of this world and put on Christ.

"Wake up," Paul shouts, "for the coming of our salvation is nearer now than when we first believed. . . . So don't live in darkness. Get rid of your evil deeds. Shed them like dirty clothes. Clothe yourselves with the armor of right living, as those who live in the light" (Rom. 13:11, 12, NLT).

Help us today, our God, to trade in the cesspools of sin for Your banquet table. Amen.

STARVING EVIL VERSUS FEEDING IT

Don't think of ways to indulge your evil desires. Rom. 13:14, NLT.

EVIL DESIRES JUST SEEM to be there. A person may be doing nothing when out of the blue a not-so-nice thought arrives. It just kind of shows up in your head. You didn't have to think about it, encourage it, or even want it. It's just there, because, as Ellen White so picturesquely puts it, we have a "bent to evil" (*Education,* p. 29). Beginning with Adam's fall the human mind has lost its goodness and wholeness and instead tends toward the unhealthy in life.

OK, you may be thinking, *I got the point. We have bent minds. We don't have to want evil desires—they're just there, spontaneous. So what?*

Good question. Because it is the "so what" that Paul has in mind in today's verse, when he tells us not to "think of ways to indulge your evil desires."

He knows you don't have to prompt the desire itself. He was plain on that point in the second half of Romans 7.

But Paul also knows that you can do one of two things once you realize the presence of an evil desire. First, you can starve it and toss it out. Of course, evil desires are like nine-lived cats—they just keep resurrecting. That's where prayer comes in. We can pray for God's grace to put the nasty little thing away and to focus our minds on something more constructive. You may even decide to pray more than once about it, even up to "seventy times seven."

The second way to handle an evil desire is to feed it and cherish it. That is what Paul discusses in today's text. Don't feed your evil desires. When we do, they grow up to be addictions that demand constant feeding.

James hits the target when he writes that "each person is tempted when he is lured and enticed by his own desire. Then desire when it has conceived gives birth to sin; and sin when it is full-grown brings forth death" (James 1:14, 15, RSV).

Don't feed it! Starve it! But don't try to starve it by yourself. Only God's grace can lead us to victory in the struggle with sin.

Today, O Father, please help me stay close to You. Amen.

Lesson Number Seven in Transformed Living

As for the man who is weak in faith, welcome him,
but not for disputes over opinions. Rom. 14:1, RSV.

WITH ROMANS 14 WE enter into Paul's longest section of advice on how to live the transformed life (Rom. 12:1, 2), the life based on the law of love (Rom. 13:8-10). The core of that advice is not to be judgmental of others in the church who may not agree with you on various points not central to the Christian message.

Paul has been preparing his readers for this chapter from the beginning of the book. In the first chapter he raised the issue of Jews and Gentiles in the church. Then in chapter 2 he condemned one person's censuring of another. Those who passed judgment on others, he noted, actually pass judgment on themselves (Rom. 2:1).

Romans 14 raises an issue of central importance to the church in every age. As Leon Morris points out, "the church was never meant to be a cozy club of like-minded people of one race or social position or intellectual caliber. Christians are not clones, identical in all respects. One of the difficulties the church has always faced is that included in its membership are the rich and the poor, the powerful and the powerless, those from every stratum of society, the old and the young, adults and children, the conservatives and the radicals."

One of the most natural things in the world is for me to want everyone in the church to believe and act as I do. After all, I'm right and have a text or 10 quotations to prove it. Thus the matter is settled!

That is just the attitude that Paul meets head-on in Romans 14. From the outset of the chapter we need to realize that the "strong" and the "weak" are both church members and that Paul has quite definite testimony for both of them. It is also true that even though he identifies with the strong (Rom. 15:1), he has a great deal of understanding and sympathy for those whom he deems "weak in faith" (Rom. 14:1, RSV).

Romans 14:1 also makes it clear that not every belief held by church members is of equal importance. Some of them Paul identifies as "opinions" (RSV) or "disputable matters" (NIV) or "doubtful disputations" (KJV). The problem comes in when we hold that everything that *we* believe is of equal importance and then try to force our concepts on others.

A PLEA FOR TOLERANCE

*The man who eats everything must not look down on him who
does not, and the man who does not eat everything must not
condemn the man who does, for God has accepted him. Rom. 14:3, NIV.*

INTOLERANCE IS ONE of the church's most dreadful sins. If I were the devil I would get the various members picking away at each other. I would get some to look down their "justified noses" at others, whom they deem weak because of their scruples about this or that, and I would get those with scruples to condemn everyone who doesn't live as they do—to look down their "holier-than-thou noses" at the rest of the church. And I might get both sides to exclaim that God can never bless the church until the "others" shape up and believe right and/or live right.

As we can see, the devil has been quite busy throughout church history. Unfortunately, he has been not only active but quite successful. The devil has too often captured the day by moving the church from central issues to the peripheral. Paul feels so deeply about such attitudes that he gives us an extensive exposition on the problem in Romans 14 and 15.

Today's text concerns being judgmental and/or condemning toward those in the church who eat differently than we do. We should note that it has a very definite context. Romans 14:2 indicates that "one man's faith allows him to eat everything, but another man, whose faith is weak, eats only vegetables" (NIV).

No, Paul is not speaking about Seventh-day Adventists or those who are vegetarians for health reasons. In fact, he really doesn't have in mind diet at all. His main point is people's *attitudes*. Diet is merely an illustration.

In the illustration he is not condemning vegetarianism but rather those who had given up eating flesh foods for the wrong reason—that is, because they had weak faith. We don't know exactly what the dietary issue was in Rome. But we do know that in Corinth disagreement had raged in the church between those who would not eat meat sacrificed to idols and those who did. In that situation some whom we might regard as the "weak in faith" refrained from eating any meat because they could never be positive that someone hadn't offered it to an idol. Paul responded that it really didn't make any difference, since a firmly grounded Christian knew that an idol was nothing.

The problem in Rome was not exactly the same as in Corinth, but it may have been related. Paul's main point in Romans 14:3 is that intolerant condemnation and arrogance in the church must cease.

THE ULTIMATE SIN

Who are you to pass judgment on the servant of another? It is before his own master that he stands or falls. And he will be upheld, for the Master is able to make him stand. Rom. 14:4, RSV.

WHO ARE YOU TO PASS judgment on anyone? Excellent question! Especially in the light of the words that immediately precede today's verse: "God has accepted him" (Rom. 14:3, NIV). Am I the judge of someone whom God has already accepted and justified? If so, who made me the judge? Am I capable of judging another because I am better than they are on the basis of what I eat or don't eat?

Definitely not! Such teaching flies in the face of what Paul took so much time to teach us in Romans 1–5. We are all sinners, no matter how good we think we are or what our lifestyle practices may be. And because we are all sinners, we all get what we don't deserve—salvation by grace freely—if we are willing to receive it by faith. And God accepts every person who takes His gift.

It is flat land at the foot of the cross. No one is superior to another. All have in the past been slaves of sin and Satan. Now all through God's gift in Christ have become slaves of God and righteousness (Rom. 6). And if we are all slaves, we all have one Master. And it is He alone who passes judgment.

Passing judgment on another Christian is the ultimate sin, because it places ourselves in the role of God. To see ourselves as superior to other Christians is pure arrogance. It is judging those whom God has already accepted, and it is doing so by our personal standards rather than God's.

The Lord in Romans has already set forth the only standard for acceptance—taking His gift in Christ through faith.

Yet church members down through the ages have wanted to create new standards for their brothers and sisters. A perennial one has had to do with diet. Diet is important to health, but Paul is quite clear that "the kingdom of God is not a matter of eating and drinking, but of righteousness, peace and joy in the Holy Spirit" (Rom. 14:17). We will have more to say on that important passage in a few days.

In the meantime, it is time to start taking the apostle seriously.

Our place is to be faithful servants in the church and not to judge those whom God has already accepted.

Help me today, Father, to learn the lesson of Romans 14:3, 4. Help me not to usurp Your role as judge.

DIFFERENCES AMID UNITY

One person regards one day above another, another regards every day alike. Each person must be fully convinced in his own mind. He who observes the day, observes it for the Lord. Rom. 14:5, 6, NASB.

DIETARY ISSUES WERE not the only ones that divided the Roman church. People also fought over the observance or nonobservance of certain days.

Paul doesn't explicitly state their nature, but it was apparently not the weekly Sabbath, since the Sabbath was one of the Ten Commandments, and Paul has already spoken in Romans several times to the importance of the Decalogue in the Christian life (see Rom. 13:8-10; 7:12, 14, 16; 3:31).

The most likely candidates for the dispute were the feast days and yearly sabbaths. The debate between the Jewish and Gentile Christians over issues related to the Jewish ceremonial regulations had already led to the conference between Paul and the leaders of the Jewish Christians in Acts 15. On other occasions we find Paul dealing with the issue of special days and feasts in Galatians 4:10, 11 and Colossians 2:16, 17. In that latter passage, as in the present one, Paul had to deal with church members passing judgment on fellow believers regarding both food and disputed days. But there he explicitly notes that the festivals and sabbaths in question were "only a shadow of what is to come" (RSV). That language implies the yearly ceremonial sabbaths, symbols pointing forward to Christ. The weekly Sabbath of the Decalogue, by way of contrast, directed attention backward to God's work of creation (see Gen. 2:1, 2; Ex. 20:8-11).

With that distinction in mind, even though undoubtedly differences existed between the problems in Rome and those in Colossae, Paul tells his Roman readers that those whose faith had enabled them to immediately leave behind all ceremonial holy days should not despise others whose faith wasn't as strong. Nor should the latter criticize those who had given up the Jewish feasts when they came to realize that, like the Passover, they all pointed forward to Christ.

Beyond the debate over days, Paul sets forth an important lesson for all Christians in Romans 14:5, 6 (only partially quoted above). Each person must live by their own convictions. God is leading each person who chooses to be led. But all don't have the same background or move at the same speed. It is important for a Christian to have convictions, but it is equally vital that those convictions come from the Lord. In nonessentials, Paul reminds the Romans, the church cannot expect uniformity.

DOING ALL WITH GOD

*We do not live to ourselves, and we
do not die to ourselves. Rom. 14:7, NRSV.*

IT IS TRUE THAT "no man is an island," that we constantly touch and influence the lives and decisions of others. But that is not what Paul has in mind in today's verse.

His thought is that all that we do must be in relationship to God. It is really an expansion of the discussion in Romans 14:5 and 6 that whether people eat or don't eat or whether they keep a Jewish holy day or don't observe it, they do it "unto the Lord." That is true because they have based their convictions on their understanding of His will, and they give thanks to Him for their course of action.

What Paul seeks to get across in today's verse is that we are never separate from God. It is not just a matter of disputed dietary ideals or ceremonial sabbaths, but in everything the Christian does it is all "unto the Lord." As A. Graham Maxwell notes, "it is the aim of his [a Christian's] entire existence to live not 'to himself,' for his own pleasure and according to his own desires, but 'unto the Lord,' for His glory and according to His will. . . . His whole life, to the very last moments, belongs to the Lord."

And beyond life itself, each Christian must at some future time "give account of himself to God" (Rom. 14:12, RSV). Each person shall someday "stand before the judgment seat of God" (verse 10, RSV).

The fact that everything we do in life as Christians we do with and for the Lord is a powerful point. It is all-inclusive. As Paul wrote to the Corinthians, "Whether therefore ye eat, or drink, or whatsoever ye do, do all to the glory of God" (1 Cor. 10:31).

In short, it is the Christian's relationship to God that directs every action in his or her life. A Christian is one who lives for God. There are no holidays from being a Christian. Taking time off from being a Christian is what the word "hypocrisy" is all about.

Today will you join me in the rededication of our lives to God? I want to live for Him in all that I do or say or think. I want my life immersed in the principles of His kingdom. I want to live the transformed life that Paul has been talking about. And I want to live the life of love that is the very essence of Christian ethics (Rom. 13:8-10).

JESUS IS SAVIOR AND LORD

Whether we live, we live unto the Lord; and whether we die,
we die unto the Lord: whether we live therefore,
or die, we are the Lord's. Rom. 14:8.

JESUS IS SAVIOR! No Christian ever denies that. Without Christ as Savior Christianity cannot exist.

But is Jesus also Lord? That is an important question.

Jesus as Savior means that He has saved us from our sins. He has forgiven and justified us. But Jesus as Lord means that He is our Master and that we are His slaves. Too many Christians forget that Jesus as Savior and Jesus as Lord must go together.

Paul flagged that thought in the very first verse of Romans, when he identified himself as a slave of Jesus Christ. Then in chapter 6 he applied the slave analogy to each Christian. "Do you not know," he penned, "that . . . you are slaves of the one whom you obey, either of sin, which leads to death, or of obedience, which leads to righteousness? But thanks be to God, that you who were once slaves of sin have become obedient from the heart to the standard of teaching to which you were committed, and, having been set free from sin, have become slaves of righteousness" (Rom. 6:16-18, RSV).

Christ is both Savior and Lord. Christians not only follow His will and do His bidding, but—and this is one of Paul's major points in Romans 14:5-8—they get their marching orders from Him. It is Christ through the Spirit who brings a Christian to conviction regarding personal duty on a particular point (Rom. 14:5). And when Christians put conviction into practice they do it "unto the Lord," giving thanks all the while (verses 6, 7).

In Romans 14 Paul concerns himself with those Christians who want to become Lord to their brothers and sisters, those who want to be mind and conscience for their fellow church members.

Ellen White had the same concern as Paul. "In matters of conscience," she wrote, "the soul must be left untrammeled. No one is to control another's mind, to judge for another, or to prescribe his duty. God gives to every soul freedom to think and to follow his own convictions. 'Every one of us shall give account of himself to God.' No one has a right to merge his own individuality in that of another. In all matters where principle is involved, 'let every man be fully persuaded in his own mind.' (Rom. 14:12, 5)" (*The Desire of Ages,* p. 550).

STANDING BEFORE THE JUDGMENT SEAT

*Why do you pass judgment on your brother? Or you, why do
you despise your brother? For we shall all stand
before the judgment seat of God. Rom. 14:10, RSV.*

WHO AM I TO pass judgment on another Christian? The answer should be obvious by now. I have no right to condemn anybody.

The plain fact is that I myself will someday "stand before the judgment seat of God." Thus, far from being a judge of others, I myself will become the subject of God's tribunal.

That thought brings us back to Jesus' picture in Matthew 7, which indicates that we need to be extremely careful in making any judgments of others. Our primary task, according to Jesus, is to get the log out of our own eye. Church history and contemporary congregations are cluttered with disastrous examples of those with a log in their eye seeking to pronounce judgment on others. Unfortunately, such blind ophthalmologists not only have failed to see themselves in the mirror of God's law of love, but have pushed many other Christians right out of the church. In fact, it was such "log carriers" who put Jesus on the cross. Humans who take upon themselves the role of God are in reality the agents of Satan.

Fortunately for each of us, God can forgive our judgmental attitudes toward others and enable us to overcome them. For that we need to come to Him on our knees, asking Him to perform eye surgery on us.

God is our judge. "But," you may be asking, "why is there a final judgment for God's people? Didn't Jesus say that Christians have 'passed from death to life,' already have 'eternal life,' and will 'not come into judgment' [see John 5:24, RSV]?"

Those things are all true. No person who continues to accept Christ will ever come under judgment in the sense of "condemnation" (John 5:24, KJV), but Paul makes it abundantly clear in today's text that there *will* be a final judgment.

Daniel makes that same point. But he is quite straightforward in saying that God's judgment will be "for the saints of the Most High" (Dan. 7:22). The final judgment of Christians is in effect a legal statement to the universe that they have accepted God's grace and thus have a right to immortality. For a Christian the judgment is part of the good news.

IT'S NOT WHAT YOU THINK ABOUT ME THAT COUNTS

It is written: "As I live, says the Lord, every knee shall bow to Me, and every tongue shall confess to God." Rom. 14:11, NKJV.

I HAVE OFTEN SAID of those who have passed judgment on me and criticized me that I am not really concerned about their opinions. But I am intensely interested in God's opinion and judgment of me.

Quoting from Isaiah 45:23, the apostle proves the point he has been making regarding the future judgment of every individual. At the end of time not only will every person come before the judgment seat of God but they will also be constrained to confess that God's judgments are true and just.

Paul, like Jesus in Matthew 7, did not seek to avoid the doctrine of the final judgment. He wrote that "each man's work will become manifest; for the Day [of judgment] will disclose it" (1 Cor. 3:13, RSV).

Again he wrote: "With me it is a very small thing that I should be judged by you or by any human court. I do not even judge myself. I am not aware of anything against myself, but I am not thereby acquitted. It is the Lord who judges me. Therefore do not pronounce judgment before the time, before the Lord comes, who will bring to light the things now hidden in darkness and will disclose the purposes of the heart. Then every man will receive his commendation from God" (1 Cor. 4:3-5, RSV).

Even though each person will eventually stand at the judgment seat of God, the good news for Christians is that we won't be alone. As William Barclay points out, "we stand with Jesus Christ. We do not need to go stripped of everything; we may go clad in the merits that are his." If we have lived with Christ in life, He will accompany us in judgment.

We can praise God for His grace even in His judgment. Without His continuous mercy we would have no hope. After all, if all have sinned, He has a perfect right to condemn us. But He has made a way of escape through Christ's life, death, resurrection, and ministry in heaven. Through Christ God gives us forgiveness rather than condemnation. He asks us to do the same for our fellow believers. Far from being their judges, we are to pass on God's forgiveness to them as we live God's love (Matt. 6:12; 18:21-35).

Thank You, Father, for the good news of the judgment. Thank You that You are willing to be on our side. Help me to hold on to You as my hope and my Redeemer.

LIFE'S FINAL AUDIT

So then every one of us shall give
account of himself to God. Rom. 14:12.

FROM TIME TO TIME businesses, charitable institutions, and governmental agencies receive a visit from an auditor. The auditor's task is periodically to examine the financial records to verify their accuracy. In short, businesses and other agencies that handle money must give an account of their actions. The very fact that an audit will happen undoubtedly encourages some officials to be more honest.

But let's face it, a crafty person can sometimes find ways to "fix" the books so that they look right when they aren't. Human auditors are fallible.

Paul tells us that God will also conduct an audit or accounting for each life. Each of us (Paul included himself) will have to "give account of himself to God." But a difference exists between the divine Auditor and all others—He is infallible. He can't be fooled. No one can fix the books with Him. As the wise man said: "Fear God, and keep his commandments; for this is the whole duty of man. For God will bring every deed into judgment, with every secret thing, whether good or evil" (Eccl. 12:13, 14, RSV).

But remember that in the final audit the bottom line is not whether you have merely kept God's commandments, but whether you have accepted Christ as Lord and Savior. It is within that context of a faith relationship—and only within it—that commandmentkeeping has any Christian significance.

And at the heart of Paul's discussion so far in Romans 14 is one particular commandment—the injunction to stop judging our neighbor. It is unfortunate that those who honestly have a concern with the keeping of all of God's commandments too often forget the one not to be judgmental. In that forgetfulness they actually break the Ten Commandments in the sense that they have usurped God's role and thus have put themselves in His place, a transgression of the first commandment.

Listen up! says Paul. We have one Judge, and each of you "self-appointed" righteous ones will someday stand before His throne for your final audit.

The moral: Stop judging and start modeling God's love. Judging tears down, modeling builds up. Accountability is a sobering message, but an important one.

A SECOND REASON NOT TO JUDGE

Let us therefore cease judging one another, but rather make
up our minds to place no obstacle or stumbling block
in a fellow-Christian's way. Rom. 14:13, REB.

THUS FAR IN ROMANS 14 Paul has presented one basic reason for not judging our fellow believers—such judgment is God's alone. Therefore, people are not accountable to one another but to Him. As a result, to judge another person is to put oneself in God's place. Thus reason number one is serious indeed.

In today's verse Paul supplies us with a second motivation to stop judging others. This second reason derives from Christian love. Believers who are strong in faith, because of their love, will be considerate of the consciences and scruples of their weaker neighbors in the church, who may not have figured out which are salvational issues and which are not. As a result of their faith and love, Paul emphasizes in Romans 14:14-23 that the "stronger" believers will exercise care not to offend the weaker.

In effect, Paul now begins an argument that implies that if there is to be any judging, it should not be criticism, but rather a determination not to cause another to stumble or fall.

The words the apostle uses for "stumbling block" are interesting. He employs two of them in today's passage, the first of them translated as "obstacle." That word also appears in 1 Corinthians 8:9, in which he gives the same warning, again in relation to food. After noting that food offered to idols shouldn't be an issue for Christians, he goes on to add "take care lest this liberty of yours [to eat such food] somehow become a stumbling block to the weak" (RSV). The main idea behind the word is to strike one's foot against something and thus stumble.

The second word originally meant the bait stick on a trap. Later it came to represent the trap or snare itself. Paul uses the term in a way that suggests that a Christian should not do those things that arouse prejudice or become a hindrance in such a way that they cause others to fall.

A Christian, therefore, must live with care. Christians, in spite of their liberty, will not do anything, including judging and condemning others, that will harm a brother or sister. That thought reminds us of the words of Christ, who said that "it would be better" for those who hurt the weak ones "to have a great millstone fastened around his neck and to be drowned in the depth of the sea" (Matt. 18:5, 6, RSV).

CONTEXT IS IMPORTANT

I know and am convinced by the Lord Jesus that there
is nothing unclean of itself; but to him who considers
anything to be unclean, to him it is unclean. Rom. 14:14, NKJV.

TODAY'S VERSE IS AN interesting one. The New International Version translates the passage as "no food is unclean of itself." While the word "food" does not appear in the Greek of Romans 14:14, it is in the next verse and is obviously what Paul is talking about.

But, we need to ask, what kind of unclean foods does he have in mind? We don't know for sure, but of one thing we can be certain—that he is not referring to the unclean food prohibitions of Deuteronomy 14 and Numbers 11. How do we know that? From the context. The issue Paul lays out in 14:1, 2 is not between eating unclean and clean meats but rather between eating unclean meats and no meat at all.

Of course, since the cross no foods have been ceremonially unclean. But that does not mean that all foods are healthy. Those foods that were unhealthy before the cross are still unhealthy today.

C. H. Dodd helps us here when he writes that it is "quite illogical" to take Paul's teaching as meaning that "nothing is good or ill, but thinking makes it so." Paul is not teaching that everything is good for people to eat or that unhealthful eating is a figment of one's imagination.

The context is all-important in understanding Romans 14:14. Rather than discussing unclean foods forbidden to the Jews in Deuteronomy, Paul refers to foods that had become an issue of conflict in the Roman Christian community. As we noted above, it probably involved foods offered to idols that may have found their way into the marketplace. For Paul, that possibility was not a problem, since an idol was nothing anyway. Thus, as a "strong" believer, he didn't worry about such things.

But not everyone shared Paul's position on the topic. Some definitely held that such food was wrong to eat. The apostle doesn't condemn such people, even though he believes they are wrong. Rather, he respects their conscientious convictions.

We find a lesson for us here. We need to respect other people for their convictions, just as we would like them to do the same for us. While we may not always agree, we can still live together.

If the church followed Paul's advice it would be a much more pleasant place.

KEEPING OTHERS IN MIND

*If your brother is distressed because of what you eat, you are
no longer acting in love. Do not by your eating destroy your
brother for whom Christ died. Do not allow what you
consider good to be spoken of as evil. Rom. 14:15, 16, NIV.*

WE ARE DEALING WITH an important point in these verses. William
Barclay sums up Paul's counsel as *"it is a Christian duty to think of everything, not as it affects ourselves only, but also as it affects others."*

That thought represents an important aspect of Christian love. After
all, we are in a sense the keepers of our brothers and sisters in the faith.
What we do has an impact upon those around us.

Paul here paints a picture of a scrupulous Christian who sees another
church member doing something the first one believes to be wrong. As a
result, the more scrupulous member feels a "holy horror." The other's actions deeply wound him or her. It is as if someone with whom he or she
had close ties had committed a serious sin and made light of it. In such a
situation the more scrupulous Christian, seeing everything as a matter of
salvation, might become spiritually disoriented. Or worse yet, decide to
do the same thing while being conscientiously opposed to it.

Such results would be spiritually destructive to a person for whom
Christ had given His life. Thus Paul's admonition to love by refraining
from a given action on the part of the "stronger" Christians.

But wait a minute. Do the strong in faith always have to forgo anything about which a weaker person may have qualms? After all, in a world
containing so much variety there is hardly anything that you or I might do
that some other believer will not object to. Beyond that, on most issues,
believers exist on both sides. "If," as James Montgomery Boice puts it,
"we were to listen to what all these other Christians have to say and try to
live by their standards, we would either fall into a new legalism or go
crazy trying to balance thousands of conflicting claims on our behavior."

Barclay helps us here when he writes that "Paul is not saying that we
must always allow our conduct to be dominated and dictated by the views,
and even the prejudices, of others; there are matters which are essentially
matters of principle, and in them a man must take his own way. But there
are a great many things which are neutral and indifferent" rather than essential parts of life or conduct. "And it is Paul's conviction that in such
things we have no right to give offence to the more scrupulous brother."

PAUL'S DEFINITION OF THE KINGDOM

The kingdom of God is not food and drink but righteousness
and peace and joy in the Holy Spirit. Rom. 14:17, RSV.

THIS TEXT USED TO offend me back in the days when dietary issues stood at the center of my religious experience. Only gradually did I come to see that while diet and good health were instrumental to balanced religion, we should not confuse them with religion itself. Diet and health are means to an end rather than the end itself. But great confusion has reigned in the church because of those who have confused ends and means.

Paul is quite sure that the central issues of religion are "righteousness and peace and joy in the Holy Spirit." "Righteousness" is one of the most important words in Romans. It is the word that Paul utilizes to sum up the salvation that comes through Jesus. To him righteousness through Christ is the very heart and soul of the Christian religion. Without Christ's righteousness accepted into the heart through faith Christianity simply cannot exist. Paul had little sympathy with those ascetics who sought to put food and drink at the center of their religion. On the other hand, he was willing to bend over backwards in order not to offend those who were struggling as they sought to separate themselves from the taboos of their Jewish heritage—as long as they didn't confuse those taboos with religion itself.

One of the fruits of righteousness in Paul's mind was peace. He refers to two kinds of peace in his Epistles: peace *with* God and the peace *of* God. The first we came across in Romans 5:1, in which he writes that "since we have been justified through faith, we have peace with God" (NIV). The second he mentions in Philippians 4:6, 7: "Do not be anxious about anything, but . . . present your requests to God. And the peace of God, which transcends all understanding, will guard your hearts and your minds in Christ Jesus" (NIV).

A second fruit of righteousness is joy. One of the sad facts of life is that so many Christians look so miserable. One wonders where the center of their religion lies. Paul, by contrast, was joyful even in adversity. Why? Because Jesus was his Savior and Lord.

The order of Paul's threefold definition of religion is all important. Too many people want the joy and peace without the righteousness. But they come only in the train of a right relationship to God.

GOD CALLS PEACEMAKERS

*Let us therefore make every effort to do what leads
to peace and to mutual edification. Rom. 14:19, NIV.*

"BLESSED ARE THE peacemakers," Jesus said, "for they shall be called sons of God" (Matt. 5:9, RSV).

Peace is an important word in Romans. In the book's initial greeting Paul blesses his readers with grace and peace (Rom. 1:7), and in the last few verses of Romans he refers to God as the "God of peace" (Rom. 16:20). But the most important thing about peace in Romans is that every person who accepts the sacrifice of Jesus by faith has peace with God (Rom. 5:1). Having been forgiven and justified, they no longer have to fear God. The alienation is over. They know that God loves them, and that in turn frees them to love Him with all their heart, mind, and soul (Matt. 22:37).

The Bible makes it absolutely clear that when we love God we will also love our neighbor (verse 39). The person who claims to love God and to be at peace with Him, yet who fails to live out God's love in peaceful relationship with other people—even people who differ from him or her racially, ethnically, or theologically—has something wrong.

Those who have met Jesus will be peacemakers. They will pass on the peace they have found with God. This business of peace presents only two options. Either we will be peacemakers or we will be among those who increase alienation in the world and the church.

That alternative brings us to Paul's second main point in Romans 14:19. Christians should be involved in "mutual edification." The word *edification* comes from the same root as edifice. An edifice, of course, is a building. Paul repeatedly refers to the church as a building. And in Romans 14:19 and 20 he points out that we can do two things to that building called the church. First, if we are peacemakers, we will participate in "mutual edification" or upbuilding of the church. Second, we can tear down God's building and "destroy the work of God" (Rom. 14:20, RSV).

Paul's concern in Romans 14 is related to those who have so put dietary and other noncentral issues at the focus of their religion that they have become destructive of the church itself. Unfortunately, the church across the ages has had members who become critical and judgmental of others over issues that are not central to Christianity. Paul is appealing for a halt to such attitudes. He wants us each to be peacemakers and upbuilders, even with those with whom we disagree.

HEALTH REFORM IS GOOD IF . . .

*Do not tear down the work of God
for the sake of food. Rom. 14:20, NASB.*

HEALTH IS A PRECIOUS thing. And the health reform movement is one of God's blessings. In no time in modern history have people had such good health, thanks to the principles of health set forth during the past 150 years.

Unfortunately, all those concerned with health haven't been healthy themselves. In fact, some are unbalanced. Just as there were those with "forceful" ideas on dietary issues in the days of Paul, so they have always existed in the history of the church.

Ellen White had to face off with those who were tearing "down the work of God for the sake of food" in her day.

"Statements," she penned, "are made that some are taking the light in the testimonies upon health reform and making it a test. They select statements made in regard to some articles of diet that are presented as objectionable—statements written in warning and instruction to certain individuals who were entering or had entered on an evil path. They dwell on these things and make them as strong as possible, weaving their own peculiar, objectionable traits of character in with these statements and carry them with great force, thus making them a test, and driving them where they do only harm.

"The meekness and lowliness of Christ is wanting. Moderation and caution are greatly needed. . . .

"Health reform, wisely treated, will prove an entering wedge where truth may follow with marked success. But to present health reform unwisely, making that subject the burden of the message, has served to create prejudice with unbelievers and to bar the way to the truth. . . .

"We see those who will select from the testimonies the strongest expressions and, without bringing in or making any account of the circumstances under which the cautions and warnings are given, make them of force in every case. . . . There are always those who are ready to grasp anything of a character which they can use to rein up people to a close, severe test, and who will work elements of their own characters into the reforms. . . . Picking out some things in the testimonies they drive them upon every one, and disgust rather than win souls. They make divisions when they might and should make peace" (*Selected Messages,* book 3, pp. 285, 286).

God, please grant us balance as we use Your gifts. Amen.

MY RESPONSIBILITY TO YOU

*It is wrong to make others fall by what you eat; it is
good not to eat meat or drink wine or do anything that
makes your brother or sister stumble. Rom. 14:20, 21, NRSV.*

PAUL'S MAIN TOPIC IN Romans 14 is *not* eating or drinking or any other lifestyle issue. Rather, he is writing about the responsibility of each Christian not to be offensive to other Christians.

As we noted some days ago, the issue at hand is not the distinction between eating or not eating the so-called clean and unclean animals of Deuteronomy 14, but rather between eating meat and eating absolutely no meat at all. We saw in 1 Corinthians that some of the early Christians had become vegetarian for the wrong reason; not for health reasons but because they feared that the meat might have been offered to an idol. Paul believed such a practice was wrong headed, since idols were not really gods. Thus consuming meat offered to them was a nonissue to him. But in order not to offend "the weak" he was willing not to eat in their presence those things that offended them (1 Cor. 8).

As we have said before, we don't know the exact problem among the Roman Christians, but a high probability exists that it was similar in nature to the issue in Corinth. In today's text Paul also raises the topic of wine in the same context with that of the so-called unclean foods. Once again he doesn't tell us what the exact problem is, but it is probable that some of the Romans found themselves troubled by the fact that some wine sold in the marketplace had been offered to a pagan deity as a libation. Thus Paul is not talking about abstinence as such, but abstinence for a *wrong* reason.

His real point is the responsibility that Christians have for one another. In today's passage he advises those he terms "strong." They have a responsibility not to be a stumbling stone to those who haven't really grasped the core of the Christian message and are thus concerned with such peripheral issues as food and drink offered to idols.

And what should their course of action be? That of peacemakers. Rather than entering into dispute or flaunting their understanding, those who have a better grasp of the uniqueness of Christ and the gospel of salvation should, as their neighbors' keepers, live in such a way as not to offend others with a less adequate faith.

That advice is still needed today. As a Christian I want to build up each of God's children.

Some Beliefs Are Personal

So whatever you believe about these things keep between
yourself and God. Blessed is the man who does not
condemn himself by what he approves. Rom. 14:22, NIV.

PAUL HAS BEEN SPEAKING to the strong in Romans 14:21. He has told them not to do anything that will cause their fellow believers to stumble and fall. Thus he is quite certain that those who aren't quite as sensitive on certain lifestyle issues that he has been discussing have a responsibility to those who are more scrupulous in their convictions.

But he now goes on to write in today's passage that the weaker brothers and sisters also have an obligation. They should not make an issue of all their various beliefs. The King James Version appears to suggest that they are to restrict their faith to themselves. But that translation, since some might read it in a general way that implies that they shouldn't witness, is obviously inadequate. Rather, they are to keep their faith on the noncentral, disputed issues to themselves. Or as the New International Version implies, they are to limit their ideas on the disputed topics to between themselves and God.

That is, they are not to be constantly advocating their particular convictions on this or that lifestyle issue as if it were a matter of salvation. Think how different the church would be today if everyone followed Paul's advice not to make their personal convictions on behavioral standards the norm for everyone.

But even though Paul tells the "weaker" members not to agitate their views, he never downplays their importance to them as individuals in their walk with God. If they truly believe that God has convicted them on these matters, then it is wrong for them to transgress their beliefs. Paul writes that "blessed is the man who does not condemn himself by what he approves. But the man who has doubts is condemned if he eats, because his eating is not from faith" (Rom. 14:22, 23, NIV).

We must not skim over these words lightly. Each of us is accountable to God for living up to our convictions. Even if they are mistaken, we need to be honest to them until God shows us a better way. To do otherwise would make us hypocrites in our own eyes and be detrimental to our faith in God.

Paul's lessons in chapter 14 are important to us. The church with its various strong-minded people had a difficult time getting along in Paul's day. It still does. And the answer to that problem is still the same.

YOUR CONSCIENCE IS IMPORTANT

Whatsoever is not of faith is sin. Rom. 14:23.

WE NEED TO TAKE that forceful statement in its context. The first part of the verse, as we saw yesterday, notes that those who feel convicted about something yet go against that conviction stand condemned. The condemnation is not merely in their own eyes but in God's also. God's condemnation does not come from the eating or from the doing, but from doing something that one believes to be wrong; that people don't live up to their own convictions.

Phillips' translation helps us see the point: "If a man eats meat with an uneasy conscience, you may be sure he is wrong to do so. For his action does not spring from his faith, and when we act apart from our faith we sin."

Douglas J. Moo's comments also are helpful: "What [Paul] here labels 'sin,' . . . is any act that does not match our sincerely held convictions about what our Christian faith allows us to do and prohibits us from doing." Or as Herman Ridderbos puts it: "For a Christian not a single decision and action can be good which he does not think he can justify on his Christian conviction and his liberty before God in Christ." We need to pay attention to our consciences. But we must also carefully read God's Word so that our consciences are as adequately informed as possible.

Some interpreters have viewed Paul's words "whatsoever is not of faith is sin" to mean that whatever a person does outside of a justifying relationship to Christ is sinful, no matter how good the action itself. Such an interpretation goes beyond what Paul is talking about and cannot be based upon Romans 14:23.

On the other hand, it is true that Paul teaches faith in Christ as Lord and Savior as the only ground for Christian living. To Paul it is a living faith in Christ that leads to obedience. Thus Paul begins and ends Romans by speaking about the obedience of faith (Rom. 1:5; 16:26). Obedience flows out of faith. It is also true in Paul's overall writings that those who don't have faith in Christ stand condemned. Thus there is a sense in which even the good actions of those who don't have justifying faith are sin. But that is not Paul's point in Romans 14.

In this great chapter, which we need to study more than we generally do, Paul provides the "formula" for a healthy church. Part of his solution is for Christians to be tolerant with one another on the "nonessentials" of Christianity.

LET OPPRESSORS BECOME SERVANTS

We who are strong ought to bear the weaknesses of those
without strength and not just please ourselves. Rom. 15:1, NASB.

PAUL'S ADVICE GOES against the trend of all of human history in every culture. Nearly everywhere the strong have tended to use their strength as a way to ease their personal burdens by making the weak bear them as well as their own. The strong rise to the top of any pyramid, and the weak become their servants. In fact, the "strong" in most systems see taking advantage of their own strengths as a natural right. "Society," so the thought goes, "owes me certain rights and privileges because of my talents, my education, or my powerful connections." The oppressor mentality stands at the heart of "normal" living.

But Paul tells us that the "normality" of a sinful world is not to prevail in the church. Christians who are truly Christians, he asserts in various places, live by the law of love rather than the law of the jungle (see Rom. 13:8-10). Instead of living by the accepted standards of a sinful world in which "might makes right," Christians are to live "transformed" lives through the renewal of their minds in the ways of God's kingdom. They are to become "living sacrifices" in God's service (Rom. 12:1, 2).

That was one of the hardest lessons for the disciples to learn. The strongest among them, such as Peter and John, contended for the supreme places. Through their strength they sought to dominate. One of Christ's most forceful lessons was that they were not to copy the world's patterns in such matters. Rather, Jesus said, they were to let their self be crucified. In the new model the strong would be the servants of the weak.

One thing that Christianity teaches us is that God does not give us our strengths and talents and gifts for self-aggrandizement, but that we might more effectively help others. What a wonderful place the church would be if we each let God "baptize" our strengths for service.

Of such is the kingdom of God. And it will be the principle of the kingdom when Christ comes again. In today's verse Paul tells us that the strong, among whom he included himself, needed not merely to tolerate the misunderstandings and foibles of the weak, but also to help them carry their burdens. A person of great talents, Paul gave his life to serving those less capable than himself.

God is calling each of us today to that same ministry.

REALLY DOING "GOOD" FOR OTHERS

Let each of us please his neighbor
for his good, to edify him. Rom. 15:2, RSV.

HERE PAUL SEEMS TO be speaking to both the strong and the weak. It is the responsibility of each church member to seek to build up every other member. Paul has now moved beyond the negative advice with which he began his extended treatment in Romans 14:3, in which he told the strong not to look down their noses at the scruples of the weak, and the weak not to condemn those who weren't as strict as they were.

The apostle has now shifted from the negative to the positive. Everybody must work in unity to build up both those who agree with them and those who disagree.

Paul notes that we should aim at helping others for their "good." The point he is making is that we as Christians constantly need to seek to do for others what is for *their* good rather than ours.

Leon Morris claims that it does not mean that the weak (those with the most sensitive consciences) should control the church. A situation in which the weak (those majoring in minors, who focused on sidelines off from the center of the gospel) dominated the church would be detrimental to the health of the church itself. All they would have to do was express a scruple and all would rush to conform. That is not Paul's definition of "good." In fact, Morris notes, "that would mean that the church would be permanently tied to the level of the weak and that life and growth would cease."

Paul is not writing here about control, but rather setting forth a principle of tender concern. The strong are to respect the weak, and vice versa. The strong must not hurt or take advantage of the weak, but must strive for their good. Likewise, the weak must desire the good for the strong.

Of course, in Paul's mind (remember, he has linked himself with the strong [Rom. 15:1]) genuine concern for the weak (those with an immature faith) will mean an attempt to strengthen them by leading them out of their ill-founded scruples so that they will also be strong. He spent much of his ministry building up and enlightening those weak in their faith and understanding.

The definition of "good" for Paul in today's passage is related to building up or edifying. Each of us has a ministry to every other person to strengthen them in Christ Jesus.

SERVING AS JESUS SERVED

For Christ did not please himself; but, as it is written, "The insults of those who insult you have fallen on me." Rom. 15:3, NRSV.

TODAY'S VERSE CENTERS ON Christ's life, but it points in two directions. First, the word "for" at the beginning of the verse points us back to the preceding verse, which stated that "each of us should please his neighbor for his good, to build him up" (NIV).

Thus Christ is our example in how to treat other people. Think about it. He could have come to earth with the attitude that in His Christian liberty He had a right to do what He pleased. After all, He didn't have to put up with all the foolish weaknesses of Peter and the other disciples. Christ could have said, "I have a life to live. Why should I be burdened with your stupidity? After all, I have already given you sufficient instruction."

Yet He didn't take that course of action. Patiently and repeatedly He bore the weaknesses of others. "His way," F. F. Bruce observes, "is to consider others first, to consult their interests and help them in every possible way." Paul notes that "Christ did not please himself." If He had done so, His life would have been like the lives of other people. The apostle's point is that Christ did not assert His rights. He put the interests of others before His own. Jesus Himself captured that idea when He noted that "the Son of man came not to be served but to serve, and to give his life as a ransom for many" (Matt. 20:28, RSV).

Christ is not only a Christian's Savior; He is also an example. And just as His life was one of service for others, so will be the lives of His followers. In the light of the context of our passage, Paul is suggesting that, given the example of Jesus, the strong in the church will not push for their rights to do what they want in spite of the scruples of the weak. Nor will the weak condemn others. Both groups will work toward unity.

Today's verse also points us toward service to God. Jesus not only served human need, He also served God, a concept reflected in the quotation from Psalm 69:9 in today's verse. He came to do the Father's will, to serve the Father in spite of the insults that such service brought from both those inside the church and from those on the outside.

Christ's life of service, Paul reminds us, is to be a motivation for each of us as we seek through God's grace to serve both God and our fellows.

Today, Father, please help me to be more like Jesus. May His life of service to God and others be my model. Amen.

THE IMPORTANCE OF THE OLD TESTAMENT

Everything written in the Scriptures was written to teach us,
in order that we might have hope through the patience and
encouragement which the Scriptures give us. Rom. 15:4, TEV.

ROMANS 15:4 APPEARS in a chapter filled with quotations from the Old
Testament. We just saw one in verse 3, and Paul will use five more in
verses 9, 10, 11, 12, and 21. In today's passage the apostle provides us
with his justification for appealing to the Jewish Bible so often.

We can learn several things about the Old Testament Scriptures from
this verse. First, God gave them to "teach us" as Christians. That may
seem obvious to you, but not to some Christians. Back in the 1960s I
pastored in Fort Worth, Texas. In that area one of the largest Christian
groups proclaimed that God had done away with the Old Testament at the
cross, that the "Old Bible" had only historic value for Christians, and that
the "New Testament" was all that a Christian needed.

Such thinking couldn't have been further from Paul's mind. The apostle had no doubt that the Old Testament had a function in teaching
Christians (see 1 Cor. 10:11).

A second thing Paul tells us about the Old Testament is that God
meant it for our encouragement. And how does the Old Testament encourage us? Personally, I find my faith strengthened when I see how God
faithfully led His people down through Jewish history. They didn't always
follow, they didn't always do His will, but God never gave up on them.
He continued to love them in spite of themselves. I find that encouraging,
because I live in a church equally less than perfect. God is still leading, in
spite of some of our individual and corporate blunders.

Third, the Old Testament provides us with hope. Jeremiah speaks of
God as the "hope of Israel, its saviour in time of trouble" (Jer. 14:8, RSV),
and the psalmist says "for God alone my soul waits in silence, for my hope
is from him" (Ps. 62:5, RSV).

In a world that from a human perspective looks hopeless, we can be
thankful for a God who through His Word inspires us with hope. Just as
the Old Testament pointed to the first coming of Christ, so the New points
to the Second Advent. And we need to remember that the second is just
as certain as the first.

WHY CAN'T EVERYBODY BE RIGHT LIKE ME?

*And now may God, the source of all patient endurance
and encouragement, give you a spirit of harmony among
yourselves as you follow Christ Jesus. Rom. 15:5, NT.*

PAUL'S ARGUMENT IN Romans 15 is an interesting one. First, in verses 1 and 2 he exhorts the Romans to build up each other. Second, in verse 3 he quotes a Scripture text to prove his point. Then, after an explanation in verse 4 as to why he cited the text, verse 5 finds him praying for his readers.

Note the pattern: (1) exhortation, (2) Scripture support, (3) prayer. Here is a model we do well to remember in our own dealing with other people.

The apostle was a man of prayer, a fact that shows up throughout his writings. In his prayer in today's verse he asks God, the source of all patience and encouragement, to bless the Romans with a spirit of harmony as they follow Christ.

I suppose that he added the part about God being the source of patience and encouragement because those qualities are just what the Romans needed in their life together. I don't know about you, but I am easily discouraged when it comes to working with some of the "block-heads" in the church. (Please note, it is always *others* who are the block-heads.) How can they move so slowly? How can they be so dense? Why can't they see the "truth" of what I have told them?

In short, I need all the patience and endurance I can get in living and working with such people. Of course, in my more sanctified moments I recognize that they also need patience and endurance from God in working with me. (But I don't really know why, since I am always right.)

Paul's hope for the church is that it might have "harmony." Some versions render the word translated "harmony" as "unity." But the idea Paul is expressing in the context of Romans 14 and 15 is closer to harmony than to unity in all things. As Donald Grey Barnhouse put it: "Although God wants us to be brethren, he does not mean that we are to be identical twins."

Throughout his writings Paul focuses on variety in the church. Thus even though Christians are of one body they represent various strengths. Likewise, in Romans 14 and 15 Paul is trying not to plow under the opinions of either the weak or the strong, but to get them to respect each other so that they can live in harmony. That is still God's ideal for His church.

THE PURPOSE OF THE CHURCH

That ye may with one mind and one mouth glorify God,
even the Father of our Lord Jesus Christ. Rom. 15:6.

WE FIND A MOST interesting picture of the church in Romans 14 and 15. The various members obviously have differences that they believe to be quite serious. In times past those viewpoints have led to divisions in the church, with each perspective judging and condemning the others. They have genuine disputes on several issues that some of them believed were important to their Christian faith. Paul didn't agree that everything some of them desired to have unity on were as vital as they thought. On the other hand, he didn't want them to change unless they felt genuinely convicted to do so. Rather he counseled mutual tolerance.

Why? So that they might with one mind and one voice glorify God. The point is—and it is an important one—that they didn't need to agree on every detail of belief or on every one of the lifestyle issues that had been dividing them. They could by demonstrating Christian love and tolerance for each other still exist in harmony.

If they continued to beat each other up over their differences, they could hardly glorify God in their community. But if they could gracefully allow for individual perspectives on those points not central to the Christian faith, they could be a genuine witness for God to others.

The real purpose of the harmony among believers that Paul has been calling for is that "God, even the Father of our Lord Jesus Christ" might be glorified and honored. Unfortunately, constant bickering among church members glorifies no one except the devil himself. Paul here makes a heartfelt call for Christians to put away those differences that aren't central to their faith and to begin to live as Christians should.

God wanted them to have the character of Christ, expressed in such fruit as love, joy, and peace. Yet they, in their desire to do everything "right" on the one hand and to live in Christian freedom on the other, presented a picture to non-Christians of anything but love, joy, and peace.

Let them who have ears listen to what the Spirit says to the churches. Put your differences to one side so that your life and your congregation might truly be a glory to God rather than a wart in the kingdom.

GOD'S ACCEPTANCE AND MINE

Accept one another, then, just as Christ accepted you, in order to bring praise to God. Rom. 15:7, NIV.

"ACCEPT ONE ANOTHER." With those words Paul returns to the beginning of his argument in Romans 14:1. In fact, he sandwiches the extended, closely reasoned discussion about the strong and the weak between two cries for acceptance: "accept him" (Rom. 14:1) and "accept one another" (Rom. 15:7). The apostle addresses both pleas to the whole congregation at Rome, even though the first urges the church to welcome the weaker brother and the second entreats all church members to accept each other.

John Stott points out that both pleas for acceptance have firm roots in a theological rationale: "The weak brother is to be accepted, *for God has accepted him*" (Rom. 14:3), and the members are to welcome each other *"just as Christ accepted you"* (Rom. 15:7).

Paul has stopped dividing his readers into the strong and the weak. The apostle, we should note, intimately relates their acceptance of each other to justification by faith. Just as Christ has received other believers on the basis of their faith in Christ, so are we as fellow believers to accept one another. Or, as Paul put it earlier in his argument: "God has accepted him. Who are you to judge someone else's servant?" (Rom. 14:3, 4, NIV). When Christ has accepted someone, who am I to say that I will not take him or her as a Christian brother or sister?

Those are important questions. And they raise once again the spiritual arrogance of those who have assumed a throne and made themselves judges over their fellow church members. Have we forgotten that we were also unworthy and still are unworthy? Has it slipped our minds that our own membership in the community is on the basis of grace rather than that of our accomplishments?

Our acceptance of others also rests upon the gospel of grace. Of course, some of "those people" are disgusting. But then, so are you! So am I! Christianity is not a religion of the big head. It leaves no room for spiritual pride.

No! Just as God accepted me with all of my faults, so must I accept others on the same basis. *Christianity is a religion of living the transformed life (Rom. 12:2), of demonstrating God's grace and love in daily practice. When we forget that truth we have forgotten what the point of it all is.* By that time we may already be gobbling down camels while spitting out gnats.

343

BACK TO RACIAL DIFFERENCES

*For I tell you that Christ's life of service was on behalf
of the Jews, to show that God is faithful, to make his
promises to their ancestors come true, and to enable even
the Gentiles to praise God for his mercy. Rom. 15:8, 9, TEV.*

WITH THIS VERSE Paul has picked up a theme that has run throughout
the book from chapter 1—the issue of the tension between Jews and
Gentiles. Please note that he has rather subtly shifted his discussion from
the weak and the strong back to the Jews and the Gentiles. "This suggests," Ernst Käsemann points out, "at least that the conflict depicted earlier [in chapter 14] has something to do with the diverse composition of
the church at Rome, or, more precisely, that it involves the relationship
between a Jewish-Christian minority and the Gentile-Christian majority,"
the weak and the strong, respectively.

Thus the lines of separation that ran through the Christian community
in Rome did not merely involve theological differences, but also racial,
ethnic, and cultural ones. All of that seems rather modern. Paul's counsel
to the Romans is just as needed today as when first written.

One of the most important things we can realize about the Bible is the
universal applicability of its basic principles. The faces, names, and na-
tionalities of the people involved may change, but the problems of individuals and groups remain basically the same across time and space. So it
is also with the Bible's solutions to those fundamental difficulties. While
the particularities reflecting unique times and places might lose their rel-
evance, the great principles set forth in God's Word are eternal.

For that reason the Bible is able to speak across the millennia and
across cultures. While it is true, for example, that I am not Peter, the Bible
still speaks to the "Peter characteristics" in me. One can think of other illustrations, but the main point is that God's Word has a message for us in
the twenty-first century. And that statement is nowhere truer than on our
need to accept those who differ from us. It makes no difference whether
the differences are theological or racial; we as people who live God's love
need to surrender our hearts so that His love might manifest itself in our
daily lives.

*Today, dear Father, I rededicate my life, through Your grace, to mov-
ing beyond the barriers that separate me from those brothers and sisters
who differ from me racially, culturally, or in any other way. Amen.*

FOUR GENTILE QUOTATIONS

"From the root of Jesse, One will arise to become the ruler of the Gentiles, and they will put their hope in Him." Romans 15:12, NT.

IN ROMANS 15:9-12 WE find Paul building on verse 4, in which he told his readers that God inspired the Old Testament Scriptures so that we might have hope today. Verses 9-12 present four hope-filled quotations from the Jewish Bible, at least one from each major division of the Old Testament. One quotation comes from the Law, one from the Prophets, and two from the Writings. Through them the apostle asserts that all the recognized divisions of Scripture witness to the fact that the Gentiles have their place in God's salvation.

There appears to be a definite progression as Paul moves through his four quotations. The first quotation (verse 9) is one in which the psalmist praises God among the Gentiles. While it is natural to find a Hebrew singer praising God, Paul selected this particular one because it moves the singing of praise from a restricted Jewish context to the nations as a whole. Thus Paul selects his quotation from Psalm 18:49 to demonstrate that more than just the Jews will sing God's praises.

The second quotation, taken from Deuteronomy 32:43, calls on the Gentiles to rejoice with Israel. The original passage emphasizes joy as Moses summons the nations to praise God for His greatness and the defeat of His enemies. For Paul the significant thing is the call to the Gentiles to rejoice along with Israel. As Leon Morris points out, "God has brought the blessings of salvation to both, and it is well accordingly that they rejoice together."

Paul's third quotation, from Psalm 117:1, finds the Gentiles praising God independently of Israel.

The fourth quotation, from Isaiah 11:10, goes back to the foundation of salvation for both Jews and Gentiles. It speaks of "the root of Jesse," the only One in whom sinners can hope. "From the root of Jesse, One will arise to become the ruler of the Gentiles, and they will put their hope in Him." The name of Jesse, of course, pointed Paul's readers back to the great king David. David belonged to the lineage of Jesse, and the Messiah, the Christ, was to come through the same line. The significance of Isaiah 11:10 for Paul is that it explicitly stated that the Messiah would be not only for the salvation of the Jews but also the Gentiles.

Praise God that none of us have been left out of His plan of redemption.

THE GOD OF HOPE

May the God of hope fill you with all joy and peace as you
trust in him, so that you may overflow with hope by
the power of the Holy Spirit. Rom. 15:13, NIV.

PAUL HAS FINALLY REACHED the end of the massive argument that he began in Romans 1:18. For 15 intense chapters he has hammered home his points on what it means to be a Christian.

Now he is ready to stop. But how shall he conclude? Given the power and logic of his arguments he could have ended with a triumphalistic "I'm right and you're wrong" or "Now you have the real truth, so roll over and quit arguing."

But the apostle is out to win souls, not arguments. Thus he concludes the most influential presentation of salvation in the history of Christianity with a prayer.

He begins with the pregnant phrase "the God of hope." Hope expresses a central part of what the gospel is all about. A Christian is one who has hope. On what basis? "The God of hope." Everett Harrison points out that it is God who both "inspires hope and imparts it to his children." Because God is faithful we can trust Him to fulfill His promises.

Paul prays that "the God of hope" will fill his Roman readers (and us) with joy and peace as they trust in Him. Here we have three more of Paul's favorite words. Paul uses "joy" more than any other New Testament writer. I wish that the church today could catch that emphasis. Too many churches I go to look like morgues rather than places of rejoicing. Why? The saved have more than enough to rejoice about. They have not only joy but also "peace" because of their reconciliation to God. All of a Christian's blessings are related to "trust in Him" who is hope Himself.

Paul closes his short prayer with the wish that those who trust in God will "overflow with hope" through "the power of the Holy Spirit." Here we find the third mention of hope in two verses. Paul knew that the world of his day was hopeless. More than anything else people needed hope. Things haven't changed. The world still longs for hope. That is why the gospel is so important. It is a message of hope, joy, and peace for those who through the Spirit learn to trust in the "God of hope."

Paul, we want to join you in your prayer. We also want to pray for both others and ourselves, that we might have the confirmed hope of salvation and the joy and peace that flow out of that hope.

STEP 7
Saying Goodbye

Romans 15:14–16:27

TAKING A SEVENTH
STEP WITH PAUL

I myself feel confident about you, my brothers and sisters,
that you yourselves are full of goodness, filled with all
knowledge, and able to instruct one another. Rom. 15:14, NRSV.

WE HAVE JOURNEYED a long way with Paul this year in the book of
Romans. The great apostle has provided us a tour de force on the plan of
salvation. After meeting Paul and the Romans (Rom. 1:1-17) he immediately introduces us to the basic problem of all humanity—*sin* (Rom.
1:18–3:20). It is that problem that sets the stage for the rest of his Epistle.

The third step on Paul's tour took us through the wonders of justification by grace through faith in the sacrifice of Christ (Rom. 3:21–5:21).
We discovered that justification by faith is for Paul the basic platform on
which everything else in the Christian life rests. And, he was careful to
show us, just as every person is a sinner, so the only hope for every person is God's gracious gift in Jesus.

From justification Paul took us on a tour of the way of godliness, or
what we might call living the sanctified life (Rom. 6:1–8:39). From there
he went on to point out that salvation was for everyone—both Jews and
Gentiles (Rom. 9:1–11:36). And finally he presented us with a word picture of what it means to live God's love in the real world of our personal,
civic, and church life (Rom. 12:1–15:13). For Paul, getting saved was not
an esoteric experience related to some private realm of the religious. To
the contrary, the saved person lives as a saved person. It affects every aspect of existence.

With Romans 15:14 Paul is ready for the last step in our tour. He has
finished his presentation of salvation. Now he is about to say goodbye.
Between Romans 15:14 and 16:27 he will provide us with some of his reasons for writing the letter (Rom. 15:14-22) and his future travel plans
(verses 23-33), and he will send greetings to the people he knows in Rome
(Rom. 16:1-27).

In today's verse Paul warmly expresses his personal confidence in the
believers in Rome. He sees hope in them even though they, like other
churches, have their problems. But the apostle wants them to move beyond their problems and differences and into a fuller Christian life. Like
us, Paul's first readers were also walking with him to the kingdom.

WANTED: BALANCED WITNESSES

On some points, I have written to you very boldly by way
of reminder, because of the grace given me by God to
be a minister of Christ Jesus. Rom. 15:15, 16, RSV.

PAUL IS IN MANY ways the model of the faithful preacher. He didn't beat around the bush. Knowing what his message was, he didn't hesitate to give it, because he knew it was from God. In the course of his argument in Romans he had spoken "boldly" on many points. Not the least were his emphatic pronouncements on the universality of sin, the uselessness of human effort, the inclusion of both Jews and Gentiles on the basis of the gospel, and, of course, his forthright treatment of the problems between the strong and the weak.

In his bold writing he followed the advice he provided for Timothy. As his mentor, Paul had told the younger minister to "preach the word, be urgent in season and out of season, convince, rebuke, and exhort, be unfailing in patience and in teaching" (2 Tim. 4:2, RSV).

In today's passage Paul realizes that he himself has not lacked the essential boldness of a faithful servant of God, but now that he has completed his argument he admits that he has probably stepped on everyone's toes.

With that admission we begin to see another aspect of Paul's pastoral ideal—tact. A true Christian leader not only can fearlessly rebuke sin and error, but he or she also has a tact softened by love and care for those who are the object of ministry.

Both boldness and tact (see Rom. 15:14) need to blend in those who work for Christ as either laypeople or clergy. I know of some who have boldness but lack tact. Such know how to scourge the people but are unable to win their love and confidence. On the other hand, some are so tactful that they never get to the point. They are so fearful of offending anyone that they are unable to give the trumpet its sound of certainty.

A study of Paul's characteristics is of great value because he exemplifies the needed balance between tact and boldness. One might say that he had tactful boldness and bold tactfulness. The two must go together.

Father, help me today to be a balanced person. Help me to let You so mold me that I can be an effective witness for You. Help me to grow in both tactful boldness and bold tactfulness. Amen.

PAUL'S PRIESTLY MINISTRY

*[God] made me Christ Jesus' servant, sent to the Gentiles. I have
the priestly duty of telling them the Good News from God, so that
I may offer up the Gentiles as an acceptable offering to God,
made pure by the Holy Spirit. Rom. 15:16, NT.*

HERE PAUL EMPLOYS ideas explored nowhere else in the New Testament.
He tells us, for one thing, that he has a "priestly duty" to believers.

Priestly duties in the Bible are a function of the Levitical priests in the
Old Testament and the duty of Jesus as our High Priest in the New. A
priest in the Old Testament was one who stood between God and the sinner. But in the New Testament the priesthood is finished. Every believer
is a priest before God (1 Peter 2:9) in the sense that he or she can come
directly to Him through Jesus. Since Christ's offering on the cross all
other offerings and all sacerdotal priesthood have ended, except for that
of Christ Himself, as the book of Hebrews makes plain.

If the priesthood is a thing of the past, what does Paul mean by saying that he has priestly duties? The answer, as usual, we find in the context. Paul mentions two specific duties in relation to his "priestly"
statement. The first is that of instruction. He had the duty of proclaiming
the gospel. But he didn't have to describe that function in priestly terms.

It is the second duty that appears to be connected to Paul's use of
priestly language. He tells us that part of his task is to "offer up the
Gentiles as an acceptable offering to God."

Apparently Paul is taking us back to the language of Romans 12:1, in
which he urged the Romans to "offer" their "bodies as living sacrifices"
(NIV). Thus he preached the gospel to the Gentiles so that they might
offer themselves to God. Instead of bringing some animal to God, they are
to present themselves—body, soul, and spirit—as a "spiritual act of worship" (Rom. 12:1, NIV).

But how could they know that God would accept their sacrifice?
Because, says the apostle in today's verse, they had been "made pure by
the Holy Spirit."

Praise be to God! The Spirit still makes us acceptable to God, as we
receive God's justification through the sacrifice of Christ. The plan of salvation is so important that Paul pictures all three members of the Trinity
as being involved in it. The apostle was *Christ's* servant in making an offering to *God the Father* that had been made pure by the *Holy Spirit.*

GOOD BOASTING

Therefore I glory in Christ Jesus
in my service to God. Rom. 15:17, NIV.

THE "THEREFORE" IN today's verse refers us back to Romans 15:15 and 16, in which Paul spoke of his successful ministry to the Gentiles, who offered themselves to God because of the apostle's preaching of the gospel.

The word that he used for "glory" we could better translate as "boast." Paul has been adamant throughout the book of Romans that people have nothing to boast about. After all, they are hopelessly lost sinners. And they can't even boast about their salvation, since it was totally a gift of God.

On the other hand, he has earlier told us that he glories in God. And now he declares that he glories or boasts in what God has done through him for the salvation of others.

We need to note Paul's use of boasting carefully, because there is both a sinful type of boasting and a healthy one. The sinful variety focuses on our own accomplishments. "Look at me," it says. "What a great person I am."

Paul had had the sinful type prior to meeting Jesus on the road to Damascus. "If anyone else thinks he has reasons to put confidence in the flesh," he wrote to the Philippians, "I have more: circumcised on the eighth day, of the people of Israel, of the tribe of Benjamin, a Hebrew of the Hebrews; in regard to the law a Pharisee; as for zeal, persecuting the church; as for legalistic righteousness, faultless" (Phil. 3:4-6, NIV).

Paul had been a proud, boastful man. But when he met Jesus on the road to Damascus he realized that he was truly nothing.

Of course, in one sense he was wrong. He came to realize that each of us is something if we let God save us, transform us, and use us in His service. But at that point it is not we who deserve the boasting or glory, but the God who does the saving, transforming, and empowering. It is in relation to that very insight that we find Paul boasting in Romans 15:17: "I glory in Christ Jesus in my service to God."

He is not glorying in himself, but in what God has been able to do through him in bringing men and women to Jesus.

May each of us realize our nothingness so that Paul's God can use us for His glory. And may we also learn the lesson of "good boasting"—of boasting in God's power for salvation. May we learn to glory in Christ Jesus as we glorify the Father for His marvelous work for each of us.

THE MARKS OF A PREACHER

I will not make free to speak of anything except what Christ has accomplished by me, in the way of securing the obedience of the Gentiles, by my words and by my deeds, . . . by the power of the Spirit of God. Rom. 15:18, 19, Moffatt.

IN ROMANS 15:17 PAUL asserted that he boasted only in his service for God. In today's passage he explains the nature of that boasting. In the process he reveals at least four marks of the faithful preacher.

First, he took no credit for himself. He was not bragging about what he had accomplished as an apostle, but in what Christ had done through him. From what we find in the New Testament, Paul seemingly had more to boast about than any of the other apostles, including John and Peter. The greater part of Acts focuses on his ministry, and he contributed more to the New Testament than any other author. Beyond that, his missionary journeys had largely spanned the empire. His background and education had uniquely prepared him to fill a slot in the interface of Jewish and Gentile cultures that no other apostle was equipped to accomplish.

Paul had plenty to brag about, had he been so inclined. But he gloried only in what Christ had accomplished. Often we find that those who have achieved the least have the most to say about themselves, not so with Paul.

Second, he proclaimed a full message. He not only preached the gospel of justification by faith, he also put before his converts the importance of obedience. Thus the fact that he had secured "the obedience of the Gentiles" was important to him. It was so significant that he mentioned it explicitly in his general introduction to the book of Romans (see Rom. 1:5). Paul was well aware of the fact that a call to obedience was a part of Christ's gospel commission to the disciples. They were to teach observance of all He had commanded (Matt. 28:20).

A third mark of the faithful preacher is personal integrity. Paul notes that his influence on the Gentiles came about through his words and his deeds. His life matched up with his words. Part of the power of his message was that he had avoided a life of hypocrisy on one hand and self-righteousness on the other.

A fourth mark of the faithful preacher as exemplified by Paul was that his work succeeded only "by the power of the Spirit of God." There is nothing so pathetic as Christians seeking to do good through their own power. Our greatest need today is God's Spirit to bring life to our efforts for Him.

THE FIRST GREAT MISSIONARY

*From Jerusalem and round about as far as Illyricum I have
fully preached the gospel of Christ. Rom. 15:19, NASB.*

ONE OF THE LAST acts of Christ before His ascension to heaven was
the giving of what has become known as the "gospel commission" to His
disciples. "All authority in heaven and on earth," He told them, "has been
given to me. Go therefore and make disciples of all nations, baptizing
them in the name of the Father and of the Son and of the Holy Spirit,
teaching them to observe all that I have commanded you; and lo, I am with
you always, to the close of the age" (Matt. 28:18-20, RSV).

Several years later Christ met Paul on the road to Damascus and
commissioned him with a special assignment. Speaking to Ananias, who
was to help Paul during his transition period as he moved from Judaism
into Christianity, the Lord said, "Go, for he [Paul] is a chosen instrument
of mine to carry my name before the Gentiles and kings and the sons of
Israel" (Acts 9:15, RSV). At a later date, while Paul was in Antioch, "the
Holy Spirit said, 'Set apart for me Barnabas and Saul for the work to
which I have called them.' Then after fasting and praying they laid their
hands on them and sent them off" (Acts 13:2, 3, RSV).

The apostle Paul was a man with a calling from God. From the time
of the laying on of hands at Antioch he would be a missionary for Christ.

In today's passage Paul tells us that he had proclaimed the gospel of
Christ to the Gentiles (see Rom. 15:18) "from Jerusalem all the way
around to Illyricum" (verse 19, NIV). The problem with that passage is
that Paul never had a mission to the Gentiles in Jerusalem. Nor did he ever
preach in Illyricum (today's Albania and the various divisions of the old
Yugoslavia). Apparently what he meant was that he had evangelized from
one to the other. It would be like people saying that they had traveled all
over the United States from Canada to Mexico. Such a statement does not
claim that they had traveled in either Canada or Mexico but that they had
traveled throughout the land in between.

Given the complexity of travel in the first century, Paul's three missions, which took him to Turkey, Macedonia, and Greece, were a stupen-
dous accomplishment. He was obeying both the Great Commission and
his special calling. Paul became the model missionary par excellence.

Even to this day, 2,000 years later, young men and women (and older
ones also) still follow in the footsteps of the first great missionary.

PAUL THE CHURCH PLANTER

It has always been my ambition to preach the gospel where Christ was not known, so that I would not be building on someone else's foundation. Rom. 15:20, NIV.

EXCITING THINGS ARE happening in the Adventist Church today. Church planting is finding a new life—a fact especially important in such places as North America and Europe, where it had become a lost art. But now hundreds (and even thousands worldwide) of new congregations start each year. The annual SEEDS convention held at Andrews University helps people learn how to plant churches in new territory. And now SPROUTS, an organization to help develop programs to nourish the new church sprouts that have grown from the spreading of the seeds, has joined the trend. The aim is to capture new territory for Christ.

Paul could have identified with these movements. The most well-known church planter in Christian history, he was what we would currently term a "pioneer missionary." His ambition was to preach the gospel where Christianity was still unknown. He had no desire to build on anyone else's evangelistic work.

In saying that, the apostle was well aware that not all Christians or even Christian missionaries had a pioneering role. He recognized the differentiation of function in God's service. Thus he could write to the Corinthians that some plant and others water and that there are those who lay a foundation and those who build upon it (1 Cor. 3:6-14).

While he appreciated the division of labor in the missionary enterprise, he firmly believed that his divine calling was to be that of pioneer to the unreached pagan world. Of course, he also at times worked with congregations that he had not founded. The very letter to Rome itself is an example of his aiding Christians in an already established community.

But Paul's personal burden was pioneer work. He wanted to reach those who had never heard the name of Christ.

That is still one of the great demands and challenges of the Christian church. It is to that need that such organizations as Adventist Frontier Missions are responding. God has people reading this message today who need to become involved in church planting through either their talents or their means. One of them may be you.

THE SMOKE OF A THOUSAND VILLAGES

As scripture says, Those who had no news of him shall see, and those who never heard of him shall understand. Rom. 15:21, REB.

WE HAVE COME TO the last quotation from the Old Testament in Romans. The apostle has repeatedly quoted from the Jewish Scriptures to nail down his points. In fact, Romans has more Old Testament quotations than any other New Testament book. The next in line is Matthew, with 61 quotations. But, we should point out, Matthew is more than twice as long as Romans. Thus the density of Old Testament material in Romans is much greater. The reason appears to be that the material presented in Romans, in the light of the ongoing controversy between the Jews and the Gentiles in Rome, needed to be thoroughly substantiated from the Jewish Bible. In the process, the apostle Paul shows himself to be a man of the Book.

Today's passage has a quotation taken from Isaiah 52:15. Romans 15:21 carries on the theme of Paul's dedication to pioneering missionary work, and it provides Old Testament grounding for it: "Those who had no news of him shall see, and those who never heard of him shall understand."

In our day many still need to see and understand. The role of the pioneer missionary is not a path followed by many, but the past 200 years have seen a constant stream of them as Christianity has circled the earth.

One was David Livingstone, who pioneered for Christ in eastern and central Africa. When the London Missionary Society asked him as a young man where he wanted to go, he answered: "Anywhere, as long as it is forward." After reaching Africa, he noted that the smoke of a thousand villages stretching off into the distance haunted him.

The smoke of thousands of villages and cities still stretches off beyond the horizon. The great lands of the Islamic, Buddhist, and Hindu faiths have multitudes who have never heard the name of Christ. Much the same can be said for the postmodern, post-Christian enclaves of the West, where for millions the name of Christ is a cultural anachronism.

The world still needs Pauls. It still requires those prepared to take the gospel message to earth's remotest bounds. And it still seeks those willing to support pioneer missions with their influence and finances.

PLANNING PLANS FOR GOD

*Now, since I no longer have any room for work in these
regions, and since I have longed for many years to come to you,
I hope to see you in passing as I go to Spain. Rom. 15:23, 24, RSV.*

PAUL HAS COME TO another turning point in his letter. In 15:14-22 he laid out his basic reasons for writing to the Romans. Now he turns in the rest of the chapter to his future plans. He intends to begin pioneer work in Spain, and on the way he hopes to visit Rome. But before then he needs to go to Jerusalem. Unfortunately, that visit will lead to his arrest and his appeal to Caesar. In the end he will reach Rome not as a pioneer missionary on his way west, but as prisoner of the Roman government.

Meanwhile, Paul had a *plan,* one that never came true. That frustrated scheme raises the question of planning in the Christian's life. Some Christians act as if it is some sort of sin to figure out things beforehand; that God will lead them step by step without any direct involvement on their part. Such people infer that planning is wrong. Here they disagree with Paul. While he was open to God's special guidance, he also believed in careful planning as he sought to accomplish God's work. Well-laid plans shaped his daily life and provided a vision for his future.

If a first characteristic in Paul's planning was to devote a place for it in his life, a second was that he kept himself flexible. He operated on the basis that God could open and shut doors in his life. He planned, yet he also followed God's leading providence.

A third characteristic of Paul's planning was that he was persistent. He notes in Romans 15:22 that he had "often been hindered" (RSV) from going to Rome, but that was still his intention. No matter how long it took, he still kept plodding toward his goal. The same was true of Spain. We don't know if he ever got there, but its evangelization remained his heart's desire.

Christians today need to dream dreams and plan plans for God. Of course, it's true that some of our dreams may fail of fulfillment. But as one author puts it: "It is better to dream great dreams for God, even if they are not fully realized, than to dream no dreams at all. One thing is certain, unless we see visions, dream dreams, and make plans, there will be no great steps forward in the work of the gospel."

Lord, help us today to dream dreams and plan plans for Your kingdom and Your glory. Amen.

LEARNING FROM PAUL'S EXPERIENCE

*I hope to visit you while passing through and to have you
assist me on my journey [to Spain], after I have enjoyed
your company for a while. Rom. 15:24, NIV.*

PAUL PLANS TO VISIT Rome on the way to Spain. He looks forward to
two things during that visit: (1) Christian fellowship and (2) assistance.
We, of course, know what Paul didn't at the time. That is, that events
would frustrate his plans.

What can we learn from Paul's experience? One is that God often ful-
fills His will in ways we neither anticipate nor desire. Take ancient Israel,
for example. Who would have thought that God's way of making the Jews
into a great nation would have been through the imprisonment of Joseph
and the enslavement of the Jewish people? Or who would have supposed
that God would bring Paul to Rome through his arrest in Jerusalem? God's
ways are not ours, and we need to keep our minds open as we serve Him.

Also we need to remember when our world is falling apart that "in all
things God works for the good of those who love him" (Rom. 8:28, NIV).
That came home to me with renewed force last Sabbath. Two years ago a
classmate of one of my sons died in an accident while serving as a student
missionary. The death was tragic, but unbeknown to us, God was able to
use it to begin to wake up the young woman's grandfather. An agnostic,
he for the first time began to think seriously about religion when faced
with her death. That man was in my congregation last Sabbath, and once
again I was impressed with the fact that God does indeed work in all
things for the good of those who love Him.

We never know what sort of blessing God will bring out of what appears to be a misfortune in our lives. Yet, like Paul, we can continue to
trust in Him in spite of outward appearances.

Another thing that we can discover from Paul's experience is that the
God who can work miracles to supply the needs of His missionaries usually supports them through the gifts of His people. Paul, we note in today's
passage, desires the assistance of the Romans for his work in Spain. Earlier
he had relied on support from Antioch for his evangelism in Asia Minor
and on help from Philippi for his mission in Greece. He depended upon
home bases to supply many of his needs throughout his ministry.

God still works the same way today. Some of us go to the ends of the
earth, while others of us support them with our prayers and gifts.

FINAL JUDGMENT
TURNS ON ONE POINT

I am going to Jerusalem in the service
of God's people there. Rom. 15:25, TEV.

BEFORE PAUL COULD visit Rome he first needed to go to Jerusalem in order to distribute the offering for the poor in the heartland of Judaism that the Gentile churches had collected. For Paul that act of mercy not only had implications for the healing of some of the misunderstandings between Jews and Gentiles, it also was an expression of his service motif.

Love expressed in caring acts of mercy to those in need stands at the very heart of what it means to live God's love. One of my favorite assignments is to have people read the parable of the sheep and the goats in Matthew 25:31-46. As they read, I ask them to count the question marks. You see, we will find lots of surprised people in the final judgment of God.

On the one hand, you have those who unexpectedly get saved. "How come?" is their cry. "We weren't perfectionistic on the law like the Pharisees," they point out. In fact, they admit, "we have some real problems."

"But," says Jesus, "you have done what counts. When I was hungry you fed Me in the person of the poor, when I was in prison you visited Me. You have internalized the great principle of the law of love. As a result, you will be happy in heaven."

About that time the Pharisees pipe up. "You have to save us," they declare, "because we kept the Sabbath, paid tithe, and ate the right things."

"But," says Jesus, "when I was in need you didn't care. You have not internalized the great principle of love. You have not absorbed the only thing that counts. You wouldn't be happy in heaven."

The Desire of Ages provides a fascinating insight on Christ's portrayal of the final judgment. After quoting Matthew 25:31, 32, it says: "Thus Christ on the Mount of Olives pictured to His disciples the scene of the great judgment day. And He represented its decision as turning upon one point. When the nations are gathered before Him, there will be but two classes, and their eternal destiny will be determined by what they have done or have neglected to do for Him in the person of the poor and the suffering" (p. 637).

Christ's word picture is not one of salvation by works, but of received love being passed on. Caring for others is the natural response of those who realize how much God has cared for them.

A UNIFYING GIFT OF FELLOWSHIP

*Macedonia and Achaia have been pleased to make a contribution
for the poor among the saints in Jerusalem. Rom. 15:26, NASB.*

PERHAPS THE MOST widespread tension in the church in Paul's day
was the racial/religious issues between Christians of Jewish and Gentile
backgrounds. We have seen the tension between the two groups all
through the book of Romans. Paul has gone to great pains to explain how
the plan of salvation works, how it includes both groups on the same
basis, how it relates to the Jewish Scriptures and patriarchs, and how it relates to Old Testament law.

Paul, as the apostle to the Gentiles, had been at the very center of the
conflict between the two groups of believers. He had done his best to help
the Jewish Christians of his day see how Christianity and salvation by
grace through faith touched both the moral and the ceremonial laws. The
book of Romans itself is an excellent example of his sensitive approach to
the continuing tensions.

The apostle was doing all he could to bring unity to the two groups,
while at the same time being faithful to the truth of the gospel. One of his
major overtures was to get the Gentile Christians to help out their Jewish
brothers and sisters in a tangible way. To that end, Paul developed an extensive program to collect an offering throughout the largely Gentile churches
he had founded to help relieve the suffering of the poor in Jerusalem.

Cut off from the usual sources of Jewish charity because of their new
beliefs, the Christians in Jerusalem had experienced poverty from the earliest days of the church (Acts 6). Many who had had property had sold it
to try to alleviate the situation (Acts 4:34-47), but that was only a temporary solution. Once the money was gone, they had nothing to fall back on.

It is into that void that Paul comes with his relief plan. But for the
apostle his program was more than for just physical relief, it was to help
build the unity of the church. Thus it was of crucial importance to the spiritual health of those on both sides of the racial divide.

As a result, when Paul says that the Gentiles made a contribution he
uses a word that really means "fellowship." What he was saying was that
the gift was not a soulless one. To the contrary, it was but an outward expression of the deep love that binds Christians into one body, the church.

A church that continues to face various internal tensions still needs
that spirit.

SHARING IS A TWO-WAY STREET

*They were pleased to do this, and indeed they owe it to them; for if
the Gentiles have come to share in their spiritual blessings, they ought
also to be of service to them in material things. Rom. 15:27, NRSV.*

PAUL REINFORCES THE idea that the Gentile believers were "pleased"
to help out their Jewish relatives in the gospel. Of course, the apostle, as
demonstrated in his Corinthian correspondence, did bring some pressure
to bear to generate the collection. But that persuasion doesn't mean that
the Gentiles weren't pleased when they finally fulfilled their obligation.
Rather it illustrates the fact that "fellowship means something more than
enjoyment, it calls for effort, and if necessary self-sacrifice."

The Gentiles had a good reason to sacrifice for the Jews. After all, the
gospel had reached them through the Jews. Paul had earlier pointed out in
Romans that the promises of God had come through Abraham and his descendants (Rom. 4:13). Beyond that, as Paul has repeatedly reminded his
readers, the Scripture promises of the Savior, and even the Savior
Himself, emerged through the Jewish line. Israel was indeed the tree into
which the Gentiles had been grafted (Rom. 11:7-24). Beyond that, as Acts
demonstrates, it was the Jewish-Christian communities who initiated the
sending of missionaries to the Gentiles, and it was generally a core of
Jewish believers who became the foundation of each new congregation.

Thus the Gentiles had received much from the Jews. In fact, without
the Jews they would not have the gospel. With that in mind, it is of little
wonder that Paul bluntly states that the Gentiles "owe" a debt to the Jews.
The Jews had shared their spiritual blessings with the Gentiles. It was only
right for the Gentiles to share their material blessings with the Jews. Paul
holds that Christian sharing is a two-way street.

But for Paul the Jewish acceptance of the gift from the Gentiles was
fraught with an even deeper meaning. The Christian church had changed
rapidly in the few short years of its existence. Starting out as almost a sub-
set of Judaism, it had rapidly become predominantly Gentile in membership, with Paul as the foremost missionary to the Gentiles. Receiving a
financial gift from the Gentiles by the hand of Paul would signify the
Jewish Christians' acceptance of the new state of affairs. With that important issue on his mind, Paul goes on to request the prayers of the
Romans on his behalf as he travels to Judea (Rom. 15:30). Above all, he
hoped that his mission there would result in peace and unity.

A CASE OF PRIORITIES

Therefore, when I have finished this, and have put my seal on this fruit of theirs, I will go on by way of you to Spain. Rom. 15:28, NASB.

PAUL WAS OBVIOUSLY eager to move on to Spain. He had been seeing visions and dreaming of what God could do through his ministry in a land as yet untouched by the message of Christ. Obviously he had been planning his new work for some time and, as we saw in Romans 1, he probably wrote the entire book of Romans to introduce himself and his theology to the church that he hoped would become his home base for missions westward.

A man of passion, goals, and energy, the apostle was also a man of priorities. He knew that no matter how important or how enticing the prospects in Spain, he needed first to bind off his work in the east. As one author has noted, "planning for future ministry must never cause a present ministry to suffer."

With his priorities firmly in mind, the apostle told the Romans that he first had to "put my seal on this fruit of theirs." That strange expression probably had to do with the commercial practices of the times. We know, for example, that merchants put such produce as wheat and barley in sacks. When the sacks had been checked they had a seal put on them, certifying their contents. The seal indicated that all was in order. John Knox points out that when Paul has delivered the fund for the Jewish Christians in Jerusalem "and it has been received in the hoped for spirit, Paul will have ended his divinely appointed work in Asia Minor and Greece" and "the 'fruit' of his mission will have been 'sealed.'" At that point, he would be free to move on to new challenges and opportunities.

We can find some lessons for each of us in Paul's attitude. First, a Christian is one who completes the important tasks that he or she undertakes. It is a part of our service to other people and to God to be thorough workers in all that we undertake. Second, Paul's experience teaches us an evangelistic lesson. Too many times we stop our efforts for new converts after they have joined a congregation. But at that juncture the work of integrating them into their new life is only partly done. It isn't ready for the "seal" yet. Third is the lesson of priorities. As Christians who serve a faithful God, we need to always keep our own priorities in proper balance.

Help us today, Father, to be thorough workers for You, workers who understand our task and who have our priorities straight. Amen.

So Long to the Gospel of Wealth and Health!

When I come to you, I know that I shall come with
a full measure of the blessing of Christ. Rom. 15:29, TEV.

REALLY PAUL? HOW can you say that "you know" that when you arrive in Rome you will have "a full measure of the blessing of Christ"?

Don't you realize what's going to happen to you? Don't you understand that you will reach Rome as a prisoner, and then only after having been in chains for at least two years? How can you possibly say that you will arrive "with a full measure of the blessing of Christ"?

With those kinds of questions it looks as if we need to revise our ideas of God's blessing. Certain television preachers have a lot to say regarding the "gospel of health and wealth." Listening to some of them, you almost feel unfaithful and lost if you are not both wealthy and healthy.

But such a teaching couldn't have been further from Paul's mind. His obedience to Christ had cost him dearly both financially and physically. Because of his service to Christ, he suffered imprisonment, beatings, stonings, dangers from both Gentiles and Jews, and a host of other hardships (see 2 Cor. 11:23-27). But none of those outward problems could rob him of God's inward blessing.

To the contrary, the apostle wrote to the Philippians that "what has happened to me has really served to advance the gospel, so that it has become known throughout the whole praetorian guard and to all the rest that my imprisonment is for Christ; and most of the brethren have been made confident in the Lord because of my imprisonment, and are much more bold to speak the word of God without fear" (Phil. 1:12-14, RSV).

It looks as if Paul was right after all. He did arrive in Rome in the fullness of God's blessing. You see, God's blessing is not so much an outward matter as an inward one. No matter what our external condition, we can still have the fullness of God's blessing in our lives.

So long to the gospel of health and wealth. God has something more important, something of more value than silver or gold. That something more is the blessings of salvation and the spiritual blessings that accompany salvation.

Today, O Father, help me to desire the most important of Your blessings. Baptize my mind that I might walk with You. Amen.

PRAYER IS MORE THAN
A HARMLESS LITTLE EXERCISE

I urge you, brothers, by our Lord Jesus Christ and by the love of the Spirit, to join me in my struggle by praying to God for me. Rom. 15:30, NIV.

OFTEN PAUL IN HIS letters asked his readers to pray for him. "You must also help us by prayer," he wrote to the Corinthians (2 Cor. 1:11, RSV); "pray at all times in the Spirit" "and also for me," he penned to the Ephesians (Eph. 6:18, 19, RSV); and "pray for us," he asked the Thessalonians (1 Thess. 5:25, RSV; see also Col. 4:3; 2 Thess. 3:1).

"I urge you," he pens. That is strong, but then he adds, "by our Lord Jesus Christ and by the love of the Spirit." Paul is serious about their need to pray. He is not calling for a tepid, formal prayer, but one that entails whole-hearted involvement. The apostle wants them to join him in his "struggle," a word originally used of athletic events, especially gymnastics, in which the various contestants, such as wrestlers or boxers, struggled against each other.

Prayer, as Paul saw it, is a major weapon in the great controversy between good and evil. The apostle pictured himself locked in a death struggle with those forces that opposed the gospel. And he wasn't wrong. After all, his advocacy of the gospel would eventually cost him his life.

How many modern Christians see prayer as a life and death struggle? Most of us probably consider it as a kind of harmless little exercise we perform before meals, when getting up or going to bed, or, more formally, in church. For most of us it is a comfortable routine, but also an almost mindless one. That is just the way the devil would have it.

But Paul knew the power of prayer. That is why he "implored" (NEB) the Romans in the names of Christ and the Spirit to struggle with him in prayer. The apostle recognized that he was battling supernatural powers and that he needed supernatural strength from God.

As twenty-first-century Christians we need to realize that too many of our prayers are nothing but harmless little practices. God calls upon us to feel the urgency of prayer as we struggle against Satan for the eternal lives of our children, spouses, parents, neighbors, and so on. He calls upon us to become prayer warriors for Him. The Lord longs for us to tap into the most powerful force in the universe. He wants us never to forget that prayer "in the hand of faith" unlocks "heaven's storehouse" (*Steps to Christ*, p. 94).

PAUL AS BABYLON

[Pray] that I may not fall into the hands of the unbelievers
in Judaea, and that the Jerusalem Christians may welcome
the gift I am taking to them. Rom. 15:31, Phillips.

IN ROMANS 15:30 PAUL asked the Romans to pray for him. He now comes to the content of what he would like them to ask for.

He sees two dangers in particular. First, the unbelieving Jewish leaders, who view Paul as their number one troublemaker, a man at the forefront of spreading throughout the empire what they considered to be a heresy. Nobody is more hated than a person who trades sides in the midst of a struggle. And here was Paul, the one who had been at the forefront of those persecuting Christians, now the head of the new religion's missionary outreach. As the book of Acts demonstrates, some of the Jews would be willing to lose their own lives if they could get rid of this troublemaker.

But Paul also sees possible problems among the Jewish Christians. Why? we might ask. Wasn't he bringing them food? Don't his letters show how much energy he had expended to raise money for the poor Christians in Jerusalem? What is the problem?

Paul has to deal with an issue that has faced the church many times in its long history. According to the Jewish Scriptures he knew he was correct in his teachings, but certain conservatives saw him as an apostate, or, as we might say, "Babylon." Why? Because he had not stuck by the old-time theology that they held. Some regarded him as a dangerous innovator. Thus they might consider taking his money as a buyoff or bribe, wherewith, notes Leon Morris, "the apostle hoped to buy a condonation of his breaches of the [ceremonial] law." Therefore, by accepting his money they would be endorsing his teachings among the Gentiles. To them Paul was spreading "Babylonish" teachings—he was the enemy.

Paul, of course, realized that the Jewish Christians hadn't yet fully grasped the meaning of what Jesus had done on the cross for their ceremonial system. He hoped in prayer and faith that his bringing of aid from the Gentiles would help them see that all were indeed on the same side of the great struggle against the powers of darkness.

His experience has an important lesson for our day. It is all too easy to label someone as "Babylon." In all such situations it is crucial to listen to one another, to pray with and for one another, and to seek to bring God's peace through an understanding of His Word. The church still needs healing.

CHRISTIANS NEED PEACE TOO

Now the God of peace be with you all. Amen. Rom. 15:33.

PEACE IS AN IMPORTANT word in Romans. Paul first uses it in the greeting of Romans 1:7, in which he writes, "grace to you and peace from God." Altogether he employs the word 11 times in Romans, and in addition uses "peaceably" once, when he admonishes his readers to "live peaceably with all" (Rom. 12:18, RSV).

The concept of peace was absolutely central to Paul because it is the attribute missing in a world gone wrong, a world under sin's disruptive influence and power.

A primary characteristic of the world in every age since Eden has been the lack of peace between nations, between family members, between fellow workers, and even, unfortunately, in the church. The result is war, divorce, intrigue, and squabbling.

But that is not God's will for us. He desires our peace. As a result, He sent Jesus to earth. His sacrifice on Calvary opened the way for the reconciliation of each person with God (Rom. 5:10). Because of that reconciliation, those who have accepted Christ's sacrifice by faith can have peace with God (verse 1).

That is what Paul's gospel is all about—being at peace with God. Of course, he realizes that once we are at peace with God, then the way exists for the first time for men and women also to live peaceably with one another (Rom. 12:18).

Paul refers to the Lord as the "God of peace" in today's verse. That is the fourth description he uses for God in the present chapter. We also find Him called "the God of steadfastness," the God of "encouragement," and "the God of hope" (Rom. 15:5, 13, RSV). What a beautiful picture of God.

The God of peace wants to bring peace into each of our lives today. To that end He offers us both hope and encouragement. His peace is ours for the taking. Right now He wants us to let go of those worries and fears and animosities that trouble us. He longs for us to learn to trust in Him.

The good news is that the God of peace not only wants to give us peace, but He intends that we pass it on to those we live with, work with, and go to church with. He desires that we become peacemakers.

Our Father in heaven, please help us today to have Your peace in our hearts. And may that peace flow out into our lives so that all might know that we are truly Your children. Amen.

A WOMAN IN GOD'S SERVICE

*I commend to you our sister Phoebe, a deaconess of the church
at Cenchreae, that you may receive her in the Lord as befits the
saints, and help her in whatever she may require. Rom. 16:1, 2, RSV.*

THAT IS AN INTERESTING translation of Romans 16:1, because one of
its important words does not appear in the Greek original. The word "deaconess" is not there, but has been added. The actual word is *diakonos,*
translated correctly by the King James Version as "servant" and in such
places as Philippians 1:1 as "deacon." The reason "deaconess" is wrong is
because the Greek word has a male rather than a female ending.

Now, as you might guess, in an age that has hotly debated the role of
women in the church, today's passage has received its share of attention.
Was Sister Phoebe a "servant" or a "deacon"? In other words, did she hold
an official office, or was she a servant in the general sense that all
Christians are servants?

It is impossible from this particular text to solve the issue, although
some have argued that the words "of the church at Cenchreae" appear to
suggest that she was a church official or "deacon."

What I find fascinating about today's verse is that Paul lists Phoebe
first in the greetings. That primacy probably implies that she carried the
letter from Paul to the church members in Rome.

The New Testament depicts females as playing an influential role in
the early Christian community. Not only did Phoebe bring Paul's precious
Epistle to Rome, but she had been "a great help to many people," including Paul (Rom. 16:2, NIV).

It was Mary Magdalene who had heard Christ's prediction of His
forthcoming death, whereas all of the disciples had been blinded to it by
their prejudices. As a result, she anointed Him for death.

Again, it was women who stood close by Christ on the cross, while the
disciples largely distinguished themselves by their invisibility. Likewise,
women became the first heralds of the good news that Christ had risen.

God has used women alongside men down through church history.
One of the most remarkable examples was the ministry of Ellen White,
which did so much to shape Adventism through her 70 years of service.

God is still calling both men and women to service in our day. Thus
Phoebe, the "servant" or "deacon," was merely one of a long line of females who will accomplish much for God through the end of time.

LESSONS FROM A LIST OF NAMES

Greet Priscilla and Aquila, my fellow workers in
Christ Jesus. They risked their lives for me. . . . Greet also
the church that meets at their house. Rom. 16:3-5, NIV.

THE GREETINGS GO ON and on throughout this last chapter of Romans. Because of the *Pax Romana* (Roman peace), travel was relatively easy in the Mediterranean basin. Thus Paul had many acquaintances in Rome even though he had never been there.

His greeting tells us several things about the early church. One is the fact that women must have been fairly active. Of the 26 people that the apostle greets, 9 of them are women—Phoebe, Priscilla, Mary, Junia, Tryphena, Persis, the mother of Rufus, Julia, and the sister of Nereus. That is a remarkable proportion in a society dominated by males.

A second thing that we learn from his list is that it speaks of a house church. When we in the twenty-first century think of churches, we envision large structures that hold an entire congregation. That wasn't so in the early church. The first church buildings of which we have knowledge did not appear until the third century. Early Christians worshiped on a regular basis in the homes of leading members. Such groups not only were intimate for the members but apparently represented nonthreatening environments in which to do evangelism.

Down through church history many effective movements have utilized variations on the "house church" theme. The highly successful Wesleyan movement grew up around what they called "class meetings." And many churches in our day employ "cell groups" to help make Christian fellowship more vital and evangelism more effective.

The lesson: God can use a variety of means, and those of us who think that a thing can be done only one way haven't really grasped how the early church worshiped, fellowshipped, and did evangelism.

Beyond house churches, Paul speaks as if the church in Rome was also a unified congregation. That may have been so, but if it was, we have no information on how they may have maintained their unity or where they may have met to do so.

God wants us as Christians to keep our minds and hearts open to His leading. In different contexts He works through His people in a variety of ways. We as Christians need to remain flexible so that He can most effectively use us as new doors open for experimentation.

THE MIRACLE OF IDENTITY

Greet Rufus, chosen in the Lord, and
his mother and mine. Rom. 16:13, NKJV.

RUFUS! WHERE HAVE I heard that name before?

Back in Mark 15. Mark mentions that the Roman soldiers "compelled a passer-by, Simon of Cyrene, who was coming in from the country, the father of Alexander and Rufus, to carry his [Jesus'] cross" (verse 21, RSV).

The Gospel writer obviously made his comment because his readers knew Rufus and Alexander. The addition of their names gives his gospel a personal touch. Keep in mind that it has generally been held that the Gospel of Mark was written primarily for the Christian community in Rome, and we can begin to see that the Rufus in Romans 16 just might be the same Rufus whom Mark calls the son of Simon of Cyrene.

Of course, we cannot prove the connection. And the name Rufus was a common one. Thus the link at present is merely an intriguing possibility.

But what we can demonstrate by the two uses of the name of Rufus is that God knows each of His children personally. We won't get lost in the cracks of a large church of innumerable other Christians. God remembers even Rufus, whose father had such an interesting part to play in Christ's crucifixion. He thinks even of Rufus in the church at Rome. The most significant thing from a Christian perspective is not the possibility that they were the same person, but that they were remembered at all.

As Jesus one time put it, God numbers even the hairs of our heads. We are personal to Him. He knows us by name, whether that name be Bonnie, Bill, Sonia, Frank, or even Rufus. Each of us is significant to Him as individuals.

Rufus, Paul tells us, was "chosen in the Lord." That is true of every Christian, so he must have meant that Rufus had a special responsibility for God.

Paul also notes that Rufus's mother was his mother. I doubt that he and Rufus were blood brothers. Rather Paul is stating his closeness to her and the fact that all Christians belong to the family of God. We have many brothers and sisters in the faith, as well as mothers and fathers and sons and daughters. And as in our earthly families, as Christians we have responsibilities to our relatives in the faith.

Part of the good news is that we belong to the family of God, and that you and I have personal significance to the Ruler of the universe. Praise God!

AND WHAT HAPPENED TO THE HOLY KISS?

Greet one another with a holy kiss. All the
churches of Christ greet you. Rom. 16:16, NRSV.

HOLY KISSING! When is the last time you got a kiss in church? I remember one time I received a kiss in church. I was greeting people who were exiting from the sanctuary when a woman grabbed me and placed a rather interesting kiss right on my lips. She later caught me off guard out in front of my university's administration building. Once again I experienced her "special treatment." After that second incident I made it a point to remember what she looked like and to watch both directions every time I went anywhere on campus. I fear that her greeting was a perversion of the holy kiss. In fact, it seemed to resemble an "unholy kiss."

Be that as it may, the New Testament Epistles make it plain that the holy kiss was a common form of greeting in the early church. Thus Paul closes off 1 Corinthians with the injunction for them to "greet one another with a holy kiss" (RSV), and Peter at the end of his first letter admonishes his readers to "greet one another with the kiss of love" (1 Peter 5:14, RSV; see also 2 Cor. 13:12; 1 Thess. 5:26).

Well, then, you may be thinking, *How come we don't practice holy kissing in our churches today?* Several reasons have led to the change. One was that the forms of greeting have altered across time. In the days of the early church the kiss was a common form of greeting in society at large. Judas utilized that custom to identify Christ to the group that went out to arrest Him. Today the handshake, the warm smile, and more recently a hug hold a similar place to the holy kiss of the early church.

As we might expect, a second reason that the holy kiss went out of fashion is that it tended among some believers to be abused. Clement of Alexandria (c. 150-c. 215) writes of people who "make the churches resound" with kissing. He then points out that "the shameless use of a kiss . . . occasions foul suspicions and evil reports" (*Instructor* XI).

Thus in some groups the holy kiss had degenerated, but the principle remains. People need a warm greeting when they attend church. One of the most unfortunate experiences is visiting a strange church and not being greeted warmly or even greeted at all. Such experiences raise the question of whether we are in the house of the God who cares.

DIFFERENTIATING BETWEEN A "WILD BOAR" AND A PROPHET

*I appeal to you, brethren, to take note of those who create
dissensions and difficulties, in opposition to the doctrine which
you have been taught; avoid them. Rom. 16:17, RSV.*

ROMANS 16:17-20 CATCHES us by surprise. Here right in the middle
of a series of cordial greetings we find a strong warning against false
teachers. Why?

Paul had just spoken in verse 16 about the holy kiss of peace, signify-
ing the church's unity. But he knows the problems caused by dissenters in
some of his churches. His concern for the Roman church and the potential
dangers it faced brings forth the impassioned warning that we find in
verses 17-20. He wants to do all he can to protect the Christians in Rome.

That pastoral concern has influenced church leaders across the 20
centuries of Christian history. Pope Leo X, for example, issued a papal
bull against Martin Luther in the early 1500s, complaining that a "wild
boar" was ravishing God's "vineyard." Luther, of course, was not doing
that. To the contrary, he was more like an Old Testament prophet calling
a wayward church back to its biblical roots.

But wild boars really do ravish the church from time to time. That is
what Paul warns about in today's verse. If that is so, we need to ask, How
can we distinguish between "wild boars" destroying the unity of the
church and prophetic voices calling the church back to the truth?

We find the answer in our passage. Paul notes that those causing the
problem are out of harmony with the doctrine they have been taught.

Here is an important test that we can apply to all so-called reformers.
Do their teachings agree with the doctrines of Christ and the apostles as
reflected in their teachings preserved in the New Testament?

The false teachers that I have run across invariably either stress ideas
not emphasized in the Bible, or flatly contradict its teachings. Many of
them show up with a fistful of texts and quotations and declare the church
apostate. But when we carefully and unemotionally compare their claims
with the main themes of Scripture, they stand exposed as wild boars rather
than true prophets.

Things haven't changed all that much over the past 2,000 years.
Paul's warnings are still important today. So is his solution.

370

THERE ARE STILL
WOLVES AMONG THE SHEEP

Such people are not serving our Lord Christ, but their own
appetites. By smooth talk and flattery they deceive the
minds of naive people. Rom. 16:18, NIV.

JESUS WARNED US TO "beware of false prophets, which come to you in sheep's clothing, but inwardly they are ravening wolves" (Matt. 7:15). Paul is saying something similar in today's text. Not everyone that claims to have the "truth" really has it. Some of them are just plain charlatans.

Today's text reveals the motivation for some of these people as "their own appetites." Such false teachers may seem to be sincere and caring, but their primary concern is not Christ or the church but self-interest and self-gratification. Sometimes they seek fame. At other times they may want influence or financial gain. But at the bottom of it all is the problem of self-centeredness.

Jude pronounces a withering condemnation on such false prophets: "These men are blemishes at your love feasts, eating with you without the slightest qualm—shepherds who feed only themselves. They are clouds without rain" (Jude 12, NIV).

A few years ago one of America's most popular TV programs was *PTL.* The official name was *Praise the Lord,* but before the arrest of its "star pastor," many had begun to call it *Pass the Loot.* The program made constant appeals for more and more money as its leaders fed "their own appetites."

Paul speaks not only of the motivation of the false teachers he had in mind but also of their methodology. They deliberately set out to delude the unwary: "By their smooth and flattering speech they deceive the hearts of the unsuspecting" (NASB).

The church has never, unfortunately, been short on the type of people Paul is talking about. They always want to "help" us. They always have the "truth." They always tell us that everybody (including the church) is wrong except them. And they are often smooth and convincing. If we could only help them by supporting their ministry, they suggest, then the truth could get out, and Jesus could come. The result, as in Paul's day, is that sincere, "unsuspecting" believers send in their money.

Just as in the days of Paul, Christians need to be wise. In giving, we will receive a blessing, but God expects us to be careful in that giving.

PREVENTION IS BETTER THAN CURE

The report of your obedience has reached to all;
therefore I am rejoicing over you. Rom. 16:19, NASB.

IN MANY WAYS, as we noted near the beginning of our year in Romans, the letter's conclusion reflects Paul's greetings at the beginning of the book. It is so in today's passage, which commends the Romans for their faithful obedience, the knowledge of which has reached "to all." Paul also raised that idea in Romans 1:8, in which he thanks his God "for all of you, because your faith is proclaimed in all the world" (RSV).

The apostle is obviously dealing with a church that is basically sound. True, they have some issues to settle, as his Epistle to them makes evident. But on the whole the church in Rome is a healthy congregation. They have faith, and that faith has led them into a walk with Christ that is obedient to God's will. Whatever problems the Roman church may have had, they hadn't as yet flared out into serious proportions.

It is that exact point that the apostle seems to be speaking to in Romans 16:17-20. Being a wise leader, Paul realizes that prevention is better than a cure, that it is better to head off a problem rather than to have to deal with its ugly complexities once it has invaded the church.

All too often a congregation or even an entire church allows a bad situation to develop because no one has the courage to confront it; and often, as William Barclay points out, "when the situation has fully developed, it is too late to deal with it. It is easy enough to extinguish a spark if steps to do so are taken at once, but it is almost impossible to extinguish a forest fire."

In Romans 16:17-20 the apostle provides us with a strategy for dealing with problems before they become all-consuming. First, we need to understand our Bibles and what they teach (verse 17). Second, we must be discriminating rather than naive in the face of those who would lead us astray (verse 18). Third, we should remember that prevention is nearly always better than a remedial cure. And, fourth, as Paul illustrates in today's verse, we need to commend God's people whenever we can truthfully do so. Too many just tear down. God is looking for followers who can build up His church.

My Father, help me today to be a Christian who is willing and able to follow the strategy for dealing with problems that You set forth through Paul. Both in my church and in my other relationships, help me to be a part of the solution rather than a cause of the problem. Amen.

HARMLESS AS A SERPENT AND WISE AS A DOVE

*I want to see you experts in good, and not
even beginners in evil. Rom. 16:19, Phillips.*

TAKEN IN ITS CONTEXT, today's verse is a further admonition to avoid Satan's traps. It reminds us of Jesus' saying in Matthew 10:16: "Behold, I send you out as sheep in the midst of wolves; so be wise as serpents and innocent as doves" (RSV).

On a more general level, the Bible makes it plain that Christians will not be free from the presence of sin and its allurements until Christ comes again. In the meantime, if we are to be "experts in good" while "not even beginners in evil," we need to follow Paul's advice in other places. "Hate what is evil," he has earlier told the Romans, "hold fast to what is good" (Rom. 12:9, RSV). Again, he wrote to the Philippians, "whatever is true, whatever is honorable, whatever is right, whatever is pure, whatever is lovely, whatever is of good repute, if there is any excellence, and if anything worthy of praise, let your mind dwell on these things" (Phil. 4:8, NASB).

We build character day by day as we make choices. People wonder at the violence in the world today. For the past few years some of that violence has erupted as a rash of school shootings. But why should anyone be surprised when their daily diet is violent entertainment and violent spectator sports?

How can we and our children fashion characters that focus on goodness and abhor evil unless we take a conscious stand to reject the values of the predominant culture in which we live? As Christians we need to be more genuinely countercultural. If we don't, we are liable to end up as harmless as serpents and as wise as doves.

By way of contrast, Ellen White writes, "the greatest want of the world is the want of men—men who will not be bought or sold, men who in their inmost souls are true and honest, men who do not fear to call sin by its right name, men whose conscience is as true to duty as the needle to the pole, men who will stand for the right though the heavens fall" (*Education*, p. 57).

That kind of character doesn't come about by accident. It is a day-by-day construction as we individually allow God to make us into "experts in good" but "not even beginners in evil."

Whether I am wise as a serpent and harmless as a dove or harmless as a serpent and wise as a dove will be determined by my daily choices.

GENESIS 3:15 FULFILLED AT LAST

The God of peace will soon crush
Satan under your feet. Rom. 16:20, NIV.

THAT'S QUITE A STATEMENT. The God of peace will crush Satan. It hardly sounds peaceful.

The idea behind the text comes from Genesis 3:15. After Adam and Eve sinned in Eden, God promised them that eventually Satan would be defeated. As the passage itself puts it in a verse directed at Satan, God "will crush your head, and you will strike his heel" (NIV).

The underlying meaning is that in the end God would be victorious and that the results of Satan's attacks against Him would in the long run be inconsequential.

God will be victorious. That is good news. It is a part of the gospel. But how can we consider a Satan-crushing God as the God of peace? The answer to that question lies in the fact that His ultimate goal is the total destruction of those things that cause disruption, alienation, and death in our world. They all came in through the rebellion of Satan. Humanity will not have true peace until the results of Satan's work have been removed. We can have no hope for peace until the rebellion is put down once and for all. Thus God in His desire for peace needs to move aggressively against Satan and the forces of evil. In the process of gaining ultimate peace in a world gone wrong, the God of peace must destroy those who disrupt that peace.

The first step in crushing Satan took place on Calvary's cross, where Christ died for the world's sins. When Jesus exclaimed, "It is finished," He signified that the defeat of Satan had been ultimately settled.

But even though the victory has been won, it hasn't been consummated. That will take place after the millennium, when God eradicates Satan and evil (Rev. 20:9-14). At that point in time God will "make all things new" (Rev. 21:5). He "shall wipe away all tears . . . ; and there shall be no more death, neither sorrow, nor crying, neither shall there be any more pain: for the former things are passed away" (verse 4). Finally, Satan will have been fully "crushed," and God can re-create this earth to represent the peace that stands at the very center of His character.

Father in heaven, we look forward to the day when this old world is history. We long for the peace that You want to give us. Help us to be peacemakers in our hearts that we might be ready for Your realm of peace. Amen.

A FINAL LOOK AT GRACE

The grace of our Lord Jesus Christ be with you. Amen. Rom. 16:20.

GRACE IS ONE OF the great words of Romans. We came across it first in Romans 1:5, in which Paul ties it to his own apostleship. Then, of course, it featured at the very center of Paul's understanding of justification and righteousness by faith. The use of grace in today's passage is the final appearance of the word in Romans.

Some of Paul's great words in his letter have been faith, hope, joy, peace, justification, obedience, and grace. They are, of course, all linked together. Faith is how we individually accept or take hold of God's grace. The result of that acceptance is justification or righteousness. Other consequences are peace with God, joy in the Holy Spirit, and hope in the final solution to the sin problem. Paul also makes it clear that justification leads to obedience to God's will.

But at the bottom of all Paul's favorite words is "grace." Without grace all of his other favorite words have no meaning and content.

Grace stands at the very foundation of Paul's theology. In its essence it represents God's free gift to those who are under the power or rulership of sin and have no hope without it. It is God's radical answer to the sin problem. Without grace each person stands under the condemnation of a broken law. And without grace each person who has not accepted Christ's sacrifice by faith will die eternally.

But God doesn't give sinners the death that they deserve. No, He provides us what we don't deserve—grace, eternal life. That's Paul's gospel.

Grace is so central that we can't understand the apostle without grasping that word. It has more than one expression in our lives. Prevenient grace wakes us up to our sinful condition and our need of Christ. Justifying grace forgives us of sin and cleanses us so that God looks upon us as if we had never sinned. Transforming grace provides us with a new heart and mind, so that we desire to live for God and according to His principles rather than for ourselves and the principles of Satan's kingdom. Sanctifying grace gives us the power to live God's love. And eschatological grace will in the end save us from this old world.

Grace, Grace, God's grace. If you could ask Paul, he would tell you that that is what the book of Romans is all about.

PAUL IS NOT ALONE

Timothy, my fellow worker, greets you. . . . I Tertius, the
writer of this letter, greet you in the Lord. Rom. 16:21- 23, RSV.

SO FAR IN ROMANS 16 Paul has greeted those whom he has some acquaintance with in Rome (Rom. 16:1-16) and he has given them a firm warning regarding false teachers (verses 17-20). Now in verses 21 to 23 he sends greetings from those who are with him as he writes.

One of the things that we learn from this second list of greetings is that Paul didn't work alone. For him ministry was a team effort. That was true from his early mission with Barnabas up through the end of his life. Paul not only regularly labored with others, but he had warm feelings for them.

That connection of warmth in many ways met its apex in Timothy, whom Paul referred to as "my beloved and faithful child in the Lord" (1 Cor. 4:17, RSV). Apparently Paul's ministry had converted Timothy and his family in Lystra. Before long the younger man had become Paul's intern or apprentice in ministry.

The two men had an especially warm relationship and provide us with an excellent example of an older pastor training a younger one. "I hope," Paul wrote to the Philippians, "to send Timothy to you soon. . . . I have no one like him, who will be genuinely anxious for your welfare. They all look after their own interests, not those of Jesus Christ. But Timothy's worth you know, how as a son with a father he has served with me in the gospel" (Phil. 2:19-22, RSV).

Second Corinthians, Philippians, Colossians, 1 and 2 Thessalonians, and Philemon list Timothy as coauthor with Paul. And, of course, Paul wrote two very special letters to his apprentice in the Lord.

We see the personal aspect of Paul's relationship with his coworkers also indicated by the fact that he allows Tertius, who actually wrote down the letter to the Romans as Paul dictated it, to add his own greetings.

The personal, warm, affectionate side of Paul's ministry is important for us. The apostle was not an austere man who stood alone. He was not merely a conveyer of truth or the head pastor. No, Paul was a man of great warmth who lived God's love as he worked with his fellow Christians in preaching the gospel. In that warmth he modeled after Jesus, who had a close relationship with His disciples. God wills for each of us collegial relationships as we labor for Him.

THE GOD WHO IS ABLE

Now to him who is able to strengthen you according to my gospel and the preaching of Jesus Christ. Rom. 16:25, RSV.

GOD IS ABLE!

That phrase is one of the most important in the entire book of Romans. God is not merely willing to save and strengthen us, but is capable of doing so.

The proof of His ability is the resurrection of Christ. It was at His resurrection that Christ was "designated Son of God in power" (Rom. 1:4, RSV). And through His resurrection Christ attained "the keys of Death and Hades" (Rev. 1:18, RSV). His resurrection is a guarantee not only of our resurrection, but of God's power to save us completely and fully.

God is able! And because He is able we who have accepted Christ can have assurance that the one in whom we have believed will fulfill every promise in the gospel.

Paul began this Epistle with statements regarding the gospel and God's power to save, and he ends it in this final doxology with the same thoughts. The Epistle's very first verse used the word "gospel." That word provided Paul's theme throughout his letter to Rome (see Rom. 1:15-17). And now at the end Paul uses the word "gospel" for the last time. But just as he did in chapter 1, once again he ties it to the idea of power. God is able to do what He has promised to do. That is the best part of the good news.

But God isn't in the business of salvation by Himself. As in Romans 1:1, our text for today links God the Father with Christ in the gospel plan. The preaching of Jesus, as Paul repeatedly asserts, is all-important because He died in our place at Calvary. He died for our sins that we might have His righteousness. And He died the death that was ours that we might have through faith the life which is His.

God is able because of Christ. Because of Christ's life and death God is in a position to give us saving grace freely. "The wages of sin is death, but the free gift of God is eternal life in Christ Jesus our Lord" (Rom. 6:23, RSV). That's the gospel.

God is able! That's also the gospel. It is the best of the good news.

Today, our Father, we want to surrender our hearts and lives to You, the God who is able. Help us to grasp more fully what You want to do for us and in us. Thank You.

THE MYSTERY REVEALED

According to the revelation of the mystery, which was kept secret since the world began but now has been made manifest, and by the prophetic Scriptures has been made known to all nations. Rom. 16:25, 26, NKJV.

PAUL REFERS TO THE gospel as a "mystery hidden for long ages past, but now revealed and made known through the prophetic writings" (NIV).

When we encounter the word "mystery" in our day we usually think of something incomprehensible. The biblical idea is somewhat different. Rather than being something that can't be understood, it is rather something previously hidden but now made known.

But what, we might ask, is the mystery that Paul is talking about? In the context of the book of Romans it appears to be the gospel of salvation from sin through the work of Christ.

Wait a minute, you may be thinking. *Didn't Paul begin Romans with a statement that the "gospel of God" had been "promised beforehand through his prophets in the holy scriptures" (Rom. 1:1, 2, RSV)? And didn't we see that the entire sanctuary service with its sacrificial system pointed to Christ's sacrifice? How can it be that the gospel has been hidden for long ages past if the prophets had already revealed it?*

The answer to such questions is that while the sacrificial service pointed to Christ, it was only a mere "shadow" of the real thing. While the Israelites could learn much from the shadows of things to come, a great deal of how God would eventually fulfill His purpose still remained unknown.

But Christ cleared up those mysteries when He actually came to this earth. As the book of Hebrews says: "In many and various ways God spoke of old to our fathers by the prophets; but in these last days he has spoken to us by a Son" (Heb. 1:1, 2, RSV).

Christ is the fullest revelation of the gospel. Whereas the Old Testament could point in words at what the Lord would do, Christ hanging on the cross and crying out, "It is finished," demonstrated in concrete action what God had done.

The mystery hinted at and pointed to by the prophets was at that point in time fully revealed. As Christians we stand in the full light of the cross.

Help us, dear Lord, to appreciate that light.

THE OBEDIENCE OF FAITH—AGAIN

[God's mystery has been made known] by the command of the everlasting God to all the gentiles, that they might turn to him in the obedience of faith. Rom. 16:26, Phillips.

"OBEDIENCE OF FAITH." Haven't we seen these words somewhere before?

The answer is yes. Paul used them in the very first paragraph of his letter to Rome. Speaking of Christ, the apostle noted that he had "received grace and apostleship to bring about the obedience of faith for the sake of his name among the nations" (Rom. 1:5, RSV).

Some of Paul's contemporaries saw red when he repeatedly emphasized grace. They got upset, assuming that he was doing away with law and obedience. Many people still see red on the topic today. If someone speaks of free grace, they mumble snide remarks about "cheap" grace. Beyond that, just as in Paul's day, they often become aggressive toward the preachers of grace, treating them as if they have apostatized.

So what else is new? Things haven't changed much since the days of Paul, including misunderstandings of grace.

But if we follow Paul we don't have much to worry about. After all, "free grace" is not the same as "cheap grace." Cheap grace is grace without response or cost, but God's free grace is the most costly thing in the world. It not only required the life of the Son of God on Calvary, but it demands the self-centered lives of those who accept it.

The apostle makes it clear in Romans 6 that accepting free grace means a total transformation of our whole being—a death to the old ways and a resurrection to a new way of life based on a new set of principles.

Paul had it right. We don't earn salvation by works or lawkeeping, but those who are saved through faith will obey. They will have the obedience of faith and will love God's law.

It is no accident that Paul's great letter on salvation in its first and last paragraphs speaks of the "obedience of faith." The concept remained one of his themes all through the Epistle. Obedience has no value outside of a faith relationship, but inside that relationship obedience is vital.

We can be thankful that Paul the ex-Pharisee wrote his book. In it he has exposed us to some of the issues that he had wrestled through in his own experience. The issues that Paul raised in Romans should be topics of contemplation for every Christian every day.

379

THE FINAL DOXOLOGY

To the only God, who alone is all-wise, be
glory through Jesus Christ forever! Rom. 16:27, TEV.

WHAT A BOOK!

And what a way to end a book! Paul knows what it is all about. He understands that God is Himself the very epicenter of Christianity. His praise is everlastingly to God the Father and Christ Jesus the Son.

Some question exists as to whether we should translate today's passage as "the only God, who alone is all-wise" or as it is in the New International Version: "the only wise God." We don't really know Paul's precise meaning here, but without doubt the apostle thinks of God as both the only God and as the only God who is wise.

It is to his God that Paul offers his final doxology. Giving glory to God is a fitting way to end a book. It is also a proper way to begin a church service. When I read Romans 16:27 this morning, I immediately thought of "To God Be the Glory," a Fanny Crosby hymn familiar to most Christians.

"To God be the glory, great things He hath done;
So loved He the world that He gave us His Son,
Who yielded His life an atonement for sin,
And opened the life gate that all may go in.
Praise the Lord, praise the Lord, let the earth hear His voice;
Praise the Lord, praise the Lord, let the people rejoice;
O come to the Father, through Jesus the Son,
And give Him the glory, great things He hath done."

One of the most important things that we can say about Paul is that He put God at the center. What the Lord had done for him personally in Christ was never far from his mind. He knew where the center was. I have no doubt that he thought that doctrines and lifestyle were important, but for Paul they were never most important. Everything he believed stood in relationship to the grace of God, the sacrifice of Christ, and the ongoing work of the Holy Spirit.

Christianity for Paul was the extreme opposite of self-centeredness or those religious practices that lead people to focus on themselves and *their* achievements for God. For Paul God was all in all, and even human achievement reflected what He does in people.

With God at the center, it is little wonder that Paul started his book by referring to himself as a slave to Christ and ended it with praise to God.

THE FINAL AMEN

Amen. Rom. 16:27.

WE HAVE COME TO the last Amen in Romans. Paul has used the word five times in the book (Rom. 1:25; 9:5; 11:36; 15:33; 16:27), each time in connection with God and His salvational work in Christ.

It is fitting that Paul ends his letter with "Amen." The word means "truly" or "most certainly." As such, it is an affirmation of all that Paul has so beautifully stated about God and His plan in Romans. By concluding with "Amen," Paul is saying that it is without question true and certain. I can add my own amen to that.

We have come to the end of our year of walking with Paul through Romans. In some ways it seems our journey has been but a few days, but in others it has seemed much longer than a year.

Our time perceptions, however, matter little. The fact is that the year is over today, and tomorrow we start a new one. The real question is whether we will end our walk with Paul or continue on.

This past year we have been confronted with the most influential book in world history. But in the end we each face the question that Pilate put to the Jews: "What shall I do with the man whom you call the King of the Jews?" (Mark 15:12, RSV).

I see you fidgeting over there. But let's face it, fidgeting doesn't solve the issue. What are you going to do with the salvation through Jesus that Paul has put before you? What are you going to do with Jesus?

The answer of the Jews to Pilate was loud and clear: "Crucify Him! Crucify Him!" And Pilate did.

That is still a live option for us. The other option is that we will let Him crucify us and resurrect us to a new way of life.

God is waiting for our response. He realizes the depth of our need. But He also knows the depth and height and breadth of the riches of His grace. It is ours for the acceptance.

Today, Father, we thank You for the journey. But more than that, we want to recommit our lives to walking with You in the path of faith for the coming year.

We need Your blessing, we need Your help, we need Your guidance, we need Your salvation—we need You. Amen!

Coming by
GEORGE R. KNIGHT

If you like Bible study

you will want a copy of George Knight's

EXPLORING HEBREWS

scheduled for release spring 2003.

*E*xploring Hebrews is a devotional commentary that takes its readers step by step, in clear, simple language, through one of the most difficult books of the New Testament.

THIS IMPORTANT BOOK BRINGS TO ITS READERS

- A fresh translation of the entire Epistle from the Greek
- A commentary that explores every paragraph in Hebrew in sections short enough (four to six pages each) to be easily read and digested.
- Not only an explanation of the main theological ideas of each paragraph, but also their devotional and practical application for daily living.

The publication of *Exploring Hebrews* is especially timely, since the Sabbath school lessons for the third quarter are on Hebrews. Also great for small group study.